THE PRESIDENT AND PROTEST

THE PRESIDENT AND PROTEST

Hoover, MacArthur, and the Bonus Riot

by

DONALD J. LISIO

Fordham University Press
New York
1994

Copyright © 1994 by Donald J. Lisio
All rights reserved
First Edition, The Curators of the University of Missouri, 1974
Second Edition, Fordham University Press, 1994
LC 94-19465
ISBN 0-8232-1571-7 (hardcover)
ISBN 0-8232-1572-5 (paperback)

Library of Congress Cataloging-in-Publication Data

Lisio, Donald J.
   The President and protest : Hoover, MacArthur, and the Bonus Riot
: with a preface to the 1994 edition / Donald J. Lisio.—2nd ed.
     p.   cm.
   Includes bibliographical references and index.
   ISBN 0-8232-1571-7.—ISBN 0-8232-1572-5 (pbk.)
   1. Bonus Expeditionary Forces. 2. Hoover, Herbert, 1874–1964.
I. Title.
F199.L57   1994
973.91'6'092—dc20   94-19465
                                     CIP

Printed in the United States of America

TO SUZANNE
AND OUR FAMILIES

Contents

Preface to the Second Edition

Since the publication of this book in 1974, it has occurred to me from time to time that a brief summary of its major findings in a preface would enhance its value to scholars and students alike. Now Fordham University Press has graciously given me that opportunity. Thus, before discussing some manuscript sources that were closed when my research was undertaken in the late 1960s and 1970s, a short summary will acquaint the reader with the book's scope, thesis, and major conclusions.

Following World War I, two new veterans' organizations, the American Legion and the Veterans of Foreign Wars, steadily intensified their congressional lobbying for increased veterans' benefits. In 1924 Congress avoided a third presidential veto by delaying payment of a World War I "bonus" until 1945, when compound interest from a trust fund could pay an average bonus of $1,000.00.

In March 1929, when Herbert C. Hoover became the thirty-first President of the United States, the country was "bright with hope." As he took office, Hoover was known widely as "the Great Humanitarian" for his efforts to provide European relief during and after World War I. But by October 1929 the stock market had crashed, ushering in the Great Depression. That same year renewed lobbying generated more than forty pending veterans' bills. In response, Hoover convinced Congress to create the Veterans Administration and to increase benefits for all the ex-servicemen. But the veterans severely criticized him when he opposed their demand for immediate payment of the bonus, which would have amounted to $4 billion—equivalent to the entire federal budget. Chapters 1 and 2 of this volume analyze the history of the bonus legislation and Hoover's efforts on behalf of veterans.

After the American economy collapsed in 1929, millions of Americans lost their jobs, their homes, their sense of dignity. Many took to the rails, roaming the country by freight car looking for work. One such depression-weary group, the Bonus Army, carried its entreaties to Washington and became the depression's largest and most famous protest.

During the spring and summer of 1932, the "army" of more than 20,000 bonus marchers made their way to the nation's capital, where they camped for two months lobbying Congress for passage of the bonus. Hoover secretly protected the marchers' civil liberties and secretly provided food, tents, equipment, and an army field hospital, while steadfastly resisting demands to evict them.

The House passed a bill for immediate payment of the bonus, but the Senate overwhelmingly rejected it. In mid-July, as Congress adjourned and its members went home, many believed that the issue was settled and that further petitioning was futile.

A small portion of the Bonus Army had illegally occupied a group of condemned buildings on the south side of Pennsylvania Avenue. A demolition contractor had earlier purchased the salvage rights to these buildings. He lost money daily as the squatters lingered on, and as his own debts mounted, he threatened to sue the federal government for not evicting the bonus marchers from his buildings. Under this pressure, Hoover agreed to a Treasury Department request for the limited eviction on July 28 of a small contingent of veterans from the condemned buildings. As the police attempted to remove them from their makeshift quarters, some of the veterans attacked the police with bricks and rubble. Later, a small group of protesters again attacked the police, who shot and killed two of the veterans. Frightened police demanded that federal troops be summoned.

Hoover specifically directed that the Army operations be limited to the small riot area and that the troops only surround the riot area and assist the police, who were to remain in charge. But when Army Chief of Staff General Douglas MacArthur took command, he deliberately disobeyed Hoover's written order limiting the scope of the Army's assistance, and he later ignored the President's repeated oral messages to stop all operations. Instead, he directed his troops to attack the other veterans' camps as well, driving the unarmed, discouraged bonus marchers, along with their wives and children, out of the nation's capital.

The expulsion of the bonus marchers delivered an irreparable blow to Hoover's reputation, as most people assumed that he had ordered the brutal dispersal. In the immediate aftermath and for years later, MacArthur falsely justified his disobedience to the President by insisting that his troops had faced armed insurrectionists. MacArthur and Secretary of War Patrick J. Hurley met with Hoover, after the fact, and convinced him of the grave danger that the nation supposedly had faced. Hoover acquiesced to their explanation, took full responsibility, and did not publicly discipline his disobedient Chief of Staff. But as weeks passed and neither MacArthur nor any federal agency could prove a Communist plot, Hoover bore the blame for the cruel rout.

In 1967 I published an article widely cited by scholars of this event, which established MacArthur's disobedience. In 1974 the first edition of this book appeared. Other historians who have also investigated this subject and accepted my interpretation include Joan Hoff Wilson, David Burner, Ellis Hawley, and Martin L. Fausold. It is not unusual during a twenty-year span for new manuscripts or documentary evidence to be uncovered. Yet since the publication of this book in 1974, little new evidence or scholarship has emerged.

Subsequent work attempting to analyze press reaction, rather than the event itself, has tended to become mired in the possibly unprovable question of the impact of the rout on the 1932 election. John Tebbel and Sarah Miles Watts, *The Press and the Presidency: From George Washington to Ronald Reagan* (New York: Oxford University Press, 1985), p. 431, conclude: "While editorial opinions differed politically on this episode . . . the bald facts as related in news columns . . . did more . . . to diminish Hoover's reputation and solidify his negative image than anything else while he was in office."

Louis Liebovich, "Press Reaction to the Bonus March of 1932: A Re-Evaluation of the Impact of an American Tragedy," *Journalism Monographs* (August 1990), pp. 1–32, presents an opposite viewpoint and attempts to claim that the rout of the marchers helped rather than hurt Hoover, as measured by the initial press reaction. As newspaper editors had been consistently opposed to the bonus march, it was easy for them initially to accept the administration's claim that MacArthur's troops had put down an insurrection attempt. Thus, Liebovich correctly concludes that the press at first was generally, though not en-

tirely, favorable to Hoover's explanation of the rout. But his trac-
ing of press reaction virtually stops in mid-August, when the
press was still supportive. He mentions two unfavorable articles,
one in September and one in October. Otherwise, he does not
analyze the other anti-Hoover criticism between September 10
and the election, when the administration's defense of the brutal
dispersal collapsed.

On September 13 Police Chief Pelham D. Glassford attacked
the administration's defense and correctly charged that the
administration had misled the American people on the character
of the bonus marchers. Even Hoover's press secretary, Theodore
Joslin, concluded in his book that by September 15 "there was
no question that the President was hopelessly defeated." Then,
on October 30, Glassford published the first of a series of articles
which claimed that Hoover had deliberately provoked the riot
as a "pretext" to turn troops against the marchers and thus con-
coct a law-and-order campaign issue. The police chief's late
October charge was incorrect, but it received considerable coverage and was widely repeated by Democratic politicians. More
important, although knowledge of immediate press reaction is
useful, it has clearly limited value. Long after the editorials
ceased, the damage to Hoover's reputation was perpetuated in
speeches, campaigns, recollections, scholarly and popular accounts, college textbooks, and "documentaries."

Textbook writers have gradually incorporated my evidence of
MacArthur's disobedience of Hoover and have gradually softened the previous use of the rout to convey the impression of
Hoover as a mean-spirited leader of the "old order." Much more
comprehensive has been the work of television producers, who
have even more fully incorporated this scholarship.

In 1990 Meredith Woods and Eric Neudel, a production team
from Blackside, Inc., traveled to the Herbert Hoover Presidential Library in West Branch, Iowa, to investigate the possibility
of making a documentary film on the bonus march and rout.
Meredith Woods had mastered the scholarly literature and arranged a long interview with me during which she and Neudel
asked numerous well-informed questions centering on the interpretation of the evidence and its historical meaning. Then they
spent several days at the Hoover Library examining documents,

photographs, and film accounts. Ironically, the Hoover Museum at that time regularly showed a dramatic biographical film about Hoover which repeated MacArthur's outrageous lie that he had driven the veterans and their families out of Washington on Hoover's orders.

Blackside produced two documentary films about the depression of the 1930s which included long segments on the bonus march. The first documentary, produced for "The American Experience," was shown by Boston's WGBH. Entitled "After the Crash," the one-hour examination quickly sketched the impact of the depression on farmers, on industrial laborers, and on Washington, D.C., where the bonus protest centered. About one-third of the documentary told the story of the bonus march, graphically presenting the interpretation in this book. Excellent footage conveyed the dramatic and poignant nature of the protest, the meager conditions of the huge Anacostia camp, "the depression's most famous Hooverville," and the cruel and tragic rout. Also important in the presentation was the clear and repeated fact that MacArthur had violated Hoover's orders, which limited the use of troops to the small downtown area near the riot. The film shows MacArthur's troops driving the veterans away from central Washington, across the river, and, along with their families, out of the large Anacostia camp. The documentary cites Franklin D. Roosevelt listening to radio reports of the rout and concluding that Hoover had already lost the election.

In 1993 Blackside expanded on the footage from "After the Crash" in "The Great Depression" series. This documentary added the recollections of Alonzo Fields, one of the White House butlers, who reinforced the proof that Hoover overrode Secretary of War Hurley and insisted on helping the homeless veterans during their long encampment. According to Fields, who heard the breakfast discussions of Hoover and his Cabinet, Hurley protested that providing army kitchens for the campers would be "accommodating" them "and we would just get more and more and more and more." But Hoover ignored his objections and provided the aid secretly. Fields also recalled MacArthur's dispersal of the marchers and said that the next day at the breakfast table Hoover was "very much upset." According to Fields, Hoover exclaimed, "Why did we have to use so much

force against unarmed veterans? Why did we have to do that!"
The production skillfully presents both Hoover's and MacArthur's actions during the bonus protest, and for the first time
in over sixty years an historically accurate documentary is now
available to the general viewing public.

Three manuscript sources which were closed to scholars when
I was researching this book have finally been opened. All of
them support this interpretation. The papers of Attorney General William D. Mitchell add little but do reveal his anger and
dismay at the handling of the eviction and with the odious assignment of having to defend it. The diary of Campbell B. Hodges,
Hoover's military aide, offers little of relevance, but it does contain one interesting vignette of the publicity-seeking Secretary
of War Hurley and Chief of Staff MacArthur. Hodges was present
when Hurley emerged from a Cabinet meeting on Saturday, July
30, two days after the brutal rout. As the press surrounded him,
Hurley bragged about his great pride in the manner in which
the Army had conducted itself during the dispersal. "And I want
to tell you," he added, "Mac [MacArthur] was there—he was
there like four aces and a king."

The diary of Theodore Joslin, Hoover's press secretary, is
somewhat more useful. It reflects the great work load under
which Hoover was laboring in the days immediately preceding
the riot. With five appointments remaining to the Reconstruction Finance Corporation and to the Home Loan Board, the
writing of his acceptance speech, and numerous other duties,
Hoover complained to Joslin, "I have never been so damned
pressed for time. I don't see how I can get the work done that
I have got to do. Everything seems to be crowded into the next
week or two." Rather than focusing his attention on the bonus
marchers so that he might craftily manipulate their expulsion
for maximum political advantage, as Glassford and one historian
have argued, Hoover did not pay enough attention to the potentially explosive situation. Thus, when the police were attacked
and the D.C. Commissioners called for federal troops, Hoover
relied on Hurley and MacArthur, who unexpectedly yet repeatedly disobeyed his orders.

According to the Joslin diary, during the Bonus Riot of July
28 Hoover worried about violence and bloodshed, especially

after the police had shot two of the veterans. In agreeing to the District Commissioners' second request for troops, Hoover "insisted to Hurley that the soldiers come without their guns." As I have already established, Hurley repeatedly ignored Hoover's explicit orders and obviously encouraged MacArthur to do so as well.

After the rout, when Hurley and MacArthur finally convinced the President of their insurrection thesis, an unfortunate change took place in Hoover. He became defensive and conspiracy-oriented, lashing out at the bonus marchers and his critics as well. Like Hoover, Joslin also readily accepted MacArthur's argument that the Army was faced with armed insurrectionists. As press secretary, Joslin was preoccupied with the presence of Communists among the protesters, even though there were only about 200, and with their persistent efforts to gain publicity for themselves and to generate publicity unfavorable to Hoover. According to conspiracy theorists, the Bonus Riot was supposed to be the beginning of a Communist coup. Yet, as this volume shows, the Communist leader, John T. Pace, concluded that there were only about twenty-five of his followers whom he could trust. Only one Communist took part in the first riot, none participated in the second attack on police, and none challenged the Army troops which swept the veterans out of Washington. Moreover, the ineffectual Communists were disrespected and continually abused by the other bonus marchers. Therefore, although as press secretary, Joslin had reason to feel perturbed by the sensational Communist propaganda, his diary overemphasizes both their presence and their importance.

Conspiracy theories have always been popular, even today. Several proliferated in the press after the dispersal of the bonus marchers, emanating both from Hoover's critics and from the administration itself. The two most important partisan fabrications were the administration's erroneous charge that Communists or criminals, or a combination of both, had conspired to overthrow the government, and the equally incorrect conspiracy charge by Glassford that Hoover had diabolically planned the rout in order to manufacture a campaign issue. The historian's craft dictates careful gathering and weighing of the evidence, thus separating sensational claims from the actual events. The story of the bonus march illustrates the complexity of such charges and countercharges of conspiracy, while at the same time this volume examines the depression's largest protest, and the conflicting roles in that event of President Herbert Hoover and General Douglas MacArthur.

D.J.L.
Cedar Rapids, Iowa
May 1994

Acknowledgments

Many individuals and institutions have assisted me since the spring of 1966, when I began work on this study. First, I am happy to thank the National Endowment for the Humanities for the Younger Scholar Fellowship in 1969–1970. The fellowship came at a crucial time, enabling me to complete the first draft of the manuscript. I am grateful to the American Council of Learned Societies for a grant which further aided my study. Over the years Coe College has also encouraged me through research grants and leaves of absence. My colleagues and students, too, have been most considerate and supportive. Collectively, they have created a liberal arts college where one can enjoy both teaching and scholarship.

Foremost among the archivists who have assisted me are the highly competent staff members of the Herbert Hoover Presidential Library. Because of their professional dedication, the resources made available to scholars have steadily enlarged. Robert Wood, Charles Corcoran, and Carole Sue DeLaite were especially helpful in calling new materials to my attention. Thomas Thalken, Dwight Miller, Ruth Dennis, and Mildred Mather have also been most cooperative. Other professionals who have assisted my searches include Mary Hawley of Coe College; Edwin H. Kaye, Ann Mitchell, Elizabeth W. Smith, Wilbur Smith, and Saundra Taylor of the University of California, Los Angeles; Jack D. Haley of the University of Oklahoma; Elizabeth B. Mason of the Oral History Collection, Columbia University; John E. Wickman and Brenda Reger of the Dwight D. Eisenhower Library; J. C. James of the Franklin D. Roosevelt Library; Philip D. Brower and Robert H. Alexander of the MacArthur Memorial; William C. Marten of the State Historical Society of Wisconsin; and Warren MacDonald, Special Assistant to the Administrator of Veteran Affairs. In addition, I want to express my appreciation to the staff members of The Library of Congress, the National Archives, the American Legion National Headquarters, the Coe College Library, the University of Iowa Library, the Georgetown University Library, the Minnesota Historical Society, the Washington, D.C., Public Library, the

Knox College Library, the Iowa State Department of History and Archives, the Memphis, Tennessee, Public Library, the University of Colorado Library, and the Idaho State Historical Society.

Others who have been helpful in a variety of ways and who merit special thanks include Guy Alchon, Violet Swanson Anderson, Martin Blumenson, David Burner, Frederick Bates Butler, Robin Byrnes, F. Trubee Davison, John S. Eisenhower, Seth Harkins, Allen Hoover, Mrs. Graham Hoyt, Thomas V. Hull, Franz Lassner, A. K. Macdougall, Joseph E. McCabe, Janet and Joseph Miller, John J. Murray, Leo L. Nussbaum, Congressman Wright Patman, Byron Price, John J. Rumbarger, Martha M. Smith, James Van Zandt, Carson W. Veach, and Robert M. Warner.

Several scholars have helped me during the various stages of this study. Paul Glad has been generous with his advice and support, and I owe a special debt to Irvin G. Wyllie for his many efforts on my behalf. Ellis Hawley read portions of the manuscript and offered important suggestions. Charles K. Cannon read the entire manuscript and made valuable comments, as he has done and continues to do for others at Coe. I am deeply grateful for their assistance.

For over twenty years, since 1952, when I began my undergraduate studies, David M. Pletcher has been my good friend and mentor. In the course of becoming a distinguished historian, he has unselfishly given to his students his time, energy, and encouragement. The entire study has been aided by his thoughtful advice and detailed criticisms.

My wife, Suzanne Swanson Lisio, has been of inestimable assistance, and to her I owe my greatest appreciation. While not a professional historian, her probing questions and editorial skills helped sharpen my analysis, and her boundless enthusiasm transformed revisions from an arduous task into an engrossing pleasure.

D. J. L.
Cedar Rapids, Iowa
November, 1973

Footnote Abbreviations

ALP—American Legion Papers, American Legion National Headquarters, Indianapolis, Indiana

ASCF—Adjusted Service Certificate File. This designation is used in both the Patman Papers and the American Legion Papers.

BEF—Bonus Expeditionary Forces

DCP—District Military Relations, Bonus Marchers File, District of Columbia Commissioners Papers, District of Columbia Building, Washington, D.C.

EL—Eisenhower Papers, Dwight D. Eisenhower Library, Abilene, Kansas

FDRL—Franklin Delano Roosevelt Library, Hyde Park, New York

FTH—Frank T. Hines

GMP—George Van Horn Moseley Papers, The Library of Congress

GP—Pelham D. Glassford Papers, Institute of Industrial Relations, The University of California, Los Angeles

GP 679—Pelham D. Glassford Papers, Division of Special Collections, Collection Number 679, Powell Library, University of California, Los Angeles

GT—*Glassford, Testimony Before the Grand Jury*

HH—Herbert Hoover

HHPL—Herbert Hoover Presidential Library, West Branch, Iowa

HHPW—*The State Papers and Other Public Writings of Herbert Hoover*, ed. William Starr Myers

HP—Riot Folder, Patrick J. Hurley Papers, The University of Oklahoma, Norman

HSUS—*Historical Statistics of the United States, Colonial Times to 1957*

HUAC, CTVG—House Un-American Activities Committee, *Hearings, Communist Tactics Among Veterans Groups*

LC—The Library of Congress, Washington, D.C.

MP—MacArthur Papers, MacArthur Memorial, Norfolk, Virginia

MTGJ—*Memorandum of Testimony Presented to the Grand Jury, District of Columbia*

NA—The National Archives, Washington, D.C.

PDG—Pelham D. Glassford

PP—Presidential Papers. The collections at the Hoover Library are divided into major categories such as Commerce Papers, Post-Presidential Papers. The box number follows the abbreviation.

RCS—"Report of Chief of Staff, United States Army, to the Secretary of War on the Employment of Federal Troops in Civil Disturbances in the District of Columbia, July 28–30, 1932."

RG—Record Group

TP—Elmer Thomas Papers, The University of Oklahoma, Norman

WP—Robert Wagner Papers, Georgetown University, Washington, D.C.

Introduction

In the continuing reevaluation of United States history, Herbert Clark Hoover remains one of the most familiar presidential villains; much of his characterization is rooted firmly in his reputed role in the bonus march. According to the usual scenario, on July 28, 1932, Hoover deployed infantry, tanks, cavalry, and troops armed with tear gas to drive thousands of unarmed and penniless men, women, and children out of the nation's capital. A decade earlier the men had been heroes, the victorious veterans of World War I, but now, almost three years following the stock market crash, they were beaten and destitute, most having lost their homes, savings, jobs, and even self-respect. They had marched on Washington in the spring of 1932 to petition Congress for immediate payment of the bonus for World War I veterans that was scheduled for distribution in 1945; they were, therefore, known as the Bonus Army. To many citizens, they were forgotten heroes as well as representatives of the poor and needy. With the aid of a benevolent police chief they had sustained a peaceful demonstration for two months, but at the end of that time, on a slight pretext, Hoover turned the Army upon them. So goes the script.

This cliché-ridden, partisan, inaccurate, yet surprisingly durable story has been accepted by historians and nonhistorians alike. In the wake of the Bonus Riot many Americans viewed Hoover as a diabolical, cruel, or at best extremely fearful Chief Executive. The rout of the ragged army intensified the widespread frustrations and disillusionment caused by the depression. Hoover had already been discredited as a political leader and as the instigator of the "New Era" of prosperity, but within a few months after the rout he also lost his reputation as a man of integrity. Some of his more extreme critics argued that he had deliberately planned and provoked the riot, then rushed troops against the protesters in order to claim that he had saved the Republic from a revolutionary coup—all of this,

1

so he could fabricate a law-and-order issue for the 1932 presidential campaign.

The story of Hoover's Presidency has been peopled with villains and heroes, usually with Hoover acting as the chief villain and, in this event, the veterans and the kind police chief as the heroes. The bonus march, the most massive protest that the capital had known and among the longest, became one of the most compelling human-interest stories of the depression era. But the confrontation of President and veterans was not a simple villain-versus-heroes collision: Hoover's relations with the veterans and the events of the march were far more complex than historians have yet recognized. As one evidence of this complexity, the President has frequently been both praised and faulted for the wrong reasons. The event is significant for the numerous misconceptions it has fostered, for the personal change it worked in Hoover, and for the explanations based on suppositions of conspiracy that it produced. The depression ruined Hoover's reputation as a leader, and his aloof, introverted nature further handicapped him, but the rout of the bonus marchers shattered the remaining credibility of his administration, seriously damaged his reputation as a man of integrity, and significantly hampered his future effectiveness within the Republican party. His personal reputation might have weathered some of the discontent engendered by the depression if federal troops had not attacked unarmed, hungry petitioners—victims of that depression.

As the bonus protest passed into folklore, an extensive literature developed. Almost without exception the major accounts both by scholars and partisans reveal the passions the rout of the marchers generated. The bibliographical essay examines the more important accounts. The evidence concerning the event is widely scattered, highly emotional, often self-serving, and usually imbued with implications of conspiracy, if not outright accusations of various plots. The two most important sources are the papers of Police Superintendent Pelham D. Glassford and of President Herbert Hoover. Both are exceedingly valuable, yet both present their own particular and conflicting theories concerning conspiracy, as examined in the bibliographical essay. Because scholars could not consult the most extensive and revealing source of information until 1966, when the Herbert Hoover Presidential Library opened, they sometimes minimized the significance of the protest and often perpetuated the standard anti-Hoover interpretations.

Since 1966, when I first began research for this volume, my purpose and scope of analysis have steadily expanded. I sought first to evaluate and place in proper historical context this fateful event of the Hoover Presidency. I soon discovered that the President's stereotype had influenced me more than I cared to admit. However, evidence from various sources worked a change in my thinking, and my article written in 1967 established that Hoover had actually tried to prevent the rout of the protesters and that it was his Chief of Staff, Douglas MacArthur, who decided to drive them out. In so doing, MacArthur knowingly and repeatedly disobeyed presidential orders.

Other evidence I have gathered since 1967 has produced further changes. Hoover's generous and reformist program for the veterans, his substantial aid given secretly to the protesters, his protection of their civil liberties, the absence of any plot, and his behind-the-scenes efforts to avoid violent confrontations are facts that destroy the old stereotype and help open the way toward less biased, more dispassionate analyses of the man and his administration. Further, just as Hoover's characterization as a fearful, scheming President must be altered, that of the bonus marchers must be changed from that which appears in depression-era lore. To be sure, the protesters were a tattered and poignant group, tragic people down on their luck, but they were not "forgotten heroes" and certainly were not spokesmen for the nation's poor. Yet, in any discussion of the bonus march, this mistaken symbolism must be reassessed, for it has accentuated the impression of Hoover as a mean-hearted, craven, plotting man.

This book is not intended as a full-scale revision of Hoover or of the history of his administration. It should, however, illumine significant misconceptions about the President, while recognizing that there was also much in his conduct to criticize. The government's reaction to the protest movement was badly mismanaged, and especially after MacArthur drove the protesters out of the city, Hoover and his advisers made serious mistakes in governance, especially in presenting and defending their case. Most reprehensible, the administration attempted to cover up its blunders and silence its critics. One of the central themes of this study is Hoover's change, after the rout of the marchers, from a man of restraint and relative tolerance on the red issue to one incensed by the eventual belief that a Communist conspiracy had been the cause of the Bonus Riot.

A related purpose is to analyze the most neglected and among the more important aspects of the protest—the various allegations of conspiracy that arose in the midst of the 1932 presidential campaign, which surfaced again in the early McCarthy era, and which have persisted for two generations. The complex circumstances leading to the violence on July 28, 1932, and the administration's catastrophic effort to cover up its blunders encouraged such explanations by partisans on both sides of the controversy. They led to gross distortions of the event as well as to significant errors in assessing the careers of President Hoover, Police Superintendent Pelham D. Glassford, Secretary of War Patrick J. Hurley, and Army Chief of Staff Douglas MacArthur. Until now these major explanations of the Bonus Riot, which depend on conspiracy theories, have not been carefully analyzed and thus have often been allowed to masquerade as history.

1

Hoover and Forgotten Heroes

Central to Hoover's relations with the bonus marchers was his earlier three-year encounter with veterans' lobbies. From both the veterans' and Hoover's point of view the relationship was unfortunate, ironic, and abortive. Months before the stock market crash Hoover had realized that action by the powerful veterans' lobbies would pose one of his most formidable political challenges, yet he had no idea how bitter the fight would be. Indeed, in early March 1929, when he became the thirty-first President of the United States, he expressed high hopes for his administration and the nation. The unprecedented national prosperity was seemingly endless and constantly expanding. The mood of the nation was correspondingly festive, lending a large measure of joy and optimism— even euphoria—to the Inauguration.

To the majority of Americans it seemed especially appropriate that Hoover should lead the nation. He was a progressive who had been courted by both the Republicans and Democrats, for eight years a popular and dynamic Secretary of Commerce, a self-made millionaire, and a respected humanitarian. After his landslide victory over his Democratic opponent Al Smith, there was little that could dampen the exuberance of the new President. His Inaugural Address was the most optimistic of his entire public career, and it reflected the mood of most Americans. "I have no fears for the future of this country," he exclaimed. "It is bright with hope." [1]

1. Herbert Hoover, *The State Papers and Other Public Writings of Herbert Hoover*, William Starr Myers, ed., 2 vols. (New York: Doubleday, Doran and Co., 1934), I, 3–12 (hereafter cited as HHPW); Harris Gaylord Warren, *Herbert Hoover and the Great Depression* (New York: Oxford University Press, Inc., 1959), pp. 3–18.

The sense of energetic initiative and momentum which Hoover tried to convey in his first presidential address was more than mere rhetoric. With Republicans in control of both the House and the Senate, the Democratic party seriously divided, and no foreign threats to the nation, he confidently assumed that he could achieve the resolution of a variety of pressing national problems. In addition to his plans to call a special session of Congress to act on agricultural relief, he outlined some important long-term goals. One of these was to reshape the federal bureaucracy. But before he could fully initiate the sweeping reorganization and less than eight months after his inauguration, the nation suddenly plunged from unprecedented prosperity toward unprecedented economic collapse, requiring the President to expend virtually all of his time in vigorous efforts to end the crisis.

Although he did not have much opportunity to restructure the Executive branch during his Presidency, Hoover did sponsor an often overlooked yet highly important reorganization—the establishment of the Veterans Administration. It was his only major bureaucratic reform, yet ironically it did little to smooth his relations with the veterans. Hoover had known that, even more deeply than Harding and Coolidge before him, he was about to be dragged into the thickets of veteran politics. To meet this challenge he first directed the consolidation of the three competing veterans' agencies. At the same time he created a top-level committee to establish policy guidelines for handling the numerous piecemeal, often contradictory, veterans' pension bills. In spite of these efforts toward standardization of benefits, Hoover's handling of the numerous veterans' bills brought little appreciation from the ex-servicemen.

When Hoover took office in March 1929, the veterans were testing their strength with Congress. After the stock market crash in October of that year, a badly frightened Congress approved a host of costly pension and hospitalization bills, frantically hoping to curry favor with the politically potent, well-organized veterans' organizations as the 1930 general elections approached. In the face of nationwide panic, the approaching congressional elections, and veterans' demands, Hoover personally tried to ensure justice to all the veterans at a price a nation in economic crisis could reasonably be expected to pay. Both his intentions and the cost and quality of the bills passed during his term, Hoover believed, demonstrated that he had been more generous than any previous President. Ironically, however, despite his best efforts the veterans increasingly came to look upon him more as an enemy than as a friend.

As Secretary of Commerce, Hoover had witnessed the punishing congressional battles over the bonus for veterans of World War I. For almost five years, beginning in 1919, the newly founded American Legion made issuance of the Adjusted Service Certificate, popularly referred to as "the bonus," its principal legislative goal. In its drive, the Legion subjected Congress to increasingly effective pressure. The bonus would, in addition to the veteran's regular pay that he had received as a soldier, entitle him to $1 for each day of duty in the United States and $1.25 for each day of duty overseas. From the veterans' viewpoint this added compensation did not appear too much to ask, especially as many of those who had remained in civilian life had earned far more at considerably less risk. Their argument was reasonable in the period following the Armistice. At that time the nation could afford the payment, and as the ex-servicemen felt that the nation had not treated them fairly, they demanded not a "bonus," but what they considered to be the belated payment of hard-earned wages. Some congressmen held that opposition to the bonus was "a well-organized, concerted conspiracy, concocted by the big moneyed interests." [2]

According to opponents of the bonus, however, the two to four billion dollars required, at a time when the total yearly federal income was just slightly over four billion dollars, seemed exorbitant, especially to those who demanded early elimination of wartime taxes and retirement

2. Roger Daniels, *The Bonus March: An Episode of the Great Depression* (Westport, Conn.: Greenwood Press, Inc., 1971), pp. 37–39.

of the World War I national debt. The bipartisan opposition emphasized the fear that immediate payment would necessitate a crushing tax burden. Thus it was not difficult for two successive Secretaries of the Treasury, William Gibbs McAdoo and Andrew Mellon, to convince Presidents Wilson, Harding, and Coolidge that immediate payment of the bonus would be an outrageous burden on the nation. At Mellon's insistence both Harding and Coolidge vetoed bonus bills.

In 1924, however, under renewed pressure from the Legion, Congress agreed to a skillfully devised compromise measure. Rather than insisting on immediate payment, the veterans settled for a twenty-year endowment fund, which could be financed without raising taxes and which would accumulate enough money through compound interest to pay an average individual bonus of about one thousand dollars in 1945. Coolidge vetoed the bill, but Congress overrode him, clearly demonstrating the new political muscle of the well-organized, fast-growing, and henceforth immensely influential veterans' lobby. The compromise resulted in a substantially larger bonus because the veterans were willing to wait until 1945, and thus it appeared that the issue had been settled.[3]

Within a month after taking office Hoover learned that over forty veterans' pension bills had been introduced during the preceding session of Congress and that a majority in both the House and Senate were already committed to enacting a general pension program. Still, at that time most Americans were enjoying the prosperity of the late twenties and did not want it marred by increased taxes. The American Legion did not favor a general pension bill, but, an adviser warned, should the Legion decide to support pension legislation, passage would be certain.[4]

3. For an excellent discussion of the congressional bonus battles during the early 1920s, see Arthur L. Hennessy, "The Bonus Army of 1932" (Ph.D. diss., Georgetown University, 1955), pp. 10–87; Richard S. Jones, *A History of the American Legion* (Indianapolis: The Bobbs-Merrill Co., Inc., 1946), pp. 165–80; Daniels, *Bonus March*, pp. 37–39.
4. Royal C. Johnson to HH, April 1, 1929, PP 295, HHPL.

Hoover wasted no time in launching an immediate investigation of veteran affairs. What he discovered was not encouraging. While his suspicion of pension illegalities similar to those in previous years proved unfounded, it was evident that the government had no central control over the three agencies that were handling these matters. Each, with large staffs and overlapping functions, operated independently of the others. The United States Veterans Bureau, the National Home for Disabled Volunteer Soldiers, and the Interior Department's Bureau of Pensions together employed over 30,000 workers and were duplicating records and efforts without the administrative and budgetary control necessary for better service and care at less cost to the people.[5]

As soon as Hoover alerted his cabinet to the need for consolidation of the administration of veterans' affairs, he faced a bureaucratic power struggle. The initiator of the struggle was his close friend, Secretary of the Interior Ray Lyman Wilbur. Wilbur controlled the inefficient and costly Bureau of Pensions, which represented 70 per cent of the Interior Department's annual budget. Not wanting to lose the Pension Bureau, Wilbur urged the President to consolidate all three veterans' agencies within his department. To counter Wilbur, Secretary of Labor J. J. Davis, who also favored eliminating the large Veterans Bureau, proposed distributing the duties among four cabinet departments—one, of course, being Labor. Since Davis's suggestion offered the antithesis of consolidation, Hoover brushed it aside.[6]

At first Wilbur had powerful allies among both veterans and congressmen. William Williamson, chairman of the House Committee on Expenditures in the Executive De-

5. HH to Secretary of Interior, April 8, 1929, PP 10; FTH to HH, April 20, 1929, PP 156, HHPL.
6. Ray Lyman Wilbur, *Memoirs of Ray Lyman Wilbur*, Edgar Eugene Robinson and Paul Carroll Edwards, eds. (Stanford: Stanford University Press, 1960), pp. 466–68; U.S., Congress, House, Committee on Expenditures in the Executive Departments, *Hearings on H.R. 6141, Consolidation of Veteran Affairs*, 71st Cong., 2d sess., January 8, 1930, pp. 43, 46, 62; William A. DuPuy to Wilbur, March 9, 1929, Wilbur Papers, HHPL; Rice C. Means to HH, March 20, 1929; and James J. Davis to HH, March 29, 1929, PP 156, HHPL.

partment, pledged his support. Since Williamson would control the committee through which the reorganization bill must pass, Wilbur appeared to be in an especially strong position.[7] That circumstance and his seemingly favored relationship with the President led Wilbur to underestimate the effectiveness of the chief of the Veterans Bureau, Frank T. Hines.

A balding, firm-jawed ex-brigadier general, Hines was earnest, thorough, and competent as an administrator, and he enjoyed overwhelming his listeners with his vast knowledge of the intricate laws governing veterans' benefits. A master bureaucrat, Hines had maintained excellent relations with the American Legion, the Veterans of Foreign Wars, and influential congressmen; he had no intention of letting either the Interior or Labor Department suddenly devour his highly efficient Veterans Bureau. Hoping for a delay during which he could rally his influential friends, Hines suggested that Hoover appoint a committee to investigate the entire question of reorganization.[8]

Faced with a choice between Hines and Wilbur, and uncertain which alternative the powerful veterans' organizations would support, Hoover accepted Hines's suggestion. It was the easiest and theoretically the safest way to avoid what promised to be a politically sensitive battle. After eight years as Secretary of Commerce, during which someone had dubbed him "Under-Secretary of Everything," Hoover recognized the value of delaying decisions until the opposing forces and their arguments became unmistakably defined. To that end, he decided to give the contending advocates their day in court by appointing a committee consisting of two of his personal aides and the three principal administrators of veteran affairs, Hines, Wilbur, and Gen. George H. Wood, chief of the National Soldiers Home.[9]

From mid-June until October 1929, while Congress bat-

7. William Williamson to HH, July 23, 1929, PP 156, HHPL.

8. HH to FTH, March 9, 1929, PP 283; FTH to HH, April 20, 1929, PP 156, HHPL.

9. HH to Secretary of Interior, May 23, 1929, PP 156, HHPL.

tled over the tariff and farm relief, the Committee to Coordinate Veteran Affairs met periodically in an atmosphere poisoned by mutual suspicion and jealousy. Finally, after continual disagreements and quarrels, the committee's chairman Wilbur suggested that the group had too often been "lost in the bush" and that the President himself should decide exactly how to effect the coordination. The exhausted members of the committee could agree at least on that point, and on October 1, 1929, they advised Hoover to proceed as he saw fit.[10]

Secretary of Interior Wilbur was well aware that this suggestion might possibly work to his advantage. As a trusted cabinet member and old friend of the President, he apparently felt confident of convincing Hoover to reorganize veterans' affairs within the Interior Department. To his surprise, however, Hines had expertly usurped his favored position during the months while the committee met. Hines had also recognized that William Williamson was a key congressional chairman, but unlike Wilbur, did not rely on personal persuasion as much as on a skillful campaign waged by the lobbyists for both the American Legion and the Veterans of Foreign Wars. This support was the crucial factor. While the committee had been quarreling, Hines had lined up the unanimous backing of the major veterans' organizations.[11]

Before long, Congressman Williamson completely reversed his position; he now favored consolidating the veteran agencies in Hines's control. In fact, Williamson was so eager to effect his plan that he introduced his own reorganization bill—without consulting either the President or Hines—on December 3, 1929, the same day that Hoover called for consolidation of veteran agencies in his first State of the Union message. The timing of William-

10. "Minutes of the Committee to Coordinate Veteran Affairs," July 26, 1929; September 25, 1929; and October 1, 1929, PP 156, HHPL.

11. FTH to the National Commander of the Disabled American Veterans of the World War, June 10, 1929, PP 283, HHPL. House, Committee on Expenditures in the Executive Departments, *Hearings*, 71st Cong., 2d sess., January 8, 1930, pp. 32–35.

son's move strongly suggested approval by the President, and Williamson actively circulated the impression that, according to secret word from Hoover, Hines, not Wilbur, would be chief of the new agency.[12]

In effect, the battle for control of the Veterans Administration was over, and at that point Hoover should have called a halt to the struggle by insisting that Wilbur drop his opposition to the new consolidation bill. Yet, for some inexplicable reason—possibly to soothe his friend's feelings—Hoover refused to restrain his Interior Secretary and agreed to allow him to testify against the Williamson bill. That was a mistake, for it cast an easily avoidable shadow over Hoover's relations with the veterans. Now it was no longer an internal feud between competing bureaucracies. Wilbur found himself involved in a public debate in which he was pitted against not only Williamson and Hines but the Legion and VFW as well. Although Wilbur favored consolidation under his own department, his testimony against the Williamson bill created the impression that he was generally opposed to the veterans' interests. Some naturally suspected that he must be speaking for the President—a strange turn of events, since Hoover's State of the Union message had called for consolidation. Speaker after speaker had supported Hines, and Edwin S. Bettelheim, chief lobbyist for the VFW, warned Hoover that the veterans' organizations "were rather taken back to hear the testimony from the Secretary of Interior . . . a member of the President's official family." [13]

The fight over the Veterans Adminstration epitomized the many hidden ironies that plagued Hoover's handling of veteran affairs. Although the President had initiated the drive for reorganization and consolidation, the Secretary

12. Copies of H.R. 6141 are in PP 157, HHPL, in Legislative Records, No. 46, 233, NA; and in HHPW, I, 162; Williamson to Edward H. Balevre, February 15, 1930, Legislative Records, No. 42, 223, NA.

13. House, Committee on Expenditures in the Executive Departments, *Hearings*, 71st Cong., 2d sess., January 8, 1930, pp. 5–35, 46; Edwin S. Bettelheim to Walter Newton, January 30, 1930, PP 157, HHPL.

of Interior's opposition during the public congressional hearings suggested to powerful veteran leaders that Hoover might actually be obstructing their interests. For a brief time the President managed to overcome this suspicion. He worked closely with Williamson in personally drafting another bill, which allowed Hines full powers to consolidate all three agencies into the new Veterans Administration. The bill passed Congress without debate.[14] Unfortunately, much damage had already been done to the President's reputation among veterans. In reality the plan and the initiative had been Hoover's, but it appeared that he had acquiesced only after intense pressure from the veterans.

In Hoover's handling of the reorganization can be seen one source of his problems, not only with the veterans, but increasingly with the country as a whole. Time and again Hoover would support the veterans' demands for increased benefits only to discover that he had garnered more disfavor than credit. His unhappy tendency to attract criticism for his efforts resulted, in part, from his growing ineptness in communication and in political action. In sharp contrast to his extraordinarily successful public relations efforts while Secretary of Commerce, now, especially after the stock market crash, he seemed unaware of the importance of political appearances. Faced with complex problems, he seemed unable to predict or even to concern himself with the political effects of his words and actions.[15] Because of his repeated fail-

---

14. Williamson to HH, March 11, 1930, PP 157, HHPL. Copy of H.R. 10630, Legislative Records, No. 46, 233, NA; U.S., Cong., House, *Consolidation of Veterans Activities*, Report No. 951, 71st Cong., 2d sess., March 21, 1930; Senate, *Consolidation of Veterans Activities*, Report No. 1129, 71st Cong., 2d sess., June 28, 1930; House, *Congressional Record*, 71st Cong., 2d sess., 1930, 72, pt. 8, pp. 7791–8011; Senate, *Congressional Record*, 71st Cong., 2d sess., 1930, 72, pt. 11, pp. 12049–52.

15. Theodore Joslin, *Hoover Off the Record* (New York: Doubleday, Doran and Company, 1934), pp. 2–4, 68–69; James E. Pollard, *The President and the Press* (New York: The Macmillan Company, 1947), pp. 737–72; Paul Y. Anderson, "Hoover and the Press," *Nation*, 133 (October 14, 1931), 382–84; Craig Lloyd, *Aggressive Introvert: A Study of Herbert Hoover and Public Relations Management, 1931–1932* (Co-

ures to dramatize his supportive actions and because of his tendency to make offensive moral pronouncements, he continually found himself judged harshly and for the wrong reasons by the very men he was trying to help.

Congress had further handicapped Hoover's efforts by the exceedingly haphazard fashion in which laws concerning veterans' benefits were considered.[16] When Hoover had created the Committee to Coordinate Veteran Affairs, he had also instructed its members to give thought not only to the reorganization of veteran agencies but to the broad question of legislative policy as well, with special emphasis on ways to weed out the many injustices in existing laws and to ensure greater equity in future legislation.

Laws concerning veterans had long been a subject of bitter complaint among ex-servicemen, and the vast inconsistencies and flagrant discriminations Hoover uncovered confirmed the validity of these complaints. A renewable government life insurance policy was available for veterans of the World War, for example, but not for those of prior wars. Old soldiers, on the other hand, could claim pensions of from twenty to ninety dollars a month, but not veterans of the World War. One provision allowed treatment for venereal disease contracted many years after discharge; other soldiers with more serious ailments could not obtain hospitalization unless space were available—simply because they had served in the wrong war.[17]

Hoover condemned such "conflicts and injustices" and the "tremendous number of discordant and unequal treatments." [18] Disabled men who had served in the World

lumbus: Ohio State University Press, 1972), pp. 166–70. Lloyd's book is an outstanding analysis of Hoover's use of the press as an instrument of governance.

16. U.S., Congress, House, Committee on World War Veterans Legislation, *Hearings on H.R. 7825*, 71st Cong., 2d sess., January 16, 1930. For copies of other bills, see PP 207, and FTH to Newton, April 12, 1930, PP 296, HHPL. Hines sent Hoover a list of 42 bills pending in Congress.

17. "Brief of Major Inequities in Veterans Legislation" and "Chronological Resumé of Veteran Laws 1861–1932," PP 286A, HHPL.

18. HH to FTH, April 12, 1930, PP 296; FTH to HH, April 22, 1930, PP 297, HHPL.

War were being admitted to veterans' hospitals, whether their disability was connected to their service or incurred many years later, but Civil War and Spanish-American War veterans did not enjoy the same privilege. They were admitted with nonservice-connected disabilities only if the hospitals happened to have empty beds. As a result, only 10 per cent of the men from the less favored wars could get needed hospital treatment. The other 90 per cent of these veterans waited in vain for space and were forced to seek private medical aid or to receive no aid at all. It was theoretically possible for a young man ten years removed from the World War to obtain immediately a hospital bed and treatment for a recently acquired case of syphilis—a disease classified as resulting from personal "vicious habits"—yet a Civil War veteran who had sustained a heart attack might be forced to wait several months for admittance, or he might be turned away, with no hope of government assistance.

Veterans also complained, with justice, that the Army had done a poor job of diagnosing and recording medical problems. Thus, many service-connected illnesses did not appear in their medical files, and legitimate benefits were denied. Numerous inequities reflected the almost total lack of rational, consistent policy, yet neither Congress nor veteran leaders made a serious effort to correct the abuses. In fact, they resented Hoover's efforts to standardize policy. Instead, each of the competing veterans' lobbies seemed interested only in gaining more benefits for its own members.

In May 1930, the House and Senate overwhelmingly passed a bill that illustrated to Hoover the evils inherent within the existing laws. It was a pension bill for veterans of the Spanish-American War and of what Congress euphemistically referred to as the Philippine Insurrection and the China Relief Expedition. At an estimated cost of $11.7 million annually the Spanish-American War bill increased disability pensions and extended them to all veterans of that war who had become disabled, whether or not the disability had resulted from military service. It also reduced the ninety-day-service requirement to sev-

enty days.[19] By contrast, World War I veterans could receive hospital treatment for nonservice-connected infirmi-
ties, but not disability pensions. They were also required
to prove they had served for ninety days. To the former
doughboys, the Spanish-American War pension bill was
obviously discriminatory. Moreover, Hoover realized that
if he signed the bill or allowed it to become law, he
would have little basis on which to oppose future bills of
a similarly inequitable character.

Beyond the bill's injustices the President had to consider its potential for arousing new and still more expensive demands from competing veterans' groups. Rather
than eliminate inequities and discriminations, rampant
logrolling might well lead each veterans' group to make
increasing demands for its own members, liberalizing the
laws to be sure, but also perpetuating inequities for other
veterans' groups. If any attempt to arrive at a more uniform and just policy were to be made, Hoover knew that
he must act immediately. Therefore, on May 28, 1930, in
the face of mighty congressional support for the Spanish-
American War bill, he penned his first veto.[20]

Hoover based the veto on three guidelines, which he
hoped would govern and standardize all future legislation
for veterans' benefits: that no man be given benefits
whose disability resulted from his own so-called "vicious
habits"; that ninety days, not seventy, be the required
minimum period of service; and that beneficiaries must
prove need as well as disability. The first two criteria were
readily accepted even by the veterans' lobbyists. Unfortunately, however, the President's message was written in
his unique, sanctimonious style, which emphasized the
issue of morality rather than the more meaningful one of
equity. Most irritating of all was the last of the three criteria, the question of need. Hoover's critics accused him
of forcing on veterans "a pauper's affidavit," which could

19. A copy of the bill and petitions are in PP 207, HHPL.
20. HH, "Message to the United States Senate, May 28, 1930, Veto
of S. 476, Spanish War Veterans Pension Bill," PP 207, HHPL; HHPW,
I, 302–3; "Minutes of the Committee to Coordinate Veteran Affairs,"
PP 156, HHPL.

not be effectively administered. Others suspected a more sinister motive, nothing less than an attempt "to take away from the veterans the pensions that they now have." [21]

Hoover had included a need provision in his criteria on the strong recommendation of the Veterans Bureau chief, Frank T. Hines, and the Committee to Coordinate Veteran Affairs. Despite the high moral tone of his veto message, the President may actually have been more flexible than his words suggested. According to Walter Newton, his principal political secretary, Hoover had earlier passed the word to congressional leaders that if Congress included the "vicious habits" stipulation and ninety-day requirement, he would be willing, if necessary, to sign the bill without insisting on a need clause. Apparently Hoover did consider the issue of need important but not vital. Furthermore, he had good reason to believe that the need clause would not be especially troublesome anyway. Hines had earlier vigorously advocated that provision before the American Legion national convention, and neither then nor in the months that followed had there been a protest.[22] Clearly, he had not expected the intense reaction that came from congressmen and veterans alike.

Only four days after the veto, on June 2, 1930, the Senate interrupted its debate on the tariff and unanimously agreed to limit discussion of the veto to one hour. A few senators, notably Arthur Vandenberg of Michigan, suggested that the President's position on "vicious habits" and the ninety-day requirement had some validity, but condemned the need clause as "wholly and entirely

21. "Minutes of the Committee to Coordinate Veteran Affairs," PP 156; George H. Woods to C. B. Hodges, PP 207; HH, "Message to the United States Senate," May 28, 1930; copies of letters sent to congressmen by Edward S. Matthias, chief lobbyist of the United Spanish War Veterans; copy of letter distributed to veterans by Rice W. Means; Coe to Newton, June 7, 1930, PP 207 (numerous letters of protest are included in this box), HHPL. Coe was National Commander of the United Spanish War Veterans.

22. Newton to William T. Coe, June 13, 1930, PP 207, HHPL; FTH to George Akerson, September 24, 1929, PP 283, HHPL. Akerson was one of Hoover's secretaries.

beyond any compromise." George Norris, the old progressive from Nebraska, chided Hoover's denunciation of "vicious habits." He thought it absurd to force men who had experienced the horrors of war "to prove that they were Sunday-school boys." As the hour ended and no one offered an effective defense, the Senate easily overrode the veto. On the same day, without mention of the President's objections to the bill, the House quickly followed suit.[23]

Nevertheless, many Americans felt that Hoover's indignation had been well justified. Newspaper editors took up Hoover's defense in strong editorials, championing his criteria and castigating the veterans for their costly special-interest politics during a time of national crisis. The *Times* of Leavenworth, Kansas, echoed the tone of more influential newspapers. After scolding congressmen who had voted "in favor of granting pensions for gonorrhea, syphilis, and alcoholism," the editors concluded that Congress's submission to the voracious veterans' lobbies had made a mockery of representative government. Instead of holding fast against the smaller, disunited veterans' organizations of the earlier wars, Congress had actually encouraged their audacious raids on the federal Treasury. With the onset of hard times for everyone, Americans were in no mood to continue depleting the federal Treasury for the veterans' special interest.[24] Later, when the veterans of World War I would begin agitating for immediate payment of the deferred bonus, liberals and conservatives alike would agree in their opposition to the veterans' demands.

On June 9, 1930, just twelve days after he signed the veto, Hoover missed an excellent opportunity to demonstrate that he had been speaking in good faith. Congress passed another veterans bill, this time equalizing and

23. Senate, *Congressional Record*, 71st Cong., 2d sess., 1930, 72, pt. 9, pp. 9852–71, 9868–76; House, *Congressional Record*, 71st Cong., 2d sess., 1930, 72, pt. 9, pp. 9811–9914.

24. Philadelphia *Inquirer*, June 3, 1930; St. Louis *Post-Dispatch*, June 4, 1930; *The Christian Science Monitor*, June 4, 1930; newspaper clippings in PP 207; D. R. Anthony to Newton, June 8, 1930, PP 207, HHPL. Anthony was editor of the Leavenworth (Kansas) *Times*.

substantially increasing pensions for Civil War veterans. Hoover approved the measure, merely signing the estimated $12.1 million bill into law with little ceremony and even less public notice. He favored the increases, yet just as he had been unable to explain effectively his veto of the measure for Spanish-American War veterans, he seemed equally incapable of advertising his substantial positive efforts to help old soldiers of the Civil War. In the lingering furor of his earlier veto, his silent support for the later legislation went virtually unnoticed.[25]

The highly popular Rankin bill for World War I soldiers was another example of the inequities that resulted from logrolling by veterans' groups. The Rankin bill for disability benefits extended the presumption date for service-connected disability from January 1, 1925, to January 1, 1930, and revised as well the list of diseases that could be treated under veterans' benefits. From a medical viewpoint the new presumption date was as meaningless as the previous arbitrary date. Further, the bill was so vaguely worded that even obesity would qualify as one of the diseases of a "chronic, constitutional character." However, other disabilities were not included. Theoretically, a man who became disabled by obesity before January 1930 could qualify; another, who suffered from a more serious infirmity or who became disabled after that date, could not. Hines considered the provisions of the bill detrimental to all veterans, based on "wrong principles," and a "stupendous" burden on the taxpayers. It is little wonder that Hoover was appalled with the inequities in veterans' legislation. He informed Congress that, while the bill would grant additional pensions to 100,000 veterans with "acceptable" diseases, it discriminated against 200,000 others who had also been disabled in civilian life in ways not covered in the bill. Since the bill created more inequities, Hoover pleaded with Congress for time to establish a general disability policy that would ensure justice for all veterans. Nevertheless, on the following day,

25. For a copy of the bill and letters thanking Hoover for his support, see PP 207, HHPL.

June 25, 1930, the House ignored Hoover's plea, accepted the Senate version, and sent the Rankin bill to the White House.[26]

This time Hoover was prepared. He vetoed the bill and emphasized its "long train of injustices and inequalities." He called for "a square deal between veterans," with no special favors for special groups. If Congress insisted on pensions for nonservice-connected disabilities, then all disabled veterans must be included, not merely the 100,000 who had been stricken with specified diseases before January 1, 1930. To the surprise of many legislators, Congress sustained the veto by 4 votes. Then, immediately after the vote, Royal C. Johnson, chairman of the House Committee on World War Veterans and a trusted ally of the President, moved to suspend the rules and quickly approve a new Disability Act—which was in reality Hoover's substitute bill. Caught off guard, John Rankin of Mississippi, who had helped sponsor the vetoed bill, was furious. The choice now became Hoover's bill or nothing, and Rankin therefore reluctantly advocated passage, in the confident expectation that the Senate would offer substantial changes.[27]

The President's bill went far beyond any measure Congress or the veteran lobbies had yet advocated. It entirely eliminated the presumption of service-connected disability and struck out the deadlines and list of acceptable diseases. This was the "square deal" the President had proposed. To be sure, the benefits were significantly lower

26. Jones, *American Legion*, p. 145; O. L. Bodenhamer to Royal C. Johnson, telegram, June 30, 1930; Johnson to Bodenhamer, June 20, 1930; FTH to Newton, April 22, 1930, PP 296; FTH to HH, June 18, 1930, PP 297; FTH to HH, June 21 and 25, 1930, PP 284, HHPL; Senate, *Congressional Record*, 71st Cong., 2d sess., 1930, 72, pt. 11, pp. 11461–500; Andrew W. Mellon to HH, June 25, 1930; FTH to HH, June 25, 1930, PP 297, HHPL; HH to James E. Watson, June 21, 1930, HHPW, I, 320–22; "Press Conference," June 24, 1930, HHPW, I, 322; House, *Congressional Record*, 71st Cong., 2d sess., 1930, 72, pt. 11, pp. 11693–94.

27. HH, "Message to House of Representatives, June 26, 1930, Veto of H.R. 10381," PP 284, HHPL; also in HHPW, I, 323–28; House, *Congressional Record*, 71st Cong., 2d sess., 1930, 72, pt. 11, pp. 11828 (the new Hoover bill was H.R. 13174), pp. 11829–42.

for nonservice-connected disabilities, and the bill limited one with full civilian disability to a $480-a-year pension as against a possible $2,400-a-year payment to a fully disabled veteran who had been wounded on active duty. Nevertheless, Hoover's bill, conservatively estimated at $64 million, was the most sweeping, equitable, and generous proposal that had been made. It was especially generous at a time when approximately 65 per cent of Americans earned less than $3,000 a year.[28]

As Rankin had predicted, the Senate amended the bill after an extended and often bitter debate; fully expecting the House–Senate conference committee to agree to its amendments, the Senate passed the bill on July 1, 1930. But the elation among Hoover's opponents was premature. In his capacity as presiding officer of the Senate, Vice President Charles Curtis appointed the Senate conferees to the House–Senate conference committee. As might be expected, the committee quickly eliminated the amendments and reported Hoover's bill back in its original form. Outraged, critics in the Senate heaped abuse on the conference committee's decision and the President. Each vied with the other to prove that he, not the President, was the true friend of the veteran, but they could neither rescue the amendments nor prevent the bill's passage. The costly new World War Disability Act was exceedingly generous, and it was Hoover's bill.[29]

If Hoover had sought to cast himself in the role of true friend and generous benefactor of the veterans, he need only have informed the public of his behind-the-scenes role in passing the 1930 Disability Act. Two years later,

28. House, *Congressional Record*, 71st Cong., 2d sess., 1930, 72, pt. 11, pp. 11829–33, especially section 200, pp. 11830–31; U.S., Bureau of the Census, *Historical Statistics of the United States, Colonial Times to 1957* (Washington, D.C.: Government Printing Office, 1960), p. 165 (hereafter cited as HSUS). The income level is based on 1929, the closest year for which statistics are available. The five-year estimate was $319,714,650 or about $64 million a year. "Veteran Relief," April 8, 1932, PP 296, HHPL.

29. Senate, *Congressional Record*, 71st Cong., 2d sess., 1930, 72, pt. 11, pp. 12058–61, 12198–99, 12387–418; House, *Congressional Record*, 71st Cong., 2d sess., 1930, 72, pt. 11, pp. 12460–62.

during his reelection campaign, at least one veteran leader lamented Hoover's continued silence concerning his authorship of the Disability Act. At that time Hoover faced intense criticism for driving the bonus marchers, who were World War I veterans, out of the capital at gunpoint. Therefore, argued Roy Cookston, senior vice commander of the Louisiana and Mississippi VFW, Hoover should inform the veterans of his role in passing the Disability Act. "If it is capitalized on," he urged, "it will bring more ex-servicemen back to the Republican ranks . . . than anything that could have happened." [30]

Hoover was never in a good position to capitalize his generosity, however—neither in 1930, after he had demanded sharp cuts in federal spending, nor in 1932 after the rout of the Bonus Army. Nor was he especially proud of the bill. Over the strenuous objections of both Hines and the American Legion he had abandoned the old principle of service-connected disability, and during a great economic crisis, while exhorting the nation on the need for rigid economies, he had secretly sponsored an extremely expensive piece of legislation for the veterans. It was a compromise, Hoover later argued, a necessary compromise "in order to avoid passage over the veto of another bill [the Rankin bill] which would have called for three times the annual expenditure." But each organization had its own pet requests, and fearing that the cost of Hoover's legislation would hamper its own long list of new, more expensive demands, the Legion vigorously and publicly condemned it. "This added cost," a Legion official later claimed, "is the responsibility of the Administration." [31]

Consequently, few thanked Hoover for his efforts. The American Legion complained about the expense the bill entailed; Hines lamented the end of the service-con-

30. Roy Cookston to Ernest Lee Jahncke, July 12, 1932, PP 296, HHPL.

31. Jones, *American Legion,* pp. 145–48; HH to Grenville Clark, July 22, 1932; "Legislative Proposals of American Legion," Memo, PP 296, HHPL. The minimum cost was put at $153,190,000 a year and the maximum yearly cost at $181 million. New York *Times,* July 13, 1932.

nected disability requirement; and the National Economy League voiced its strong opposition. An influential, fiscally conservative watchdog, the vocal League demanded sharp cutbacks in federal spending, especially on veterans, and was outraged that treatment of nonservice-connected disabilities should cost the government more than $450 million annually. By June 30, 1932, 407,584 World War veterans with nonservice-connected disabilities had been added to the pension rolls at an annual additional cost of $73,470,000; [32] even so, the veterans would not admit to being pleased.

With the one exception of his abortive veto of a Spanish-American War pension bill, Hoover had been quite successful in his efforts to provide increased benefits to the veterans and more efficient administration of veteran affairs. He had without fanfare approved over $12.1 million for veterans of the Civil War; he had signed four special acts totaling $5.4 million for new construction of soldiers' homes as well as two acts for hospital construction at $15.9 million and $20.8 million; and he had favored increased pension and hospital benefits for soldiers of every war since 1861.[33] The most costly of the pension bills was his own $73 million Disability Act—radical in its departure from the listing of specific diseases and in its attempt to establish equity and justice for all ex-servicemen, whether or not their disability was conclusively service-connected.

Hoover's approval of large expenditures for veterans' benefits and his efforts on their behalf have never been adequately recognized. One impression was that Hoover slighted the ex-servicemen but that pressure from legionnaires and from the Hearst-owned papers for immediate

32. Bodenhamer publicly denounced the expensive legislation. Senate, *Congressional Record*, 71st Cong., 2d sess., 1930, 72, pt. 11, pp. 12055–56. Clark to HH, July 19, 1932; National Economy League, "Declaration of Purposes, June 29, 1932," President's Personal File, 1998; FTH to HH, June 30, 1932, PP 286; "Disability and Death Compensations," Memo, September 3, 1932, PP 296, HHPL.

33. "Veteran Relief," Memo, April 8, 1931, and copy of hospital construction bill, PP 296; for a resumé of all benefits to veterans, see FTH to HH, September 13, 1930, PP 284, HHPL.

payment of the bonus "made it difficult for the Republican leadership to continue to do nothing." Obviously, from the record, the President was not an obstructionist as his congressional and veteran critics charged. In almost all instances he had not resisted, but had encouraged, signed, and even sponsored legislation to assist the country's veterans. Furthermore, he had created the new Veterans Administration to ensure providing more efficient service to both ex-servicemen and the nation.[34]

The discontent engendered by the depression was partly responsible for the growing alienation between the President and the ex-soldiers; the estrangement was also as much a product of Hoover's unfortunate political style as of his opposition to ill-planned expenditures for the veterans. Busy with the numerous problems of the economic collapse, the shy, introverted President was incapable of practicing artful politics and benefiting from them. His behind-the-scenes sponsorship of the World War Disability Act, his failure or unwillingness to advertise his support for the Civil War bill and for various hospital acts, his offensive, moralizing veto of the Spanish-American War bill, and his earlier decision to allow his Secretary of Interior to testify against the consolidation bill made him appear, not as a friend, but as an opponent of the veterans' interests.

Confronted by the ex-servicemen on one side and the National Economy League on the other, his positive efforts in their behalf did not impress the veterans. Equally convinced of the need to promote stricter economies and of the justice of many of the veterans' requests, he could hardly demand a balanced budget and at the same time publicize his generosity to the veterans. By his silence he risked the enmity of the veterans' pressure groups, which had tested their power in Congress and had found it to be mighty. As the nation sank deeper into the depression, the veterans were to increase their demands and their

34. Daniels, *Bonus March*, p. 43. Daniels does not examine Hoover's efforts on behalf of the veterans. William D. Mitchell to HH, July 10, 1930, PP 284, HHPL; HHPW, I, 356–57.

complaints that the federal government had not been generous enough. Ironically, the chief reason for this stingi-
ness, they came to believe, was their chief benefactor,
Herbert Clark Hoover.

2

The Depression and the Bonus

Since the passage of the World War Omnibus Bill in 1924, an "era of good feelings" had characterized relations between Republican Presidents and veterans' organizations.[1] Hoover's generosity logically should have extended that era far into the future, for within less than a year and four months he approved a succession of costly bills for construction of soldiers' homes and hospitals and for hospitalization and pensions. During that period he signed new benefits of more than $118 million, and his expensive Disability Act abandoned the sacrosanct service-connection principle. The Spanish-American War bill provided another $11.7 million. Added to past benefits, the new veterans' laws shot total annual benefits to $675.8 million.[2] These provisions awarded the veterans more than 16 per cent of the total federal income, yet they

1. Richard S. Jones, *A History of the American Legion* (Indianapolis: The Bobbs-Merrill Co., Inc., 1946), p. 140.

2. See U.S., Bureau of the Census, *Historical Statistics of the United States, Colonial Times to 1957* (Washington, D.C.: Government Printing Office, 1960), p. 740 (hereafter cited as HSUS). As *Historical Statistics* tabulated figures in fiscal year increments, the effect of Hoover's new legislation is not immediately apparent. In 1930 expenditures for veterans jumped from $665.3 million to $675.8 million; in 1931 to $752.8 million; and in 1932 to $835.4 million. In 1933, after Hoover's defeat, FDR cut benefits significantly. Hoover approved $118 million in new legislation in less than a year and four months, between December 1929, when he signed two hospital construction acts totaling $15.9 million, and March 1931, when he approved additional hospital construction totaling $20.8 million as well as four special acts for construction of soldiers' homes at $5.4 million. His approval in 1930 of the Civil War Act ($12.1 million) and of the Disability Act ($64 million) brought the total of Hoover's newly signed benefits to an estimated $118.2 million. The Spanish-American War bill, which passed over his veto, added another $11.7 million. For a summary of benefits, see "Veteran Relief," Memo, April 8, 1931, PP 296, and FTH to HH, September 13, 1930, PP 284, HHPL.

represented less than 4 per cent of the population. Hoover's quick approval of more than $118 million in new benefits represented an 18 per cent increase over annual expenditures before he became President.[3] In addition, the creation of the Veterans Administration promised greater efficiency and service for ex-soldiers.

On the basis of his support for ex-servicemen, Hoover should have been among the veterans' favorite Presidents; the "era of good feelings" should have continued. Instead, in 1930 it came to an abrupt end. Hoover's moralistic veto of the Spanish-American War pension bill and his ineptness at public relations had helped create an atmosphere of suspicion and misunderstanding. More im-

---

3. HSUS, p. 711. In 1930 the federal income was $4,177,942,000; in 1931 and 1932 government income dropped to $3,115,557,000 and $1,923,913,000, respectively. Using the higher 1930 federal income, expenditures for veterans for that year ($675.8 million) absorbed 16.1 per cent of the federal income, and in Hoover's subsequent years as President, when federal income decreased and veterans' benefits increased, the new legislation for ex-servicemen claimed a larger percentage. The U.S. population in 1930 was 123,188,000. There were 4,680,000 veterans in civilian life—3.7 per cent of the population. HSUS, pp. 7, 738. Estimates at the time of passage were more startling than *Historical Statistics* figures, which were tabulated years later. Hoover claimed that "total outlays for all services to World War veterans are nearly $600,000,000 a year and to veterans of all wars nearly $900,000,000 per annum." "Address to the Twelfth Annual Convention of the American Legion," October 6, 1930, in Herbert Hoover, *The State Papers and Other Public Writings of Herbert Hoover*, William S. Myers, ed., 2 vols. (New York: Doubleday, Doran, and Company, Inc., 1934), I, 388 (hereafter cited as HHPW). Hoover's figures are open to question, since he did not cite their sources. He often obtained estimates from Hines, and Hines probably based his computation on the forecast of the number of eligible veterans expected to apply for benefits. Hines frequently cited five-year estimates, and both Hoover and Hines tended to think in terms of the number of eligible veterans. Not all eligible ex-servicemen took advantage of their benefits, which may account for the lower figure recorded in HSUS, 1960, p. 740. Nevertheless, during Hoover's term the President and Congress dealt with projected costs, and using Hoover's figure of $900 million, expenditures for veterans would have represented 21.5 per cent of the federal income. In that context Hoover and many liberal congressmen opposed further spending for veterans. In 1928, the year Hoover was elected, annual expenditures for veterans stood at $652.7 million. His approval of $118 million in new legislation represented an 18 per cent increase in benefits.

portant, perhaps, Hoover felt obligated to uphold the earlier decision to defer payment of the bonus until 1945.
The logical time to have paid the bonus was during the
prosperous twenties, but the nation had then been unwilling to recognize the long-range costs of waging wars. With
the coming of the depression, veterans became more
strongly determined to demand immediate compensation.
Certainly they deserved the bonus; but most political and
financial leaders believed that further expenditures for
veterans' benefits must be deferred until prosperity returned. Thus, instead of enjoying a climate of continued
good relations between ex-servicemen and Republican
Presidents, Hoover faced a situation that promised increasing conflict.

The leader who finally brought the veterans' tempers to
a boil was an obscure, newly elected Democratic congressman from Texas. Except for local publicity, Wright
Patman's election in 1928 went almost unnoticed.[4]
Boyish-looking at thirty-six, Patman entered Congress
with all the zeal and determination of a successful district
attorney and the convictions of a Baptist prohibition cru-
sader.[5] While working as a tenant farmer, he had scraped
enough money together to begin his legal studies, worked
his way through law school, won election as prosecuting
attorney in the Fifth Congressional District of Texas, and
served two terms in the state legislature. No doubt to the
amusement of his new Washington colleagues, he aptly
described himself as a "missionary Baptist." Missionary
he was; the cotton farmers of northeastern Texas and his
beloved comrades of the World War had elected him, and
it was their interests that he came to Congress to represent. Patman thought of himself as a champion of the

4. Some of the information on Wright Patman's early career is based
on his private collection of local Texas newspaper clippings. When either the name of the newspaper or the date of publication is not clearly
indicated, the citation refers to the scrapbook in which the clipping is
located; for example, Patman, Scrapbook, I.
5. Patman, Scrapbook, I. At the time I consulted the Patman papers
they were in Congressman Patman's possession and in considerable
disarray. Since that time they have been transferred to the Lyndon
Baines Johnson Presidential Library in Austin, Texas.

"plain people" and therefore a dedicated enemy of trusts, monopolies, big bankers, and plutocrats in general.[6]

The young Texan wasted little time in displaying his evangelistic fervor. As Congress raised the nation's already high tariff, Patman steadfastly denounced protection as a device to line "the pockets of the few who already own and control a majority of the wealth." In almost the same breath, however, he demonstrated a bewildering inconsistency by demanding federal subsidies for cotton farmers and an import tariff on cotton cloth as justice to the people. Then, lacking the restraint that ordinarily characterizes freshman congressmen, he vigorously attacked Hoover's new attorney general, William D. Mitchell, for delaying legal action against the cottonseed oil trust. Patman believed that Republican administrations had encouraged monopoly. The Attorney General's failure to launch an immediate investigation of the Federal Trade Commission's alleged favoritism toward the trust convinced Patman that Mitchell was obviously too lax in rooting out conspiracy and corruption in big business; Mitchell was already "following in the footsteps of Harry Daugherty," Harding's attorney general who was tried for corruption twice but escaped conviction each time.[7]

During May 1929 Patman initiated what became a long personal crusade that soon absorbed almost all of his time and energy. This project was his bill to provide immediate cash payment at full value of the Adjusted Service Certificates—"the bonus." [8] Under Coolidge, the veterans had accepted a compromise on the bonus that provided for distribution in 1945. The twenty-year endowment fund would, of course, substantially increase each veteran's payment, but Patman wanted the full face amount

6. Texarkana *News*, February 10, 1928; Dallas *Morning News*, October 12, 1929; Texarkana *Gazette*, November 30, 1929.

7. Texarkana *Gazette*, May 13 and July 20, 1929; Laman (Texas) *Echo*, March 28, 1930; Houston *Post-Dispatch*, May 4, 1930.

8. For a copy of HR 3493, see Adjusted Service Certificate Files, May 28, 1929, Patman Papers (hereafter cited as ASCF); U.S., Congress, House, *Congressional Record*, 71st Cong., 1st sess., 1929, 71, pt. 2, pp. 2146, 2480.

on the certificate, and he wanted it immediately. Amidst the numerous veterans' benefit bills introduced during Hoover's first year of office, Patman's bill at first received little notice. His arguments before the House stressed that immediate payment would help blot out the memory of billions of dollars in federal subsidies to war profiteers and belatedly do justice to the nation's real heroes.

Already engaged in a reorganization of veteran agencies and under heavy pressure from veteran lobbies for more hospitals, increased pensions, and expanded disability allowances, Hoover had privately rejected Patman's proposal, especially as the American Legion showed little interest.[9] At that time the stock market crash was still five months in the future, and as many Americans were enjoying unprecedented prosperity, Patman's class-conscious appeal at first went almost wholly unheeded.

Patman realized that without the organized support of the American Legion his effort was doomed. The Veterans of Foreign Wars were willing to make the bonus their special crusade, but the Legion's officers had their own favorite pieces of legislation, and they were in no hurry for the bonus. The much more powerful Legion preferred to concentrate its efforts on increasing benefits for veterans disabled in the war and for their widows and dependents.[10] Patman was a loyal legionnaire and a past commander of a local post, but he considered the Legion's policy to be much too narrow. With the same degree of inconsistency that moved him to denounce higher tariffs as favors to special interests while at the same time demanding cotton subsidies and import quotas on cotton cloth, he championed every effort to increase veteran

9. FTH to HH, November 16, 1929; HH to James C. Roop, November 16, 1929; Roop to HH, December 3, 1929; FTH to Newton, March 7, 1930, PP 297, HHPL; Patman to FTH, November 26, 1929, ASCF, Patman Papers.

10. On March 24, 1930, Patman sent a letter to each congressman asking him to join a drive for full payment of the bonus. For a copy of the letter, see Patman, Scrapbook, I. Daniel De Coe, "An Open Letter to Mr. Hoover," *Foreign Service*, 19 (November 1931), 10–11; interview with James Van Zandt, former National Commander of the VFW, April 14, 1972; New York *Times*, September 25, 1931.

benefits while refusing to concede that the organized veterans' lobbies were themselves special-interest groups.

To Patman's way of thinking, the veteran was the common man, defended by veterans' organizations such as the Legion against the predatory rich, who ruled the country to their own advantage. He ignored the fact that many veterans were affluent middle-class Americans and that they could not claim to represent the interests of "the common man"—at best an amorphous term. But to a crusading politician with a dramatic flair, ex-servicemen were "the people," while the Mellons and Hoovers protected the nation's exploitive monied class. Irritated by opposition from the Legion's national officers, Wright Patman headed back to the source of his strength, back to the Texas Legion. From that power base he hoped to launch a drive that would win over the national organization during its forthcoming convention in October 1930.[11]

While Patman corralled supporters at the Texas state Legion convention, Hoover decided that he would attend the national convention. It was a belated attempt to capitalize on his Disability Act and at the same time to mend political fences with the ex-servicemen. His advisers, including John Thomas Taylor, chief Legion lobbyist on Capitol Hill, recommended that, since most delegates were "highly idealistic" men, the President should appeal to patriotism, the maintenance of law and order, the duty of community service, and the glories of the Legion. Should anyone offer resolutions that might embarrass the administration, Hanford MacNider, a wealthy Iowa farmer, popular past national commander, and Hoover's minister to Canada, could be relied upon to silence the opposition.[12]

In his speech before the Boston convention Hoover adhered to the suggested emphasis on idealism and patrio-

11. U.S., Congress, House, *Congressional Record*, 71st Cong., 2d sess., 1930, 72, pt. 6, pp. 6842–46; Patman, Scrapbook, I and II; Texas *Legion News*, November 10, 1930.

12. John Thomas Taylor to Lawrence Richey, August 27, 1930, PP 59, HHPL; George Akerson to Hanford MacNider, September 13, 1930, MacNider Papers, HHPL.

tism. Complimenting the legionnaires at great length, the President reminded them that the government was already spending $600 million a year for World War veterans and $900 million a year for all veterans. He also stressed the public's already heavy tax burden. An address by the President was a sign of immense prestige and a source of gratification to an organization founded only eleven years earlier, and while Hoover seemed incapable of arousing deep emotion in any of his public appearances, the speech was definitely a success. He had created the impression of a benign and cooperative Chief Executive who would not forget the sacrifices of the soldier or slight the dignity of the Legion. His message was clear; when economic conditions improved, the Legion would find a sympathetic listener in the White House.[13]

After the pleasantries of speechmaking, the administration engaged in a tough power struggle behind the scenes. Hoover's supporters convinced the Resolutions Committee that it should withhold action on the bonus until it had polled the convention, which in effect delayed the proposal for at least a year. Patman's greater influence on the legislative subcommittee, however, led to a minority report before the entire convention, where Patman's support was the strongest. Expecting the floor fight and adept at managing conventions, Hanford MacNider and John R. Quinn, another past national commander, immediately moved that the minority report be tabled, thus cutting off debate and confounding the advocates of the bonus.[14]

Circumvented, Patman urged every Democratic nominee to make the bonus an issue in the November congressional election. Bonus politics in the 1930 congres-

13. *Summary of Proceedings*, Twelfth Annual National Convention of the American Legion (Boston, Massachusetts, October 6–9, 1930), pp. 8–11, American Legion Papers (hereafter cited as ALP).

14. Patman, news release [?], n.d., ASCF, Patman Papers; House, *Congressional Record*, 71st Cong., 3d sess., 1931, 74, pt. 3, pp. 2469–70; *Summary of Proceedings*, Twelfth Convention, American Legion, p. 58, ALP.

sional election involved far more than Patman's anger and frustration. He knew that he had a political issue with great potential, and his political astuteness became a matter of real concern for his foes. Edward Lewis, an important veterans' lobbyist, was convinced that the Republicans would also jump on the bandwagon, and he predicted that Hoover "was only awaiting the psychological moment to spring it before the November election." [15] The President, however, refused to "spring" the bonus, and Republicans lost control of Congress. Amelioration of the depression, not the bonus, had been decisive in the elections, but now the bonus loomed larger as an issue.

Patman's supporters celebrated the election results and informed him of a swelling tide of support from veterans, bolstered by thousands of letters and petitions and thirty new bonus bills introduced in the House. After the election the Hearst newspapers opened a hard-hitting campaign to make the bonus a national issue, and Patman enthusiastically predicted that with Hearst's support he and his allies could "put this proposition over in sixty days." [16]

With estimates on bonus legislation ranging up to $4 billion, the total federal yearly income at that time, Hoover had reason to be critical of the measure.[17] As often happened when he felt righteous anger, however, he played into the hands of his political enemies. At a news conference on December 9, the President made one of the most politically inept statements of his career. Without clearly identifying the bonus bills as his chief

15. Patman, Scrapbook, I; Patman, To All Democratic Nominees, n.d., mimeographed letter, Patman Papers; Edward Lewis to Ralph T. O'Neil, October 20, 1930, Veterans Welfare, ASCF, ALP; Chicago *Herald Examiner*, November 17, 1930.

16. Patman to Col. Frank Knox, November 30, 1930, ASCF, Patman Papers. For numerous articles, see Scrapbook, II.

17. HH to Ogden Mills, November 28, 1930; Arthur H. Vandenberg to HH, December 29, 1930, PP 297, HHPL. Hoover informed Mills that it "might be desirable to write him [Vandenberg] as to how impossible this is." Many letters to Mellon, Mills, and Hines are in Records of the Department of the Treasury, Secretary's Correspondence, Soldiers' Bonus, RG 56, NA.

targets, he charged that special-interest groups had introduced bills amounting to $4.5 billion, "under the guise of giving relief of some kind or another," and that such measures, rather than providing relief, would cause a tax increase and thus retard recovery. He warned that prosperity could not be restored "by raids on the public Treasury," nor would the American people be fooled by those who were "playing politics at the expense of human misery." [18] Because he did not specifically denounce the bonus or direct his anger at the veterans' demands, some critics felt that Hoover had attacked all the needy who sought relief as well as the congressmen who were trying to help them.

While Senator Arthur Vandenberg of Michigan attempted in vain to convince Hoover that the Republican party should take a more positive stance on the bonus, Patman's drive steadily gained momentum. To Patman's way of thinking, the economic problems of Americans were due to more than the depression; they were caused by nothing less than a war that was being waged against the people by a conspiracy which placed "property rights above human rights." A vote against the bonus was a vote against the people, a vote for the exploitive rich, a vote for property rights over human rights. By advertising the bonus issue as one of wealth versus need, class versus class, Patman captured nationwide attention, and the number of signatures on his petition to discharge his bill from the House Ways and Means Committee quickly jumped to 100.[19] The fallacies in such a sweeping analogy were obvious to any thoughtful observer, but it made for good politics in a depression, and the folks back home loved it.

Patman's mustering of parades, bands, and Hearst articles had begun to yield results. He was further encouraged by unexpected and enthusiastic support from Father Charles E. Coughlin, the conspiracy-oriented, De-

18. "Press Conference Statement," December 9, 1930, in HHPW, I, 459–60.

19. Vandenberg to HH, December 29, 1930; HH to Vandenberg, December 30, 1930, PP 297, HHPL; House, *Congressional Record*, 71st Cong., 3d sess., 1930, 74, pt. 3, pp. 897–902, 1064, 1314.

troit-based Roman Catholic radio priest, who was fast becoming a powerful political force in his own right. Next,
early in January 1931, Patman sounded out Ralph T.
O'Neil, national commander of the Legion. O'Neil replied
that the results of the Boston convention had precluded
support for the bonus as part of the Legion's official legislative program, but he added that the organization would
not oppose it. Without hesitation Patman immediately
read O'Neil's letter to the House, then led a fife-and-drum
corps and a host of Hearst reporters and legionnaires
down Pennsylvania Avenue for a rally at Capitol Plaza.[20]

By January 25, following prolonged debate, the
Legion's executive committee released a declaration of
support for the bonus, and although it did not give special
endorsement to any one of the many bonus bills, congressional action was now certain. Congressional hearings on
all of the various bonus bills—including those introduced
by House Speaker John Nance Garner, Hamilton Fish of
New York, John Rankin of Mississippi, and many others—
posed an obvious threat to Patman's bill. The numerous
bills also meant that a compromise short of full payment
was entirely likely. Still, *Time* observed that with Legion
support "a little, suppressed idea burst upon the nation as
a full-fledged legislative movement." [21]

During the hearings on the various bonus bills, the administration concentrated its attacks mainly on Patman's.
Mellon and Under Secretary of the Treasury Ogden Mills

20. Charles E. Coughlin to Patman, December 30, 1930; Patman to
Coughlin, January 1, 1931, Patman Papers. Coughlin claimed that Patman had "millions of people" supporting him. O'Neil to Patman, January 9, 1931, ASCF, ALP; House, *Congressional Record*, 71st Cong.,
3d sess., 1931, 74, pt. 2, pp. 1969–70; Patman, Scrapbook, I; *Herald*,
January 22, 1931; *Daily News*, January 21, 1931. For Washington, D.C.,
newspapers, the city is omitted from the citation.

21. *Herald*, January 22, 1931; O'Neil to Edward Spafford, January
17, 1931; O'Neil to Alvin Owsley, January 17, 1931; "Resolution," National Executive Committee, January 25, 1931, ASCF, ALP. For the influence of the Texas Legion in securing the resolution, see Patman,
Scrapbook, I; Texas *Legion News*, February 10, 1931. "Bonus Bust,"
Time, 17 (February 9, 1931), 11, 12; "The Veterans Bonus—Calamity
or Blessing?" *Literary Digest*, 108 (February 4, 1931), 5–6. The Legion
switch, concluded the *Literary Digest*, gave the bonus drive "tremendous impetus."

trotted out a long procession of worried, glum-looking bankers and financiers, who repeated Mellon's argument that full payment of the $3.4 billion would shatter the securities markets, undermine public credit, and retard recovery. In support of the gloomy testimony—or perhaps as a result of it—the bond market dropped sharply.[22]

Patman's strategy, on the other hand, was to overpower the House Ways and Means Committee with a solid, determined phalanx of veterans to support his bill, thus blunting the somber testimony of Mellon and the bankers and forcing Congress to choose between Wall Street and the doughboys. But to Patman's surprise and irritation, the most effective witness against full payment turned out to be John Thomas Taylor, a veteran lobbyist for the American Legion and one of the most influential and skillful in Washington. Sporting a walking stick, snap-brim hat, spats, and a black cigar, Taylor cut a dapper figure. He commanded an expert knowledge of congressional procedure, carefully cultivated personal relations with powerful committee chairmen, and maintained an extensive file on the voting record of every legislator.[23]

During the first year of the Hoover administration, Taylor had sought a position on the Civil Service Commission, and Hoover had been favorably inclined toward the appointment until several congressmen called Taylor's character into question, complaining of his "numerous drunken orgies" that allegedly disturbed the entire neighborhood. For a while all action on the appointment was delayed. As Hoover was thought to be pleased with Taylor's cooperative attitude on the Legion's legislative proposals, however, the possibility of an appointment was an inducement that might well work to the administration's advantage, especially if, as rumored, that position would

22. "Veterans Bonus," *Literary Digest*, p. 5; "Bonus Bust," *Time*, p. 12. Patman to William Randolph Hearst, telegram, January 28, 1931, Patman Papers; U.S., Congress, Senate, Committee on Finance, *Hearings on Payment of Veterans Adjusted Service Certificates*, 71st Cong., 3d sess., January 26–29, 1931, pp. 1–29, 257–63, 354–65, 367–80, and *passim*.
23. "Heroes," *Time*, 25 (January 21, 1935), 21.

be secretary to the President. Patman's other witnesses performed as expected, but when John Nance Garner questioned Taylor, the Legion's chief lobbyist refused to champion full payment, and without his support, Patman's bill quickly lost ground.[24]

Convinced that Taylor had betrayed him and the veterans, Patman sought to force his removal as chief lobbyist for the Legion and further charged that Taylor had performed this service while under consideration for appointment as one of Hoover's secretaries. Taylor replied that as the Legion's executive committee had pointedly refused to endorse any specific bill, he had no right to comment favorably on any of them. His critics were not able to force his resignation, yet they evidently created enough ill will to prevent his appointment to an important government position.[25]

Even if Taylor had supported Patman's bill, it would still have faced a barrage of criticism. For once, the liberal segment of the press agreed with Mellon and Hoover. *The Nation* endorsed their opposition to immediate payment and applauded the bankers who testified before the House Ways and Means Committee. Their testimony informed Americans that the bonus would depress the bond market by absorbing funds needed for municipal, state, and industrial construction, dangerously affect the solvency of hard-pressed banks by draining off bank deposits for investment in safer government bonds, and thus retard recovery and deepen the depression. "It is not, however, mainly because of its serious economic consequences that the proposed cash payment is vicious, but because it has no real moral justification." The proponents' argument

24. Joseph T. Robinson to HH, July 15, 1929, PP 97; HH to Walter F. Brown, July 24, 1929; Newton to HH, memo, n.d., PP 931; A. M. Free to Richey, July 29, 1929, PP 97; O. L. Bodenhamer to HH, February 4, 1931, PP 293; David A. Reed to HH, January 31, 1930, PP 931, HHPL. U.S., Congress, House, Committee on Ways and Means, *Hearings on Veterans Adjusted Service Certificates*, 71st Cong., 3d sess., January 29, 30, 31, and February 2, 3, 4, and 5, 1931, pp. 120–24, 128–42, 151–67, 184–203.

25. House, *Congressional Record*, 71st Cong., 3d sess., 1931, 74, pt. 2, p. 4348; Taylor to O'Neil, February 3, 1931, ASCF, Taylor File, ALP.

that the bonus was unemployment relief was, *The Nation* charged, a "palpable fraud." It would not go to unemployed women, for example, or to others who were more destitute than many veterans. As a means of unemployment relief it was "complete dishonesty . . . a Treasury grab." *The New Republic* echoed this stand, calling the veterans "mercenaries of patriotism." [26]

On February 12, 1931, one week after the hearings, an executive session of the House Ways and Means Committee unexpectedly rejected all the bonus bills and within a matter of several hours reported out a new bill authorizing loans on the Adjusted Service Certificates of up to 50 per cent at 4½ per cent interest. This action raised the amount that could be borrowed from an average of $225 to $500. Patman erroneously suspected an administration compromise, yet he could not actively oppose it. Despite Hoover's opposition, even Republicans supported the loan bill, and it passed the House by a vote of 363 to 39. Soon afterward it passed the Senate by 72 to 15.[27]

Hoover had solemnly, hopelessly, fought the loan bill's confirmation. He correctly predicted that the loans could not be financed solely from the $700 million reserves already accumulated in the bonus sinking fund—a favorite point made by supporters of the bill and a source of considerable misunderstanding. In the first place, $700 million would not be enough. In fact, Hoover soon had to request and Congress quickly approved the appropriation of almost $200 million more to replenish the depleted bonus sinking fund.[28] Moreover, the original $700 million had been invested in securities, and to raise the needed

26. "Cash for Veterans," *Nation*, 132 (February 4, 1931), 113; "Bonus Raid," *Nation*, 132 (February 18, 1931), 170; "Mercenaries of Patriotism," *New Republic*, 66 (February 25, 1931), 30–31.

27. Andrew W. Mellon to Willis C. Hawley, February 13, 1931; FTH, "Press Statement," February 12, 1931, PP 298, HHPL; U.S., Congress, House, Committee on Ways and Means, *Increase of Loan Basis of Adjusted Service Certificates*, Report No. 2670, 71st Cong., 3d sess., February 14, 1931, pp. 1–8; Senate, *Congressional Record*, 71st Cong., 3d sess., 1931, 74, pt. 5, pp. 5357–86.

28. Paul Y. Anderson, "Hoover Suffers in the House," *Nation*, 132 (March 11, 1931), 268; House, *Congressional Record*, 72d Cong., 1st sess., 1931, 75, pt. 1, pp. 714–16; Senate, *Congressional Record*, 72d

cash the government would be forced to sell those securities on the open market. The problem with sale of these securities, Hoover argued, was that the money for expanding "public construction, for assistance to unemployment and other relief measures" must also be raised through the sale of securities. These demands were being made at the same time the government also needed to raise $500 million to cover the federal deficit and was legally required to retire "a billion dollars of early maturities of outstanding debts." To soften his opposition Hoover acknowledged that relief for the 200,000 to 300,000 unemployed veterans was an "appealing argument," but he reminded Congress that, since more than that number of nonveterans were unemployed, the bill was highly discriminatory.[29] In fact, although Hoover did not mention it, only about 6.4 per cent of the veterans were unemployed in 1931, and these represented only 3.7 per cent of the total unemployed.[30]

More than two thirds of each house had voted for the loan bill, more than enough to override a presidential veto. If Hoover held any hope of stopping the measure, he needed to propose some sort of compromise. A compromise strategy had worked less than a year earlier when Hoover had substituted his Disability Act after vetoing a less equitable one. Congressman William E. Evans of California suggested a substitute bill that would limit loans

Cong., 1st sess., 1931, 75, pt. 1, pp. 916–17; New York *Times*, December 10, 18, 20, 1931.

29. HH to Reed Smoot, February 18, 1931, PP 297, HHPL. Hoover based his estimate of $1 billion for the cost of the 50 per cent loan bill on Hines's letter of February 17, 1931, PP 297, HHPL. Smoot released the letter to the press; HHPW, I, 507–9.

30. HSUS, pp. 73, 738. Hoover made an effort to determine the number of unemployed veterans. George F. Getz to Robert P. Lamont, February 21, 1931; James L. Fieser to HH, February 23, 1931; FTH to HH, February 26, 1931, PP 297, HHPL. Hines informed Hoover that the Veterans Administration survey revealed an 8 per cent unemployment figure but he believed 6 per cent would be more accurate. Congressman Hamilton Fish of New York offered an unsubstantiated claim that veterans represented 15 per cent of the unemployed although they were less than 3 per cent of the total population. House, *Congressional Record*, 71st Cong., 3d sess., 1931, 74, pt. 5, pp. 5074–75, 5079.

to unemployed veterans. Such a gesture would also soften any impression of "harshness and lack of sympathy" on the part of the administration.[31]

On February 26, 1931, Hoover sent his veto to Congress. Unable to stop the relentless financial drain, he became rigidly opposed to any bonus measure, especially when there seemed no end to the ex-servicemen's demands. With the National Economy League watching his every move, and with financial advisers and the press—liberals and conservatives alike—demanding economy, especially when expenditures to veterans were involved, Hoover was in a quandary. To propose a substitute measure would have been more politic, especially as the Legion had finally thrown its power behind the loan bill. Although a veto was almost certain to be overridden, Hoover firmly refused to compromise on further disbursements to veterans. The veto message rehearsed his familiar themes: the need to balance the budget and the danger of funneling vitally needed capital to nonproductive channels. In conclusion, he remarked bluntly that by providing "an enormous sum of money to a vast majority who were able to care for themselves," Congress was breaking down "the barriers of self-reliance and self-support of our people." [32]

Many participants and historians have justly criticized the President's sanctimoniousness, his fiscal conservatism, his astigmatic favoritism toward business, and his refusal to support direct federal relief on the oft-repeated moral grounds that it would break down the self-reliance of the people. However, most of these same critics have failed to acknowledge adequately the fact that some congressional supporters of the bonus and other spending for veterans also voiced a questionable public morality. They assumed their own unconvincing moralistic stance with

31. William E. Evans to HH, February 23, 1931; Frederic C. Walcott to HH, February 20, 1931, PP 297, HHPL.

32. Letter from Legion National Commander Ralph T. O'Neil to all congressmen and senators, February 25, 1931, ASCF, ALP; HH, "Message to the House of Representatives," February 26, 1931, HHPW, I, 512–17.

the rallying cry, "Justice for the ex-serviceman!" To be sure, Patman and several others were genuinely devoted to the cause, but it is doubtful that justice was really the chief concern of some of the veterans' supporters. Indeed, although many congressmen rightfully condemned Hoover's moralizing, they also scorned his efforts to standardize the chaotic, haphazard, and inequitable manner in which they had devised and passed legislation for the veterans. While criticizing the President, they themselves offered no guidelines for equity and justice.

Only when Roosevelt became President were standards improved. FDR insisted on guidelines similar to Hoover's and was somewhat more successful in enforcing his wishes with Congress and holding veteran lobbies in check. In the Hoover years, however, the logrolling and inequities continued regardless of the President's objections; the political power of the competing veteran lobbies strengthened, Congress acquiesced, and the poor—who had no lobby to plead for them—remained without representation. Despite the often-heard pleas for justice for the veterans, some observers suspected that many a congressman's chief concern was votes. Pressure groups were having a field day on Capitol Hill, and Walter Lippmann, disgusted with the nation's legislators, pointedly observed that the "forgotten man was completely forgotten by every Senator whose constituents desired a special privilege." [33]

Despite the plausibility of the arguments against the new legislation for the veterans, it was a foregone conclusion that Hoover's veto could not stop the bonus loan bill. The humiliatingly wide margins with which both houses overrode the veto justified *Time*'s conclusion that he "had suffered his most serious Congressional reversal." [34] The President's frustration was understandable, especially

---

33. Walter Lippmann, *Interpretations, 1931–1932*, Allan Nevins, ed. (New York: The Macmillan Company, 1932), p. 281.

34. "Needy Served First," *Time*, 18 (March 9, 1931), 11–12. Joslin agreed that it was a serious blow to Hoover's prestige. Theodore J. Joslin, *Hoover Off the Record* (New York: Doubleday, Doran, and Co., 1934), p. 66.

considering the wide spectrum of antibonus sentiment.
When Congress passed the loan act, *The New Republic*
was furious. "Are the sufferings of unemployed veterans
any more appealing to sympathy than . . . men . . . either too old or too young to have served, or . . . unemployed women . . . any more deserving than farmers and
their families near starvation in the drought stricken
areas?"

According to *The New Republic*, the veterans' demands
needed to be placed in proper perspective, for the veterans considered themselves a privileged group with extraordinary rights. They were not at all concerned with
the plight of the needy or with social reform. Instead,
when they were not advancing their own interests, they
preferred "to search out and punish persons who recom-
mend changes in our political and social order, to serve
any cause which may be favored by reactionaries. They
are part of the social complex which includes the D.A.R.
and all witch-hunting bodies." By passing the loan bill,
Congress had blatantly attempted "to buy off the more energetic" at the expense of the needy. Still, more people
read Hearst papers than *The New Republic*, and Wright
Patman was the man of the hour. Though the drive for his
own bill seemed ended, he was the acknowledged leader
of the bonuseers, and he could take much of the credit for
the new loan bill.[35]

In May 1931 Credit-Anstalt, Austria's largest bank, suddenly closed its doors, and a full-scale panic ensued in
Europe. Hoover considered the panic a crucial turning
point in world affairs and believed that the collapse of
European economies was the true cause of economic difficulties in the United States, a theory that has been
vigorously challenged. The magnitude of the domestic
crisis was now clear to him. He initiated the moratorium
on debts, and in the ensuing months responded to the
crisis by offering his boldest, most dramatic leadership.[36]

35. "Mercenaries of Patriotism," *New Republic*, pp. 30–31; "Needy
Served First," *Time*, p. 12.

36. Herbert Hoover, *Memoirs*, 3 vols. (New York: The Macmillan
Company, 1951), III, 2–4, 58–59, 69–70.

At the same time, Patman launched another drive for full and immediate payment of the bonus. At first Hoover was not greatly worried. The authors of the loan bill had stolen Patman's thunder, and the Legion's national officers were solidly opposed to any new bonus legislation. However, on September 13, 1931, only one week before the convention opened in Detroit, Gen. John J. Pershing, the commander of the American Expeditionary Forces during the World War, informed Hoover that Legion officers were no longer certain that they could prevent "the other side from carrying the convention for the bonus." Pershing had canvassed the leadership at Hoover's request, and he now wrote that only a personal address by the President could prevent the Legion's approval of the bonus. With the convention only a week away and with conflicting opinions about the wisdom of a personal appearance, Hoover faced a difficult decision. In fact, on Friday evening, September 19, less than three days before the convention, Hoover consulted with his Secretaries of Treasury, State, and Commerce. Weighing their advice, he journeyed to his weekend vacation retreat in West Virginia to consider the matter a bit longer.[37]

Originally, Hoover had decided that MacNider and Theodore Roosevelt, Jr., could deal with the opposition by controlling the Resolutions Committee, but on Sunday, September 21, one day prior to the convention, newspaper reporters suddenly learned that a special train had arrived in Martinsburg to carry the President to Detroit. For Hoover, it was a dark, somber time. The events swirling around him were, he later recalled, nightmarish. On that

37. For a copy of H.R. 1, "Emergency Adjusted Compensation Act, 1932," introduced on December 8, 1931, see ASCF, Patman Papers. Patman believed the printing of fiat money would increase popular support for his bill. Patman to Emory L. O'Connell, May 27, 1935; Patman to William Randolph Hearst, October 23, 1931, Patman Papers. Patman to S. Lovenbein, June 12, 1931; Frank W. Clark to Patman, June 29, 1931; Lovenbein to Patman, July 24, 1931, Bonus Committee File, Patman Papers. John J. Pershing to HH, September 13, 1931, PP 297; J. Edgar Hoover to Richey, September 4, 1931; Newton to J. Edgar Hoover, September 14, 1931, PP 60, HHPL; New York *Times*, September 21, 1931.

same day Great Britain had announced its intention to abandon the gold standard. With international finance in almost complete disarray and the United States plunging deeper and faster into the economic maelstrom, his earlier confidence for a quick economic recovery now appeared ill-founded, even naive. Now he felt more strongly compelled to stop the latest bonus effort. To add to his unease, on the way to the train a long line of Sunday motorists who had been slowed to a crawl by the President's motorcade expressed their displeasure by persistently blowing their horns. Everyone seemed dissatisfied, most of all the man who had not yet completed the speech he did not want to give before a convention packed with thousands of disgruntled veterans.[38]

On the following morning the exhausted, haggard, deeply worried President stood silently at the podium and stared at his large audience. For almost two minutes he maintained a stonelike silence before he launched into a ten-minute address. A slight smile flickered on his round face. He was noticeably hesitant and obviously uncertain. Once again, he laid the entire responsibility for the depression squarely on events in Europe and appealed to the Legion to enlist in another battle, a "war against world depression." In one of his rare moments of eloquence he spoke of happier days, of more prosperous times, and of the sound character and high ideals of the delegates who had fought for and, he believed, always would defend the nation in times of great crisis.

There was some initial booing, but most of the audience responded with cheers. At first the cheers startled him, but then his uncertain smile quickly changed to a friendly, more confident one. Their applause reassured him—all the more because he had not expected a friendly reception. More important to the President, however, was the fact that the Legion officials solidly opposed the bonus, and Pershing's fears of new enthusiasm for the

38. Hoover, *Memoirs*, III, 83; MacNider to Theodore Roosevelt, Jr., September 2, 1931, MacNider Papers, HHPL. MacNider encouraged Hoover to attend. New York *Times*, September 21, 1931; Joslin, *Hoover*, pp. 64–65, 121–22.

bonus proved unfounded. Resolutions for benefits to disabled veterans, widows, and dependents were more popular. Despite Patman's considerable victory in forcing out a minority report, the convention easily repudiated the resolution for the bonus.[39]

Patman was understandably and openly bitter about his setback. A strong prohibitionist, he erroneously charged that the administration had swung the delegates against the bonus by promising them legal beer. *The Nation,* however, was delighted with the President's "courage and leadership." *The New Republic* agreed, but it found the necessity of a presidential address before the Legion's convention "a portent of sinister significance." [40]

With demands for the bonus seemingly laid to rest, Hoover spent most of October and November of 1931 putting together a legislative program to combat the depression. He organized the National Credit Corporation, a private group of big bankers, and cajoled it into pooling $500 million for loans to shaky banks that were holding sound securities but were dangerously illiquid. But when bank failures increased from 298 in September to a new high of 512 in October, the reluctant bankers became frightened, and a bitter President acknowledged defeat for his cherished voluntarism. In early December, prodded by Eugene Meyer, Jr., he instructed Congress to establish the Reconstruction Finance Corporation, and on January 22, 1932, he signed the bill creating the agency that was to lend millions of dollars to the nation's leading businesses, banks, and railroads. On December 8, 1931, as the new Congress convened, he had also requested additional capital for the Federal Land Banks, action to free deposits in closed banks, more flexible Federal Reserve discount rates, creation of Home Loan Discount Banks, aid to the nation's railroads, revised banking laws, and

39. New York *Times,* September 22, 23, 1931. *Summary of Proceedings* of the Thirteenth Annual National Convention of the American Legion, Detroit, Michigan, September 21–24, 1931, pp. 9–10, ALP.

40. Columbia (South Carolina) *Record,* December 22, 1931; *Nation,* 133 (September 30, 1931), 319–20; "The Lesson of the Legion," *New Republic,* 68 (October 14, 1931), 221–22.

more stringent economy. With the regrettable exception of direct federal relief for the unemployed it was, for its time, considered to be an ambitious program. These bills had been worked out in consultation with the leaders of both parties during October and November, and eventually, during the summer of 1932, most of them won congressional approval.[41]

Within one month after Hoover had unveiled his new legislative effort, Wright Patman returned to the attack. Imitating his methods in earlier successes, he went straight for Andrew W. Mellon, who had been dubbed by his party the greatest Secretary of the Treasury since Alexander Hamilton. Patman told an excited House that he had uncovered proof that Mellon's ownership of ocean vessels doing business with the federal government violated a 1789 law that forbade the Secretary of the Treasury from engaging in commerce and trade. Patman's listeners could always expect a good show, but they were undoubtedly caught off guard when he dramatically demanded Mellon's impeachment for "high crimes and misdemeanors." The embarrassing controversy did not subside until February 4, 1932, when Hoover abruptly announced that Mellon was needed as ambassador to Great Britain. Then, at the height of the well-publicized controversy, Patman introduced his newest bonus bill, an inflationary bill that required no bonds or other financial securities to support the additional dollars.[42]

The flood of letters and petitions from veterans worried the President. He warned Congress once again of his unalterable opposition to a bonus and reminded congressmen that the Legion supported his position. He insisted

41. Harris Gaylord Warren, *Herbert Hoover and the Great Depression* (New York: Oxford University Press, 1959), pp. 139–43; Gerald D. Nash, "Herbert Hoover and the Origins of the Reconstruction Finance Corporation," *The Mississippi Valley Historical Review*, 46 (December 1959), 455–68; Warren, *Hoover*, pp. 155–58.

42. For extensive documents and correspondence, see Mellon File, Patman Papers. New York *Times*, January 7, 14, 15, 1932; *Time*, 19 (January 25, 1932), 10–11; (February 15, 1932), pp. 16–17; copy of H.R. 7726, 72d Cong., 1st sess., January 14, 1932, is in the Henry T. Rainey Papers, Box 11, LC.

that Patman's bill would destroy his efforts to promote recovery and to sustain the government's credit. Patman
fired back quickly: "The millions released by the Reconstruction Finance Corporation went to the big boys by
way of New York," he said, and it was high time to put
millions into the hands of "the little fellows in every nook
and corner of the nation." Inflation, furthermore, was exactly what the nation needed. Elmer Thomas in the Senate agreed and for lack of another supporter, came to be
recognized as the leader for the bonus in the upper house.
Thomas made the necessary genuflections to veterans'
rights and worked closely with lobbyists for the VFW, but
his overriding interest was inflation. Prominent economists rejected his arguments, however, and Thomas made
few converts. Patman and Thomas were backed by John
Rankin, the Mississippi Democrat and chairman of the
House Veterans Committee. "Of course we're going off
the gold standard," he chortled, "and the sooner the better." [43]

Throughout much of April 1932, the members of the
House Ways and Means Committee listened patiently to a
long parade of witnesses favoring and opposing Patman's
inflationary bonus bill. "General" Jacob S. Coxey of
Coxey's Army and Father Charles E. Coughlin championed immediate inflation and denounced the big
bankers. Most of the committee members were horrified,
nevertheless, by the proposals to print and issue money
without backing it with either bonds or gold. Despite the
criticisms against aiding business recovery, the committee
remained unimpressed. More petitions and parades were
ineffectual. On April 17, Henry T. Rainey, the Democratic
floor leader of the House voiced a widespread fear that
Patman's bill would result in a near-worthless dollar,

43. Records of the Secretary of the Treasury, Secretary's Correspondence, Soldiers' Bonus, 1932, RG 56, NA; American Legion Post
File, Patman Papers. Hoover, *Memoirs*, III, 83; "Press Statement,"
March 29, 1932, PP 284, HHPL; "Pro Bono Politico," *Time*, 19 (April
11, 1932), 19; Elmer Thomas to Bernard Baruch, April 9, 1932, Legislative Correspondence, Box 26, Thomas Papers, University of Oklahoma,
and numerous letters to economists and leading financiers in Boxes
25 and 26.

much like the inflated German mark in the wake of the
World War. Visions of wheelbarrows full of dollars ex-
changed for a loaf of bread were called to mind by the dismal anti-inflation testimony. Speaker Garner, a major con-
tender for the Democratic presidential nomination, and
Senate Democratic Leader Joseph T. Robinson were also
adamant in their opposition.[44]

For that matter, Roosevelt also opposed the bonus. Critical of Hoover's deficit spending, FDR campaigned on a
platform of stricter economies and a balanced budget. Indeed, twice during his first term he too vetoed the bonus.
The political realities of 1932 united congressional liberals and conservatives firmly against fiat inflation. Part of
the frustration among advocates of the bonus undoubtedly
resulted because some expansion was occurring, but not
as quickly or in the manner that they would have it. In
mid-April 1932, James H. MacLafferty, Hoover's congressional liaison man, informed the President of Patman's
recognition of this expansion. More important, MacLafferty recorded that Hoover was not only well aware of the
currency expansion by the Federal Reserve but had
vigorously supported it and that Patman now feared that
its effect would "dampen our [the bonus advocates'] enthusiasm, perhaps, to the point of destroying it." [45]

Overriding these matters, in the minds of many observers, was the question of priorities, a question that cannot
be lightly dismissed as mere fiscal conservatism. Liberals
and conservatives alike, led by Representative Fiorello
LaGuardia of New York, insisted that Congress had indeed been generous to the veterans, and now, the liberals
contended, it needed to turn to relief for all of the unemployed. Although he overstated the case, Walter Lippmann expressed the anger and fears of the opposition.

44. U.S., Congress, House, Committee on Ways and Means, *Hear-
ings on Payment of Adjusted Service Certificates*, 72d Cong., 1st sess.,
April 11–29 and May 2–3, 1932, pp. 1–841; Jacob S. Coxey to Patman,
April 12, 1932; Patman to Sgt. Alvin C. York, April 29, 1932, Patman
Papers; New York *Times*, April 17, 1932; Henry T. Rainey to A. F. Bur-
bage, May 12, 1932, Box 11, Rainey Papers, LC.

45. James H. MacLafferty, Diary, April 16, 1932, MacLafferty Papers,
HHPL.

Congressional favor to the veterans during the last ten years, he charged, had "created a privileged class, a class of men who have rights which no other citizens possess." As he put it, Congress had been constantly buying the veterans' vote, and with one-fourth of the federal income already allotted to the ex-servicemen, it was evident that "this mounting burden of expenditures to a special privileged class of voters is a menace not only to the budget but to popular government itself." [46]

Without sufficient backing from his own party or from the American Legion, and with the leadership of both the Democratic and Republican parties determined to kill the bill in committee, Patman was powerless to do more than repeat his usual arguments. On May 6, 1932, his effort to win support of the Legion's national executive committee failed, and on the following day the House Ways and Means Committee issued an adverse report.[47] This time, Patman had been defeated by a more powerful bipartisan coalition than in the past. With the congressional leadership, the administration, and the Legion allied against him, the latest bonus drive had been decisively stopped.

Nonetheless, the speeches, the petitions, the Mellon impeachment controversy, and the parades all had had an effect no one could have predicted. They had popularized for ex-doughboys an issue that, neither in the beginning nor in the end, was powerful enough to attract widespread support. Most important, the constant barrage of publicity had helped to convince thousands of discontented veterans that a banking conspiracy did exist and that they were indeed being cheated. As one influential veteran leader put it, "Stalin needs no emissaries in America. Those who destroy the Constitution at the behest of Wall Street are his most effective agents." [48] To

46. House, Committee on Ways and Means, *Hearings*, pp. 305–24, 605–21; Arthur Mann, *LaGuardia: A Fighter Against His Times, 1882–1933* (New York: J. B. Lippincott Company, 1959), p. 308; Lippmann, *Interpretations*, pp. 128–31.

47. James F. Barton to R. E. Jackson, May 31, 1932, ASCF, ALP.

48. *B.E.F.News*, July 9, 1932; David Brion Davis, ed., *The Fear of Conspiracy: Images of Un-American Subversion From the Revolution*

the former soldiers this latest defeat was the signal for a dramatic march and the most explosive demonstration that Washington had ever experienced.

The bonus fights were only one segment of the larger fabric of veteran demands and legislative battles. The history of Patman's bills or of the various other bonus bills is relatively insignificant. The importance of these lengthy battles lies in Hoover's prior relations with the veterans, in the march that all the publicity inspired, and the ways in which that march raised crucial questions about protest and the balance between civilian and military authority. The protest, moreover, was to become significant in another sense: It marked a turning point in Hoover's thinking. From a position of tolerance and restraint—heretofore unrecognized and unappreciated—he would eventually come to believe that the nation had faced a Communist conspiracy to overthrow the government.[49]

to the Present (Ithaca, N.Y.: Cornell University Press, 1971), pp. xiv, xxi. Davis cites a similar notion "of hidden aristocracy, lulling and duping the common people" that appears in the "anti-Masonic, Jacksonian, and populist movements."

49. Hoover's defensiveness is noted at various places throughout this study. Others have noted his tendency to react defensively toward criticism or to explain events in terms of conspiracy. Craig Lloyd, _Aggressive Introvert: A Study of Herbert Hoover and Public Relations Management, 1912–1932_ (Columbus: Ohio State University Press, 1972), pp. 166–70; Jordan Schwarz, _The Interregnum of Despair: Hoover, Congress and the Depression_ (Urbana: University of Illinois Press, 1970), pp. 51, 82–85, 90–91, 127. Schwarz demonstrated that many congressmen were also prone to think in terms of plots, especially when their pet legislative efforts were involved. It is significant, however, that Hoover had modified his earlier tendency to view protesters or Communists as dangerous threats to the Republic. Hoover's tolerance and restraint toward protest have not yet been recognized (see Chapter 3); in light of his changed attitude after the rout, one might incorrectly conclude that he was consistently fearful.

3

Hoover and Protest

The greeting the bonus marchers would receive in the capital depended to a large extent on the attitude of two men, the President and Pelham D. Glassford, the new Superintendent of Police. Glassford was the son of a cavalry officer who had carefully prepared him for military service. He and his brother William spent their early years on Western army posts until at the age of seventeen Pelham won appointment to West Point.[1] Like his brother, who selected Annapolis and later became an admiral, young Pelham adjusted easily to the rigorous demands of the Academy. His innate good humor and sunny disposition soon earned him the nickname "Happy." The young plebe made friends quickly.[2] One of them, also the son of a career officer, especially impressed him as a leader of great ability, and in September 1902, at the beginning of Glassford's second year, he was enormously pleased by the announcement that Douglas MacArthur had been appointed First Captain of the Academy. He respected MacArthur so highly that he predicted then (and later reminded his old friend) that MacArthur would some day be President. Until the day Glassford died, it was a dream he held for his friend.[3]

1. The principal collection of Glassford Papers is housed in The Institute of Industrial Relations, University of California, Los Angeles; these papers will be cited as GP. Another collection of Glassford Papers is in the UCLA Powell Library, Department of Special Collections, Collection Number 679; these will be cited as GP 679. PDG to Walter E. Barnes, August 6, 1932, GP. Peter Clark MacFarlane, "Heroes All," *The Saturday Evening Post* (August 19, 1919), p. 17.
2. Fleta Campbell Springer, "Glassford and the Siege of Washington," *Harper's Magazine*, 165 (November 1932), 642.
3. PDG to Douglas MacArthur, December 17, 1945; April 26, 1951, MacArthur Papers.

The youngest member of the Class of 1904, Pelham Glassford was also one of the more fortunate. Because of his skill in topography and graphic arts, he was appointed after graduation to a position on the West Point staff, where he served for five years. It was as a commander of artillery rather than as a teacher, however, that he was to make his mark. On June 15, 1918, Glassford took command of the 103d Field Artillery, a Rhode Island outfit whose outstanding combat record in France soon won him promotion and the distinction of being the youngest brigadier general in the U.S. Army. During this service Glassford earned a reputation for individualism and showed a flair for the dramatic. Astride his two-cylinder motorcycle, he would suddenly burst beyond the front lines to survey enemy battle positions, dart back under fire, and quickly move his artillery so close to the forward positions that the grateful infantrymen referred to his big guns as "Glassford's trench mortars" and joked of equipping them with bayonets. His tactics were novel and risky, and on at least two occasions—at the second battle of the Marne and at Chateau Thierry—he was forced into a hasty retreat. His men revered him and respected the Distinguished Service Cross that he earned at the front. He was a stern disciplinarian who rewarded efficiency and bravery with promotions and unexpected favors—a leader who was fair, kind, and always in command.[4]

Following the Armistice Glassford's rank reverted to major. He retained some of his appetite for adventure, and after years of army routine without a break he suddenly collected months of leave time, hopped on a motorcycle, and set out to hunt for excitement. He took odd jobs, such as in a circus where he was a barker, electrician, and sign painter, and for three months he worked as a newspaper reporter on the San Francisco *Examiner*, an experience that was to prove most helpful later, when

4. Springer, "Glassford," p. 642. For his talent in graphic arts, see Pelham D. Glassford, *Pelham D. Glassford and His Watercolors* (n.d., n.p.), GP 679; Providence (Rhode Island) *Journal*, August 7, 1932. Glassford commanded the Rhode Island 103d Field Artillery until February 1919.

as the District of Columbia's police chief his understanding of the reporters' needs won the loyalty of the
press. In 1931, after thirty-one years of army life, the forty-
seven-year-old soldier resigned his commission and journeyed to Arizona where he planned to serve as adjutant
general of the state militia and to help his father, a retired
colonel, raise horses in the Salt River Valley. Two weeks
after he arrived in Arizona, his father unexpectedly died,
and Glassford's plans for ranching turned sour. A long
personal letter from his friend, the Army's new Chief of
Staff, Gen. Douglas MacArthur, brought him some conso-
lation, but Glassford was deeply depressed and he soon
left the ranch.[5]

In Washington, D.C., on a fund-raising trip for the
Veterans of Foreign Wars, the most evangelical of the
groups that advocated the bonus, Glassford happened to
talk with Maj. Gen. Herbert H. Crosby, one of his former
commanding officers. Crosby had been appointed by the
President as one of the three commissioners who gov-
erned the District of Columbia, and he offered Glassford
the position of Superintendent of Metropolitan Police.
Since the District police force had been racked with repeated scandals and charges of corruption, Crosby assured Glassford complete independence and his full support in reorganizing and rehabilitating the force. It was
a challenging prospect—more attractive than raising
horses—and Glassford decided to remain in the capital.
He took the job, he later recalled, because it promised
"plenty of fun and games." [6]

Glassford was immediately popular with the police
force. His easy manner, modest, intimate, and friendly
style complemented the disciplinary and organizational
skills he had gained from his years of command. In no

5. Springer, "Glassford," pp. 642–43. "Book Material Folder";
Douglas MacArthur to Mrs. William A. Glassford, September 2, 1931,
GP.

6. "Glassford–Boyd Manuscript," pp. 1–2, GP; Springer, "Glassford,"
pp. 642–43. The Boyd manuscript is apparently a draft of a biography
of Glassford that he read and annotated but that was never completed
or published. Also see *Times*, October 20, 1931. For Washington, D.C.,
newspapers the city is omitted from the citation.

time he won the loyalty and enthusiastic support of the
scandal-stained department. Some of the older officers
who had hoped to be named superintendent looked on
him as an outsider, but they offered no outward resistance
to his authority. He was accustomed to command and to
rivalries among men, and it seemed that his experience as
an army officer would make the transition to police chief
relatively easy.[7]

There was, however, one crucial aspect of his job for
which Glassford was totally unprepared. In the center of
the nation's political life he developed an immediate and
strong dislike for anything that smacked of "politics." A
lifelong military person, he had little understanding or appreciation of the ways of democratic politics or of its devoted practitioners. From his first day as police chief he
found himself ensnarled in what he referred to as a
"jungle" of political intrigue, and like Hoover he felt intensely uncomfortable. He quite rightly warded off
requests for special favors from congressmen and locally
prominent groups, but his naivete showed in the intensity
of his shock and disgust that such requests should be
made. He clearly had much to learn about Washington.[8]

From the beginning Glassford's new job presented
him with a constant series of challenges. In the last few
months of 1931 fear of Communist efforts to embarrass
and disrupt the government ran high. On October 17, a
month before Glassford assumed command of the Metropolitan Police, Assistant Attorney General Nugent Dodds
had alerted the outgoing police chief, Henry G. Pratt, that
the Communist party was organizing a protest march on
Washington. Agents of the Justice Department had confirmed reports that the Communists planned to arrive in
early December with the opening of the new Congress.[9]

7. *Evening Star*, November 18, 1931; *The Washington Police Post*,
November 10, 1931.
8. "Glassford–Boyd Manuscript," pp. 1–4, GP; PDG, "Speech to
United Veterans Political League," July 16, 1933, Box 15, GP 679.
9. Nugent Dodds to Henry G. Pratt, October 17, 1931; Henry Pratt
to Nugent Dodds, October 22, 1931; Department of Justice, File 95-16-
26, RG 60, NA. The Justice Department was obviously concerned over
Communist efforts to promote a series of hunger marches.

For that matter, a smaller group of reds arrived on October 30, considerably ahead of the expected December march. Members of the Workers' Ex-Service Men's League, a New York-based Communist veterans' organization, they picketed the White House, a tactic that greatly alarmed the Secret Service. The demonstrators dispersed peaceably, however, after stating their demands for unemployment insurance and, more significantly, for the full and immediate payment of the bonus.[10]

On the same day that the Communist pickets marched in front of the White House, Ralph M. Easley, a fervent anti-Communist and chairman of the National Civic Federation, informed Hoover that the Communists were plotting to assassinate him within the next several months.[11] Despite the demonstration planned for December, the President was not alarmed by Easley's warning. Quite obviously, Easley was an alarmist, and besides, Hoover was accustomed to the constant barrage of criticism directed against him from both directions—the Communists and those who wanted the party outlawed.

Immediately following the World War, the Soviet Government had honored Hoover for saving thousands of Russians from starvation, but he did not long remain a Russian hero. As a leading symbol of capitalistic prosperity during the 1920s, he shortly became a special target for Communist denunciation.[12] Although fully cognizant

10. Sol Harper to FTH, October 30, 1931, PP 296, HHPL. Harper was chairman of the Workers' Ex-Service Men's League delegation.

11. Ralph M. Easley to Lawrence Richey, October 30, 1931, PP 297, HHPL. Easley was chairman of the Executive Council of the National Civic Federation and a vehement anti-Communist.

12. For reports on Communist activities in the United States, see Commerce Papers, 549; Francis Ralston Welsh to HH, August 13, 1925, Commerce Papers, 546, HHPL. Hoover had good reason to dislike the Communists. As Earl Browder, presidential candidate of the Communist party U.S.A., put it, Hoover's "very name . . . has become the symbol of degradation and misery for the masses." The Communists launched a determined campaign of character assassination. Earl Browder, *Communism in the United States* (New York: International Publishers Co., Inc., 1935), p. 94. For more on the Communists' efforts to smear Hoover, see Jane Degras, *The Communist International: Documents, 1919–1943* (New York: Oxford University Press, 1965), III, 10, 165; James O'Neal and G. A. Werner, *American Commu-*

of these negative attitudes, he did not become in his Presidency a nervous, panicky reactionary, fearful of a Communist revolution, as several historians would have us believe. He did not think that rhetoric, even if it was an expression of revolutionary intent, constituted a serious threat to the nation. In fact, while he detested the Soviets' methods and disbelieved their claims, he firmly resisted demands to outlaw the Communist party in the United States. He also discouraged overzealous police, who would arrest Communists while they were picketing the White House, on the grounds that dramatic arrests would only bring the Communists the publicity and sympathy they wanted.[13]

Hoover was determined to avoid a repetition of the vicious red hunts that had marred the last months of the Wilson administration. As early as May 1928 he informed one zealous editor that his own book, *American Individualism*, was "a little out of date as it was written when we were somewhat more exercised over socialistic and communistic movements than we need to be today." His attitude became disturbingly evident to Republican leaders soon after he took office. In June 1929 prominent party leaders, including Republican National Committee Chairman Hubert Work, Senate Majority Leader James E. Watson, and Congressman William R. Wood, endorsed a loudly trumpeted crusade against internal "destructive

nism: A Critical Analysis (New York: E. P. Dutton Co., Inc., 1957), p. 96.

13. For letters requesting that he outlaw or in other ways hinder the activities of the Communist party, see PP 102-B, HHPL; *Evening Star*, November 24, 1931; White House Press Release, December 14, 1929, and letters protesting his leniency, PP 102-B, HHPL. George B. Lockwood to HH, May 14, 1926; HH to Lockwood, May 17, 1926, Commerce Papers, 546; Fred W. Salmen to HH, May 20, 1931; HH to Salmen, May 25, 1931, PP 102-B, HHPL. The latest examples of historians who have accused Hoover of being fearful of the Communists are Roger Daniels, *The Bonus March: An Episode of the Great Depression* (Westport, Conn.: Greenwood Press, Inc., 1971), p. 172; D. Clayton James, *The Years of MacArthur 1880–1941* (Boston: Houghton Mifflin Company, 1970), pp. 386, 407; Richard Hofstadter and Michael Wallace, eds., *American Violence: A Documentary History* (New York: Alfred A. Knopf, Inc., 1970), p. 360; and Martin Blumenson, *The Patton Papers 1885–1940* (Boston: Houghton Mifflin Company, 1972), p. 894.

radicalism." The *National Republic*, semiofficial monthly of the GOP, planned to wage the publicity campaign, and Ohio Congressman Frank Murphy assumed the task of raising funds. In his zeal Murphy assured potential contributors that the President was "doing his part splendidly"—a warping of Hoover's stance.

Hoover had witnessed the red-baiting tactics of Attorney General A. Mitchell Palmer and no doubt recalled the denunciation of such tactics by leading Republicans as well as civil libertarians generally. Hoover shared their revulsion and now moved quickly to squelch the budding red hunt. The President's ire became known both to party leaders and to the entire nation. He denounced red hunts generally, refused to allow his administration to participate in the new crusade, and warned that such misguided drives served to obscure the real issues facing the nation. The leaders of the aborted scare quickly ran for cover.[14]

Nor was Hoover as unresponsive to the persecution of radicals as some have believed. In the aftermath of the 1916 Preparedness Day bombing in San Francisco, Thomas J. Mooney, thereafter celebrated as a radical, was convicted of complicity. Many observers were convinced that Mooney's conviction had been illegal, a belief supported by President Wilson's inquiry into the probability of improper judicial proceedings during the trial. But California's governor resisted those who petitioned a full pardon of Mooney's life sentence, whereupon President Hoover became interested in the continuing controversy. Hoover consulted with his Attorney General, William D. Mitchell, about the measures he, as President, might properly take. Mitchell was unalterably opposed to either direct action or indirect pressure by the President. He insisted that Hoover had no authority to interfere with state courts or state justice; as a result, Hoover dropped the idea of intervening. Later, however, he reaped bitter criticism for his silence. In a last effort to influence the Presi-

14. HH to Homer Guck, May 8, 1928, American Individualism File, Commerce Papers, HHPL. Hoover's book was published in 1922. "Red Hunt Quashed," *Time*, 14 (July 8, 1929), 14.

dent, Mooney's aging mother visited the White House in 1932. Unknown to Hoover, his secretary Lawrence Richey refused her permission to make her appeal directly to the President—an act that greatly angered both Hoover and his critics and that contributed significantly to the impression that he feared radicals and was insensitive to the plight of the underdog.[15]

Hoover's unworried attitude toward radical and communist activities became a source of some concern to one of his trusted advisers, who warned him of the communists' aggressiveness in the United States.[16] Likewise, the Secret Service was far less sanguine than Hoover about the intentions of radicals and protesters generally, and W. H. Moran, chief of the Secret Service, protected the President with a show of force that on occasion elicited comment from reporters. In late November 1931, for example, well before the expected Communist march in December, Moran feared an assassination attempt, and he hurriedly assembled a heavy guard around the White House. No untoward event happened.

Five days later, on November 29, Moran triumphantly informed newsmen that the Secret Service had concluded a six-week investigation of a carefully plotted national march "backed by Communists, anarchists, and professional agitators of the worst type." He expected the marchers in December to climax their demonstration with a riot at the Capitol Plaza while Congress was in session. Moran had long been nervous over what he believed to be a widespread disinclination to take threats against the President seriously. No threat, he believed, was "too fantastical [not] to be taken very seriously." Police Chief Glassford immediately canceled all leaves, and federal

15. Mark Requa to Richey, August 12, 1930; HH to The Attorney General, October 18, 1930; Ray Lyman Wilbur to Richey, September 26, 1929, Secretary's File, Thomas J. Mooney, HHPL. Mother Mary Mooney to HH, March 5, 1932; Homer G. Utley to HH, March 19, 1932, HHPL. Hoover drafted his own reply but sent it over Theodore G. Joslin's signature. Joslin to Utley, March 26, 1932. Senate Resolution 116, December 21, 1931, to HH and the Attorney General's reply sent to Richey January 5, 1932, Secretary's File, Thomas J. Mooney, HHPL.

16. Edgar Rickard, Diary, May 25, 1931, Rickard Papers, HHPL.

forces prepared for a large-scale disturbance. While some predicted the beginning of the Communist revolution, others, including Hoover, were not alarmed. The Baltimore *Sun* cautioned federal officials not to panic. Like Hoover, the *Sun* contended that if the march was led by Communists, they would prefer the publicity of cracked skulls to their rights of free petition and assembly, and only "a very stupid community" would accommodate that desire.[17]

In marked contrast to his later reputation for redbaiting, Hoover took steps to ensure that the Communists' right to protest was fully protected, even promoted. Police Commissioner Crosby promised the Communists police protection against unsympathetic residents, while cabinet officers assured newsmen that they were not worried about the arrival of the reds. Attorney General Mitchell, for example, responded to a reporter's question about Communist pamphlets, which advocated insurrection, with calm disdain, and Secretary of War Patrick J. Hurley informed the press that, although the Army was ready if needed, he felt confident that such drastic measures as the use of armed force would be entirely unnecessary.[18]

In a more significant effort to ensure calm during the Communist demonstration, the administration made elaborate preparations. Fully cooperating with the new police chief, Hoover ordered his principal subordinates to take all measures necessary to guarantee a peaceable protest, indeed to provide Glassford with the Army tents, cots, blankets, rolling kitchens, and other equipment needed to care for the expected 15,000 demonstrators.[19] In addition, U. S. Grant, III, Director of Public Buildings and Grounds and one of Hoover's trusted lieutenants,[20]

17. *Evening Star*, November 24, 1931; November 29, 1931; *Post*, November 29, 1931; W. H. Moran to Richey, February 21, 1930, Treasury Secret Service File, HHPL; Baltimore *Sun*, December 1, 1931.

18. *Post*, December 3, 4, 1931.

19. *Herald*, December 4, 1931; New York *Times*, December 7, 1931. Correspondence in Hunger Marchers, November–December, 1932, File, HHPL.

20. U.S. Grant, III, had Hoover's greatest confidence and operated under his direct command. U.S. Grant, III, to HH, September 12, 1932, French Strother Papers, HHPL; HH to James W. Good, March 6, 1929;

opened federal campsites for the reds. The Sixth Marine Barracks were vacated so that 500 of the marchers could be quartered there, and that military unit also provided medical facilities, which treated over 100 of the protesters for a variety of ills.[21] When Herbert Benjamin, the leader of the Communist "hunger marchers" arrived in the capital to make arrangements for his approaching band, he was surprised to find Glassford fully prepared to offer him all the facilities necessary for a successful demonstration, including parade permits. At first Benjamin was somewhat skeptical of Glassford's motives for providing so much assistance, but finally he agreed to cooperate.

While the White House remained under heavy guard, Glassford mounted his big blue motorcycle and led the rather bizarre procession down Pennsylvania Avenue. The former general, now police chief, headed the column, and behind him four thousand Communists dramatized their opposition to the administration with a band dressed in Russian uniforms, red flags waving, and voices straining as they sang the "Internationale." For two days the Communists cooperated with cops and reveled in their own display of anticapitalist zeal. They sang of hanging Herbert Hoover from a sour-apple tree and cheered their favorite speaker, William Z. Foster, leader of the party, who praised the Soviet Union and heaped abuse on the President. Although Hoover agreed to receive a petition as the men marched past the White House, both the President and Congress refused to meet a delegation.[22]

The Washington *Post* was outspokenly enraged by

HH to William D. Mitchell, April 23, 1930, War Department, Public Buildings and Public Parks File, HHPL. Hoover informed his Attorney General that Grant was "an official under my immediate direction." Grant had also been chairman of Hoover's 1928 Inaugural Committee. When Colonel Grant's Army rotation was due, Hoover insisted that he remain Director of Public Buildings and Grounds.

21. New York *Times*, December 7, 1931; *Post*, December 7, 8, 1931. Benjamin later recalled the food, shelter, and good treatment he and his hunger marchers had received. Edward T. Folliard, "When Reds Invaded Washington," *Post-Herald*, December 2, 1956. This and other related articles are filed in EL.

22. *Evening Star*, December 7, 1931; *Times*, December 3, 1931; *Herald*, December 7, 1931.

the event, the permissive tactics employed, and indirectly by Hoover's refusal to deal more harshly with the Communists. "Some authorities," the *Post* thundered, "cherish the notion" that they could outwit the Communists by treating them gently. "These officials would feed the communists and their dupes, and provide them with housing at public expense, in the hope that the reds would thereby be induced to refrain from stirring up riots." The editors expressed the view of many of Hoover's more militant friends and supporters—that it was "a foolish and deadly mistake to coddle the Communists." Public safety and public order were being bartered away by a police chief and President who instead ought "to crush violence with the sledge hammer of law, not in belated or wavering fashion, but instantly, on the spot, whenever any hand is raised against the public peace." [23]

In spite of these thunderings, after the Communists had departed most residents were grateful and relieved for the peaceable handling of the demonstration, and they disregarded the *Post*'s fulminations. The entire credit, newsmen assumed, belonged to Glassford, and they enthusiastically praised the new chief. One month later Glassford's skill and Hoover's support were again put to the test. The Chief had already made good progress toward ridding his department of the taint of scandal, and now after only two months in office, he was faced with a second protest march. On January 6, 1932, Father James Cox, a Roman Catholic priest from Pittsburgh, arrived at the head of 12,000 unemployed workers. Cox was a popular spokesman for the destitute of his city, and his march received a great deal of publicity. Hoover again provided Army equipment and opened federal buildings for quarters. He also invited Cox to a cordial welcome at the

23. *Post*, December 7, 1931. "Communists," unpublished manuscript in GP. This 7-page manuscript was apparently intended as a chapter in Glassford's biography. The "Glassford–Boyd" manuscript contains a brief description of the march, p. 4. Further intense criticism of Hoover for "coddling" the Communists is in the correspondence in PP 102-B, HHPL. The officers of the National Civic Federation were especially angry.

White House, where he publicly expressed his "intense sympathy" with the marchers' plight and assured Cox that he was devising a legislative program to help all of the unemployed. Meantime, Glassford was busy arranging parade routes, additional lodging, and meals. Again all went smoothly. After his conference with the President, Cox led his group back to Pittsburgh, and Glassford again received the city's praise. The District's residents were overjoyed to have a police chief who knew how to handle dissenting and potentially disturbing groups so effectively.[24]

Glassford's success during the two winter demonstrations was, in part, aided by his military experience. His ability to command men and to arrange for the numerous details of their care were both important. So was his revitalization of the police department. In addition to new equipment and structural changes in the department, he tried to reshape the thinking of the force by ordering his men to read Lincoln Steffens and Clarence Darrow. A less obviously effective reason for his growing renown, one that would become increasingly significant, was his surprisingly good relations with the Washington press corps. At the very time that Hoover's rapport with the newsmen was rapidly deteriorating, Glassford's was just as rapidly improving. His three-month experience as a reporter on the San Francisco *Examiner* now proved invaluable. He understood newsmen and made himself an accessible source of news copy, as Hoover had been when he was Secretary of Commerce under Harding and Coolidge. An equally vital reason for Glassford's success has remained unrecognized by scholars: Hoover's little-noticed but important cooperation. Not eager to dramatize his considerable aid to the protesters, the President was content to allow the praise to fall on Glassford—a generosity that was to be ill rewarded.

In contrast to the first two protest marches, the Bonus

24. Hartford (Connecticut) *Courant*, December 9, 1931; *Herald*, December 10, 1931; Springer, "Glassford," p. 643; for details of the interview, see Secretary's File, James Cox, HHPL. "Glassford–Boyd," p. 4; *Herald*, January 7, 1932.

Army, now forming and preparing to march on Washington, posed a more difficult problem, one that quickly transformed the Police Chief into a major political figure and, ironically, one of the President's harshest critics. While Hoover had willingly talked with Father Cox about the plight of the unemployed, he saw the veterans who were organizing the Bonus Army as special-interest lobbyists with whom he would refuse even to discuss the bonus. He had traveled to two American Legion conventions, outlined his views in the message that accompanied his veto of the 50-per-cent loan bill, and disseminated public letters from his cabinet officials detailing the administration's reasons for opposing further benefits to the veterans. As he saw the matter, there was nothing further to discuss. At first, therefore, he was intentionally uncooperative with this latest drive for the bonus. He threw the responsibility for handling the protesters on the District Commissioners and Glassford. This march, he declared, was "a local problem," with which the administration would have nothing to do.[25]

Alarmists faulted Hoover for coddling the Communists and being soft on both the December and January protests. By contrast, the President at first stood firm against the much more conservative bonus marchers. In doing so, he created the impression of hostility. After the Bonus Riot many observers were to consider him a fearful panic-stricken man, deeply worried about a Communist revolution. In fact, most historians have begun their assessment of Hoover and his reaction toward protest by focusing first on the brutal dispersal of the bonus marchers under his administration. Their next step, using hindsight, is to assume that he was a hostile or apprehensive man. Some even suggest that Hoover plotted against the bonus marchers. However, both interpretations—the hostility and the fear—have been misleading, for these accounts have not examined Hoover's role in both the Com-

---

25. Theodore J. Joslin, *Hoover Off the Record* (New York: Doubleday, Doran and Co., 1934), p. 263. There had been rumors of a veterans' protest march as early as 1929. Ray Lyman Wilbur to HH, July 16, 1929; FTH to Richey, August 13, 1929, PP 295, HHPL.

munist march and Father Cox's, evidence which clearly establishes that he did not fear either protesters or Communists. To understand his initial attitude toward the bonus marchers, one must place that protest within the context of his earlier legislative encounters with veterans. Soon, however, even that attitude was to soften, and Hoover's unrecognized aid to and support of the Bonus Army proved even more beneficial to the veterans than his leniency toward the earlier protests.

Few thought that the bonus marchers would stay long in Washington. Wishing to discourage others from joining their ranks, Hoover decided to ignore the gathering. He hoped that official nonrecognition would somehow dampen the marchers' enthusiasm, and although ultimately disastrous, the decision at that time did not seem altogether without merit. The Bonus Army apparently lacked both leadership and funds, and it could not sustain itself for long without substantial outside help. As had the previous demonstrations, this one might in all probability dissolve, once its initial momentum had been spent. However, the President and his advisers could not have anticipated the galvanizing efforts of the Police Chief and of Walter W. Waters, commander of the marching veterans.

Waters was a former sergeant who almost singlehandedly sustained the initially faltering march toward Washington. Once in the capital, the demonstration prevailed largely through the efforts of Glassford, the unorthodox police chief. Ironically, it was also aided at first by the very neglect the President had hoped would cause its early demise and then by Hoover's unrecognized, quiet, but substantial assistance. The three men—Waters, Glassford, and Hoover—had different goals and methods and would eventually become adversaries, but through their individual, uncoordinated efforts the bonus march became the largest demonstration in the capital's history.

In March 1932 a small gathering of the National Veterans Association in Portland, Oregon, had listened to an address by a thirty-four-year-old unemployed drifter.

Walter W. Waters's physique was not extraordinary—slight stature, wavy blond hair, steel-blue eyes, a haggard yet still youthful appearance—but his intent expression was that of an evangelist. The ex-sergeant challenged the men he would one day command to acknowledge the miserable failure of their letters and petitions to a Congress that obviously had no intention of approving the full bonus. When big business wanted action on vital legislation, he declared, it did not content itself with merely sending letters; it sent people. Congress understood and feared determined lobbyists. Business succeeded because its lobbyists insisted that its interests be recognized. Rather than sending three hundred petitions, a band of men organized into a strictly disciplined army should march on Washington, growing along the way until, a thousand strong, it entered the national capital in a dramatic and forceful confrontation. This was Walter W. Waters's first public speech. He had written and rewritten it with great care and, while walking the empty night streets of Portland, had committed it to memory. But his audience was clearly uninterested. Dejected, the former sergeant stepped down from the rostrum and returned to his accustomed routine, looking for a job.[26]

Born in Oregon in 1898 and raised in Idaho, Waters had yearned for something more than his humble background had offered him. At eighteen he joined the Idaho National Guard. In the winter of 1917, as a medic with the 146th Field Artillery, Waters's company boarded a troopship that carried the advance elements of the American Expeditionary Forces into war against the Kaiser. Later, he served with the occupation forces in Germany.

When he was discharged in June 1919, he had had his fill of war, yet his ambitions for a fuller life as a civilian were repeatedly frustrated. The transition from three years of military regimentation to the freedom and uncer-

26. Walter W. Waters, as told to William C. White, *B.E.F.: The Whole Story of the Bonus Army* (New York: The John Day Company, Inc., 1933), pp. 13–15 (hereafter cited without further reference to William C. White). A photograph of Waters is in the Preface.

tainties of civilian life was not easy for the young soldier. He was never physically strong, and his uncertain health and lack of either profession or trade were serious handicaps. He searched constantly for a job that would give him personal satisfaction, a living wage, and social respectability. Automobile salesman, garage mechanic, farm laborer, baker's helper—Waters began each new venture with renewed hope, but each ended "as an equally dismal failure." His seeming inability to find a satisfying vocation was a source of deep worry and humiliation to the sensitive young veteran. At first, he ascribed his difficulties to the unsettling effects of the War. Writers of the Lost Generation were expressing for their contemporaries the disillusionment and disorientation that followed the war to end all wars, but like other "little guys" Waters spoke only for himself, and he, too, was haunted by a sense of idealism gone bad. It was a cruel blow to be a success and a hero as long as the war had lasted, but a nonentity and failure at its end.

During a brief stint in the Washington harvest fields Waters met his future wife. They were married, and they moved to Oregon, where he started anew in a canning factory near Portland. He was happy in his marriage, and he advanced in his steady job. For a while he experienced the security and respectability that had long evaded him after his discharge. In December 1930, however, as the economy steadily declined, Waters lost his job and was forced to move his wife and two children into a small, dingy apartment in nearby Portland, where they lived, first off their savings, then by pawning their possessions, and finally by accepting charity while he fruitlessly sought employment. By March 1932 he had little left except a grim determination to somehow regain a steady job and the bonus the government had promised him for serving his country. To the beaten young family man, 1945 was too far in the future.

Other veterans had also naively assumed that the justice of their cause would prevail, but by early May 1932, when the Ways and Means Committee shelved Patman's bill, they were outraged. Four days later, on May 11,

1932, Waters joined three hundred of them as they set out to carry their protest to the distant capital.[27]

The men hastily formed forty companies and elected officers and a so-called commander-in-chief, who was to travel ahead by automobile with their meager funds to arrange for food and rail transportation. The commander-in-chief—and their money—soon vanished. The railroads were unimpressed with their appeal, and as the last train from Portland sped past the stranded men, their initial buoyancy gave way to confusion and dissension. In desperation, the men blocked the Union Pacific tracks, commandeered foul-smelling freight cars, and rocked and swayed over the mountains to Pocatello, Idaho, where they were temporarily sidetracked to wait for another train. During that time the dissension that broke out convinced Waters that unless order were established soon, the men "would reach no destination other than the local jails." At that point, as he recorded the event, he climbed to the top of a boxcar, dramatically ordered the bugler to sound assembly, both chided and flattered the men, and demanded the formation of a strictly disciplined army. In response, the men shouted their decision to make him their new commander.

Waters proved to be as effective a leader for the expedition as he was a pacifier. He was determined to end dissension and to forge an authentic army attitude among the men. To enforce his oft-repeated insistence on law and order, he appointed a former prize fighter as chief of a quickly organized military police. He next delegated responsibility for securing transportation and food to selected committees, and he then completely reorganized the companies under officers elected by the men but responsible only to him. He experienced some difficulties in maintaining control and further trouble with uncooperative railroads, but he was a determined leader, and for the most part, the Portland band was by this time

27. Waters, *B.E.F.*, pp. 7, 3–7, 8–20; George Kleinholz, *The Battle of Washington: A National Disgrace* (New York: B.E.F. Press, 1932), p. 6; Daniels, *Bonus March*, pp. 77–78.

more than willing to cooperate with any leader who could keep them moving toward Washington.

The trip lasted eighteen days, spent mostly in dirty freight cars or in jostling trucks—too brief and relatively uneventful to form a basis for more than a few of those anecdotes that fill the pages of popular history. Waters recalled some high points on the way: a parade in Pocatello, the men walking with outstretched hats, that netted twenty dollars; the men volunteering en masse to give blood to a critically ill little girl in Council Bluffs, Iowa; a Saint Louis police chief who refused to evict them and gave Waters five dollars instead; and a Mississippi River toll collector who declined to ask the men for money. Without much notoriety, the original contingent of the Bonus Army soon reached East St. Louis, Illinois, where they became national news.[28]

In East St. Louis the Baltimore and Ohio Railroad was ready for a battle. Supported by well-armed local police and the company's security force, railroad officials greeted Waters with a court injunction forbidding the group's usual tactics of uncoupling cars and blocking the tracks. For three days the veterans besieged the railroad yards, but the B. & O. refused to back down. Thirty-eight years earlier, federal injunction had failed to stop Coxey's Army from the civil disobedience of hopping freights; finally, at the request of the governor of Montana, President Cleveland sent troops to impede that march on Washington. In 1932, however, despite the urging of prominent Republicans, Hoover refused to intervene.[29]

Newspapers throughout the country carried the most

28. Waters, *B.E.F.*, pp. 22, 39.
29. Donald L. McMurry, *Coxey's Army: A Study of the Industrial Army Movement of 1894* (Boston: Little, Brown and Company, 1929), pp. 40–62, 199–205, 214–26. Troops and federal marshals were used against elements of Coxey's Army more than once and prompted Attorney General Richard Olney to request a deficiency appropriation of $125,000 from the Congress. Bennett Milton Rich, *The Presidents and Civil Disorders* (Washington, D.C.: The Brookings Institution, 1941), pp. 88–89, 174. For one example of Hoover's refusal to intervene, see Bruce Barton to HH, June 6, 1932; HH to Bruce Barton, June 7, 1932, Barton Papers, State Historical Society of Wisconsin. A copy of the letter is also in HHPL.

dramatic story of the march, the "Battle of East St. Louis." The B. & O. hoped to circumvent the marchers by switching car after car to the little neighboring town of Caseyville, Illinois, where it planned to reassemble whole trains without the marchers. But the veterans discovered the plan, and with the help of automobile rides from people who had come out to watch, they carried their battle eastward. Finally, local union leaders arranged truck transportation across Illinois to Washington, Indiana. There the men were again surrounded by armed guards and enclosed by barbed wire, until the governor of Indiana, fearing violence and a massive relief problem, established a precedent by trucking them to the Ohio border. Each state was anxious to be rid of the burden. As undesirable intruders the men were trucked as quickly as possible to the next border, from Ohio to Pennsylvania to Maryland, and finally into the District of Columbia.[30]

National headlines originating from the "Battle of East St. Louis" and the growing number of other bands wending their way toward the capital clearly frightened the Secret Service, which kept the marchers under surveillance and warned Waters against leaving his men for an hour. Their chief concern was that some of the men, if left without discipline and command, might try to assassinate the President. Although memories of McKinley's assassination had faded, and American politics had been comparatively free of such attempts, the assassination of two of Japan's most prominent leaders as well as of the President of France in the spring of 1932 deeply worried those charged with protecting Hoover. Moran was unmistakably earnest in his exclamation that no threat was "too fantastical [not] to be taken very seriously." Nevertheless, one day out of Washington, Waters disregarded the warning and, in response to a telegram from Patman, secretly journeyed ahead to ascertain the type of reception awaiting his men.[31]

30. Waters, *B.E.F.*, pp. 41–63; Kleinholz, *Battle of Washington*, pp. 7–11.

31. W. H. Moran to Richey, February 21, 1930, Treasury Secret File, HHPL. *Time*, 19 (January 18, 1932), 17; (March 14, 1932), 25; (May 16,

Actually, Patman wanted no part of the Bonus Army. His desire to dissociate himself from the marchers reflected the growing fear and, in some instances, anger among congressmen over their advance on Washington. The triumphal march had definitely ended; rough weeks of encampment lay ahead, and apparently no one wanted them in the capital. According to Waters, Patman was "very nervous lest he be credited in any way with having inspired the march." [32] For years Patman had fought through legislative channels for his veterans, but he had not encouraged the march, and undoubtedly aware of its potential explosiveness, he was several times to urge the men to return home.

After assuring the congressman that he could honestly protect him against charges of inspiring the march, Waters proceeded to a meeting with the District's Chief of Police, who had already publicly decreed that the bonus marchers must leave the city within forty-eight hours after their arrival.[33] No doubt because of that stern ultimatum, Waters was surprised when he entered police headquarters on May 29. Pelham D. Glassford was six feet three inches tall, "a lithe, straight-carriaged, springy," extraordinarily handsome man, who "exuded intense vitality." He was a natural conciliator, whose countenance "gave an impression of deep soul-searching thought, a burning quality." [34] Rather than the "hard-boiled disciple of the old police school" Waters had envisioned, Glassford impressed him by his courteous and "above all humanely considerate manner."

More surprising was the thoroughness with which Glassford had prepared for the veterans' arrival. He had

1932), 21–23; (May 23, 1932), 18; Waters, *B.E.F.*, pp. 59–60. Memoir of Gardner Jackson, The Oral History Collection of Columbia University, pp. 375–76 (hereafter cited as Jackson, OHC). Jackson was a prominent journalist, a close observer of the BEF, and very friendly with Glassford.

32. Waters, *B.E.F.*, p. 62; Patman to W. C. Pullen, June 18, 1932; Patman to Hugh Carney, August 5, 1932, Patman Papers.

33. *Post*, May 26, 1932. PDG, "Chronology of Bonus Army Invasion," GP. Glassford recalled making the statement on May 28, 1932.

34. Jackson, OHC, pp. 383–84.

secured an old vacant store for their quarters, ordered a hot meal upon arrival for the tired, hungry men, and made arrangements with the governor of Maryland to deliver them directly to their new quarters rather than six miles away at the District of Columbia border. This was as cordial a welcome as Waters could have hoped. Glassford did not want the marchers in the capital, and he hoped to be rid of them quickly. Still, it was obvious from the beginning that he was an unusually skilled and kind policeman.[35]

Not at all obvious was the patience and sympathy or forthcoming assistance of the aloof Chief Executive. After slightly more than six months in office Glassford, for all the public knew, faced his third and most serious challenge alone. In the first two marches he had received Hoover's cooperation, but this time Hoover had repeatedly indicated publicly that no help would be forthcoming, a vivid impression that convinced not only contemporaries but also later historians. The former mining engineer elected President, the World War hero appointed police chief, and the ex-sergeant elevated to commander of the marching veterans had one strong desire in common: Each of them was determined to avoid violence. Together, in a strange, often complicated, and uncoordinated fashion the three men were to ensure two months of peaceful protest.

35. Waters, *B.E.F.*, pp. 62–64, 71–72; Kleinholz, *Battle of Washington*, pp. 11–12.

4

The Poor People's March

Hoover's initial refusal to cooperate with Glassford created the impression of a heartless, uncaring President and propelled the Chief into newspaper limelight. Faced with the responsibility for controlling this third and largest demonstration without the usual federal aid, Glassford quickly set in motion his own one-man lobby. First, he issued numerous press releases and sent telegrams to state governors and veterans' organizations, pleading with them to halt the marchers. When few responded, he personally urged rapid congressional action on the bonus from James Watson, the Republican floor leader in the Senate, Henry T. Rainey, the Democratic floor leader in the House, and Wright Patman, who had already begun circulating another petition to force immediate consideration of his bill.

Next, Glassford went directly to the White House, where he talked with Walter Newton, the President's political secretary. Finally, after receiving from Newton little assurance of help, he began complaining to the press about the administration's uncooperativeness. The unorthodox police officer's concern for his former comrades-in-arms made appealing news, and reporters, if not the politicians, were positively delighted with the unusual chief.[1]

Unable to do more to stop the marchers without the cooperation of state governors or to provide for the men without Hoover's help, Glassford decided to control the marchers by organizing and taking command of the so-

1. "Glassford–Boyd," pp. 7–12, GP; *Evening Star*, May 26, 1932; Owen P. White, "General Glassford's Story: An Interview," *Collier's*, 90 (October 29, 1932), 10–11. In the case of Washington, D.C., newspapers the city is omitted from the citation.

called army. His superior, Police Commissioner Herbert Crosby strongly opposed this method and favored dispersing the approaching marchers by force. On May 26, two days before Waters's well-publicized entry into the city, the Chief quickly moved to take command. In a meeting at Judiciary Square Glassford informed the first arrivals of the need for a well-disciplined organization and of his plans to provide a camp, wooden barracks, and fund-raising events at a local burlesque house. With $115 of his own money he established a commissary, aided by donations from sympathetic residents. The grateful men elected him Secretary-Treasurer of the Bonus Expeditionary Force, and Glassford became the real leader of the BEF.[2]

As the number of marchers increased dramatically, Hoover withdrew his initial and widely publicized refusal to provide federal aid. Many congressmen and private citizens deplored the protest and were alarmed by it; once again they exerted immense pressure on Hoover to end the demonstration quickly. Therefore, when he reversed his earlier position, he did so without publicity— through three of his almost anonymous, yet most trusted lieutenants, Veterans Administrator Hines, the Commander of the District National Guard, Maj. Gen. Anton Stephan, and U. S. Grant, III, Director of Public Buildings and Public Grounds.[3] Secretly, he approved the loan

2. "Glassford–Boyd," pp. 7–12; White, "General Glassford's Story," p. 10. The three District Commissioners were Luther Reichelderfer, Herbert Crosby, and John G. Gotwals. Gotwals, the District Engineer, was seriously ill and under strict orders to avoid worry and stress. He therefore had nothing to do with decisions affecting the BEF; Daniel A. Reed to Newton, June 24, 1932, HHPL. PDG to William Randolph Hearst, June 8, 1932, GP; White, "General Glassford's Story," pp. 10–11; PDG, "Chronology of Bonus Army Invasion," GP; *Evening Star*, May 27, 1932.

3. On U. S. Grant, III, see Chapter 3, footnote 20. The President of the United States is Commander-in-chief of the District of Columbia Militia; Maj. Gen. Anton Stephan was under Hoover's personal command. Anton Stephan to HH, March 3, 1932, District Commissioners, National Guard File, HHPL. On September 20, 1932, Hoover personally conferred upon Stephan a medal in recognition of his forty-five years of faithful and outstanding service, further evidence of the close cooperation between Stephan and the President. For the numerous let-

of hundreds of tents, cots, bedsacks, several field kitchens, the low-cost sale of Army rations and clothing to the veterans, and the use of federal property for quarters.[4] At the same time he continued his official policy of non-recognition, hoping to discourage new arrivals.[5]

Hoover's supportive actions have been overlooked by historians. Instead, newsmen and historians have popularized the impression of a benevolent police chief and a callous President. To be sure, Glassford deserved his praise. However, without Hoover's approval, which now paral-

ters concerned with the presentation, see Subject File, Medals, 1932–1933, HHPL, especially Richey to Reichelderfer, September 15, 1932. Considering this evidence of great esteem for both men, it is difficult to believe that either Stephan or Grant would have furnished supplies and campsites without first obtaining the President's approval or that Hoover would have later conferred an honor on Stephan if he had disapproved of the aid to the marchers. Roger Daniels, *The Bonus March: An Episode of the Great Depression* (Westport, Conn.: Greenwood Press, Inc., 1971), pp. 101–2, 98, 145, suggests that Grant and Stephan acted without Hoover's permission, that it was Glassford, not the President, who persuaded them to cooperate. Lt. Col. Frederic Bates Bulter, then Grant's executive assistant, argued vigorously against allowing the marchers to use any federal land, but Grant diplomatically evaded the protest. Gen. Frederic Bates Bulter to author March 22, 1972.

4. At first the administration refused to cooperate. PDG to Patrick J. Hurley, May 28, 1932, War Department, Office of The Adjutant General, RG 94, NA. On May 30, 1932, Glassford sent Hurley a telegram again requesting aid. PDG to Hurley, May 30, 1932, HP. Very soon, however, this attitude changed; Hurley issued the first order for equipment on May 31, 1932. Telegrams and messages, May 30, 31, War Department, Office of The Adjutant General, RG 94, NA. "Glassford–Boyd," p. 7, GP, and Donald L. McMurry, *Coxey's Army: A Study of the Industrial Army Movement of 1894* (Boston: Little, Brown and Company, 1929), pp. 196–226. For evidence of substantial aid, see Senator James Couzens to Frederick Payne, June 23, 1932; Payne to John J. McSwain, June 25, 1932; Col. H. N. Cootes to The Adjutant General, War Department, June 13, 1932; Maj. Gen. R. E. Callen, "Memorandum for Chief of Staff," March 2, 1933, Office of The Adjutant General, RG 94, 240 (Bonus), Box 1180, NA. Callen discusses the canned meat, forks, spoons, knives, cups, and repair of 108 of the 116 large pyramidal tents. War Department Militia Bureau to The Adjutant General, March 17, 1933. French Strother to Arthur McKeogh, Strother Papers, HHPL.

5. Theodore J. Joslin, *Hoover Off the Record* (New York: Doubleday, Doran and Co., 1934), pp. 263–65; HH to Bruce Barton, June 7, 1932, Barton Papers, State Historical Society of Wisconsin.

leled his assistance to earlier protests, the crucial supplies would not have been available.

With the President's behind-the-scenes aid, Glassford's effective leadership, and experienced police officers initially filling a variety of important posts and providing the organizational backbone, the new army soon became a somewhat functional operation. Nevertheless, the constant influx of additional veterans forced Glassford to spend much of his time seeking more food, equipment, and medical facilities.[6] To that end and probably with the help of the administration's opponents, he persuaded members of the Senate Committee on the District of Columbia to hold public hearings on Senator Edward P. Costigan's bill, earlier passed over, which included an authorization for $75,000 to be used in the emergency care of transients in the District of Columbia.[7]

Glassford's lobbying for the bill signaled a subtle change for the cop who hated politics. More significantly, he lumped all three protest demonstrations into the same category. As far as he was concerned, the Communist protest in December 1931, the hunger march led by Father Cox in January 1932, and the bonus march all stemmed from the same fundamental economic and social upheavals, and therefore, he reasoned, they were all hunger marches; they all petitioned for relief; and it was now imperative that the federal government accept full responsibility for their care. Unfortunately, the Senate did not act

6. PDG, "Information Concerning Visiting Veterans," May 29, 1932; PDG, "Visiting Veterans," May 30, 1932; J. E. Bennett, "Report," May 30, 1931 [1932?], GP. By June 16 Glassford was pleased by the administration's increasing cooperation; PDG to Rush Sturges, June 16, 1932, GP. Relying on Glassford's later claims, Irving Bernstein concluded that Glassford did not receive any help from the administration; Irving Bernstein, *The Lean Years: A History of the American Worker, 1920–1933* (Boston: Houghton Mifflin Company, 1960), p. 444. The same impression is conveyed in Daniels, *Bonus March*, pp. 97–105.

7. A copy of S. 4781, May 9, 1932, is in GP. U.S., Congress, Senate, Committee on the District of Columbia, *Hearings on S. 4781, Emergency Unemployment Relief and Care of Persons in Distress*, 72d Cong., 1st sess., June 1, 1932, and Arthur Capper to PDG, May 31, 1932, GP.

on the Costigan bill. The bonus had encountered bipartisan opposition, and already a variety of relief bills lay before Congress, including one for federal loans to the states, which Hoover favored. Nonetheless, Glassford's testimony, widely disseminated in the press, did achieve one of its goals. It popularized a view of the veterans as hunger marchers, and they and their champion became one of the greatest human-interest stories of the depression.[8]

Glassford's testimony before the Senate District Committee and his well-publicized efforts for the veterans both embarrassed the administration and brought a prompt nationwide response. A key factor ensuring a prolonged encampment was the money that poured in from all parts of the nation. Hopes that the squatters would be unable to sustain their lobby were dashed by a $5,000 check from Father Charles E. Coughlin, the politically influential Roman Catholic priest whose radio program, broadcast from Detroit, reached millions of Americans each week. Coughlin's generosity made good publicity and undoubtedly stimulated others to send hundreds of small contributions, which enabled Glassford to purchase supplies during the month of June. Hundreds of local American Legion posts that had backed Patman during the battles at their national conventions also contributed generously and continued their intense pressure on local congressmen.[9] Added together, there was an impressive outpouring of support for the marchers.

Within a relatively short time twenty-seven encampments were formed, situated mainly in the northeastern quadrant of the city, as close to the Capitol Plaza and the

8. *Hearings on S. 4781*, pp. 5–11, 17–18; *Daily News*, June 3, 1932; *Evening Star*, June 1, 1932; *Post*, May 30, 1932.

9. U.S., Congress, House, *Congressional Record*, 72d Cong., 1st sess., 1932, 75, pt. 11, p. 12584; Charles Coughlin to H. Ralph Burton, June 10, 1932. For more information on Coughlin, see Charles J. Tull, *Father Coughlin and the New Deal* (Syracuse, N.Y.: Syracuse University Press, 1965). Tull mentions Coughlin's support of the BEF; see pp. 12–13. Patman to PDG, June 11, 1932, GP. Patman regularly forwarded money sent by BEF supporters to Glassford. "Financial Report," May 27 to June 20, 1932, GP.

downtown shopping section as the authorities and opportunity would permit. The sprawling camp on the broad
mud flats of the Anacostia River (sometimes referred to as
Camp Marks in honor of the kind police captain at the
nearby 11th Precinct) was the largest of the settlements,
with about 15,000 residents, of which 1,100 were women
and children. The others varied in population from 2,100
at Camp Bartlett to 200 at Camp Sims. Many protesters
occupied the clusters of empty government office buildings along lower Pennsylvania Avenue near the Washington Monument and farther north, nearer to the Capitol itself. Reports of the total number of veterans at any
particular time were generally unreliable, especially as
each camp commander purposely overestimated the population of his camp in order to increase the amount of
food allotted to his group, and also because there was a
constant movement of men and women in and out of the
camps during most of June and July. The estimates of the
peak number varied from about 15,000 to 25,000, with
about 20,000 as the best estimate of the average number
in July.

The relative desirability of a camp had less to do with
its comforts than with its proximity to the Capitol. Camp
Bartlett, on private land loaned by former Postmaster General John H. Bartlett, was located on a high, beautifully
wooded plot and provided excellent tents; although it was
only a mile and a half from the huge Anacostia camp, the
veterans complained of the long walk to the Capitol.
The same complaint—distance—was voiced about Camp
Meigs, near the Columbia Institute for the Deaf. The Anacostia camp was directly across the river from the Navy
Yard and within sight of the Capitol dome and therefore
preferred over Camp Bartlett. Because of their ideal location the most sought-after quarters were the empty federal
buildings scheduled for demolition, which bordered the
Mall on Pennsylvania Avenue near the Capitol. Hoover
had willingly allowed campsites in federal parks or in
nearby Army posts, but Glassford had only a limited
amount of lumber for huts. Although the District National
Guard, with Hoover's approval, had lent him all of its

available tents, more shelter was needed. The President then agreed to allow the men to occupy the vacant federal buildings temporarily.[10]

Hoover's unprecedented willingness to aid the massive protests was no inconsequential matter. Neither was his decision to impede an important federal construction project. Ferry K. Heath, Assistant Secretary of the Treasury, who was directly in charge of the $700-million top-priority office building program for the capital, had stressed its desirability in providing thousands of jobs and thus cushioning the city from the worst effects of the depression. In granting the veterans permission to occupy some of the empty office buildings, already partly demolished, Heath informed Glassford that he had instructed the Rhine Wrecking Company to delay fulfillment of its contract. This delay worked a hardship on Rhine, whose profit depended on the sale of salvageable material, and presumably on the government, for delayed contracts might well add to the expense of demolition. Heath urged that "the occupancy of the property be not extended beyond the actual need." [11] At the time, Glassford found no reason to quarrel with Heath's limitation. He was too busy caring for the men and establishing new camps. However, the veterans occupied many more buildings than Heath had authorized, including all of those on which Rhine had contracted, and they tended to view the makeshift quarters as conquered territory. The veterans cared little for Heath's cherished building program, Rhine's lost profits, or the government's need for more of-

10. B.E.F. News, July 9, 1932; George Kleinholz, The Battle of Washington: A National Disgrace (New York: B.E.F. Press, 1932), pp. 14–17; Walter W. Waters, B.E.F.: The Whole Story of the Bonus Army (New York: The John Day Company, Inc., 1933), pp. 75, 104, 111. PDG, "Press Release," June 10, 11, and July 14, 1932; PDG to John Henry Bartlett, June 11, 1932, GP. Ferry K. Heath to PDG, June 10, 1932, PP 300, HHPL.

11. Biographical information on Ferry K. Heath can be found in Records of the Treasury Department, Secretary's Correspondence, RG 56, NA; Ferry K. Heath, "Address to Michigan Bankers Association, June 11, 1930," mimeographed, ibid.; Evening Star, October 16, 1932; Ferry K. Heath to PDG, June 10, 1932, PP 300, HHPL.

fice space and desire to use the project to provide jobs. Two months later the protesters were, in fact, to challenge Heath's right to remove them, thus precipitating a violent confrontation.

Despite the desirability of the half-demolished federal buildings, the best-known, the largest, and probably the most miserable of all the encampments was the site on Anacostia's mud flats. There the ingenuity, fortitude, and good health of the men and their families were constantly put to the test. Boredom, like an illness, became a daily challenge. As only a small percentage could serve as lobbyists, many others spent their time walking the city, begging for food, improving their shelters, or merely gossiping. But boredom became the least of their problems. Crowded into a half-mile semicircle bordering the filthy river, the 15,000 campers were either baking under a merciless sun and choking on clouds of dust or sloshing in a sea of mud after one of the frequent rainstorms.

To combat the elements the veterans erected a profusion of temporary shelters. Anything that could conceivably be used to build a dwelling place was hauled from nearby dumps by roaming bands of veterans whose job it was to "requisition" materials from every likely source in the city. Old automobiles were highly prized, as were large flat pieces of corrugated iron roofing. Mattresses, wooden boxes, cardboard piano or furniture boxes, oilcloth, canvas, and bricks and lumber from the empty federal buildings were all ingeniously hammered together into lean-tos or the more common boxlike shelters, many of which had walls or roofs made of tightly woven burdock leaves. The lucky ones slept in tents supplied by Hoover through the War Department and the District National Guard, which along with the Veterans Administration, acted as conduits for the President's secret aid. Others simply curled up under the stars or rainclouds with nothing but an Army sleeping sack filled with straw for a bed, some with only newspapers for blankets. Occasionally the miniature home of a skilled craftsman graced the neighborhood with its freshly painted fences and blooming flower garden. Yet, for all the fascinating and bizarre character of the Anacostia camp, life there was generally wretched.[12]

The squatters' diet matched the poverty of their quarters. Coffee and bread in the morning, soup at noon, and an evening meal of mulligan stew made beggars out of many, despite Waters's injunction ("No panhandling, no liquor, no radical talk") and meant that many were undernourished, usually hungry, and often ill.[13] Not surprisingly, 15,000 people jammed against the filthy Anacostia River under these primitive conditions soon represented a potential menace to the health of the city.

The rapid increase of sickness among the marchers and the need for a hospital to care for them quickly generated a new sense of crisis. William C. Foster, the District health officer, was so alarmed by the filth in the camps that he took it upon himself to order all of the veterans to leave immediately. Waters charged that Foster's order was a plot to force the marchers out of the city, but as the number of sick continued to grow, both Glassford and Hoover became increasingly concerned. In addition to supplying cots, tents, bedsacks, rolling kitchens, and food and clothing at Army prices as well as allowing the occupation of federal lands and half-demolished office buildings, Hoover had further cooperated by permitting the Sixth Marine Reserve Brigade on Indiana Avenue to open an aid station where as many as 350 veterans a day received treatment.[14] Moreover, unknown to Glassford, as soon as Hoover realized the need for a hospital, he ordered Hines to establish all the necessary facilities at nearby Fort Hunt, Virginia.

12. Waters, B.E.F., pp. 105–7; "Human Side of the Bonus Army," Literary Digest, 113 (June 25, 1932), 30.

13. "The Ghost Parade of the Bonus Seekers," Literary Digest, 13 (June 18, 1932), 6–7; Herald, June 8, 1932; Post, June 8, 1932; "Human Side of the Bonus Army," Literary Digest (June 25, 1932), 28, 30; Waters, B.E.F., pp. 103–14; Mauritz A. Hallgren, "The Bonus Army Scares Mr. Hoover," Nation, 135 (July 27, 1932), 72.

14. Herald, June 10, 1932; Waters, B.E.F., pp. 86–87; Donald Knowlton to PDG, June 4, 1932; "Health Conference Report," June 10, 1932, GP.

As happened in most of his dealings with the veterans, Hoover received no credit for his efforts. Perhaps because of the President's desire to avoid establishing precedents for direct federal relief, Hines failed to inform Glassford of the President's order, and during the next four days, while a 300-bed field hospital was being assembled and erected, Hines tried to keep the construction a secret. Meanwhile, Glassford became thoroughly angry and finally issued a public appeal "In the Name of Humanity" to the District Medical Society. Surprised by the delay and undoubtedly embarrassed by the bad publicity, Hoover demanded a full investigation to determine why his orders had not been carried out promptly. When the field hospital opened on the following day, everyone received the impression that it was Glassford who had again come to the aid of the needy ex-soldiers with his skill at marshaling public opinion, and thus had forced Hoover's cooperation. Unfortunately, no one knew of the President's prior instructions to construct the hospital, but as the damage had been done, Hoover allowed the misunderstanding to remain.[15]

The poignancy of the veterans' lot was inescapable. This huge mass of tattered humanity in the nation's capital city, begging for redress, the hungry men, women, and children symbolized the country's downtrodden masses. Their appeal was not in their specific demand but in their

15. FTH to Douglas MacArthur, August 18, 1932, War Department, Records of The Adjutant General, RG 94, NA; "Record of Telephone Messages," Donald Knowlton to PDG, June 14, 1932, PP 300, HHPL; *Herald*, June 15, 1932; F. H. Payne to HH, June 15, 1932, PP 48, HHPL. For an exhaustive investigation of the unfavorable publicity concerning the need for a hospital, see Historical Studies Files, Soldiers' Bonus, Adjusted Compensation, Veterans Administration Files, Veterans Administration Building, Washington, D.C. There are numerous letters, sworn statements, and investigative reports which establish that both Glassford and the physician on duty were irritable on that day and that the newspaper reporter grossly exaggerated the conflict. J. O. C. Roberts, Solicitor to the Administrator, June 21, 1932. I am indebted to Warren MacDonald, Special Assistant to the Administrator, for locating and allowing me access to these and other hitherto unexamined documents relating to the various bonus marches. This impression is also conveyed in Daniels, *Bonus March*, p. 157.

similarity to other Americans damaged by the depression. Glassford had publicized them as representatives of the nation's poor, and Elsie Robinson, a nationally read Hearst columnist and great friend of the veterans, sympathetically reiterated this theme for the vast Hearst readership. That the veterans represented the disadvantaged finally was widely accepted—a view that has been repeated over the subsequent years.[16]

The notion that the BEF spoke for the poor has created a significant amount of confusion about both the purpose and the nature of the protest. Neither Glassford nor the Hearst stories misled thoughtful columnists and editors, who recognized that the vast majority of the men were middle-aged and middle-class—small businessmen, skilled tradesmen, and white-collar workers, with a sprinkling of professionals, such as teachers, lawyers, and dentists. Some reporters were troubled that the marchers actually felt no real sense of kinship with the other poor. But while these were disappointed that the bonus march would not spearhead a national movement for sweeping fundamental economic reforms, much of the BEF's appeal to others undoubtedly could be found in their essentially conservative, nonradical nature. On the conventional character of the BEF, newsmen, government spies, and administration officials alike could agree. Most of their talk, Hines informed the President, was "not particularly radical. The rank and file blame the banks, big business, and politicians for everything." In fact, he added, it "reminds one of much that is heard around a country store near election time." [17]

16. *Times*, June 9, 1932; John H. Bartlett, *The Bonus March and The New Deal* (New York: M. A. Donohue and Company, 1937), p. 3 and *passim;* Jack Douglas, *Veterans on the March* (New York: Workers Library Publishers, 1934), p. 364; Waters, *B.E.F.*, p. 144; *BEF News*, July 16, 1932; *Herald*, July 18, 1932. Irving Bernstein states that the BEF "was a manifestation of transient joblessness." See Bernstein, *The Lean Years*, p. 456.

17. *Times*, June 14, 1932; "Human Side of the Bonus Army," *Literary Digest* (June 25, 1932), p. 28; *Evening Star*, June 6, 1932; "The Bonus Army," *Commonweal* (June 15, 1932), pp. 173–74; Hallgren, "B.E.F. Scares Mr. Hoover," p. 71. Waters, *B.E.F.*, pp. 116–25. FTH to HH, June 24, 1932, PP 300, HHPL. Hines sent Hoover a copy of his agent's report.

The refusal of the Bonus Army to champion the needs of the nation's poor or to advocate reforms prompted even friendly reporters to take a closer look at the BEF. *Time* commented on the illusionary nature of the camps. The men had "revived the old ganging spirit of Army days as an escape from reality." One reporter, although sympathetic, emphasized the pathos of men fleeing from the cries of their children, from the nagging of their wives, from the humiliation of unemployment, and from the mysterious, cruel depression that had robbed them of their former sense of security and self-respect. He noted that the distinguishing feature of the BEF was an overwhelming need for order, security, and self-respect rather than a demand for reforms.[18]

The Nation took a slightly dimmer view, contending that the appearance of ordered stability was misleading. The marchers were characterized, not so much by their orderliness, but by their universal lack of spirit or demand for reform. Their pitiful rituals revealed the pervasive attitude of hopelessness; utter despair was the common denominator among these middle-class casualties. They knew that the bonus would never be enough to restore their old status, "but in their confusion of mind they could think of no other goal." They did not advocate legislation to combat poverty and unemployment; they were not bold, courageous protesters for the poor, nor were they dangerous revolutionaries. More accurately portraying the crisis of the middle class, they harbored "no revolt, no fire, not even smoldering resentment; at most they are but an unchoate aggregation of frustrated men nursing a common grievance." [19]

The dominant aspect of the campers' psyche was their consciousness of being special. They were not merely unemployed men, not merely poor; they were unemployed

---

18. "Heroes," *Time*, 19 (June 20, 1932), 11. *Evening Star*, June 6, 1932. David Brion Davis, ed., *The Fear of Conspiracy: Images of Un-American Subversion From the Revolution to the Present* (Ithaca, N.Y.: Cornell University Press, 1971), pp. xvii, xx. Davis makes several interesting points on the loss of self-respect and the resulting inclination to imagine plots and deliberate oppression.

19. Hallgren, "Bonus Army Scares Mr. Hoover," pp. 71–72.

veterans, and as such they demanded and received special respect. The men took great pride in the belief that
they had not come as unworthy beggars, but as a special
class of citizens demanding the payment of an honest,
hard-earned debt.[20] One incident, involving Franklin D.
Roosevelt, further refuted the popular and simple impression of the BEF. The New York Governor was steadfastly
opposed to the bonus, remained opposed during his campaign for President, and even vetoed the measure twice
after he took office. He was one of three governors who
responded to the District Commissioners' telegrams be-
seeching the states to remove their residents from the
District of Columbia. Roosevelt sent Nels Anderson as his
personal representative to persuade the large New York
contingent to return home. He offered the men generous
terms—not only free transportation home but guaranteed
employment as well. Despite this gesture, the New
Yorkers dramatically rejected the offer and determined
not to budge until they had obtained their bonus.[21] It was
a strange decision for so-called "hunger marchers" to turn
down jobs.

Thus, added to their non-radical, essentially middle-
class outlook, the marchers found kinship in their sense of
special pride and identity. Waters recognized this bond,
and repeatedly he spoke of the veterans' identity and of
the self-respect the members of the BEF derived from
having fought for democracy. Norman Thomas, the Social-
ist party's candidate for President, also recognized their
narrow focus. He told the men of his party's support for
the march on Washington and the bonus, but he criticized
the veterans for not broadening their demands to include
general relief for all of the unemployed and needy. Their
special identity was much too important to them, how-

20. "Bonus Army," *Commonweal*, p. 173; "Bonus Army Did Not Intimidate Congress," *Christian Century*, 49 (July 20, 1932), 902;
"Human Side of the Bonus Army," *Literary Digest*, p. 28.

21. PDG to Margaret A. Kerr, June 14, 1932, GP; *Post*, June 11,
1932. District Commissioners to FDR, June 9, 1932; FDR to District
Commissioners, June 10, 1932; B. Belmont to FDR, July 5, 1932;
M. Maldwin Fertig to Belmont, July 6, 1932, Office of Governor of
New York State, 1929–1932, TERC-AC File, FDRL.

ever. To an audience of thousands Waters promised, "We're going to keep ourselves a simon-pure veterans' organization," and the troops responded with a roar of approval.[22]

The most studious critics of the BEF were the editors of *Commonweal*, a liberal Roman Catholic magazine. They did not share the fears of other critics, but they were disturbed by the BEF's excessive emphasis upon military symbolism. *Commonweal* noted, "For most of them to have been a soldier is a title to glory," making them a special class. Unlike most other needy folk, the ex-soldier saw himself as a deposed "aristocrat whose status the nation cannot with impunity ignore." Although not excessively worried, the editors did point out that this insistence on "soldier's superiority" was precisely the line that Adolf Hitler was taking in Germany. Any discussion of the bonus therefore "must reckon" with the military justification behind it.[23]

Because of the BEF's insistence on military identity and its exclusive concentration on the bonus, the nation's editors had difficulty deciding exactly what the protest represented. It was clear that the demonstrators were emphasizing "the needs of veterans at the expense of others" and that under those circumstances the bonus itself was an unworthy demand.

The march to Washington had captured the imagination of millions of Americans, and the huge Anacostia encampment of improvised huts and government tents soon became publicized as the nation's most conspicuous "Hooverville." Still, the human-interest stories, however compelling, were somewhat misleading. To be sure, the veterans were poor, but they did not speak for the poor. They were hungry, but they concentrated exclusively on relief for the veteran. Despite the impression created by Glassford, the Hearst chain, and other sympathetic reporters, their appeal for aid to others was incidental.

22. *Herald*, June 13, 1932; "Heroes," *Time*, p. 11; John Dos Passos' preface to *Veterans*, pp. v–vi.
23. "Bonus Army," *Commonweal*, pp. 173–74.

At best, the Bonus Army reflected the poverty and despair among millions of Americans, but at the same time it refused to bring pressure on Congress or on the administration on behalf of all the disadvantaged. They were a visible and stirring symbol of the unemployed and destitute everywhere, but because their plight overshadowed their purpose, they were a confusing symbol. Ragged, sickly, and hungry, they bemoaned the depression and the poverty it brought. But the "army" considered itself a special class, was concerned only with its own demands, and despite appearances, it refused to speak for the poor.

5

Fears of Conspiracy

From the moment the first marchers arrived in Washington, newsmen regularly emphasized rumors that the Communist party intended to support the bonus and, worse yet, to use the veteran protest for making trouble. Some looked for violence to be incited within the Bonus Army, others an assassination attempt on the President, and still others the beginning of a bloody revolution to bring down the Republic. Not all people equated protesters with Communists, but even many of those who made the distinction were suspicious of the purposes of the intruding Bonus Expeditionary Force. During their travels across the country the marchers' reputation had fluctuated wildly in the press. Because they commandeered freight cars and forced railroad companies to provide free transportation, they appeared as dangerous, combat-hardened desperadoes who would stop at nothing to gain their objectives. When people actually saw the veterans, the attitudes of many softened immediately, and they offered sympathy and help for the men they considered as forgotten heroes of the Great War. But then, quite suddenly and for an entire week, from June 1 through June 7, a rash of reports of Communist plans led even the normally composed Police Chief to consider calling on federal troops to control the marchers.

On June 1, 1932, only three days after the arrival in Washington of Walter W. Waters and his Oregon protesters, Emmanuel Levin, one of the founders and former state chief of the California Communist party, held a news conference in which he dramatically proclaimed that it was the Communist party which had originated the bonus march, not Waters or other Fascist leaders such as Glassford, who were undermining the real power and purpose

of the veterans. Since April 15, in fact, the Workers' Ex-
Service Men's League, the veterans' arm of the party, had
been attempting to rally support for a march on Congress.
Now Levin called for massive street demonstrations at
state capitals and city halls throughout the nation to encourage nationwide support for the demonstration. He
promised that on June 8, when more veterans would have
reached the capital, he would organize a great parade,
after which the men would elect new officers and formu-
late new demands. The BEF had also announced plans
for a huge parade on the same day, and Levin's comments
led citizens, police, and congressmen alike to wonder if
the BEF were actually Communist-inspired and -domina-
ted. Even if it was not, many wondered what violence the
Communists might incite by holding their parade at the
same time. In either case, they feared impending riot and
possibly revolution, which might become widespread
enough to threaten the American democracy.[1]

The man who had planted these doubts in their minds
was an experienced Communist organizer and propagandist. In 1930 Emmanuel Levin had moved up in the party
hierarchy to a national position as one of the founders of
the Workers' Ex-Service Men's League, and later he was
named chairman of the League's Joint Provisional Bonus
March Committee.[2] The League sought to implement the
ideological and tactical aims stated at the Tenth Plenum
of the Comintern Executive Committee held in Moscow a

1. *Herald*, June 1, 1932; *Evening Star*, June 2, 1932. For evidence
that Levin's group had been active since April, see New York *Times*,
April 16, 1932; New York *Daily Worker*, April 23, 24, 1956; and clippings from the *Daily People's World* in the Levin Papers, Department of
Special Collections, University of California, Los Angeles. Levin was
also identified as a former editor of the New York *Daily Worker*. *Evening Star*, May 10, 1933. For Washington, D.C., newspapers the city
is omitted from the citation.

2. Jack Douglas, *Veterans On The March* (New York: Workers Library Publishers, 1934), pp. 177–78. Douglas was identified as a Communist, and although his interpretation of events is distorted, some of
the clearly factual information is useful. For information on Douglas,
see U.S., Congress, House, Committee on Un-American Activities,
Communist Tactics Among Veterans Groups, 82d Cong., 2d sess.,
1951, p. 1945 (hereafter cited as HUAC, CTVG).

year earlier. By the end of 1929 the Communist party in
the United States had been thoroughly "Stalinized" into
what two respected scholars have referred to as "a totalitarian monolith." At that point the Comintern boldly announced the beginning of a new revolutionary period. According to the Communist strategy, the workers would
organize "a tightly disciplined, quasi-military party . . .
in which every member would function as an obedient
soldier." A militant, revolutionary organization would
then radicalize the people through mass street demonstrations and confrontations with reactionary forces.[3] It
was a threat some people in government as well as among
the general public took quite seriously.

During 1931 and 1932 the Communists sought to create
an impression of real accomplishment within the party by
frequently staging confrontations with the police in
various parts of the nation. For rank-and-file Communists
these clashes reinforced the conviction that the party was
engaged totally against the forces of capitalistic reaction,
thus boosting the morale of the party's dedicated members.[4] The Workers' Ex-Service Men's League hoped to
fulfill this same mission in the national capital. Levin's
press conference helped to intensify the impression that
the Bonus Army was working toward that goal, indeed
that a revolutionary tide was about to sweep the country.

Widely circulated stories of the impending insurrection
caused some concern in the War Department. Brig. Gen.
George Van Horn Moseley, Deputy Chief of Staff, feared
that the presence of the Bonus Army in Washington
would precipitate serious trouble. If he trusted the *Daily
Worker's* claims that thousands of Communist marchers
were approaching the city, it is not difficult to understand
his sense of urgency. In late May, as soon as it became apparent that state and local officials were not holding back
the marchers but actually speeding them by the thousands toward the capital, Moseley became increasingly

3. Irving Howe and Lewis Coser, *The American Communist Party:
A Critical History 1919–1957* (Boston: Beacon Press, 1957), pp. 174,
178–79, 188–90.
4. Howe and Coser, *Communist Party*, pp. 188–90.

anxious. His fear of agitators was almost matched by his
hatred of Jews, and it was not uncommon for him to warn
interchangeably of Communist or Jewish conspiracies.
But, despite his fervent plea to disperse the approaching
marchers, his superior, Gen. Douglas MacArthur, the
Chief of Staff, had flatly refused to associate himself or the
Army with plans to do so.[5]

At that time the War Department's principal worries
centered on Hoover's strong support of the Geneva Disarmament Conference and the efforts of unsympathetic congressmen to make cutbacks in the Army's already slim
budget. Moseley was not certain which posed the greater
danger—the Disarmament Conference or the congressmen's attitude. In an effort to influence the conference, he
sent to Maj. Gen. George S. Simonds, one of the U.S. delegates in Geneva, documents that, he claimed, showed
"clearly how we have dwindled."

Some influential congressmen on key military committees favored still deeper cuts in the Army budget. While
this prospect was an obvious source of great concern to
the military, Moseley defiantly informed Simonds that
the War Department was not "licked" yet. "As a matter of
fact, we have not been defeated at all thus far and we
don't intend to be." Still, doubts clearly plagued him. "It
may be," Moseley concluded, "that Congress will so disarm us that they will do more than even the Disarmament
Conference had intended." [6] Under the circumstances,
Moseley's advocacy of using the Army to disperse the approaching bonus marchers may have been influenced as
much by his desire to impress Congress with the need for
a strong internal defense as by his dislike of protesters or
fear of Communists.

    5. George Van Horn Moseley, "One Soldier's Journey," un-
published diary, 2 vols., II, 138–39, Moseley Papers (hereafter cited as
GMP). Scrapbook of Selected Papers, 1889–1942, p. 503, GMP.
    6. Moseley to Maj. Gen. George S. Simonds, April 6, 1932, GMP. A
fuller discussion of the Army's reaction is in D. Clayton James, The
Years of MacArthur 1880–1941 (Boston: Houghton Mifflin Company,
1970), pp. 378–81; John Richard Wilson, "Herbert Hoover and the
Armed Forces: A Study of Presidential Attitudes and Policy" (Ph.D.
diss., Northwestern University, 1971), pp. 132–33.

Although he strongly supported the Geneva Conference, Hoover felt that the Army had indeed been cut back too drastically for national safety, a decision he reached about the time Japanese–American relations deteriorated over Manchuria. Hoover had increased Army appropriations in 1931 and 1932 by 10 to 15 per cent, but powerful congressmen applied intense pressure to reduce the number of officers, and eventually the 1933 budget was to reflect a general reduction.[7] Possibly apprehensive about Secretary of State Henry L. Stimson's insistence on a more militant policy toward Japan and about the need to be prepared for military action, Hoover warned Patrick J. Hurley, his Secretary of War, of the intense pressure for a reduced officer corps, which influential congressmen were placing on him, and of the need for the Army to retire voluntarily a greater number of its officers.[8] Feeling the many pressures, the General Staff obviously believed that it was fighting for the Army's very life.

Worried about the hostile Congress, low budgets, a reduction in officer strength, and the possible results of the Geneva Conference, MacArthur labored over a reorganization of the Army's entire structure and directed much of his energy toward convincing congressmen that a full-strength Army was essential to national defense.[9] Further reductions, he argued, would be calamitous. At that point he had little time for concern over a bunch of grumbling

7. Wilson, "Hoover and Armed Forces," pp. 150–51.

8. HH to Hurley, July 19, 1932; Hurley to Hoover, July 20, 1932, War Department, HHPL. Hoover warned Hurley that Senator David Reed, chairman of the Senate Military Affairs Committee, had talked to him about the imperative need to reduce the number of Army officers. If this were not done by the next session of Congress, Hoover warned Hurley, "We will have great difficulties." Hurley promised Hoover that this matter would receive the War Department's "closest attention." For the Army Class B Law referred to in the correspondence, see *Supplement II, Military Laws of the United States* (Washington, D.C.: Government Printing Office, 1943), p. 19. For clarification of the law, I am indebted to Col. Georgia D. Hill, Chief Historical Services Division, Department of the Army. Eight days after Hurley responded to Hoover's warning, MacArthur drove the veterans out of the city and argued that the Army had successfully put down incipient revolution.

9. James, *MacArthur*, pp. 357–58.

protesters, especially since the Army had a standard secret "White Plan" for handling any emergency civil disturbance. Nevertheless, to Moseley it was not unreasonable to expect that special plans should be made for dealing with a group of such massive size as the Bonus Army. The marchers far outnumbered the District police force, and "in the event of an emergency" it was imperative, he argued, that the Army be prepared to meet it. To be caught off guard could bring a deluge of criticism on the General Staff. At first, Moseley's advice had no effect on MacArthur, but on the following morning the Chief of Staff suddenly changed his mind. He adamantly refused to turn back the approaching marchers, but without explanation he ordered Moseley to begin making plans to handle any BEF emergency.

Delighted by MacArthur's change of heart, Moseley plunged into the task of defending the capital. First, he secretly transferred several tanks from Fort Meade, Maryland, to nearby Fort Myer, Virginia, across the Potomac from the city, and moved reserve tanks to Fort Washington, another convenient post. Gen. Perry L. Miles, commander of the brigade at Fort Meade, prepared a detailed study of troop movements which could be utilized "to meet any emergency whatsoever." At the request of the Secret Service, troops were readied to protect the White House and the Treasury "at a moment's notice." By June 1, the day on which Levin's press conference inspired sensational headlines, the Army was ready.[10] That same day, during Senate hearings on the Costigan bill for federal relief to transients in the District, Luther Reichelderfer, president of the District of Columbia Board of Commissioners, expressed the Commissioners' view that the Army ought to assume the responsibility for the bonus marchers, a view Police Chief Glassford fully supported. But although the Army was prepared to drive the veterans out of the capital, if necessary, neither Hurley nor MacArthur had any interest in caring for their former comrades while they picketed Congress.[11]

10. Moseley, "One Soldier's Journey," II, 138–39.
11. U.S., Congress, Senate, Committee on the District of Columbia,

The rapid influx of thousands of veterans, many of them accompanied by their families, was a matter of grave concern for Glassford, and considering the widespread stories of Communist activity, the Police Chief began to have some serious misgivings about the wisdom of his own tactics. To exert control over the BEF he had insisted, for example, that before new arrivals would be issued ration cards, they must register their discharge papers at BEF headquarters. These rosters supposedly ensured that only bona fide veterans received food rations, but at the same time Glassford secretly delivered the muster rolls to the Veterans Administration, the FBI, or Army Intelligence for investigation.[12]

Another important means of control was the choice of sleeping quarters, which the police could easily supervise. This potential for supervision was a crucial factor in Glassford's choice of the Anacostia mud flats, which became the BEF's largest camp. It was outside the city proper but close enough for the men to see both the Capitol dome and the Washington Monument, thus giving them the feeling that they were close to the action. Close to the action—yes; but also hemmed in. The area was enclosed on the north by the wide, filthy Anacostia River while at the opposite end of the camp was a ten-foot bluff. Near the entrance, which could most easily be reached after crossing the Eleventh Street drawbridge, was the Eleventh Precinct Police Station. A huge city drainpipe at the far edge of the camp completed the encirclement. Should a riot break out, Glassford felt he could prevent the veterans from entering the city by raising the drawbridge, posting guards at bridges farther north, and then

Hearings on S. 4781, Emergency Unemployment Relief and Care of Persons in Distress, 72d Cong., 1st sess., June 1, 1932, pp. 8, 14; New York *Daily Worker*, April 15, June 1, 1932 in PP 299, HHPL; F. H. Payne to John J. McSwain, June 25, 1932, War Department, Office of The Adjutant General, RG 94, NA. Payne was Acting Secretary of War. Arthur Hennessy, "Bonus Army of 1932" (Ph.D. diss., Georgetown University, 1957), pp. 192–93.

12. PDG to George Alman, June 5, 1932, GP; "Information From Veterans Administration Relative to Bonus Marchers," Department of Justice, File 95-16-26, RG 60, NA; FTH to HH, June 13, 1932, PP 300; MacArthur to Joslin, June 14, 1932, PP 48, HHPL.

surrounding the camp. The site was far from ideal for the marchers, for the occupants of the tar-paper and egg-crate camp were covered with choking dust in hot, dry weather and bogged down in a muddy quagmire when the rains came. Its location was undeniably strategic, however; riot control was the main purpose in Glassford's selection of the site. At the same time, he made sincere efforts to render life as tolerable for the veterans and their families as he could.[13]

The Police Chief could not believe that the men he had led and fought with in the World War could be anything but patriotic Americans. Yet the reports that kept pouring in—some obviously rumors, some from reliable sources— were too disturbing to be ignored. Fortunately, during the first weeks of the encampment his relations with Waters were open and cordial, and their cooperation enabled the two commanders to maintain control over the marchers and to prevent them from disintegrating into an unruly mob. Nonetheless, the potential for trouble was limitless. Unfortunately, the marchers did not take seriously the notion that they were subject to Waters's commands. Their real Army days were over. While all recognized the need for order, both Waters and Glassford understood that these men might at any time refuse to obey an unpopular command. Internal strife and bickering had been evident from the beginning, and as their numbers swelled and the marchers became more discontented, the likelihood of riot increased.

No sooner had Emmanuel Levin publicized his ominous suggestion of Communist domination of the BEF than the Secret Service uncovered information that reinforced Glassford's concern. On June 1, Allen G. Straight, the Secret Service's principal operative in New York, told his chief, W. H. Moran, that Levin and James Ford, the black nominee for Vice President on the Communist party ticket, as well as other Communist veterans, had organ-

13. PDG, "Information Bulletin," June 2, 1932; PDG to District Commissioners, June 3, 1932, GP; Douglas, *Veterans*, pp. 133–34, 137–38.

ized the Workers' Ex-Service Men's League "as gorillas, or shock troops" of the party. This organization, Moran learned, had been dispatched "to various places for the sole purpose of causing disturbances and promoting violence." Straight had received his information from Paul A. Williams, an editor of the New York *Daily Mirror* and a local Legion commander. According to Williams, Levin's gang of toughs would provoke the bonus marchers into a violent confrontation, during which they would "force an entrance into the White House, or on to the White House grounds and if possible draw fire from the guards." Should any of the Communists be "fortunate enough to be wounded, or killed," the incident would provide "excellent material for future activities." [14]

Only a day later, on June 2, Glassford received more news of the same nature from two of his own detectives who had been assigned to cover Communist meetings in the District of Columbia. Not only were the Communists planning to gather a mob of veterans to descend upon the White House, but at a meeting of the John Reed Club held the previous evening, Communist leaders had announced their intention to form "an organization of 100 men into a compact fighting unit to combat the police and render assistance to comrades by drilling them in the art of street fighting." [15] The news of the Communist plot created immediate and sensational editorial reaction. On June 3, the day following the detectives' report, the Washington *Post* charged that the federal authorities "have conclusive evidence that the reds are largely responsible for the bonus march" and that they had, in fact, organized the entire BEF for their own sinister purposes. The bonus issue itself was only a smoke screen; actually, the BEF was a Communist "conspiracy" that had "double-crossed" the people and that must be dealt with as a dire threat to the public safety.[16]

By June 3 Glassford was convinced that he had a poten-

14. Allen G. Straight to W. H. Moran, June 1, 1932, GP.

15. W. C. Groons and A. Friedburg to PDG, "Report on Communist Meeting," June 1, 1932, GP.

16. *Post*, June 3, 1932.

tially serious emergency on his hands. Five days after
Waters arrived, Glassford stopped soliciting funds for the
BEF and predicted that food supplies would be exhausted by noon the following day. In a secret memo to
the District of Columbia Commissioners he briefly outlined his plan for counteracting the Communists' plot. His
men would assemble all disaffected groups at the Anacostia camp, where police reinforcements equipped with tear
gas would "hold the Eleventh Street Bridge" while additional police would localize the rioting on the east side of
the river and prevent access to the bridges farther north.
With the food supplies nearly exhausted, Glassford
added, such an emergency seemed serious enough to justify calling out the National Guard or using the Army's
"White Plan" for civil disturbances.[17]

Glassford's willingness to call for federal troops testified to his uneasiness. He had repeatedly argued that he
could handle the situation, that the men were not a threat,
and that feeding them and providing quarters for them
was the best and most sensible strategy. He had argued
this moderate attitude at the cost of a permanent rift between himself and Police Commissioner Herbert B.
Crosby. Glassford's recommendation now appeared to be
a tacit admission that Crosby had been right. After having
organized the Bonus Army and having worked incessantly
to win the respect and admiration of the veterans, Glassford was in the best position to judge their reliability. If
he was highly apprehensive, it is little wonder that others
were also.

Both Glassford and Police Commissioner Crosby were
former Army generals, and they had discussed with Mac-
Arthur the problems of controlling the influx of veterans.
Crosby had also had several conferences with Secretary of
War Patrick Hurley. Glassford's respect for and trust in

17. PDG to District Commissioners, June 3, 1932, GP. For a detailed explanation of the revised "White Plan," see John W. Killigrew,
"The Army and the Bonus Incident," *Military Affairs*, 26 (Summer
1962), 60–61. A copy of the plan is in "Report of Operations Against
Bonus Marchers," Memorandum for Chief of Staff, June 4, 1932, RG
394, NA.

MacArthur was unbounded, and he had frequently sought out his old school friend for advice on methods of controlling the veterans. Later, ironically, he was to credit MacArthur, not Hoover, for helping him to secure supplies from the Army. It is entirely possible, therefore, that when Glassford advised the use of troops, he was aware of General Moseley's blueprint for deployment. At any rate, all of them felt a sense of impending crisis.[18]

On June 4 the District Commissioners announced that on June 9, the day following the already scheduled BEF parade, all veterans were to be loaded into trucks, which would take them fifty miles out of the city and presumably leave them at the mercy of state governors to reverse the earlier trans-state journey back to their homes. The Commissioners' announcement was supported fully by Hurley, MacArthur, and Glassford. Those veterans who did not want to leave voluntarily would not be forced, but they were warned that the Police Department would stop issuing food after June 9. Also, the building of barracks at Anacostia was to cease immediately, and veterans living in abandoned government buildings were to be evicted in order to prevent a developing sanitation menace. After June 9, the veterans remaining in Washington must fend for themselves. The provisions of this announcement were impossible to execute, but at least they avoided any hint of massive force. Newspapers accurately interpreted it as an ultimatum, a test of wills on which the established police powers staked their prestige, a test they were almost certain to lose without the use of troops.[19]

An obvious weakness of the ultimatum was its failure to take into account the thousands of marchers still tramping toward the city. These men, apparently forgotten for the moment, suddenly reemerged in the news the next day. On June 4 a crowd consisting of from 1,000 to 2,000 veterans clashed with police in Cleveland, Ohio, where they

18. PDG, "Information Bulletin," June 2, 1932; PDG to Joseph Choate, n.d., Box 15; Laguna Beach (California) *Post*, August 26, 1951, Box 1, GP 679.

19. *Evening Star*, June 4, 1932; *Post*, June 4, 1932; *Herald*, June 5, 1932.

had illegally occupied the Pennsylvania Railroad round-house because of the railroad's refusal to provide free transportation to the capital. Reports that marchers from Jersey City and Baltimore had also stopped trains further suggested the militancy of the protesters and the absurdity of insisting that they voluntarily accept a fifty-mile ride out of town on June 9. Clearly, they were determined to petition Congress, and nothing but an armed force would stop them. Daniel Willard, Jr., of the B. & O. appealed directly to the President to act against the veterans who commandeered trains, but Hoover refused to intervene.[20]

Newspaper reports of Communist coups, police ultimatums, and clashes in the nation's railyards heightened the sense of crisis in the capital. They also tended to obscure a more important confrontation, the test of the Bonus Army's power. By June 2, with the aid of well-disciplined bands of veteran lobbyists, Wright Patman had succeeded in securing all but 27 of the 145 signatures needed to force the Ways and Means Committee to release his bill for a vote. Gathering the signatures had not been an easy task. Rather than allowing congressmen to choose to sign or not to sign in the privacy of their own offices, the petition had been placed in the well of the House, under the watchful eyes of the leaders of both parties, who carefully noted anyone unwise enough to flaunt party loyalty. Leaders of both parties opposed the bonus. The need for each congressman to parade before the entire House to sign the petition created heavy psychological restraint.[21] If Patman failed to gain the additional 27 signatures by June 4, it was possible that the discharge rule might well stop consideration of the bill entirely for that session of Congress, since it limited the reporting out of bills from committees to the second and fourth Mondays of each month.

20. Walter Newton, telephone memo, June 7, 1932, PP 297, HHPL. Willard called the White House on June 4. Lewis I. H. Edwards to PDG, June 4, 1932, GP; New York *Times*, June 4, 5, 1932; Douglas, *Veterans*, pp. 124–25.

21. Interview with Wright Patman, June 21, 1968.

Faced with the Commissioners' ultimatum on the one hand and the discharge rule on the other, the veterans intensified their lobbying in a last desperate effort to line up signatures. They trooped through the office buildings, the halls of Congress, dining rooms, restrooms, parking lots, and went so far as to occupy the offices of wavering and, in some instances, angry congressmen, for whom they predicted certain defeat at the polls if they refused and certain victory if they signed. On June 3 fifteen congressmen yielded under the pressure; a full dozen of the most difficult legislators remained to be convinced on the final day. BEF lobbyists packed the galleries with veterans who cheered wildly each time another signer marched to the well of the House. With only a few minutes remaining before the day's adjournment, the final signature was added amidst a triumphant outburst from the galleries. The discharge of the petition assured a vote and almost certain victory for the Patman bill in the House. The veterans had won their first lobbying battle. They had accomplished a good part of their purpose in coming to Washington, and with consideration by the Senate almost certain, they now had substantial reason to prolong their stay in the city. As a result of this victory, regardless of the red scare, no one except Commissioner Crosby believed that it would be wise to try to enforce the June 9 ultimatum.[22]

Crosby was furious over the victory in the House. The veterans' success not only vindicated the march to Washington, but it also demonstrated its effectiveness as a tactic. Crosby's more immediate concern was with harassed congressmen who had opposed the discharge and who were convinced that the veterans' success would have been impossible without Glassford's helpful, cordial policy. To demonstrate their ire, a delegation of congressmen journeyed to the District Building to inform the Commissioners personally of their displeasure. Crosby had favored driving the marchers out of the capital as soon as

22. New York *Times,* June 5, 1932; *Herald,* June 4, 1932; Douglas, *Veterans,* pp. 95–96.

they crossed into the District. Now, more deeply angry that Glassford had refused to obey him, he publicly speculated that the President might insist on the Chief's immediate dismissal.[23]

Crosby's attempt to intimidate his own police chief revealed the irreparable split between the two men and, of course, reinforced the theory that the President was hostile toward the marchers and toward Glassford. Urged to action by an increasing number of congressmen and residents of the District, the Commissioners were under far greater pressure than the press indicated. It was not uncommon in Washington for congressmen to request personally that a police chief alter his policy. Glassford was in a tight spot. Demands for his removal, on the other hand, enhanced his already rapidly growing reputation as an honest, politically independent leader. One senator castigated those congressmen "who slip around in some slimy fashion," secretly attempting to get Glassford fired. Floyd Gibbon, a flamboyant former war correspondent whose column was nationally syndicated by the Hearst chain, declared that the only basis for charges of the Police Chief's "treason" was that he "hadn't ordered them clubbed or gassed or shot or even jailed." [24]

Each passing day Glassford was forced to divide his efforts among a greater number of compelling priorities in addition to his regular duties policing the District: appealing for aid from local welfare agencies, the administration, and Congress; fending off critical congressmen and Commissioners; supervising the distribution of food; securing first aid and medical facilities; organizing fundraising drives and benefits; and locating land and materials for new camps. Then, on June 5, the same day that

23. "Glassford–Boyd," pp. 10–11, GP; *Post*, June 5, 1932; *Herald*, June 6, 1932; PDG, Newspaper Scrapbook, II, 72, GP; U.S., Congress, Senate, *Congressional Record*, 72d Cong., 1st sess., 1932, 75, pt. 12, p. 13227.

24. Senate, *Congressional Record*, 72d Cong., 1st sess., 1932, 75, pt. 12, p. 13227; *Herald*, June 6, 1932; PDG, Newspaper Scrapbook, II, 72, GP.

Crosby publicly threatened to fire him, Glassford learned that Walter W. Waters had suddenly become ill and collapsed. With his resignation from command of the marchers, the stability of the Bonus Army deteriorated rapidly.

The physical strain of guiding the Oregon contingent to Washington and the first hectic week there had been too much for the frail commander. Never a robust man, he had worked long hours with Glassford and his subordinates to reduce factionalism within the BEF and to create some degree of unity in the command and control over what were otherwise constantly expanding, chaotic clusters of disappointed and disoriented men. Before resigning, Waters appointed George Alman, a powerfully built, strong-willed ex-lumberjack upon whom he had relied during the long journey to the capital. Appointing Alman rather than calling an election was presumptuous of Waters, but the ill commander possibly hoped to avoid the factionalism that was certain to erupt in a contest for command. Whatever Waters's motives, Alman's inability to win the respect of the men soon precipitated a crisis.[25]

Alman's first mistake was to discontinue the policy of requiring a detailed muster-roll roster on each man before issuing him a ration card—a victory for Alman but costly, for it started the rumor that he was no longer in Glassford's good graces. That notion greatly upset the veterans and seriously undermined the new commander's leadership, at the same time revealing the extent to which the men recognized Glassford as the real leader of the Bonus Army. Undoubtedly Alman hoped to avoid the label "Glassford's errand boy," an epithet which so irritated Waters that he eventually avoided, whenever possible, being seen in public with the Chief. But when Alman refused to denounce the Workers' Ex-Service Men's League to inquiring reporters and suggested instead that all veterans ought to band together, his seemingly tacit accep-

25. Walter W. Waters, *B.E.F.: The Whole Story of the Bonus Army* (New York: The John Day Company, Inc., 1933), pp. 66, 83.

tance of the Communists proved to be more than some of the other veterans' leaders could tolerate.[26] A secret rump session deposed Alman and substituted two new commanders, but within hours the executive committee restored Alman to temporary command, pending the results of a promised election.

As the BEF chain of command threatened to collapse completely, Glassford came under pressure from all sides. Fear of the parade now took on a heavy sense of foreboding. A New York *Times* editorial on June 6, entitled "The Siege of Washington," lambasted Congress for "giving in to the demands of a few veterans" and reminded its readers that in 1783 the Confederation Congress had scattered a similar band of unreasonable veterans, who were also demanding a bonus, by merely threatening to call out troops against them. Accustomed to far stronger criticism, the Chief could overlook the *Times*'s advice, but the repeated stories of Communist shock troops planning to strike during the bonus parade completely shattered his hopes that violence could be avoided.[27]

On June 7 Glassford and Crosby called a news conference to announce the discovery of the Communist plot, information that police and federal officials had been evaluating since June 1.[28] Telling the public about the Communist shock troops would seem to serve no constructive purpose. Apparently, their real purpose was to prepare Washingtonians and the nation for the use of troops against the BEF. For Glassford, it was as close as he was to come to an admission that his efforts to keep the veterans under control had been insufficient. Perhaps, after all, the Communists held the trump card.

The response to Glassford's news conference was immediate. For the second time in less than a week sensational headlines warned of the red menace. The Washing-

26. *Herald*, June 7, 1932. Waters, *B.E.F.*, pp. 71–73. Douglas, *Veterans*, pp. 101–2; *Evening Star*, June 6, 1932; *Herald*, June 7, 1932; *Post*, June 7, 1932.

27. New York *Times*, June 6, 1932.

28. PDG, "Press Memo," June 6, 1932; Harry C. Lear to Moseley, June 6, 1932, GP.

ton *Post* had already proclaimed that the bonus march was a Communist conspiracy plotted by agitators who had duped the veterans and "double-crossed" the nation. The whole affair "was now associated in the public mind with invidious communistic activities." [29] These warnings caused an increase in the number of guards at the White House and the secret stationing of 300 troops at the Munitions Building about a quarter of a mile away, where they could be quickly deployed either to the White House or the Capitol. With each escalation of suspicion and fear, letters from irate citizens and worried congressmen warned Hoover that the red menace must be taken seriously and must be met quickly and decisively.[30]

One of the most influential advocates of force was Secretary of War Hurley. Hurley fully supported the plans and ideas of Deputy Chief of Staff General Moseley. By June 1 Moseley had completed his strategy for defending the capital in the event of emergency, and thus prepared, he noted that thousands of the marchers were persisting in their drive toward Washington. Since friendly persuasion obviously had not impressed them, Moseley decided to ask Hoover to approve a memorandum ordering federal troops to turn the men back. The implication was that they would also be returned home by government transportation. He discussed his proposal with MacArthur and Hurley and later recalled "Hurley's saying that my memorandum contained not only a good idea, but that it was good politics as well and would have a good effect." [31] Others in Washington agreed with Hurley and increased the pressures on the President. Voices counseling

29. *Post*, June 3, 7, 1932; *Herald*, June 7, 8, 1932; New York *Times*, June 7, 1932; Douglas, *Veterans*, pp. 100–101. Douglas accused Glassford of "red baiting." David Brion Davis, ed., *The Fear of Conspiracy: Images of Un-American Subversion From the Revolution to the Present* (Ithaca, N.Y.: Cornell University Press, 1971), p. xv. Davis notes the tendency of rhetoric to polarize conflict in conspiratorial terms.

30. Theodore J. Joslin, *Hoover Off The Record* (New York: Doubleday, Doran and Company, 1934), pp. 264–65; Moseley, "One Soldier's Journey," II, 139. Royal C. Johnson to HH, June 4, 1932, PP 297; H. C. Hopson to HH, June 4, 1932, PP 300, HHPL.

31. Moseley, "One Soldier's Journey," II, 139–41.

the use of force emanated from the United States Army, the offices of the District Commissioners, angry congressmen, leading newspapers, and private citizens. The effect was to reinforce the belief that the Bonus Army was a conspiracy that threatened to topple the government.

Not all critics of the Bonus Army, however, favored the use of force. Bruce Barton, the successful and well-known advertising executive, urged the use of political rhetoric. Barton had gained nationwide fame with his best-seller, *The Man Nobody Knows*, which was notable for its identification of Jesus Christ as a salesman. He counseled that the veterans ought to be viewed as "children who had misguidedly tramped to Washington," that the entire movement was somewhat akin to a children's crusade, and therefore that the marchers ought to be treated kindly but firmly. He reminded Hoover of Calvin Coolidge's telegram to Samuel Gompers after the Boston police strike in 1919, in which he had proclaimed that neither the Boston police nor any other group had a right to strike against the public safety at any time or anywhere. The telegram had brought the obscure Governor Coolidge, who had done nothing to end the strike, to national recognition, which helped to raise him to the Vice Presidency and, upon Harding's death, to the White House. Barton urged Hoover to attack the BEF verbally in similar fashion and to declare, "There is no right by any group to attempt to intimidate the Congress of the United States," a phrase worthy of Coolidge and certain to reflect the sentiments of many citizens. But the President declined the opportunity.[32]

Hoover did not attack the marchers either with political rhetoric, as Barton urged, or with troops, as many others demanded. In fact, he privately answered all the BEF's critics with equal candor. In conferring with Hurley, Moseley, and MacArthur he firmly rejected the Moseley memorandum soliciting troops. Moseley recalled the gist of the President's reply: "The whole movement to Wash-

---

32. Bruce Barton to HH, June 6, 1932, Barton Papers, State Historical Society of Wisconsin.

ington was simply a temporary disease of the individuals concerned and it would have to work itself out in the normal way." [33] At the height of the panic on June 7, as Glassford prepared the public for the expected clash between Communist shock troops and the United States Army, Hoover remained calm. He rejected warnings of conspiracy, which he judged correctly as being based merely on presence and reported intent. He informed Barton that the veterans had not journeyed to the capital to cause violence. Instead, he argued, "except for a few New York agitators these are perfectly peaceable people that are coming in here." [34] To those guardians of America who would again accuse him of being soft on communism, Hoover affirmed that "unless some overt act should take place," the federal government had no right to intervene. In Hoover's view, the expression of ideas, even revolutionary ideas, and the presence of a few agitators, even radical agitators, were not sufficient to constitute a criminal conspiracy. Unless those ideas and agitators brought about serious overt acts, the President refused to interfere.[35]

Hoover's defense of the marchers' civil liberties during this red scare revealed a firm faith in the democratic process as well as in the protesters, a faith few people had the opportunity of knowing the President possessed. Further, despite the hysteria of the red scare that was pervading the newspapers, despite the constant stream of stories of street gangs and revolution, Hoover's faith was justified. What no one seemed to realize—but some perhaps should have guessed—was that the sensational stories of Communist activity were part of a huge propaganda build-up by party leaders to credit the Communists with organizing the BEF, to reassure the party faithful that progress was being made, and to attract the attention of

33. Moseley, "One Soldier's Journey," II, 141.
34. HH to Barton, June 7, 1932, Barton Papers.
35. Jules Verner to HH, June 9, 1932; HH to Verner, June 10, 1932, PP 102B, HHPL. Verner, the mayor of Linden, New Jersey, criticized Hoover's "extremely lenient" policy toward the Communist bonus marchers.

any veterans who might be growing impatient with their own leadership.

Emmanuel Levin, whose news conference on June 1 had dramatically touched off the red scare, had for years been an effective organizer and propagandist, and he skillfully used the scare tactics to disguise both the late arrival of the Communists and the fact that the party had failed either to initiate or control the march. Indeed, on June 1, while Levin was making his grandiose claims, John T. Pace, who was to become the Communists' field commander once he arrived in Washington, was in Detroit, preparing to stop a train. Reports of Communist shock troops and street gangs were equally explainable in terms of Levin's propaganda drive. One of the principal sources of these claims was a well-publicized meeting of the John Reed Club, which was almost certain to attract either local or federal plain-clothes agents or both, and at which listeners were informed of plans to storm the White House and form an elite street-fighting unit.[36]

Another informer may have been an unidentified reporter for the Washington *Herald* who had attended a meeting of the Friends of the Soviet Union, where the plan to disrupt the BEF parade had been openly discussed.[37] Whatever the sources, the fact that Communist security on such an important matter could be so easily penetrated by police and reporters suggested that the reds were not at all unwilling to advertise their newsworthy intentions. Clearly, the reds were exceedingly successful in disseminating propaganda through a variety of respected channels.

While President Hoover defended the rights of the marchers, he viewed the Communists' activities with distaste and was concerned about the party's possible role

36. HUAC, CTVG, 82d Cong., 1st sess., July 13, 1951, pp. 1928–29; William Z. Foster, *From Bryan to Stalin* (n.p.: International Publishers, 1937), p. 228; HUAC, *Hearings on House Resolution 282, Investigation of Un-American Propaganda Activities in the United States*, 75th Cong., 3d sess., October–November, 1938, III, pp. 2284–87; HUAC, CTVG, pp. 1931–33, 1936; See numerous confidential police reports on Communist meetings, beginning with May 20, 1932, DCP.

37. *Herald*, June 7, 1932.

in the BEF. Despite these feelings, he remained calm throughout the hysteria of the red scare. Although he unwisely refused to talk with the BEF leaders, he declined to use the situation for political advantage. Hoover's substantial aid to and defense of such a large number of demonstrators may well have been unique. In sharp contrast, Coxey's Army of unemployed protesters in 1894 had met a much harsher reception. When "General" Coxey and his marchers arrived for the May Day parade, official Washington greeted him with intense fear and open, hostile opposition. President Cleveland offered no help or recognition, and Coxey and two of his leaders were promptly arrested for walking on the grass.[38]

Hoover had tried to discourage the marchers from coming to Washington, but they had come anyway and presented a daily embarrassment to his administration. In spite of their persistence, he would not expel them. Instead, he continued to furnish part of their needs and, equally important, to give his support privately to Glassford's policies. Indeed, in light of this evidence, the claim of the President's secretary, Theodore Joslin, that Hoover "sympathized with the great majority of them, regarding them as being unfortunate and misguided," sums up his attitude fairly.[39]

By rejecting the voices of fear and the proponents of force, Hoover proved himself to be a far better man, a far wiser leader than his critics credited him. Although few realized it, his views were much closer to Glassford's than to the Commissioners'. He would not publicly approve the Police Chief's policies or issue entirely adequate supplies—which he felt would encourage more marchers to come to the city—but he did provide the unrecognized support that helped the popular Chief to become one of the best-loved heroes of the depression era. As certainly as Glassford deserved the praise, much of it was earned at

38. Donald McMurry, *Coxey's Army: A Study of the Industrial Army Movement of 1894* (Boston: Little, Brown and Company, 1929), pp. 4–5, 33, 105–26.
39. Joslin, *Hoover*, p. 265.

the expense of the President. As Joslin put it, one of Hoover's greatest failings as a leader was his "policy of silence." On June 8, as the veterans marched peaceably in their huge parade, with still no recognition from Hoover, they were to conclude that "the great humanitarian" had become of all men the least humane.[40]

40. Joslin, *Hoover*, pp. 2–4, 68–69. *Evening Star*, June 6, 1932; Douglas, *Veterans*, pp. 98–99. Thomas H. McKee to HH, June 10, 1932; Newton to McKee, June 13, 1932, PP 297, HHPL

6

Defeat of the Bonus

Their presence in Washington and the persistence of the veterans finally forced Patman's bill to a vote. The debate was in large measure a rehash of all the tedious arguments that had been repeated at great length for the preceding three years. Those who favored the bill reiterated the facts of the veterans' heroism, the justice of paying an honest debt, the benefits of inflation, and the administration's favoritism toward big business and bankers. The opponents cited the disastrous effects of cheap money in postwar Germany and predicted certain doom for the American economy if the bonus were paid. At that time, massive deficit spending, an unbalanced budget, and tampering with the gold standard were considered heresy by members and leaders of both parties.

The strongest, most convincing aspect of the debate, however, was the question of priorities advanced by the liberals in both the House and Senate and best summarized by Congressman Fiorello LaGuardia, the future mayor of New York. Disbursing $2.4 billion to less than 4 per cent of the population "would not solve a single problem with which Congress and the country are confronted." LaGuardia insisted, moreover, that Congress must first consider the plight of 8 million other equally needy unemployed men and women who lacked organized pressure groups to make a stand for them. In this light, the true nature of the bonus bill became evident. It was nothing less than a blatant example of special-interest legislation. LaGuardia believed that Congress had already treated the ex-soldiers generously. Emmanuel Cellar of New York reminded the House that one fourth of all current federal expenditures was already being used for the aid and relief of veterans, who made up only

13 per cent of the unemployed in 1932. Like LaGuardia, Cellar felt that the veterans had had their share.[1]

Relief to all the needy was an especially effective rallying cry in Congress. An immediate concern to these liberals was the detrimental effect the huge bonus outlay might have on their national unemployment relief bills long pending before Congress. LaGuardia's bill for national unemployment insurance awaited House approval, and in the Senate Robert Wagner, another New York liberal, was equally concerned. Four days earlier, on June 10, the Senate had passed and sent to the House a bill authorizing the Reconstruction Finance Corporation to grant $300 million in relief loans to the states.[2] Since May 12, well before the Bonus Army materialized, President Hoover had consulted on the bill with Wagner and Joseph T. Robinson, Democratic leader in the Senate, and by June 6 Wagner had informed Hoover that the bill had been "stripped of practically every measure of controversy."[3]

Waters later erroneously maintained that the veterans' lobby had helped to force the relief loan bill through Congress.[4] Actually, supporters of relief measures believed that the bonus threatened otherwise certain passage. Should Congress approve the huge bonus expenditure,

1. U.S., Congress, House, *Congressional Record*, 72d Cong., 1st sess., 1932, 75, pt. 11, pp. 12847–50, 12922–23. Roger Daniels, *The Bonus March: An Episode of the Great Depression* (Westport, Conn.: Greenwood Press, Inc., 1971), Chapters 2 and 3. Daniels is critical of antibonus forces.

2. House, *Congressional Record*, 72d Cong., 1st sess., 1932, 75, pt. 11, pp. 12512–49. For a good analysis of the extended and complicated battle for relief in Congress, see Jordan A. Schwarz, *The Interregnum of Despair: Hoover, Congress, and the Depression* (Urbana: The University of Illinois Press, 1970), pp. 142–73.

3. U.S., Congress, Senate, *Congressional Record*, 72d Cong., 1st sess., 1932, 75, pt. 11, pp. 12849–50; Robert Wagner to HH, June 6, 1932, Wagner Papers (hereafter cited as WP); New York *Times*, May 13, 1932; "Press Release," May 12, 1932, pp. 275, HHPL.

4. Walter W. Waters, *B.E.F.: The Whole Story of the Bonus Army* (New York: The John Day Company, Inc., 1933), p. 129; Elmer Thomas to L.S. Ray, July 22, 1932, Thomas Papers, University of Oklahoma (hereafter cited as TP). Ray was chief lobbyist for the Veterans of Foreign Wars.

advocates of the national relief efforts feared their bills would suffer from conservative arguments against further huge deficits and ruinous inflation. They knew that devoting tax and potential relief money to a special-interest group continued to be an unpopular cause.[5]

Despite all their arguments, the opposition had little effect on the final vote in the House. Wright Patman had lined up the votes before the final debate had begun. To ensure victory he accepted an amendment which allowed financing through bond sales rather than through printing additional money. The bill had thus been shorn of some of its appeal to ardent inflationists, but it was now acceptable to a larger number of congressmen. The House passed the bonus, but only by a margin of 35 votes, far short of the required two thirds needed to override a presidential veto. Both parties split on the vote, but as expected, the Democrats generally supported it, while the Republicans basically opposed it. Considering the long fight against great opposition, the march to Washington now seemed justified. It was a victory for the bonuseers, and they fully enjoyed their moment of triumph.[6]

While the BEF reveled in its victory, the persistent deputy chief of staff, General Moseley, was trying to devise ways to rid the city of them. He felt certain that the Senate would defeat the bill, so he prepared another unsolicited memorandum. This one was in the form of a presidential proclamation ordering all veterans out of the capital. Although Hoover was genuinely worried by the massive size of the BEF, he gave this second memo no more consideration than he had Moseley's first plan.[7]

On June 16, one day after the bill had passed the House, the Senate was ready to begin its debate. The leader of the bonus forces was Elmer Thomas of Okla-

5. Senate, *Congressional Record*, 72d Cong., 1st sess., 1932, 75, pt. 11, pp. 12716–17; 12919–13048.

6. House, *Congressional Record*, 72d Cong., 1st sess., 1932, 75, pt. 12, pp. 13043–54. The vote was delayed one day, pp. 12934–35; pt. 12, pp. 13053–54. Waters, *B.E.F.*, p. 89; *Post*, June 15, 1932. For Washington, D.C., newspapers, the city is omitted from the citation.

7. George Van Horn Moseley, "One Soldier's Journey," unpublished diary, II, 141, Moseley Papers, LC.

homa, a champion of inflation, who now abandoned his own bonus bill to give full support to Patman's.[8] Thomas had worked mainly with the evangelical Veterans of Foreign Wars lobby, and like Patman he had continually emphasized his belief that the battle for the bonus was essentially one between the rich and the poor, between the "bondholding creditor class" and the "debtor class," a view that impressed few of the senators.[9]

George Norris, a veteran of many legislative battles, began his attack on the bonus by conceding several of the more appealing arguments of its supporters. He admitted that Congress had granted massive subsidies to business; the bonus was an honest debt owed to the brave men who had fought honorably in that heinous war which he had voted against in 1917. The fact remained, nevertheless, that the most important problem confronting the nation was the suffering caused by increasing unemployment, and this suffering was not limited to veterans. With the credit of the government seriously threatened, the federal annual income down to $1.9 billion, and the national debt increasing, many legislators were concerned that the $2.4 billion bonus might unite the foes of unemployment relief. The vast majority of veterans held jobs; they represented only a small percentage of the total unemployed. Norris's principal concern was that, should the Senate approve the bonus, "it will be an impossibility to pass an unemployment bill at this session of Congress." [10]

The priority of national relief programs was emphasized

8. FTH to Reed Smoot, March 21, 1932; Elmer Thomas to Bernard Baruch, April 9, 1932, TP.

9. Elmer Thomas to L. S. Ray, July 22, 1932, TP; Senate, *Congressional Record*, 72d Cong., 1st sess., 1932, 75, pt. 12, p. 13144. For other details on the Senate's opposition, see Senate, Committee on Finance, Report No. 834 on H.R. 7726. It was read into the *Congressional Record*, 72d Cong., 1st sess., 1932, 75, pt. 12, pp. 13223–24, 13246, 13258–60. *Evening Star*, June 17,1932; Waters, *B.E.F.*, pp. 146–52. A fierce battle within the American Legion over whether to support the bill resulted in defeat for the advocates of the bonus. James F. Barton to A. C. Arnett, June 8, 1932, ASCF, ALP. Numerous letters pro and con are also in ASCF, ALP. New York *Times*, April 19, 1932.

10. Senate, *Congressional Record*, 72d Cong., 1st sess., 1932, 75, pt. 12, p. 13255.

repeatedly. La Follette and Costigan were as insistent as Norris in stressing their precedence. Other senators, led by Robert Wagner, were willing to pay the present cash value of the bonus certificates; firm in their opposition to the full-payment Patman bill, however, they carried their stand to the entire nation. In a press release Wagner and his allies argued that the full bonus would bring "financial ruin in the country" and would increase a hundredfold the distress of all the people. They warned that the depression was bound to intensify. It was therefore imperative to maintain government credit, so Congress could approve the relief legislation necessary to prevent widespread starvation. To these liberal senators the choice lay between a bonus for a few and starvation for many, or general relief for all needy Americans.[11]

As the debate continued into the evening hours, thousands of veterans streaming in from Anacostia and other nearby camps suddenly inundated the Capitol Plaza. From an afternoon total of about 3,000 shortly after five o'clock, the number of people in the Plaza quickly rose to over 12,000, and Glassford immediately ordered out the large police reserve he had hidden in the Capitol's basement. To the relief of responsible officials, instead of becoming disorderly as anticipated, the crowd was quiet and well-behaved.

When Waters finally came forward to announce the bill's defeat in the Senate, the men retained their calm demeanor. He softened the sad news of the "temporary setback" by renewing his pledge to "stick it out" until 1945, and the men greeted this promise with a thunderous roar of approval. Despite their disappointment, the men did not become violent or riot. Instead, 12,000 dejected veterans stood at the steps of the Capitol and sang

11. Senate, *Congressional Record*, 72d Cong., 1st sess., 75, pt. 12, pp. 13259–60; 13268; 13244–77. New York *Times*, June 17, 1932. Wagner's strongest allies were David A. Walsh and Marcus A. Coolidge of Massachusetts and Royal S. Copeland of New York. Wagner was under great pressure from New York veterans to support the bonus. See Veterans Correspondence File, 1932, and Scrapbook, Vol. I, WP. Wagner also faced oppostition from Hoover who eventually forced changes in the relief bill. See Schwarz, *Interregnum*, pp. 164–73.

"America," then quietly shuffled back to their camps.[12] In the months and years that followed, the bonus march would strike a responsive chord of sympathy in the hearts of fellow countrymen. But the host of sympathizers never supported the bonus; what they admired was the manner in which the veterans took their defeat.

The Senate crushed the bonus bill on June 17. The 20,000 lobbyists now had little reason to stay in Washington, for only a miracle could induce Congress to reconsider the bill in the month that remained before adjournment. Wagner, Costigan, La Follette, and other Senate liberals, whose efforts against the bill had been effective, turned again to a broader program of relief. Other congressmen, tired of the bonus and of the marchers, eyed their calendars nervously and hastened toward adjournment in order to begin their campaigns for reelection. The defeat of the bonus was highly praised throughout the nation, and the veterans' continued vigil would now become futile.[13]

The first massive twentieth-century protest in the capital, and certainly one of the largest, longest, and most dramatic, the bonus march had vividly illustrated how a determined minority can force its demands upon the national consciousness. For the current session the bonus was dead, however, and now the men had to face the question of their next action. Many of them believed that if they returned home, drummed up local support, organized campaigns, and worked for the election of sympathetic candidates, they could bring more pressure to bear on the next Congress. But Waters was unalterably opposed to leaving Washington or to broadening the basis of the protest to include relief for all the unemployed. His attitude caused some of his camp commanders to question his leadership, while many of the BEF's strongest

12. Waters's version is in *B.E.F.*, p. 152. Donald J. Lisio, "A Blunder Becomes Catastrophe: Hoover, the Legion, and the Bonus Army," *Wisconsin Magazine of History*, 51 (Autumn 1967), p. 38.
13. "Approval of the Bonus Bill Defeat," *Literary Digest*, 114 (July 2, 1932), 9; "The Bonus Army Did Not Intimidate Congress," *Christian Century*, 49 (July 20, 1932), 902.

backers now withdrew their support. The first indication that sympathy was waning was a sudden drop in donations of food and money, which precipitated an immediate food emergency. Since it was now futile to focus its efforts on Congress, the BEF turned inward during the seven weeks it remained in Washington. The momentum of the protest was clearly spent, and as a hot, sticky June passed into a steamier July, the make-believe army drifted into dissension and disintegration.

During the month between the defeat in the Senate and the adjournment of Congress Waters refused to believe that the issue had been decided. He was like many Americans—and especially soldiers—in that he could not bear to accept anything less than total victory. The persistent commander strode about in his khaki shirt, whipcord breeches, and riding boots, constantly urging the men to continue their lobbying efforts. He promised that he would somehow force Hoover to call a special session of Congress to reconsider Patman's bill. "We'll stay until 1945," he repeatedly shouted. But not all the veterans were favorably impressed with Waters's dramatic ways or promises. Some camp commanders had become disgusted with his dictatorial mannerisms, others with his narrow-minded focus on the bonus. These preferred to expand the protest to include relief for all of the needy. As a result, a few days after the bill's defeat the BEF splintered into several warring factions, none of them able to agree on a new set of goals or a new leader, united only by their desire to depose their present commander.[14]

As the bonuseers became more disoriented and disillusioned, some feared that the small group of Communists would be able to take advantage of the dissension, but this worry was groundless.[15] Glassford watched the party members with a special police squad.[16] Secretary of War

14. Waters, *B.E.F.*, pp. 154–55.

15. House, Committee on Un-American Activities, *Hearings on Communist Tactics Among Veterans Groups*, 82d Cong., 1st sess., 1951, pp. 1934–38 (hereafter cited as HUAC, CTVG); *Herald*, June 10, 1932.

16. PDG, "Special Order No. 25," June 17, 1932; "Daily Bulletin

Hurley had ordered the entire Army Intelligence command to investigate possible radical influence in the BEF and in all of those groups still advancing toward Washington.[17] Throughout the nation intelligence officers and Hurley's spies were sending in reports that the veterans' organizations contained no subversives and were intensely anti-Communist.[18] General MacArthur, who was later to argue that the United States had faced a serious Communist threat, personally followed the surveillance and periodically supplied information to the White House. At this time, however, he issued no warnings of revolutionary plots.[19]

As the surveillance reports indicated, the Bonus Army was in fact a bastion of anti-Communism. Eddie Atwell, the former prizefighter who was the able commander of the BEF military police, delighted in ferreting out and physically abusing known or alleged radicals. The residents of Anacostia sometimes alleviated their boredom by watching the beatings of "radicals" at the camp's speaker's platform. The BEF military police were encouraged in this activity by Glassford's policy of turning his back on their brutality. Sometimes, however, the beatings became so vicious that under pressure from the Com-

of Metropolitan Police Department," September 7, 1932, PP 300, HHPL and in GP. Glassford established a Crime Prevention Bureau or special detective squad and an Information Center, which gathered intelligence on the veterans.

17. Alfred T. Smith to The Adjutant General, June 10, 1932, War Department, Office of The Adjutant General, RG 94, NA. Hurley was under considerable pressure from Congress to care for the marchers and feared efforts to require the Army to assume responsibility for the veterans. Copies of Congressional Joint Resolutions and Frederick H. Payne to John J. McSwain, June 25, 1932, are in RG 94, NA. George A. Paddock, "Report to Secretary of War," June 8, 1932, HP.

18. For secret telegrams from Army Area Commanders, see Smith to The Adjutant General, June 10, 1932, RG 94, NA. One report indicated the presence of some Communists, but the report is unconvincing and was an exception to the overwhelming emphasis in the other reports upon the marchers' anticommunism. No definition of a Communist was included in the report.

19. Richey to MacArthur, June 24, 1932; MacArthur to Richey, June 28, 1932, PP 300, HHPL; D. Clayton James, *The Years of MacArthur, 1880–1941* (Boston: Houghton Mifflin Company, 1970), pp. 390–91.

munist leaders, Glassford stepped in to protect not only their civil liberties but also their lives. Later, Waters recalled that one of his chief concerns was to prevent the men "from almost killing any Communist found among them." [20]

Despite the claims made in sensational newspaper headlines and hysterical editorials, the Communists were poorly led, dispirited by harassment from the veterans, and decidedly of a nonrevolutionary cast of mind. Their field commander, John T. Pace, was a former small businessman who had gained some notoriety in Cleveland, where he reputedly led a band of stranded veterans in an effort to capture and hold the huge railroad roundhouse. But Pace was ideologically naive, a recent convert who believed that he could persuade the veterans to become Communists. He avoided—even feared—violence. He knew that most of his men were neither revolutionists nor good Communists and that some were government agents. At one point, Pace concluded that there were only twenty-five of his followers whom he could trust. Levin, the nominal head of the Workers' Ex-Service Men's League, was even less of an activist than Pace. He created sensational headlines, made rousing speeches filled with the party's favorite clichés, and prepared a scrapbook of newspaper clippings to send Stalin as proof of his militancy and success, but he did little more.[21]

After the defeat in the Senate, the Bonus Army almost destroyed itself, and this without any aid from the Communists. Their presence was not required to foment widespread discontent with Waters's command. In fact, the eventual revolt was brought about by Waters's handpicked second in command, George Alman. The fiery ex-lumberjack twice before had accepted temporary leader-

20. Waters, *B.E.F.*, pp. 134, 94–96, 98; John Dos Passos, "Washington and Chicago: The Veterans Come Home to Roost," *New Republic*, 71 (June 29, 1932), 177–78; PDG, "Communists," p. 2, GP.

21. *B.E.F. News*, July 16, 1932; Jack Douglas, *Veterans on the March* (New York: Workers Library Publishers, 1934), pp. 113–14. HUAC, CTVG, p. 1944; for more on the Communists, see pp. 1938–40; Pace interview, New York *Journal–American*, August 29, 1949; PDG, "Communist Highlights," GP; Waters, *B.E.F.*, pp. 90–102.

ship during Waters's resignations and had quickly gained a reputation among the men as a troublemaker for not co-operating fully with Glassford and for refusing to condemn the Communists categorically.[22] When Waters recovered his health and resumed command, he appointed Alman national billeting officer, a job which required him to find housing for new arrivals and which soon led to another clash with Glassford.

Alman knew that the men disliked Glassford's policy of concentrating them on the Anacostia mud flats across the river from the city or farther away at Camp Bartlett. They much preferred to occupy illegally the more comfortable and convenient federal buildings in the downtown area. The day after the defeat in the Senate, June 17, therefore, Alman led a popular move into more of the downtown buildings and challenged Glassford with the new battle cry, "No men across the river." [23]

Glassford's good will was indispensable to the continued success of the encampment, and for that reason Waters and the Executive Committee immediately removed Alman from his position on the Executive Committee and as national billeting officer. Alman was furious. He insisted on a public trial and also demanded a new election of all BEF officers, for, as he said, thousands of the latest arrivals had not been given the chance to express their choice. He proclaimed his candidacy for the BEF commandership with a demand that the BEF broaden its objective. Above all, he insisted, it must initiate "an active campaign for real unemployment relief, not only for the veterans but for all American citizens suffering from the present economic conditions." The BEF must speak for all of the poor.[24]

Waters vehemently countered Alman with his familiar

22. *Herald*, June 17, 1932; *Evening Star*, June 20, 1932; Douglas, *Veterans*, pp. 158–62.

23. Douglas, *Veterans*, pp. 158–62.

24. *Evening Star*, June 21, 1932. "Walde Manuscript: Waters Reorganization—B.E.F. Politics," GP. L. W. Walde was a leading member of the BEF and Khaki Shirts of America. L. W. Walde to HH, September 16, 1932, Congress of U.S., Extra Session, 1932, HHPL. Apparently Glassford collaborated with Walde on a manuscript that was

contention that the unity and power of the protesters hinged on their identity as veterans. Any effort to expand the original purpose would splinter the Bonus Army into dozens of rival organizations and thus destroy the unique character and, as Waters saw it, the political power of the protest. He steadfastly refused to concede that the bonus bill was dead, a denial many of his previously most trusted lieutenants now openly challenged.[25]

Ironically, at the time Waters disciplined his billeting officer for defying Glassford, the Police Chief decided not to force any evictions. Once again Glassford appeared to the veterans to be the epitome of reasonableness, while Alman gained temporary popularity for initiating the illegal occupation and successfully thwarting the police. The loser was Waters. By not supporting Alman, he now appeared more definitely to be the stooge of the police—an often repeated taunt that thoroughly infuriated him. More significantly, Waters's attitude toward Glassford now began to change. Increasingly he saw the Chief as a "friendly enemy." Each needed the other's cooperation, but in what became a subtle and persistent contest for leadership, the two leaders became alienated.

The mass shift from outlying camps to the buildings near the Capitol was a portentous development. After several days, when it became obvious that the police would not resist, John T. Pace led his band of Communists from Camp Bartlett into the buildings at Thirteenth and B streets near the Washington Monument. Pace later insisted that he hoped that their occupancy would provoke a violent encounter, but this claim does not ring true, considering the Communists' cautious wait. In any case, Glassford greeted them cheerily. The Chief further angered Waters by countermanding his orders to cut off the Communists' food supply and his efforts to force them back to Camp Bartlett. According to Pace, however, Glassford's strategy "didn't do our own cause any too much

never published. Parts of the manuscript are scattered throughout the Glassford Papers.

25. Waters, *B.E.F.*, pp. 123, 138, 155–57; *Post*, June 19, 1932; *Evening Star*, June 19, 1932.

good." [26] The Police Chief's tolerance won the respect of many of the reds, weakened further the desire for a violent confrontation, diminished the rhetoric about Fascist cops, and lessened the Communists' chances of radicalizing the other veterans.

Amidst the increasing factionalism and discontent, rumors of a plot to overthrow Waters—including a bloody coup—prompted the shaky commander to surround himself with a conspicuously large number of bodyguards. As he watched his leadership deteriorate and the BEF drift toward anarchy, he came to think increasingly in terms of conspiracies. Then, on June 25 Glassford abruptly informed the Bonus Army that it must leave Washington before the food supply was completely exhausted, and Waters challenged the men to make a choice. Without any warning he dramatically resigned as commander-in-chief and turned over temporary command to his good friend George Kleinholz. In the midst of a food crisis, with the men badly divided over the BEF's objectives and the choice of Waters's successor, disintegration and either voluntary or forced departure seemed probable. The reds hoped to take advantage of the confusion by backing Alman, but Waters knew of their impotence and shrewdly counted on the inability of the other factions to reach an accord or to agree on a new leader. He understood the general fear of chaos and counted on the men's indecision and fear to return him to power by popular demand.[27]

On June 28 Waters's supporters spread the rumor that one or both of his main rivals were plotting an illegal seizure of power and, using that as their justification, engineered Waters's coup. The scene of Waters's triumphant return was a well-planned mass meeting of 12,000 hungry and confused veterans at the Anacostia camp. After re-

26. Waters's account of Glassford as an enemy is rather bitter and reflects the wide gulf that eventually developed between them. Waters, *B.E.F.*, pp. 71–73. New York *Journal-American*, August 29, 1949; *Post*, June 19, 1932; HUAC, CTVG, p. 1937.

27. Waters, *B.E.F.*, pp. 139, 144, 155–57, 250; Douglas, *Veterans*, pp. 166–72. Memoir of Gardner Jackson, The Oral History Collection of Columbia University, pp. 374–76.

peated chants from his followers calling him to the stage, he appeared on cue and spoke directly to the men's fears. He warned them of the dangers of anarchy, affirmed the need for order above all else, and called for the creation of a new, more vigorous campaign against subversion. After Glassford's ultimatum and all the confusion, their old commander appeared so firm and confident that the intrigue-weary veterans responded by cheering wildly and demanding that he stand for reelection. Waters assented to their plea, on the condition that they grant him full dictatorial powers.

The men greeted his extreme demand with renewed applause and cheering, and for many, the well-staged acclamation constituted a valid election. As so often happens when fears become dominant, stability and order become more essential than political programs or even personal liberties. These men, happy to have a dictator at their head, surrendered to Waters the powers he demanded. During the balloting on the next day, the mood held and Waters won reelection almost unanimously.[28] The cost of dissent had been too high. The veterans wanted food, security, and their bonus more than political independence. Alman's attempt to redefine the bonus march as a protest for all the poor had failed. Identity as veterans and the illusion of stability were far more important to the men.

Waters promptly declared that anyone who disobeyed his orders would be driven out of the District of Columbia. That fate had been reserved hitherto for suspected Communists. Only a day earlier Glassford had warned that such an action was strictly illegal, but Waters retorted, "To hell with civil law and General Glassford. I'm going to have my orders carried out." [29]

The Communists heaped abuse on the would-be strong man, whom they repeatedly charged was involved

28. *Post*, June 26, 29, 1932; *Evening Star*, June 29, 30, 1932; Douglas, *Veterans*, pp. 172–75; "Walde Manuscript: Waters Reorganization—B.E.F. Politics," GP.

29. Waters, *B.E.F.*, pp. 157–58; *Post*, June 30, 1932; *Evening Star*, June 30, 1932. Waters later claimed that he apologized to Glassford.

in a Fascist plot against the real interests of the veterans. Waters denied the charge of a plot but urged that a national veterans' organization was needed to maintain law and order and to eliminate groups that might endanger the government. Then he again unleashed his military police who took "law" into their own hands by setting off a new wave of terror against suspected radicals.[30]

Later, on the eve of the adjournment of Congress, Waters formally announced this new veterans' organization, which would ensure law and order and eliminate subversives. He christened it the "Khaki Shirts" and promised to end the old order and institute basic economic and political reforms. His prescription remained vague, but it was evident enough that he believed that neither the existing economy nor the existing political structure was adequate to meet the new conditions. This promise of revolution made the Khaki Shirts sound almost as radical as the Communists, but the ill-chosen name and the character of the BEF suggested fanaticism of a different stripe.

Waters's thinking reflected that of the marchers' extreme right wing. He stated that his organization would uphold the nation's highest democratic principles against communism, yet few veterans seemed enthusiastic. Some of them questioned his anomalous position as dictator and compared his Khaki Shirt toughs to "the Fascisti, in Italy, and the Hitlerites, in Germany." Significantly, he brushed the criticisms aside and even suggested that the European dictators were not so bad after all. "For five years Hilter [sic] was lampooned and dirided [sic]," and "Mussolini before the war was a tramp prin[t]er [sic], driven from Italy because of his political views." Both of these men, Waters pointed out, had become national leaders.[31]

As Waters used his military police with greater frequency, he seemed to lose sight of the protest's origi-

---

30. *Herald*, July 1, 1932; "Heroes," *Time*, 20 (July 18, 1932), 11. HUAC, *Hearings on House Resolution 282, Investigation of Un-American Propaganda Activities in the United States*, 75th Cong., 3d sess., 1938, p. 2285; Waters, *B.E.F.*, pp. 90–102, 161.
    31. *B.E.F. News*, July 16, 23, 1932.

nal aim—the bonus. Most of the men, however, were too hungry to care about the commander's warnings of plots. Immediately after the Senate's defeat of the Patman bill, Hoover had quietly initiated a bill for transportation loans to enable the veterans to return home, and on July 9 he signed the $100,000 authorization into law. Originally, Congress had agreed on a deadline of five days—until July 14—but that date was soon extended to midnight of July 24 to allow a realistic time for the veterans' orderly withdrawal. Support for the loans was practically universal. The city's newspaper editors, Patman, and other supporters repeatedly urged the men to go home, and even Hearst decided that it was time for the protest to end. If the veterans cooperated, some editors and legislators suggested, Congress might eventually cancel the loan feature of the transportation plan. But, characteristically, Waters called the loans a plot to sap the strength of the BEF, "an effort to send us back to our home towns so we can starve again." [32]

Hoover believed that the transportation loan bill was the best way to relieve a hazardous situation. Thousands of the protesters, too tired and hungry to debate Hoover's motives, gladly accepted the chance to go home. Their acquiescence infuriated Waters. Each day several hundred formed long lines in front of the Veterans Administration Building to apply for transportation. Among them were many who complained to reporters that Waters's thugs had beaten them or threatened their lives. Soon the harassment became so intense that Glassford was forced to provide squads of police to guard the men and their families against attack as they stood in line and to protect them on their way to the railroad station.[33]

While Waters's jibes at Hoover were understandable,

32. Theodore J. Joslin, *Hoover Off The Record* (New York: Doubleday, Doran and Co., 1934), p. 265; New York *Times*, June 29, July 7, 9, 1932; *Post*, July 8, 1932; *Herald*, July 8, 1932; *Evening Star*, July 8, 1932; *Herald*, July 9, 1932; *Times*, July 11, 1932. Waters denounced Hearst for turning against the BEF; Waters, *B.E.F.*, p. 164. "Heroes," *Time*, 20 (July 18, 1932), 11.

33. *Evening Star*, July 11, 12, 1932; *Times*, July 11, 1932; "Heroes," *Time*, p. 11.

his reaction against his own men cast serious doubt on his judgment as a leader. He now turned the BEF against itself, using violence against Communists and comrades alike. It was a senseless policy that drew general disapproval. The BEF's chief lobbyist, Harold B. Foulkrod, echoed the widespread sense of outrage over the dictator's methods. He pointedly informed reporters that he would not "contaminate" himself "by pretending to agree with the stupid slogan: 'We Stay Here Until 1945.' " That was another example of Waters's "false, ignorant, inefficient leadership [which] has already cost the BEF the support of its best friends." The time had come "to end this farce." [34]

34. *Evening Star*, July 12, 1932.

7

The New Militancy

Waters's growing use of violence and intimidation revealed all too clearly the frustration he felt in his frantic efforts to maintain his leadership. Under constant stress the besieged commander had reached a point where further open cooperation with the police too obviously threatened his pride and his prestige. Perhaps the Communists and his rivals had made greater headway with their insults than he had with his beatings of radicals and his dictatorial powers. When Glassford warned of impending danger, Waters rather insultingly assured him that he need not be concerned, as his men "would constitute a first-line of defense" between the police and the Communists.[1]

Unfortunately, Glassford's superiors, the District of Columbia Commissioners, were as obstinate as Waters. On July 9 they informed the Chief that they were highly displeased with his cavalier enforcement of the law. Time after time they had instructed him not to allow any unauthorized occupation of abandoned federal buildings. The veterans' insistence on selecting the most convenient buildings had caused extended delays in Heath's construction program, and he had appealed unsuccessfully to Glassford to evict the men from several of the properties. The Commissioners now reiterated their earlier demands that he uphold their orders and the laws of the District without regard for the comfort of the protesters. Commissioner Crosby, who was usually the angriest, informed Glassford that he would no longer tolerate the illegal occupation of federal buildings. Pointedly he reminded the Chief that he had disobeyed specific orders to prevent

1. PDG, Memorandum, July 10, 1932, GP.

still another group of veterans from occupying buildings
at Pennsylvania Avenue and Three and One Half streets,
S.W., an area near the White House which later proved
significant. When Glassford refused again to evict the law-
breakers, Crosby concluded that the Police Chief was
using the law only to suit his own purposes.[2]

Then, on July 9 the city apprehensively witnessed the
arrival of a band of 250 Californians led by flamboyant
Roy W. Robertson. Advance reports indicated that he was
an unusual man, and his appearance seemed to confirm
them. While serving in the Navy, he had fallen out of his
hammock, broken his neck, and permanently injured his
spine. A leather neck brace, supported by a tall, steel column protruding almost a foot above his shoulders, created
the eerie impression of a man with his head perpetually
in a noose. His face was that of a man of grim determination. Judging from Army intelligence reports, Robertson
was cunning, unscrupulous, and quite possibly a Communist. The reports wrongly accused him of fraudulently
misusing the Red Cross insignia to raise money during
the trip and of being the leader of a group "under Communistic influences" who were "very anti-government,
anti-Congress, and anti-Hoover." From the beginning,
government agents marked him as a man to be watched
closely.[3]

One observer described Robertson as "a very articulate
fellow, rather slight, but alive, tense, flaming little guy,"
who lacked "political savvy" but had a "rapier-like wit

2. PDG to D.C. Commissioners, June 25, 1932; PDG, Memorandum
for Record, June 27, 1932; PDG Memorandum, July 10, 11, 1932; PDG,
"Diary," July 12, 1932; Ferry K. Heath to PDG, June 27, 1932, GP. Ira
E. Keck to Luther Reichelderfer, July 8, 1932; Ron Haworth to Reichelderfer, July 5, 1932, DCP. Glassford was severely criticized by Congressman Frank L. Brown (R., W.V.,), Times, July 6, 1932. For Washington, D.C., newspapers the city is omitted from the citation.

3. George B. Hicks to The Adjutant General, June 14, 1932; William
Nelle to Assistant Chief of Staff, June 29, 1932, War Department, Of-
fice of The Adjutant General, RG 94, NA. Nugent Dodds to H. J.
Hughes, July 22, 1932, Department of Justice, File 95-16-26, RG 60,
NA. Hughes concluded that there was no reason to continue the inves-
tigation of the alleged illegal use of the Red Cross symbol. H. J.
Hughes to Nugent Dodds, July 27, 1932, ibid.

. . . a wisecracker [who] would have gone great guns . . .
on radio and television." [4] The Californian in fact was
neither racketeer nor Communist but a high-spirited,
strong-willed independent, a political moderate, who enjoyed being a dramatic leader in the full glare of publicity. Nonetheless, those who saw a Communist in every
new dissenter regarded Robertson's arrival in the city as
the signal for the rumored deluge of insurrectionists. As
soon as he entered the capital, he quickly informed reporters that he had no liking for "all this military stuff"
and had no intention of subjecting his men to Waters's
dictatorial rule. He and his men had made the journey to
present their own petition to Congress.[5]

On July 12, after waiting three days for a parade permit,
Robertson received permission from Vice President
Charles Curtis to march to the Capitol Building, where he
presented his petition. The permit provided only for the
march to Capitol Hill and the reading of the petition, but
immediately afterward Robertson ordered his men to
sleep on the Capitol lawn. His decision alarmed Glassford; the action held the prospect of a confrontation between these men and the special Capitol Hill police
force, which had no previous experience with the bonus
marchers. Glassford arranged a hurried conference with
Vice President Curtis, who agreed to allow him instead of
the Capitol police to handle the situation. The Chief convinced the men that they must take their bedrolls to their
billets, but later Robertson decided to carry through his
original intent, and the men slept on newspapers on the
Capitol lawn.[6]

Robertson's unexpected defiance unnerved some Washingtonians, who feared that this type of confrontation
would encourage a new deluge of protesters and inevita-

4. Memoir of Gardner Jackson, The Oral History Collection of Columbia University, pp. 373–75.
5. PDG Memorandum, July 11, 1932; "Diary," July 12, 1932, GP.
Walter W. Waters, B.E.F.: The Whole Story of the Bonus Army (New
York: The John Day Company, Inc., 1933), p. 165; Herald, July 11,
1932; Times, July 12, 1932.
6. PDG, "Diary," July 12, 13, 1932, GP; Times, July 12, 1932; Post,
July 13, 1932.

ble violence. Most upset were those who were in charge of the Capitol Plaza—Vice President Curtis, Speaker of the House John Nance Garner (soon to be elected Vice President), and the members of the Capitol Police Board, which comprised the Sergeants at Arms of both the House and the Senate as well as the Capitol Architect. Although angered by Robertson's maneuver, these men for the time being accepted Glassford's advice against using force and commissioned him to inform Robertson that he must not continue to camp on the Capitol grounds or break any more laws.

Glassford realized that Robertson would not leave the Plaza voluntarily, for he had publicly committed himself to "direct action" and would not give Waters, for one, the satisfaction of seeing him meekly submit to the Police Chief's first request. Glassford understood this. Indeed, as he partially explained to the Vice President, he wanted to encourage rivalries. By reducing the veterans into small bands, he increased their dependence on him; thus, he hoped, the eventual evacuation would be an easier process. Therefore, when Robertson asked if there was any law against walking on the Capitol sidewalks, the Chief readily accepted the implied suggestion. He knew, as did everyone else, that 250 men walking around the Capitol Building, whether on sidewalks or on the grass, obviously constituted a procession. To the rulers of Capitol Hill he argued that it was perfectly legal to walk on the sidewalks and that he had allowed the men to walk single file because, in that formation, they were easier to control. Naturally, the veterans were delighted and the Capitol Police Board and Waters were outraged.[7] Thus began the Death March, as newspaper reporters dubbed it, and a suspicion, which was to grow, that Glassford had not fulfilled the trust the Capitol officials had placed in him. By effective bargaining, however, Glassford had again avoided the use of force, but at the cost of once more raising the pivotal question—was he to maintain

7. PDG, "Diary," July 13, 1932, GP. *Times*, July 13, 14, 1932.

order or to uphold the law? To entertain a distinction between law and order was probably heretical for many people, but to the extraordinary Police Chief it was the only
practical choice that made sense.

The Death March quickly captured nationwide headlines and virtually everyone's imagination, especially that
of Waters's disgruntled followers. An exceedingly impressive and novel tactic, the slow, shuffling vigil, which
lasted three days and four nights, became "one of the grit-
tiest demonstrations of the Depression." Back and forth,
up and down the asphalt sidewalks walked the men with
ever heavier tread. In his Navy overseas cap and whipcord breeches, his head held high in the rigid brace, Roy
Robertson led the determined column behind a soiled
American flag.

The first night of nonstop walking taxed the men to
their limits, and for a time it appeared that the tactic
might have to be abandoned. Then Robertson broke the
group into relays, and understanding police allowed the
off-duty protesters to doze nearby. Three times Robertson
had toppled over into the street. "Give yourself a break,"
Glassford urged, but the Californian insisted that he was
all right, and the Death March continued.[8]

The steady, silent procession made Capitol leaders intensely nervous, and what to do about the Death March
quickly became one of the chief topics on the Hill. Then
suddenly, late in the afternoon of July 14, Glassford received a telephone call from Crosby, who asked if he had
requested the use of troops against the Death Marchers.
Glassford replied that he had not, whereupon the Commissioner ordered him to a meeting at General Mac-
Arthur's office in fifteen minutes. Although MacArthur
had not requested troops, his lucid and precise review of
the legal procedure for ordering them out left little
doubt that the Army was fully prepared to move instantly.
As the meeting proceeded, Adm. Henry V. Butler, commander of the Navy Yard, entered the room and after he

8. "No Man's Land," *Time* (July 25, 1932), p. 9.

caught the drift of the conversation, casually informed the gathering that sixty Marines were already aboard a trolley car on their way to disperse the marchers at the Capitol.

Glassford immediately persuaded Butler to order the Marines back to their barracks at least temporarily, until he could obtain clarification on the sudden and unexplained order. Then, accompanied by Admiral Butler and Gen. Perry L. Miles, he arranged a quick conference with the Capitol Police Board and the Vice President. It soon became clear that it was Curtis who had called out the Marines and that, as he had acted without first consulting Glassford, he no longer trusted the Chief. The conference degenerated into a heated exchange between Glassford and Curtis. The threat of force would not produce violence, Curtis insisted; the veterans would obey the Marines without resisting. Glassford considered the risks too great to test Curtis's assumption, but the Vice President had lost his patience. He had granted permission for Robertson's men to parade, and they had repaid him by sleeping on the Capitol grounds and then by placing Congress essentially under siege. It was most embarrassing for a Vice President of the United States to be so rudely defied. The time had come, Curtis insisted, to stop the demonstration and stop it decisively.[9]

Glassford seemed at the end of his resources. If he refused to use his own police against the marchers, the Vice President could deploy the special Capitol Police or at a moment's notice recall the temporarily restricted Marines. At that point, having tried his best to avert violence, Glassford might well have washed his hands of the entire affair, but he refused to allow the Vice President's decision to stand. Leaving the conference, he went directly to the office of Senator Hiram Bingham, one of Hoover's personal friends. After listening to Glassford's account of his encounter with Curtis, Bingham telephoned the President. Hoover had not known about his Vice President's action; he immediately expressed full support of Glass-

9. PDG, "Diary," July 14, 1932, GP. Glassford revealed many of these details later. *Herald*, November 3, 1932.

ford in his insistence on using only those tactics which would guarantee a peaceful end to the demonstration. Senator Bingham next telephoned Curtis, and after some discussion the Vice President backed down.

Curtis now allowed the veterans to continue their picketing, but on the southwest side of the grounds, away from the Capitol Building itself. Robertson had no desire to engage in a violent confrontation, and, unwilling to see his highly successful tactic canceled, he accepted Curtis's terms and moved his men to the new location. On July 14, after Robertson reiterated his promise to leave when Congress adjourned, the legislators in both Houses voted to extend the time limit on the transportation loans until midnight of July 24, a ten-day reprieve by which they hoped to implement a peaceful, unhurried evacuation.[10] The marchers and the public thought little more of the incident. Few knew of the maneuvers behind the scenes— Glassford's efforts or the President's support.

Glassford's well-publicized methods naturally earned him the enmity of many observers, including Curtis and Speaker of the House Garner. With their sanction, the Capitol Police Board launched a public attack against him, accusing him of willfully disobeying orders and taking the law into his own hands.[11] Significantly, the attack also reflected the views of the District Commissioners, many of Washington's citizens, and an undeterminable number of Republican and Democratic congressmen, who were weary of the protest or who suspected that the BEF's organization and actions had been inspired by Communists.

The Washington *Star* warned that the subversive spirit of these "well known agitators against existing order,

10. PDG, "Diary," July 14, 1932, GP; *Herald*, November 3, 1932; *Evening Star*, July 14, 1932; FTH, "To All Veterans of the World War," GP. Hines informed the men of the new deadline.

11. Copy of Capitol Police Board statement, July 15, 1932, and Glassford's reply, July 15, 1932, GP. Mark Requa, Republican National committeeman and close friend of Hoover, warned the President that the BEF was "under inspiration of communists and irresponsible politicians seeking personal advantages." Walter Newton, Memorandum, July 14, 1932, PP 297, HHPL.

crafty organizers of sedition, preachers of pernicious doc-
trines, representatives of organizations seeking to overthrow the government of the United States [was as clear]
a menace to the public peace, as the whole assembly is a
menace to the public health." This gathering of men constituted a federal rather than a local problem, federal action was long overdue, and by "federal action" the *Star*
did not mean unemployment relief. The issue of law and
order threatened to make the Death March every whit as
emotional as the earlier red scare.[12] There were hotheads
among editors, the rulers of Capitol Hill, and members of
the administration. While some railed against subversion
and others clamored for Glassford's job, few knew that
Hoover had supported the Chief rather than his Vice
President. Instead, appearances suggested that the President and Glassford were on a collision course.

On July 15 the news-hungry Communist Workers' Ex-
Service Men's League tried unsuccessfully to capture
headlines by parading to the Capitol Building. They were
disappointed in their bid for publicity, for their march
was uninterrupted, uneventful, and made under police escort. The public's attention remained focused on Robertson, who retained his position center stage by issuing a
call for all veterans to join his men the following day in a
mass protest against the adjournment of Congress. Obviously vexed at his rival's activism and astuteness,
Waters became determined to regain the initiative and to
refurbish his sagging prestige. Late that evening he issued his own order for the entire BEF to meet at the Capitol Plaza at ten o'clock the next morning.[13]

At 10:30 on the morning of July 16 only 3,000 of the
8,000 to 10,000 veterans remaining in the city obeyed Waters's order to gather at the Plaza. The poor showing revealed a growing indifference to Waters's orders, but the
number was sufficient nonetheless to carry out his plan.
The commander knew that Glassford had worked out a

12. PDG, Press Release, Reply to Capitol Police Board, July 15,
1932; *Evening Star,* July 14, 1932.
13. PDG, "Diary," July 15, 1932, GP; *Herald,* July 16, 1932; *News,*
July 16, 1932; *Post,* July 16, 1932.

compromise between Vice President Curtis and Robertson which had put the large Capitol Plaza off limits to the Death Marchers. When Waters arrived, he was not surprised therefore to see his men held back from the Plaza by Glassford's police. Robertson had called for direct action, and he would have it, thought Waters, but he would not get credit for it any longer. Suddenly charging forward and waving to his men to follow, Waters bolted through the police cordon and toward the Capitol Building. Surprised and delighted by his boldness, the veterans roared their approval and swept past the dazed police. At one stroke the BEF commander had regained the spotlight.

Somehow, Glassford managed to intercept Waters as he approached the bandstand in the middle of the Plaza. He was furious with Waters's trick, as it now appeared that Glassford could no longer control the men. When Waters refused to order his men to retreat, Glassford placed him under arrest and had him taken into the basement of the Capitol Building. He then mounted the bandstand and tried to reason with the angry veterans. "I don't want any trouble, but we'll have it if you don't get back," he yelled. "I told the Vice President I'd keep the plaza clear. When I say I'll do a thing, I'll do it." The men responded with menacing chants of "We want Waters!" and "Turn him loose or we'll go in and get him!" The jeering, booing, and threats, which completely drowned out the Police Chief, resounded throughout the Senate and House chambers, where congressmen apprehensively hurried through the final bits of legislation so they could adjourn that evening.[14]

Outside, the noise, impatience, and surliness of the crowd increased, and onlookers and reporters drew back, fearing violence. After ten minutes Waters was brought outside, but he again refused Glassford's order, and the Chief sent him back into the Capitol Building. As the news of the confrontation spread, men poured into the Plaza from their various camps. Repeatedly they called for Waters and jeered the man who had been their chief pro-

14. PDG, "Diary," July 16, 1932; "No Man's Land," *Time*, p. 9.

tector for the past six weeks. The dangerous tension momentarily broke when "a buxom, yellow-haired woman" suddenly leaped onto the bandstand—a nurse who had aided the bonus marchers. Seizing a megaphone, she urged the men to sing, and before they could recharge themselves to the explosion point, Waters once more appeared.[15]

The commander had convinced his police guard that their plan to spirit him out of the side doors of the building would inevitably produce a riot. Without an alternative, the police officers brought him outside again to Glassford. The beleaguered Chief now offered to allow Waters to occupy the remainder of the Plaza, but only on condition that Waters would agree to keep his men off the Capitol steps. The commander immediately rejected the offer. He would accept nothing less than Glassford's complete humiliation. After further haggling, Glassford finally agreed to the occupation of the middle staircase. Waters also won an audience with Speaker of the House Garner to present a petition against adjournment. With great relish he moved forward to announce his triumph. "I've got permission for you to use these center steps," he said. "But you've got to keep a lane open for the white-collar birds inside so they won't rub into us lousy rats. We're going to stay . . . until I see Hoover." [16]

Seemingly he had won a victory, and Waters thoroughly enjoyed it. Later that afternoon Congress proffered another gesture of good will by passing a bill that met two of the veterans' lesser demands. The act repealed previous legislation, which had denied borrowing privileges to those who held their bonus certificates for less than two years. Thus, 215,000 additional veterans would be able to borrow as much as half the value of their certificates. The act also reduced the interest rate charged on the loan from 4½ per cent to 3½ per cent. The attack on the Plaza did not move Hoover or the Congress closer to capitulation,

15. Waters, *B.E.F.*, pp. 168–69; "No Man's Land," *Time*, p. 9; Jack Douglas, *Veterans on the March* (New York: Workers Library Publishers, 1934), pp. 208–9.

16. *Times*, July 16, 1932; Waters, *B.E.F.*, pp. 170–71, 173–74, 169–71.

however; in fact it lessened their trust in Waters's leadership. It was an action that the shaken Police Chief, his detachment of 120 officers, and scores of Secret Service and Department of Justice operatives would not soon forget. Thousands of defiant veterans had occupied the Capitol Plaza, thoroughly discredited the police authority, and confronted Congress with a frightening spectacle. Glassford never admitted that the men had unnerved him, but he was certainly angered and shaken by Waters's conduct. Mistrust now clouded the previously cooperative interchanges, and relations between the two men never quite healed.[17]

Waters's need to regain the limelight had created the unstable and dangerous confrontation. Growing numbers in and out of the government were now taking sides on the Police Chief's moderation. Earlier, the management of the protest had been a cooperative endeavor; in exchange for peaceful persuasion, Glassford and Hoover had, in their own uncoordinated ways, attempted to hold back the advocates of force. But that odd relationship had changed. Waters had temporarily silenced the Communists and seized the initiative from Robertson, but his undercutting of Glassford's authority was a heavy price to pay. Clearly, establishing his independence, refurbishing his prestige, and giving the men the illusion of progress were more important to him than the risks involved. What became evident was that the threat of violence was at least as probable from Waters as it was from the Communists or from fearful leaders like Curtis. While the various BEF factions struggled to dominate each other, the protest moved further from its goal and closer to trouble.

Imagining new-found powers, Waters returned to his headquarters and celebrated his notoriety with a rousing speech, in which he again vowed to continue the protest until 1945 and declared, "We have just begun to fight." He now insisted that the BEF represented all of the nation's unemployed and demanded, in addition to the

17. New York *Times,* July 17, 22, 1932; PDG, "Diary," July 16, 1932, GP.

bonus, federal relief for all of the poor and destitute. Obviously, this extension of aims was merely an attempt to forestall the adjournment of Congress—one last chance to add new appeal to the bonus.[18] It was clearly an afterthought. For almost six weeks Waters had celebrated the veterans' identity and had vehemently rejected every aim but the payment of the bonus. He had successfully engineered his election as dictator on that stand. Only after Robertson had artfully captured the nation's attention with his Death March did Waters formally announce the organization of his Khaki Shirts, and only then did he begin to speak of a national veteran folk movement that would somehow benefit all of the poor. Such last-minute professions of concern for the poor failed to sway Congress, which proceeded with the business of adjournment.

Waters's occupation of the Capitol steps soon gave way to a new threat by Robertson to gain prestige over him a second time. After Waters's charge, Robertson announced plans to transfer the Death March to the White House after Congress adjourned that evening—another escalation, which sent shock-waves through the ranks of police and Secret Service agents charged with protecting the President. Hoover was expected to attend the formal closing ceremonies of Congress that evening. Anticipating that more protesters would flock to Capitol Hill to await his arrival and fearful for the President's safety, in view of Waters's behavior that morning, hundreds of Metropolitan Police, Capitol Police, Secret Servicemen, and Justice Department agents hovered about the White House grounds, the surrounding streets, and Capitol Hill, while military forces stood in reserve nearby.[19]

The day's events had worked a change in the thinking of many Washington leaders. Hoover had earlier admonished guards not to arrest Communists picketing the White House; his attitude toward the threatened transfer of the Death March was now less sanguine. Everyone was edgy, but when Commissioner Crosby ordered Glassford

18. *B.E.F. News*, July 16, 1932; *Herald*, July 18, 1932; Waters, *B.E.F.*, p. 144.
19. *News*, July 16, 1932; *Post*, July 17, 1932; *Herald*, July 17, 1932.

to arrest the unauthorized pickets, the Chief objected.[20] Again, he reached Senator Bingham and asked him to explain his fears to the President. Senator George H. Moses relayed the President's wishes back to the Chief: Hoover did not comment on the instructions to arrest illegal pickets, but he did emphasize that he definitely wanted to avoid a large-scale, violent confrontation.[21] For the second time in two days the President supported Glassford's appeal for restraint.

However, this time, as insisted upon by the District Commissioners and no doubt the Secret Service, the judicious arrest of troublesome leaders became the established policy. To protect himself, Glassford demanded that Crosby put the arrest order in writing. The Chief had repeatedly argued that any show of force would surely provoke violence, and he was determined to ensure in writing that the responsibility for that violence would clearly be the Commissioners', not his.[22]

Excited reporters claimed that the massing of police power was the largest since the race riots following the Great War. Hoover waited silently in the Executive Mansion while his automobile and motorcycle escort of a dozen policemen stood by. The closed gates and drawn curtains of the White House, the bustle of security agents, and the powerful assemblage of police regiments seemed to confirm rumors that the Secret Service had called in operatives from all over the United States and that large numbers of agents had already been sent to the Capitol in anticipation of the President's arrival. These activities also supported the critics' charge that Hoover was exceedingly fearful.[23]

Shortly before ten o'clock, just as Hoover was almost

20. Lewis I. H. Edwards to PDG, July 16, 1932, GP.

21. Glassford recorded that Moses conferred with Hoover and told him of Hoover's reply. PDG to District Commissioners, July 16, 1932; PDG, "Diary," July 16, 1932, GP.

22. PDG, "Diary," July 16, 1932, GP. Also see Crosby's order handwritten in pencil on the back of an envelope and initialed H.B.C. One of the major purposes of the order was to avoid conflict of authority between the Metropolitan Police and the separate Park Police.

23. Post, July 17, 1932; Evening Star, July 17, 1932.

ready to leave for the closing ceremonies, fifty to eighty veterans marched toward the White House. The pickets, reputedly Communists, preempted Robertson's threatened transfer of the Death March to the President's front door. Police followed the marchers and then, when they arrived at LaFayette Park, subdued and arrested three who resisted, dissuaded others, and efficiently dispersed a large crowd of spectators.[24] The arrests had not brought the violence which Glassford had predicted.

The elaborate security around the White House was understandable. After Waters's siege of Congress only hours earlier and Glassford's inability to clear the Plaza, further confrontation seemed probable. Behind heavily guarded and locked White House gates the President remained in the Lincoln Study. Shortly after eleven o'clock the members of the Senate, in a most unusual procedure, passed quietly through the tunnels beneath the Capitol without notifying their colleagues in the House. All of the legislators were gone a half hour before the veterans waiting outside had any notion that the formal closing ceremonies would not take place. Congressmen and senators had heard and seen enough of the new militancy that day, and their underground escape revealed more clearly than any other action the new fears that gripped the capital.[25]

24. *Evening Star*, July 17, 1932; "No Man's Land," *Time*, p. 9; Douglas, *Veterans*, pp. 211–13.

25. "Bonus Expeditionary Force," *New Republic*, 71 (July 27, 1932), 273; *Herald*, July 17, 18, 1932; *Evening Star*, July 18, 1932; *Post*, July 19, 1932; Mauritz A. Hallgren, "Bonus Army Scares Mr. Hoover," *Nation*, 135 (July 27, 1932), 71–73.

8

Blunders Compounded

July 16 had been an especially trying day for Washington officialdom. While there had been no serious violence, Waters's charge on Capitol Plaza, the attempted picketing of the White House, and the spectacle of thousands of restless veterans perched outside Congress infused the day with an air of explosiveness and initiated a more militant phase of the protest. Once again the reputation of President Hoover—not of Waters or Glassford—was damaged by events. The number of security forces patrolling the White House grounds and nearby streets and the President's failure to attend the adjournment of Congress suggested to some commentators that he had been badly frightened, perhaps had panicked; to others, Hoover appeared merely irresolute and weak. Reports circulated that federal troops had been alerted after Waters stormed the Plaza and that Hoover had left Washington in a secret, heavily guarded, and hurried retreat. These reports reinforced the impression of cowardice and fear, and his critics exploited it.[1]

Rather than cowardice, it might be argued that Hoover had actually demonstrated patience and restraint. Only a few persons realized that the President had not ordered out the Marines in panic two days earlier. Far from turning troops against the protesters, he had held his Vice President in check, and in cooperation with Glassford, he had stopped the Marines at the Capitol. His purpose in absenting himself from the adjournment of Congress was, most probably, to avoid a confrontation and possible vio-

1. Mauritz A. Hallgren, "The Bonus Army Scares Mr. Hoover," *Nation*, 135 (July 27, 1932), 73. Baltimore *Sun*, July 26, 1932; "Bonus Expeditionary Force," *New Republic*, 71 (July 27, 1932), 273.

lence. Even when several angry congressmen had demanded that he call up troops, Hoover had remained firm and thereby had helped to end Robertson's Death March peacefully. There was no possibility that by picketing the White House the protesters could induce Hoover to call a special session of Congress. On balance, it was wiser for him to remove himself, even at the risk of being labeled a coward, than to invite a White House Death March or to retaliate with troops. Restraint continued to characterize his course, but his silence left his detractors to their own interpretations.

Despite the Communists' repeated evidences of ineffectiveness, their determination to transfer the Death March to the White House understandably caused official concern. On the evening of July 16, when the first effort was quickly and easily stopped, the size of the security force seemed far out of proportion to the actual threat, if indeed any threat existed. A secret meeting of the Communists on the following morning, however, suggested that federal officials actually did have reason for anxiety. At this meeting—not publicized like those in early June— Israel Amter, a representative from the party's Central Committee, informed his comrades that the time had come for a fresh, more militant effort. It was absolutely essential that the Communists step up their criticisms of the administration, with the President as their target. The strategy required continuous picketing of the White House. This, Amter hoped, would lead to a bloody riot into which the hungry, frustrated veterans would almost certainly be drawn. Before leaving the capital, Amter reminded Pace that if the veterans were allowed "to get out of Washington without a fight we have lost our cause." [2]

Lines lengthened in front of the Veterans Administration Building as increasing numbers of the men came to believe that their continued encampment was futile.

---

2. U.S., Congress, House, Committee on Un-American Activities, *Hearings on Communist Tactics Among Veterans Groups*, 82d Cong., 1st sess., 1951, pp. 1939–40 (hereafter cited as HUAC, CTVG). *Herald*, July 18, 1932. For Washington, D.C., newspapers the city is omitted from the citation.

Many freely expressed fear that serious trouble would develop as soon as the Communists' reinforcements arrived.[3] Even Waters was troubled. He no longer opposed acceptance of the transportation loans, and in an effort to blunt the Communists' new enthusiasm he launched another terror campaign, aimed at stopping the distribution of leaflets which called for picketing the White House and for the end of Waters's dictatorship. Waters's "military police" were so effective that Pace demanded and secured Glassford's promise of police protection.[4] Thus reassured, on July 20 Pace resolutely led his 200 men on a march to the White House.

Within several blocks of their destination, Pace's men spotted Inspector Albert J. Headley, who to his consternation found himself standing alone in the middle of the street, well in advance of his large force of police. Acting spontaneously, Headley singlehandedly confounded the approaching demonstrators by seizing Pace by the throat and hurling him against his startled followers. The brutal tactic scattered the surprised men in all directions, their self-confidence and no doubt also their faith in police protection destroyed. Although Pace managed to rally fifty of his men, they were immediately surrounded by police, who arrested him and several minor leaders for disorderly conduct and for parading without a permit. Beset by Waters's vigilante methods and by an alert, determined police force, Pace gained little but headlines.[5]

Although the Communists' attempt to lay siege to the White House had failed, Emmanuel Levin delighted in Pace's arrest. In a personal address to the faithful he ex-

3. *Evening Star*, July 20, 1932; *Post*, July 18, 1932; Walter W. Waters, *B.E.F.: The Whole Story of the Bonus March* (New York: The John Day Company, Inc., 1934), pp. 174–78.

4. J. O. Patton, "Report," July 19, 1932, DCP. Lewis B. Smith to PDG, July 19, 1932, GP. Smith complained that the recent terror campaign was a repetition of previous ones. For examples of earlier Communist demands for protection, see Emmanuel Levin to PDG, June 10, 1932; PDG, "Order to Police Force," June 28, 1932, GP. *News*, July 7, 1932.

5. A. Friedberg to PDG, "Report on Communist Meeting," July 20, 1932, GP. *Times*, July 21, 1932; *Herald*, July 21, 1932.

tolled his comrades' progress. Levin's threats of continuous confrontations at the White House may have been intended as much for recognized government spies as for his own followers, but his words and newspaper reports that a large Communist force in Philadelphia was prepared to join them emboldened his followers. Many observers now spoke openly of possible violence.[6]

To add to officials' anxieties, rumors circulated that members of the BEF were arming, and rumor also spoke of twelve machine guns and twenty-four boxes of hand grenades hidden within seventy-five miles of the capital. Officials recalled the discovery in early June of two sticks of dynamite and the persistent story that some veterans had ready access to guns and ammunition.[7] As Glassford privately told the editor of the Baltimore *Sun*, his greatest fear was that the heavily reinforced Communists "would take advantage of the situation." His inability to feed and house the new arrivals and their determination to start trouble would eventually create more disorder than his police could control.[8] Later, however, the Chief denied that such a threat had existed or that he had ever doubted his ability to control it.

Considering the Communists' new militancy and—perhaps even more dangerous—Waters's determination to dominate all rivals, the administration's decision to end the long encampment was both timely and reasonable. Congress had adjourned, and the veterans' remaining in the capital promised no constructive results. The public no longer supported the BEF. Even Waters later admitted that it had been the proper time to disperse.[9] Indeed, the veterans' strongest allies, including Patman and Hearst, repeatedly pleaded with them to initiate a voluntary, peaceable evacuation. The administration hoped that the

6. *Evening Star*, July 21, 22, 1932; *Post*, July 22, 1932; *Herald*, July 21, 1932; "Report on Meeting of Workers' Ex-Service Men's League," July 21, 25, 1932, DCP. Administration officials also kept records of *The Daily Worker*'s exaggerated account of events. PP 299, HHPL.

7. Ogden T. Davis to PDG, July 20, 1932, GP; *Evening Star*, June 11, 1932; Waters, *B.E.F.*, p. 202.

8. PDG to Editor, Baltimore *Sun*, July 12, 1932, GP.

9. Waters, *B.E.F.*, pp. 237–38, 172–74, 163–64.

men would take advantage of the transportation loan offer, which Congress had extended until midnight of July 24. Apparently to apply further pressure, Hoover decided to delay the federal building program no longer and to begin repossession of federal property. Contracts had been let, and the government was hard pressed for office space and losing valuable construction time. Certainly, if the order to evacuate were to have the desired effect, it should be made at once, before the congressional loan offer expired. Unfortunately, the administration had not prepared adequately for this new line of action, thanks to Hoover's belief that the BEF was a local rather than federal problem. Thus, his failure to appoint a cabinet member or other high-ranking official to coordinate the evacuation led to a series of embarrassing and finally dangerous blunders. Indeed, the effort was so poorly planned and so ineptly executed that deadlines were constantly rescinded, everyone became confused, and the veterans came to the conclusion that the administration could not move them out.

On July 20, the first eviction notice appeared—on the day of Pace's arrest and only four days before the transportation offer was to expire. Ferry K. Heath, the Assistant Secretary of the Treasury who was in charge of the federal building program, informed the District Commissioners and Police Chief Glassford that it was now necessary to evacuate the buildings in the area between 3rd and 4½ streets and Pennsylvania Avenue. Many of the buildings had been occupied illegally, and he recalled his letter of June 10 in which he had granted permission for the veterans to occupy some of the abandoned buildings only on the condition that they leave promptly when the actual need for them had passed. Now that Congress had adjourned, he added, the building program could be delayed no longer.[10]

10. Ferry K. Heath to PDG, July 20, 1932; Heath to Herbert Crosby, July 20, 1932, PP 300, HHPL. In his letter of authorization to Crosby, Heath stated that the area between Third and Sixth streets must be cleared in order that the demolition could be resumed and insisted that "the premises be not occupied any longer than absolutely necessary."

Heath's original proposal involved only a small area, but on the following day, July 21, another assistant secretary of the Treasury, Seymour Lowman, informed Glassford and the District Commissioners that a second repossession site was needed—that between C and D streets and Twelfth and Thirteenth streets, S.W. This section bordered the Mall and included several square blocks near the Capitol, in which were 2,500 campers, among them 500 women and children and Pace's 200 Communists.[11]

On that same day U. S. Grant, III, the Director of Public Buildings and Public Grounds, took the matter much further by directing the Commissioners to repossess all federal property. In effect, that order would eliminate all of the camps except Camp Bartlett, which was located on private property. Possibly most important, Grant's order contained no deadline. Grant had allowed the informal and illegal use of federal land while the veterans petitioned Congress, but after July 16 he considered further encampment on federal property thoroughly unreasonable.[12]

Although the three directives contradicted each other, the District Commissioners were delighted to receive them. They had waited many weeks to begin evacuating the squatters. Armed with their new authority, they lost no time issuing their own, more comprehensive decree. They did not limit the eviction to areas suggested by Heath and Lowman but used Grant's request to evacuate all federal property and added their own series of deadlines for specified eviction sites. Before consulting with either Glassford or their legal advisers, the Commissioners ordered evacuation of the first designated site, a section between Pennsylvania Avenue, Missouri Avenue, Third Street, and Sixth Street, N.W., by midnight July 22—the next night. The second deadline—only two days later—midnight July 24, correlated an order to clear the entire downtown area with the expiration of the transpor-

11. PDG to Seymour Lowman, July 22, 1932, PP 300, HHPL; *News*, July 23, 1932.

12. U. S. Grant, III, to Reichelderfer, July 21, 1932, DCP. *Evening Star*, July 21, 1932.

tation loans. All other federal property was to be vacated by August 4.[13] Obviously, the Commissioners' arbitrary deadline did not allow sufficient time to move large numbers of people from the downtown area. Only two days remained to obtain transportation loans, and while the Commissioners' motives may well have been related to this deadline, set by Congress, they created the impression of a malevolent scheme.

The Commissioners based their withdrawal orders on two false assumptions. They believed, as did the Treasury officials and U. S. Grant, III, that they had the legal authority to use local police for the eviction and that Glassford had no choice but to obey. Instead, on July 21, as soon as he received the order, and only a day before the first deadline, Glassford decided to challenge the Commissioners. First, he informed the veterans of the order.[14] Then he consulted the District's legal counsel, W. W. West, who confirmed his suspicions that the order was unlawful. The next day Glassford called together the United States District Attorney, the Corporation Counsel for the District of Columbia, the United States Marshal, and a representative for the Solicitor of the Treasury. After discussing the issues all morning, they agreed unanimously that the Commissioners did not have authority to order evictions from buildings under temporary control of the Treasury Department. Further, the department could act only after obtaining a court order or invoking the Forcible Entry and Detainer Statute—and then only if Treasury agents conducted the eviction, not local police. Glassford warned that repossession by Treasury agents would lead to "riot and bloodshed." [15]

Pressing the veterans to leave while there was still time to obtain loans would have been an eminently sensible

13. Daniel E. Garges to Major and Superintendent of Police, July 21, 1932, PP 300, HHPL; New York *Times,* July 22, 1932. All tents and rolling kitchens loaned to the BEF were to be returned by noon, August 1, 1932.

14. PDG to Commanding Officer, BEF, July 21, 1932, GP.

15. PDG to Seymour Lowman, July 22, 1932, GP; PDG to D.C. Commissioners, July 22, 1932, DCP.

strategy. Even Glassford feared the arrival of Communist reinforcements. The strategy was conceived too late, however, and the Commissioners misjudged when they imposed a twenty-four-hour deadline for the first eviction, especially without first ascertaining their powers. Glassford's startling challenge effectively put an end to the edict, and soon the Commissioners quietly abandoned their eviction schedule.[16]

Most embarrassing was the ease with which the local police chief had exposed the lack of careful planning and coordination of an important and possibly dangerous undertaking. The fiction of a "local problem" had been unwise from the beginning, and now that it was discredited, the responsibility for planning the evacuation was placed squarely upon administration officials. They were, it became clear, totally unprepared to accept it. The administration had no policy for dealing with the veterans, other than encouraging them to apply for transportation loans and hoping for a gradual, orderly withdrawal. The District Commissioners publicly exonerated Hoover of any responsibility for the short notice of the first deadline, but understandably, few could believe that the administration had been so ill-coordinated, ill-informed, and inept.[17] It appeared instead that the Commissioners were generously assuming the blame for the inadequacies of a scheming, unbending President.

Waters's reaction to the order made matters worse. He knew that Glassford opposed the use of force and had uncovered legal complications. Accordingly, Waters could have supported Glassford's maneuvers by maintaining

16. Daniel E. Garges to PDG, July 22, 1932, GP. The Commissioners retained the August 1 deadline for tents and rolling kitchens. New York *Times*, July 23, 1932; *Post*, July 23, 1932; *News*, July 23, 1932. Crosby testified to the District Grand Jury that the purpose of the July deadline was to encourage the veterans to accept the transportation loans. Reichelderfer argued that the Commissioners' order "was not put out" and was in fact rescinded. "Memorandum of the Testimony Presented to the Grand Jury, District of Columbia," Department of Justice, File 95-16-26, RG 60, NA, pp. 15–18, 36–38, 48 (hereafter cited as MTGJ).

17. *Post*, July 23, 1932; *News*, July 23, 1932.

calm in the BEF.[18] Instead, he decided to stage a dramatic defiance. After reinforcing with 500 men the first site to be evacuated, Waters vowed that the BEF would fight rather than bow to the Commissioners' decree. In an address to his men he advised them that if the need to fight should develop, they must make certain that the police would "get rough first." Implying that those circumstances would thoroughly justify full-scale retaliation by the BEF, he shouted a warning to police. Should they use force, he declared, all he needed to do was to raise his hand, and "my following of 12,000 men will act according to my wishes—either a fight or a frolic." [19]

It was Glassford's legal challenge, not Waters's rhetoric, that ended the first eviction effort, but the commander's threats added to the mounting frustration and tension. The administration's failure to enforce its wishes evoked numerous criticisms. Some detractors recalled the earlier fiasco that involved the Marines. Few took seriously the claim that the Bonus Army was the Commissioners' responsibility. Both at that time and later, the general assumption was that the President had been immediately in charge of the entire situation at all times. Other critics interpreted the confusion as evidence of Hoover's weakness and demanded that he drive out the "Praetorian Guard." [20]

Somehow, newspaper editors throughout the nation got the erroneous impression that the veterans were departing voluntarily. They reacted with relief and jubilation, for they had envisioned Fascists fighting Communists in the streets of Washington. While street fighting between extremist factions plagued European democracies, where the democratic process was under severe attack, the vol-

18. Waters had privately assured Glassford that he would cooperate on condition that either he would be allowed time to find new housing or the federal government would provide adequate shelter. PDG to Seymour Lowman, July 22, 1932, PP 300, HHPL.

19. Ogden T. Davis to PDG, July 22, 1932, GP; *Evening Star*, July 22, 1932. At first Waters advised them to employ passive resistance, then he negated this advice as he continued to harangue the veterans.

20. Morgantown (West Virginia) *Post*, July 23, 1932; Nashville (Tennessee) *Tennessean*, July 18, 1932.

untary withdrawal of the BEF seemed to justify nationwide pride in the American political system. Unfortunately, the reports of total withdrawal were based merely on wishful thinking.[21]

Ferry K. Heath initiated a second eviction effort on July 23, immediately after the Commissioners had rescinded their order and one day before the transportation offer was to expire. This time, he designated midnight of July 25 as the new deadline for evacuating three large sections near the Capitol.[22] With only $3.19 left in the BEF treasury, Waters might wisely have decided that continuing the protest was no longer feasible, but he did not. Federal agents reported to the President that Waters believed that Hoover alone was responsible for the defeat of the bonus and for the sufferings of the veterans, and he had vowed that before he would surrender he would "declare war" on Hoover.[23] At the same time Doak Carter, Waters's chief of staff, informed newsmen that his men would be ready for the predicted arrival of Communist reinforcements: The Khaki Shirts would "leap into the breach between American institutions and threatened anarchy." [24] Thus the day passed, with little attention to Heath's deadline or the expiration of the loans. At midnight on July 24, when the offer expired, only about 5,750 veterans and 463 women and children, aided by the Red Cross, had left the city. Fully 8,000 to 10,000 remained, including the majority of Robertson's men, who had refused to follow their leader back to California.[25]

21. Baltimore *Sun*, July 26, 1932; newspaper clipping files in both the Glassford Papers and the Hoover Library.

22. These were the same areas Heath and Lowman had previously indicated on July 20 and July 21. An additional area between B and C streets and Twelfth and Fourteenth streets, S.W., was also included in the new order. Ferry K. Heath, Eviction Order, July 23, 1932, GP; copy in PP 300, HHPL.

23. FTH to Richey, July 25, 1932, PP 300, HHPL. Hines sent Richey a copy of his secret agents' daily reports for the period July 22 to July 25, 1932.

24. FTH to Richey, July 25, 1932, PP 300, HHPL; *Post*, July 23, 1932.

25. FTH to HH, July 25, 1932; FTH to HH, August 2, 1932, PP 300, HHPL; *News*, July 23, 1932; James L. Fieser to HH, July 29, 1932, PP

As expected, John T. Pace could ill afford to be outdone by Waters's public declaration of war on President Hoover. To recapture the spotlight, Pace arranged another well-publicized march on the White House. At noon on July 25, twelve hours after the last loans were given and an equal time before Heath's midnight deadline, Pace launched his last offensive. Amazingly, he believed that thousands of government employees would join his march during their lunch-hour break as he led his followers into police lines. Those who tried to break through the police cordon were clubbed; one of the marchers did manage to grab a revolver from an officer's holster but was overtaken after a wild chase by a dozen angry police. During the encounter Walter Eicker, one of Pace's most active lieutenants, scrambled up a tree, from which vantage point he loudly exhorted his comrades to fight. But the half-dozen men who obeyed him were easily overwhelmed and, along with Pace, were charged with inciting to riot and jailed. There was a Keystone cops flavor to the incident, especially with Eicker, safe in a tree, urging his troops to deeds of valor. "Comrades, this is only the beginning," he shouted, while a dozen police scurried desperately to corner the artful gun-snatcher.[26]

Still, it was the most forceful show of defiance that the Communists had yet staged, one that could easily have caused bloodshed. Despite its awkward humor, the encounter lent an ominous ring to the Communists' new, more militant rhetoric. Pace remained in jail, but during a party rally on that same day two speakers openly referred to the use of guns, and Emmanuel Levin, who announced that 400 reinforcements would arrive in Washington the next day, promised that if any Communists were evicted, they would "come back fighting." [27] Like Waters's threats of "a fight or a frolic" and his declaration of war on Hoo-

300, HHPL. Glassford put the number of veterans in the District on July 28 at 8,000. New York *American*, November 4, 1932.

26. HUAC, CTVG, p. 1941; *Evening Star*, July 25, 1932.

27. "Report, Meeting of Workers' Ex-Service Men's League," July 25, 1932, DCP; *Evening Star*, July 27, 1932; New York *Times*, July 27, 1932.

ver, Levin's bombast troubled officials. Some now needed no convincing that they faced desperate, unreasonable men who would settle for nothing less than a bloody confrontation or worse.

Months, even years afterward, when participants and witnesses continued to ask questions about the events which took place three days later, during the Bonus Riot of July 28, Waters, Glassford, and other commentators have either suggested or reinforced the view that the federal officials hoped to precipitate a violent encounter with the BEF. Others charged Hoover with plotting cynically to crush the suspected subversives and thus gain a winning campaign issue.[28] The number of eviction deadlines—one issued on impracticably short notice—and the subsequent use of massive force against the protesters seemed to bear out this charge of a well-planned, sinister plot. Accordingly, Waters argued further that administration officials had been thoroughly inflexible in the evacuation efforts. A behind-the-scenes analysis of events preceding the riot, however, reveals no well-coordinated conspiracy, only haphazard bureaucratic fumbling.

An examination of two important meetings challenges the widely accepted charge that the administration was inflexible. The first involved the attorney for the BEF and Secretary of the Treasury Ogden Mills. At the second, Waters conferred with Secretary of War Patrick J. Hurley. On the afternoon of July 25 Herbert S. Ward, a local attorney who had volunteered his services to the BEF, arduously sought a postponement of Heath's midnight deadline. He appealed directly to Secretary of the Treasury Mills, who at once arranged the conference. Ward found Mills exceedingly anxious to arrive at a peaceful solution. The BEF attorney argued that the midnight

28. Waters, *B.E.F.*, pp. 180, 184, 188, 190; New York *American*, October 30, November 2, 5, 1932; *Herald*, November 6, 1932. Roger Daniels, *The Bonus March: An Episode of the Great Depression* (Westport, Conn.: Greenwood Press, Inc., 1971), pp. 141–46, 172. D. Clayton James, *The Years of MacArthur, 1880–1941* (Boston: Houghton Mifflin, 1970), p. 409, charges an administration "conspiracy to maneuver the B.E.F. into precipitate action that would justify the use of the Army to get a quick eviction."

deadline would not give Waters time to locate shelter for
the 500 women and children in the repossession area, and
in response, Mills offered to postpone his Assistant Secretary's deadline for another twenty-four hours until midnight of July 26. Naturally, the postponement would add
to the confusion, but the Treasury Secretary felt that providing for the veterans' dependents was essential.

Moreover, he agreed with Ward's suggestion that the
Red Cross might be persuaded to lend tents to the veterans until permanent barracks could be erected at Camp
Bartlett. The National Guard would be engaged in its annual maneuvers in August and would need all its equipment, but Mills hoped that the use of Red Cross tents
might enable the entire evacuation process to be concluded without confusion. He even offered to help persuade the Red Cross and then gave Waters the opportunity to present his own plan for an orderly withdrawal.[29]

Waters demanded a delay of five to thirty days, during
which he would begin building permanent quarters at
Camp Bartlett. Meanwhile his men would live in Red
Cross tents. Unfortunately, however, the national commander of the Red Cross rejected the request. The next
day, July 26, he replied that regulations forbade him to
lend the tents. He offered instead to call Army Chief of
Staff Gen. Douglas MacArthur, who also refused to lend
tents but arranged still another conference, this time with
Secretary of War Hurley.[30] On the afternoon of July 26,
still during the twenty-four-hour extension, Waters, his
chief of staff Doak Carter, and their attorney Herbert S.
Ward hurried off to meet the cabinet officer who in June
had informed General Moseley that the use of troops
against the bonus marchers was not only wise, but good
politics as well.

The odd manner in which the conferences had been ar-

29. Arthur Hennessy, "Bonus Army of 1932" (Ph.D. diss., Georgetown University, 1957), p. 312. Hennessy interviewed Ward in December, 1956. *Post*, July 26, 1932; *Times*, July 26, 1932. Significantly,
Waters does not mention this conference but concentrates on his meeting with Hurley; Waters, *B.E.F.*, p. 190.

30. *Times*, July 26, 1932; Waters, *B.E.F.*, pp. 190–91.

ranged revealed total confusion within the administration. No one seemed to know what ought to be done or who was principally responsible for establishing policy. With no coordination and with general confusion among the officials, some chance for flexibility remained. Secretary Mills's offer to postpone Heath's deadline and his willingness to help secure tents were obviously encouraging signs. Secretary of War Hurley's readiness to confer with Waters was another.

When Waters and his aides entered Hurley's office, the tall, distinguished-looking Secretary of War sat calmly behind his desk, while his Army Chief of Staff Douglas Mac-Arthur had already begun pacing the floor. Hurley was a hard-driving, self-made millionaire with a strong, stubborn will, rudimentary political instincts, and little tolerance for those who he felt were not self-reliant. He enjoyed citing his own economic success as proof of Hoover's maxims on the merits of individualism, free enterprise, and the unique spiritual character of America. In his more candid moments he admitted that the depression stemmed from the economic follies of the twenties. Privately, he argued that the depression had deepened as a result of twenty foreign revolutions during the past three years. Indeed, revolution was in the air. But the intrinsic soundness of capitalism was unquestionable, and a man's lack of success, therefore, was obviously due to his own indolence.[31]

Hurley's views on the BEF were equally firm and vehement. The long encampment of the bonus marchers in the capital had greatly irritated the Secretary. He was well aware of Hoover's generosity to the ex-soldiers and his patience with the prolonged lobby, and undoubtedly he questioned the President's judgment. Hurley could not

31. Don Lohbeck, *Patrick J. Hurley* (Chicago: Henry Regnery Company, 1956), pp. 23–60. Lohbeck's work is the authorized biography of Hurley's life and is extremely partisan. Hurley to Frank E. Murphy, July 22, 1932, Republican Election Campaign Folders, HP. The best scholarly analysis of Hurley is Russell D. Buhite, *Patrick J. Hurley and American Foreign Policy* (Ithaca: Cornell University Press, 1973).

understand why these people were not seeking employment or creating new opportunities for themselves just as he had done when he was poor.[32] More damaging in his sight than their indolence and ingratitude was the political embarrassment they caused daily during a crucial national campaign. They had indicted the Republican party, unreasonably defied repeated evacuation orders, and completely disregarded the Communists' threat. Now their audacious appeal for him to help them establish a permanent base for this organization was more than the fiery, redheaded Secretary could calmly accept. On the other hand, it is indeed curious that two days before the riot, at a time when an outbreak of hostilities seemed imminent, the intractable Secretary opened his office to the delegation from the BEF.

Waters immediately attempted to convince Hurley that the only solution short of violence required the administration to help establish a permanent camp on private property. With tents for the men's shelter and more time, he guaranteed a gradual, voluntary, nonviolent evacuation—an assurance greatly at variance with his current public statements. The commander then took undeserved credit for the number of veterans who had applied for the transportation loans, but he offered no plan for providing for those who remained such essentials as food, clothing, and medical services. Hurley rejected his solution. Waters had no means to provide for the men, and Hurley flatly refused to help him establish a permanent camp. He tried at first to intimidate the BEF commander. The Bonus Army had been orderly—"too orderly" was the phrase that Waters later recalled—but Hurley warned him that the United States Army was prepared to act "at the first sign of bloodshed." [33] Hurley also discussed his preparedness during the Communist hunger march of December 1931. Trying another tack, Waters stressed the dif-

32. Lohbeck, *Hurley*, pp. 23–60.
33. Waters, *B.E.F.*, pp. 193–97. Waters's collaborator in writing the book, William C. White, noted Hurley's denial of Waters's account in a footnote.

ficulty of providing shelter for so many people on such short notice, especially for the 500 women and children in the eviction area.

The appeal for the care of the women and children apparently touched Hurley's sensibilities. Like Secretary of the Treasury Mills, he appreciated Waters's concern and also exhibited a measure of flexibility. Probably to the surprise of everyone present, Hurley telephoned Frank T. Hines to urge that the Veterans Administration allow the women and children the use of Fort Hunt, an unoccupied Army post close to the city. Fort Hunt currently housed the field hospital Hoover had earlier secretly ordered to be constructed and which had become Hines's responsibility. Hurley's plan might have allowed both the veterans and the administration to save face and gain time needed to work out a peaceful compromise. But, surprisingly, Hines was unalterably opposed to the suggestion— perhaps because he had already been saddled with the arduous responsibility for the field hospital as well as with the red tape involved in arranging for transportation loans. Possibly, he feared that if he agreed, he would soon be required to care for all of the marchers, as he was later ordered to do by FDR during the Second Bonus March in 1933. In any case, he adamantly refused, and the idea was dropped. The fact that Hurley and Hines had disagreed over the possible use of Fort Hunt apparently did not strike Waters as particularly noteworthy. In the years that followed, he continued to lash out at the administration for complete inflexibility and for what he saw as a conspiratorial plot. Obviously, if such a plot had existed, Hurley need not have made the call to Hines; warned that troops would be used if necessary, he need not have conferred with Waters.[34]

Hurley had made at least a grudging gesture toward a possible solution, but he had no authority over Hines, just

34. Waters, *B.E.F.*, pp. 196–97, 194–95. Herbert S. Ward to Hurley, August 31, 1932, HP. Ward's criticisms of Hurley were never denied by the Secretary. Ward to Henry L. Stevens, September 1, 1932, Veterans Welfare File, ALP; "Hurley and the Bonuseers," *New Republic*, 72 (November 9, 1932), 359.

as Treasury Secretary Mills had no authority over the Red Cross. Too little time remained, and too little effective planning emerged. Rather than easing the growing sense of crisis, the conference with Hurley only intensified it. In their attempt to persuade Hurley, Waters and Doak Carter continually emphasized the likelihood of Communist-incited violence. They were unaware of a secret Army Intelligence report on the BEF that supported Hurley and MacArthur's fears and warned that "the first bloodshed by the Bonus Army at Washinton is to be the signal for a communist uprising in all large cities thus initiating a revolution. The entire movement is stated to be under communist control, with branches being rapidly developed in commercial centers." When Hurley informed them of the details of the sensational report, however, Waters did not challenge it and Carter innocently reinforced the Secretary's fears by offering the fighting services of the Khaki Shirts against the Communists. Hurley curtly informed him that he would not need the BEF's assistance.[35]

Waters left the conference well aware that the administration was now insistent upon a general evacuation and that it would use troops if the local police were unable to maintain order. The administration made no secret of its intentions. There is no proof to support Waters's later charge that the administration was "eager to turn the BEF into a mob" or Glassford's dubious claim that Hurley had given the BEF "a definite promise" to allow them the use of an Army camp at the outskirts of the city. Obviously, there is even less evidence to support historians who suggest that Hoover was seeking a pretext to drive out the veterans. The significant factor was Hoover's failure to establish a clearly stated, well-coordinated repossession and evacuation policy and to appoint a top-ranking official to carry it out. The entire affair smacked of continued *ad hoc*

35. Waters, *B.E.F.*, pp. 194–95. Conrad A. Lanza, Asst. Chief of Staff, G-2 to Asst. Chief of Staff, G-2, 2d Corps, July 5, 1932, War Department, Office of The Adjutant General, RG 94, NA. For Carter's account, see Indianapolis (Indiana) *Times*, September 12, 1932. A copy of the newspaper article is in Veterans Welfare File, 1932, ALP.

decisions made by a variety of officials at various levels, officials who had little or no idea of what was expected of them. They persisted in thinking and acting as if the veterans would ultimately cooperate in an orderly evacuation.

Neither was there anything surprising or intentionally harassing in the choice of the first site to be repossessed.[36] The initial group of buildings to be reclaimed was located along the south side of Pennsylvania Avenue between Third and Sixth streets. Despite possible appearances, the choice of this first area did not reflect a desire on the part of the administration to provoke resistance. In fact, Treasury officials selected the partially demolished downtown buildings for less dramatic reasons: economic considerations and the increasing pressures from an irritated contractor.

Assistant Secretary of Treasury Heath wanted these buildings cleared first because their demolition had been contracted by George W. Rhine, owner of a salvage company that had paid the Treasury Department $5,251 for the privilege of clearing the area. In June, when Glassford asked Rhine for the use of two of the buildings as temporary quarters, Rhine had agreed. The contractor had assumed that he could continue his salvage and wrecking operations on the other buildings in the area and that the bonus marchers would not long remain. Unfortunately for

36. Daniels, *Bonus March*, pp. 141–46, 172. Daniels contends that many police officials were spoiling for a fight and suspects that the Commissioners viewed the initial eviction plan as "a military operation" (p. 146). He later states that Hoover was willing to call out troops against the marchers "at the slightest pretext" (p. 172) and that the first site assumed inordinate significance—"like a chess game in which all the pieces are concentrated to control a key square" (p. 142). The Sixth BEF Regiment, a Texas group, occupied this site, and "man for man, they were probably as combative as any element in the bonus army" (p. 143). There is no evidence that these men were more combative than Pace's Communists, the BEF military police, or any other particular group in the BEF. The contention that federal authorities chose as the first site the quarters of the "most combative" marchers leads the reader to further speculation. Daniels does not charge a conspiracy, but his speculations and implications are suggestive. They are undocumented however, and result from a lack of familiarity with important sources.

Rhine, Glassford refused to evict the illegal squatters who quickly occupied all of the buildings in the area and who began to tear out the doors and other salvageable material on which Rhine depended for his profit.

By late July Rhine was desperate; he brought as much pressure as possible to bear on Heath and the Treasury Department to remove the veterans from the buildings. Each day his profits diminished; his sale of salvaged material quickly dropped off, his debts mounted, and his creditors eventually foreclosed on his home in Alexandria, Virginia. No knowledgeable official at the time denied Rhine's problems or failed to understand why these partially demolished buildings should be assigned first priority for repossession. Treasury officials in both the Hoover and Roosevelt administrations readily admitted that Rhine's previously profitable business had been ruined. Later, FDR's adviser Louis Howe informed Rhine's lawyer that Roosevelt would make no objection to the special bill that authorized payment to Rhine of $27,500 in compensation.[37]

At 7:30 on the morning of July 27, Glassford and a special detachment of 70 police arrived at the first eviction site. Secretary of the Treasury Mills's twenty-four-hour postponement had lapsed, and Rhine had already moved his huge crane into position. It was immediately surrounded, however, by hundreds of veterans. Hundreds more in the partially gutted buildings shouted and waved at the thousands of spectators who had gathered to witness the eviction. To everyone's surprise, Glassford refused to proceed with the repossession. He had not checked with the inept Treasury officials to see if its agents would be on hand, as required, to carry out the eviction. His responsibility was limited to protecting those Treasury agents. There was no question of his police initiating the effort, but when asked by reporters about the delay, Glassford dramatically proclaimed that

37. Lionel A. Anderson to Louis McHenry Howe, January 2, 1934; Howe to Anderson, March 12, 1934, Official File 391, FDRL; numerous related materials and a copy of H.R. 14238 are at FDRL.

he would not tolerate the "illegal use" of his police in an eviction attempt that was the responsibility of the Treasury Department. Unable to begin work, Rhine was forced to order his men off the job, and when the police in turn withdrew, the spectators and veterans suddenly joined in cheering Glassford's stand.[38]

The administration's humiliation was now complete. It had officially demonstrated lack of a formulated policy, indecision, and ineptness in a series of eviction orders that were first rescinded, then postponed, and finally bungled on a legal technicality. Indeed, the administration's poor planning was perhaps nowhere better illustrated than by the fact that Glassford had halted the eviction effort for the second time in one week on the same legal technicality. Six days earlier, on July 21, when he had refused to comply with the Commissioners' order, Glassford had informed a representative from the Solicitor of the Treasury that the law clearly prohibited his local police from evicting veterans from federal property. After such a positive statement, the absence of Treasury agents to carry out the July 27 repossession underscored the continued communicative bungling.[39] Rather than being charged with skillfully conspiring against the marchers, the administration should be criticized for its embarrassing and at the same time increasingly dangerous blunders.

Soon after he returned to police headquarters, Glassford met with the District Commissioners, their legal advisers, and Treasury Department lawyers, who sought to untangle the legal snarls and arrive at a practical plan. Crosby wanted to make another attempt at eviction that same afternoon, but the conference ended with the agreement that Treasury agents, protected by Glassford's police, would begin the process the following morning, July 28. At first Glassford won agreement to severe curtailment of the initial area. He argued that his police could better control the crowds of spectators and veterans if reposses-

38. PDG, "Events of the Day," July 27, 1932, GP; *Times*, July 27, 1932; *Evening Star*, July 27, 1932; Albany (New York) *Knickerbocker Press*, July 28, 1932.

39. PDG to Seymour Lowman, July 22, 1932, PP 300, HHPL.

sion were limited to the old National Guard Armory. In
the final order, however, Heath enlarged the eviction area
slightly to include Rhine's buildings. His decision somewhat complicated the task for the Treasury agents and police. Compared to previous orders, however, the scope of
the area was very moderate, for it significantly reduced
the number of veterans affected and settled for a token
display of the administration's resolve to begin moving
the veterans out of Washington.[40] The responsible officials hoped that, after the smaller area had been cleared,
larger camps such as Camp Marks on the Anacostia could
also be peaceably repossessed.

That same afternoon, July 27, an uncoordinated "White
House conference," conducted mostly by telephone, put
the finishing touches to plans for the next day.[41] Secretary Mills and Hurley, two of Hoover's major campaign-
ers, fully realized the political dangers of continued bungling or continued irresolution. A repetition of that
morning's humiliation could not be tolerated. Hurley insisted that troops might be needed. Only after Mills, Hurley, and Heath had argued with Hoover at great length
did the President reluctantly agree to the possible use of
troops. He insisted, however, that troops be used only if
absolutely necessary, and then only for a strictly limited
purpose.

To avoid further misunderstandings Hoover advertised
the new plan as quickly and fully as possible, a fact that
has not been appreciated.[42] Rather than acting suddenly,
as Senator James E. Watson implied, the administration
clearly set forth the exact details of the scheduled repos-

40. PDG, "Events of the Day," July 27, 1932, GP; Heath to District
Commissioners, July 27, 1932, DCP.
41. President's telephone calls, July 27, 1932, Telephone Calls File,
HHPL, and Appointments Calendar.
42. Waters, *B.E.F.*, pp. 225–26. Waters learned of the administration's plans at 5:30 P.M. on July 27. The plan was released to the press
on July 27; 6:00 A.M. final edition, *Herald*, July 28, 1932. Ogden Mills
clipped the newspaper account telling of Hoover's plans for July 28
and placed it in his personal scrapbook. Albany (New York) *Knickerbocker Press*, July 28, 1932, Ogden Mills Papers, LC, Box 196, Newspaper Clippings, Vol. 11, p. 161. New York *Times*, July 28, 1932.

session. Hoover may have discussed with Watson the advisability of using troops, but he neither attempted to keep that possibility a secret nor acted in the manner Watson's highly confused account records.[43] Hoover knew that it was imperative that no more mistakes result from faulty communication. That evening, a White House spokesman released details of the President's intentions to the press, and early the following morning Washington newspapers carried full descriptions of the exact plans that Hoover had approved, and they reported his strong reluctance to use force. The first repossession, scheduled for July 28, was to be a strictly limited eviction, involving only one square block, which included Rhine's buildings. This time the legal snarls had been untangled, and the newspapers kept the public informed.[44]

43. Watson recalled that "one night," about 10:00 P.M.—although he did not indicate which night—Hoover had telephoned him to express his concern over the bonus marchers. Watson remembered that the President spoke at great length about the illegal occupation of government buildings and the stalled construction programs with contracts running into millions of dollars. Then, according to Watson, when Hoover indicated that troops might be necessary, Watson vigorously dissented. He warned Hoover that the use of troops would be a "colossal blunder" and of the millions of votes he would lose in the presidential campaign. Watson then insisted that "a little after midnight" Hoover telephoned again to say that the District Commissioners had informed him that "riots were about to break out" and that "life would be endangered," and Hoover had "at once called out the troops." This account could be important if it were not so confused and inaccurate. By the time Watson wrote his autobiography his memory of the event was obviously hazy at best, yet Gene Smith, in *The Shattered Dream*, accepted Watson's account as reliable evidence that establishes Hoover's premeditation. Smith claims that the conversation took place on July 27, yet Watson did not say when it had taken place. If such a conversation had occurred on July 27, as Smith contends, Watson's account grossly distorted Hoover's intention. Moreover, the rioting did not take place on July 27 or "a little after midnight." As political rivals within the Republican party, neither Hoover nor Watson liked one another, especially as Watson was an Old Guard leader who had misgivings about Hoover's sudden rise to political prominence. Gene Smith, *The Shattered Dream: Herbert Hoover and the Great Depression* (New York: William Morrow & Co., Inc., 1970), p. 160; James E. Watson, *As I Knew Them* (Indianapolis: The Bobbs-Merrill Co., Inc., 1936), pp. 276–77; Harris G. Warren, *Herbert Hoover and the Great Depression* (New York: Oxford University Press, 1949), pp. 153, 25.

44. Waters, *B.E.F.*, pp. 225–26; 6:00 A.M. final edition, *Herald*, July 28, 1932; New York *Times*, July 28, 1932.

Moreover, the President had finally designated a coordinator, Attorney General William D. Mitchell, whom he placed in charge of arranging all the schedules of all future evictions. Mitchell informed his subordinates that the plans must allow for a gradual, orderly evacuation. Significant too, was the absence of any new set of deadlines. The effort would begin the next day, but no rigid timetable would complicate the process of evacuation of all sites on federal property.[45]

Hoover not only alerted the press to the administration's plans for the limited first step, he also supplied reporters with his full and exact orders concerning the possible use of troops. The news stories emphasized the administration's belief that such an emergency would not arise; should troops be needed, their role would be strictly regulated. Emergency troops would merely herd the resisters out of the downtown area toward the Anacostia camp. There they would be placed under guard until the proper investigation and legal actions could be initiated. Assistant Attorney General Nugent Dodds, who had outlined the legal aspects of imprisoning rioters, privately informed the Attorney General that if such an emergency arose, the number of arrests would not exceed the capacity of the nearby jails. Although the Attorney General publicly emphasized that the jail capacities were sufficient, he indicated that he did not expect mass arrests or any need to declare martial law.[46]

The administration took great pains to clarify and advertise its plans for the next day's limited eviction. Waters later acknowledged that the news of the federal plan was widely known as early as 5:30 P.M. on July 27, the eve-

45. "Memorandum for Mr. Caldwell," July 28, 1932, PP 300, HHPL. Attorney General Mitchell initialed this memorandum. The legal details and the order in which the sites would be evicted were carefully prepared. See Heath, "Memorandum for the Attorney General," July 28, 1932; Nugent Dodds, "Memorandum to the Attorney General," July 27, 1932; E. N. Chisolm to Edgar C. Snyder, July 28, 1932; E. N. Chisolm to William D. Mitchell, July 28, 1932; David D. Caldwell, "Memorandum to the Attorney General," July 28, 1932, PP 300, HHPL.

46. New York *Times*, July 28, 1932; *Herald*, July 28, 1932; Nugent Dodds, "Memorandum to the Attorney General," July 27, 1932, PP 300, HHPL.

ning prior to the action.[47] That fact calls into question Waters's claim that he had been promised a four-day delay. During that time, he argued, he would have voluntarily evacuated his men from the eviction site to the new quarters at Camp Bartlett. At first examination, it appears that either the administration or Waters must have been lying. Waters placed on Hoover the ultimate blame and declared that the BEF had been a pawn in a ruthless conspiracy to aid Hoover's campaign for reelection. Yet, a careful analysis reveals still more blundering. A crucial misunderstanding, in which Hoover was not involved, apparently confirmed Waters's belief that he had been double-crossed.

Waters's claim that he had been granted a four-day extension of occupancy had its roots in a secret conference that Glassford arranged at the District Building later that same afternoon, July 27. The Police Chief had spent most of the afternoon overcoming legal obstacles with Treasury Department attorneys, and he fully understood their intention to begin the eviction process the following morning. He was determined to prevent a show of force, no matter how limited the repossession. He did not realize, however, that the President was conducting his own White House discussions almost simultaneously and that the administration had finally taken command of the situation. Glassford acted as if he alone would continue to direct the operation. His sense of sole responsibility was, of course, understandable. He assumed that, if he could arrange a last-minute compromise between Waters and the Commissioners, he could then convince the Treasury Department to accept it. To that end, he had invited Waters to the secret, late-afternoon bargaining session. White House officials, on their part, had no knowledge of Glassford's maneuverings. At the time that Hoover finally decided to accept the responsibility and to reveal his intentions to the press, Glassford with equal abruptness withheld from reporters the details of his hushed negotiations with Waters and the Commissioners.

The conference was a strange, confused session, which

47. Waters, B.E.F., p. 225.

Glassford should have quickly terminated as soon as he realized the Commissioners' refusal to see Waters. Instead, he undertook the responsibility of relaying messages from one room to another. Under these circumstances, the chances of misunderstanding multiplied. The Chief desperately sought a compromise. When Waters expessed willingness to order 200 men from the repossession area to begin construction at Camp Bartlett, Glassford considered a four-day postponement to be a reasonable counterconcession. Waters needed time to erect his shelters and readily agreed to the suggestion. Unfortunately, the Chief had no authority to establish such a policy, and only a few hours earlier he had attended the meeting that had cleared the way for the next morning's eviction.[48]

The Commissioners never agreed to Glassford's proposed extension for constructing the permanent camp. Commissioner Reichelderfer denied it, and all evidence suggests that they were unalterably opposed to a permanent encampment in the District. Reichelderfer had earlier publicly denounced the idea.[49] Glassford and Waters were so eager for a solution, however, that they both eagerly clung to the "plan"; darting back and forth be-

48. PDG, "Events of the Day," July 27, 1932, GP. Glassford stated that the Commissioners had "authorized me to be the intermediary between themselves and Waters and reach some agreement to evacuate all members of the B.E.F. to Camp Bartlett at the earliest possible date." Reichelderfer and Crosby both denied that they had authorized Glassford to negotiate with Waters; MTGJ, pp. 4–5, 15–18, 25, 28–29. In his testimony before the Grand Jury, Glassford did not repeat his allegation that the Commissioners had authorized him to act as the intermediary or that they had agreed to a conference with Waters; "Glassford, Testimony Before the Grand Jury," August 1, 1932, p. 2, PP 300, HHPL (hereafter cited as GTGJ); Waters, B.E.F., p. 203. In still another important document Glassford again did not mention the Commissioners' approval of a meeting with Waters. PDG, "Circumstances Leading Up To The Use of Federal Forces Against the Bonus Army, July 31, 1932," p. 4, GP.

49. MTGJ, pp. 4–5. On July 23, in defending the Commissioners' sweeping eviction order, Reichelderfer informed reporters: "I am not disposed to turn over the whole city to these men. We have been very lenient with them. Their work here is now over, Congress having adjourned. When it comes down to making a permanent thing of it we have got to take action." News, July 23, 1932. FTH to Richey, July 25, 1932, PP 300, HHPL.

tween the rooms, Glassford led Waters to believe that the Commissioners had also agreed.

While the Police Chief was busily relaying messages between the two rooms, the Commissioners received news of the President's decision to take the first step in the plan of repossession the next morning. At that point they reputedly ordered Glassford to break off his talks with Waters and to do so, Glassford later insisted, without telling Waters about the next day's plans. Thus, according to Glassford, the Commissioners had agreed to the four-day postponement but then deliberately tricked the BEF commander. Waters left the conference believing that he had been granted an extension when in fact no such agreement existed.[50] Hoover proceeded with his well-publicized plan, with no knowledge that Glassford had offered another reprieve.

Glassford later argued that the Commissioners had consented to the four-day stay of eviction, then changed their minds, and finally ordered him to give Waters the false impression. This version does not ring true. Immediately following the abortive meeting, waiting reporters questioned the Commissioners, who denied that any agreement had been reached. Crosby added his comment that the repossession was no longer the Commissioners' responsibility, and they had no authority to alter existing plans. Obviously, the Commissioners had no intention to trick Waters when they openly denied any extension of time to the press. Aware of the "White House conference" and knowing the next day's plans, the newsmen then interviewed "serious-faced" Waters and Glassford, who followed the Commissioners out of the building. Waters spoke of "his plan," but later he admitted that the administration's intention to begin repossession the next morning was known to him and others at the time. Why he clung to Glassford's assurance of a four-day extension must unfortunately remain in question.[51]

50. Waters, *B.E.F.*, pp. 203–6; PDG, "Events of the Day," July 27, 1932, GP.
51. PDG, "Events of the Day," July 27, 1932, GP; *Post*, July 28, 1932; Waters, *B.E.F.*, pp. 225–26.

Clearly, the Police Chief should never have allowed Waters to leave the extraordinary meeting without at least casting doubt on the validity of the agreement. Exactly why he did not forewarn Waters or possibly the President must also remain in question. He had just attended the meeting that mapped out the next day's plans, and he knew full well the dangers of deliberately misleading already angry men, yet he did nothing to correct the false impression. Never before during the two-month encampment had he allowed the Commissioners' orders to interfere with his sense of duty to the veterans. On at least three previous occasions he had relayed his concerns to Hoover, bypassing the Commissioners and also the Vice President, and he could have undoubtedly done so again. In spite of his knowledge, he allowed Waters to leave the District Building with a worthless assurance. The end of the conference marked the complete and final breakdown of candor between the Chief and the commander. Of such is the stuff of tragedy and of conspiracy theories.

9

The Bonus Riot

Hoover's decision on July 27 to repossess several buildings and the administration's thorough publicizing of its plans for July 28 created the impression that the President had now almost exclusively focused his thoughts on the bonus marchers. Actually, Hoover was far less engrossed with the protest than he should have been. Within less than a week, the government's haphazard concern with the BEF had shifted from Hines to various Treasury officials, and now finally, after repeated bungling by the Treasury, Hoover assigned Attorney General Mitchell the responsibility for coordinating a gradual evacuation. The shift represented not only a lack of clear policy but also Hoover's belief that other more important problems and crises required his attention.

During the last two weeks of July Hoover struggled with a profusion of urgent national concerns. Before Congress had adjourned and the legislators had eluded the demonstrators on the evening of July 16, Congress had agreed on several pieces of vital legislation. Loans to the states for general relief and the expansion of the RFC's construction program required immediate implementation by the President. During those last weeks of July Hoover worked until after midnight on many occasions. He began reorganizing the Board of Directors of the RFC, creating a new engineering department to ensure the rapid expansion of self-liquidating projects and establishing new divisions for the distribution of loans to the states, and increasingly took additional responsibility for policy direction in these new areas.

The passage of the Home Loan Bank bill was still another measure with high priority to which Hoover gave his immediate attention. As the number of mortgage foreclosures around the nation soared, he worked to establish a board of directors and a national organization of regional discount banks. This same sense of urgency was also evident in his efforts to improve the effectiveness of his farm policy and in his daily concern with the numerous problems of coordinating federal agencies that were ill-prepared and ill-equipped to meet the challenges of an unprecedented economic collapse.

Matters of foreign policy were equally pressing and time-consuming. During June and July Hoover tried to revitalize the lagging Geneva Disarmament Conference. More important were his efforts to calm his Secretary of State, Henry L. Stimson, who was growing increasingly frustrated and impatient with Japan. Relations between the United States and Japan during these two months had deteriorated sharply. Rather than accept a policy of nonrecognition or acquiesce to Stimson's thinly veiled threats, the Japanese pressed their conquest of Manchuria.

Stimson favored stronger, more forceful efforts to curb Japan's incursions on the mainland. He advocated a major policy statement that would pledge U.S. support of action taken against Japan by the League of Nations, including the use of sanctions. Hoover was deeply concerned over Stimson's insistence on a tougher policy and therefore gave the problem "exhaustive consideration." He agreed to edit Stimson's draft of a major address the Secretary planned to deliver before the Council on Foreign Relations in New York. Indeed, on July 28, the day of the riot, Hoover scrutinized Stimson's speech, finally approving it after he had deleted several passages that he believed would tie the U.S. too closely to the League's actions or, in the extreme, provoke war. Thus, on the day when many citizens assumed that Hoover was directing the eviction of veterans from government buildings, he was in reality concentrating his energies on several other important problems.

Hammering out what came to be known as the Hoover–Stimson Doctrine toward Japan and implementing the host of new bills passed in the final days before Congress adjourned fully occupied the already overtaxed President.

He openly worried too about the failure of corrupt police departments to enforce prohibition, the lack of international cooperation in devising means to halt the depression—especially the French and British attitudes—and his forthcoming acceptance speech.[1] His critics were naturally less concerned with Hoover's burdens, however, than with the amazingly inept handling of the earlier repossession attempts. Their immediate question was Hoover's next move against the BEF, and on this they could not agree.

After observing the continually bungled eviction efforts of the past six days, Hoover watchers had become increasingly perplexed and caustic. Paul Anderson, a frequent contributor to *The Nation* and one of the President's harshest critics, charged that the administration had obviously become hysterical in its reactions to the veterans and that a violent confrontation was inevitable. "Guts and sanity are needed to avert trouble," he wrote, "but where we look for the white plume we espy only the White Feather." [2] On July 28 the *BEF News* predicted: "Historians of the future will record that the collapse of American democracy reached its final stage in 1932 and that thereupon dictatorship began. The sly man in the White House, Herbert Hoover, prepares to strike at our liberty." [3]

Another critic, Mauritz Hallgren, expressed his doubts that Hoover would ever resort to troops. He predicted that an important part of the Republican campaign strategy would be "based on the myth that under Mr. Hoover's able guidance the country has been free from violent dis-

1. Richey to Henry M. Robinson, July 15, 1932, Trip File, HHPL; Armin Rappaport, *Henry L. Stimson and Japan, 1931–1933* (Chicago: University of Chicago Press, 1963), pp. 158–77, especially pp. 168–69; Richard N. Current, *Secretary Stimson: A Study in Statecraft* (New Brunswick, N.J.: Rutgers University Press, 1954), p. 109. One of Hoover's most trusted advisers recorded the President's worries; Edgar Rickard, Diary, July 22, 23, 24, 1932, Rickard Papers, HHPL.

2. Paul Anderson, "Some Sweet-Smelling Politics," *Nation*, 135 (August 3, 1932), 102.

3. Quoted in Louis L. Snyder and Richard B. Morris, eds., *A Treasury of Great Reporting* (New York: Simon and Schuster, 1949), p. 477.

turbances." The earlier call for Marines and Hoover's "panic stricken demand for police protection" when Congress adjourned might suggest that strategy, but, Hallgren concluded, Hoover would deem the political reaction against the use of bayonets so disastrous that he would surely allow the BEF to disintegrate by itself.[4]

Commander Waters, armed with his bogus four-day extension, and the veterans agreed. Like Hallgren, they interpreted the administration's vacillation as evidence of Hoover's weakness. Despite their newspaper's rhetoric, they could not believe that he would actually use force against them. Their confidence rested, in part, on their own self-image. They were, after all, genuine national heroes identified by battle scars, medals, and love of country. They could not imagine that any official would feel threatened by men who had marched off a decade earlier to make the world safe for democracy.[5] Mark Sullivan, a noted journalist and friend of Hoover, repeated that view. On July 27, as the President publicized plans for the next day's limited eviction, Sullivan noted that anyone who walked among the men would "recognize instantly their complete harmlessness." Radical elements and the BEF's size posed dangers, but on the whole, he concluded, a "child or a lost pocketbook would be safer among them than among any average cross-section of a city population."[6]

Most of the marchers believed that the only real threat of violence came from the Communists—not from the administration, and most assuredly not from themselves. Thus, they eagerly attempted to drive the reds into oblivion. Eddie Atwell, commander of the BEF military police, recalled that "those last few days before the eviction were hideous." In a constant state of excitement, always hungry and apprehensive, the men fell victim to wild,

4. Mauritz A. Hallgren, "The Bonus Army Scares Mr. Hoover," *Nation*, 135 (July 27, 1932), 73.

5. Malcolm Cowley, "Flight of the Bonus Army," *New Republic*, 72 (August 17, 1932), 13.

6. *Evening Star*, July 27, 1932. For Washington, D.C., newspapers the city is omitted from the title.

self-generated rumors. Late one night, shouts that the Communists were advancing on Camp Marks caused near hysteria among the campers. Thousands of angry veterans prepared to defend their large camp on Anacostia's mud flats. Armed with pipes, bricks, and other crude weapons, they almost attacked a small band of their own loyal members. Each day the men grew more edgy and the situation more explosive. Yet, confident in their unchallengeable reputation for heroism and the justice of their cause, they concluded that Hoover might well cancel the eviction and perhaps call a special session of Congress.[7]

At 9:30 A.M. on July 28, as the veterans at Third Street and Pennsylvania Avenue waited apprehensively, Glassford gathered his ranking officers and a force of 100 men in another part of the city. The Chief's main concern became the predictably larger crowd of veterans and spectators who were to gather at the site to be evacuated. In charge of traffic control Glassford placed Assistant Superintendent Ernest Brown, who dispatched forty men for several blocks in all directions to divert spectators from the area. Assistant Superintendent Lewis Edwards commanded a roped-off area twenty-five yards square, which enclosed the old National Guard Armory, the first building to be evacuated. While Glassford and a dozen carefully chosen officers assisted Treasury officials, Edwards was to station his men at five-yard intervals within the roped-off perimeter.[8]

Shortly before he ordered his men to the eviction site, Glassford decided to reach John H. Bartlett in order to reassure himself that 200 of the evicted veterans would be allowed to begin construction of the new barracks that same morning. The use of Camp Bartlett was central to Waters and Glassford's agreement. The Police Chief im-

7. Edward F. Atwell, *Washington, the Battle Ground: The Truth About the Bonus Riot* (Washington, D.C.: Patriotic Publishing Society, 1933), p. 32.

8. "Statement of Lewis I. H. Edwards," August 3, 1932, DCP and in PP 300, HHPL; "Memorandum of Testimony Presented to the Grand Jury, District of Columbia," Department of Justice, File No. 95-16-26, RG 60, NA, pp. 93, 94 (hereafter cited as MTGJ).

peratively needed Bartlett's assurance. He may have believed that when Waters discovered that he had been
tricked, his need for the camp would be so acute that he
would cooperate. Then, after the token evacuation, the
administration might well agree to a compromise. Bartlett
reassured the Police Chief, but after the call he suddenly
changed his mind. "Immediately after this conversation,"
Bartlett recalled, "sensing that possibly Glassford's plan
was not approved by the administration I messaged a letter to Glassford, to the Secretary of the Treasury, and to
the local newspapers." The Bonus Army's loyal supporter
explained that he could not consent to the use of his land
for a permanent camp unless this were approved by both
the District Commissioners and the administration.[9] Obviously afraid of being caught in a political battle, Bartlett
quickly doomed Glassford's hopes. Oddly enough, neither Glassford nor Waters later revealed any bitterness toward Bartlett or charged him with destroying their plan.
Waters apparently did not learn of Bartlett's decision that
morning, but the BEF commander's reaction to another
disclosure soon ended any chance of a voluntary withdrawal.

Even on a clear, sunny morning Camp Glassford at
Third Street and Pennsylvania Avenue was an ugly sight.
Located three blocks west of Capitol Hill and a half mile
east of the White House, the partially demolished buildings stood like grotesque skeletons against the sky. Lee's
Undertaking Garage remained intact, but in May, before
the veterans arrived, Rhine's wrecking crews had gutted
several wholesale warehouses, automobile showrooms, a
restaurant, and a cheap hotel. Once the central shopping
district, the run-down area was to be renovated under the
administration's widely approved expansion of official
structures along Pennsylvania Avenue. Although current
plans apparently called for conversion of the first eviction
site into a park, new and long-awaited federal office

9. John Henry Bartlett, *The Bonus March and the New Deal* (New York: M. A. Donohue and Company, 1937), pp. 20–22. *Evening Star*, July 28, 1932.

buildings would line much of the avenue. Rhine was desperate to protect his remaining salvage in the occupied buildings, and the entire project was to provide badly needed jobs.[10]

When Waters arrived at Camp Glassford, W. J. Wilford, the camp's commander, was already suspicious of suggestions for action from any source. An hour earlier, J. O. Patton, a police detective, had solicited Wilford's cooperation and discussed voluntary withdrawal.[11] Wilford remained skeptical when the BEF commander explained his agreement to send 200 men to Camp Bartlett in exchange for a four-day extension of occupancy. By the early evening of July 27 Waters had learned of the administration's plans to start the evacuation on the morning of the 28th, but for some reason he believed that his agreement with Glassford was the latest word, and he wistfully proceeded on that ground.[12] Despite Waters's assurance, Wilford refused to surrender his camp. Only the day before, with Glassford's support, his men had successfully defied the government's wrecking crews. None of the commander's arguments could move Wilford from the hard-line policy of no surrender that Waters had created. As Waters later put it, the men were convinced that "they had bluffed the Government, an unpleasant conviction for any group to hold at any time." [13] At a loss for alternative action, he assembled the veterans at the camp speakers' platform and explained his plan. They booed and jeered him for breaking his promise and losing his nerve. Stung by their rejection, Waters struck back. He warned them of the possible use of troops, accused them of jeopardizing the lives of women and children, and returned their contempt with a taunt: "If troops do come you mugs will be the first ones to run." [14]

10. "The Battle of Washington," *Time*, 20 (August 8, 1932), 5; New York *Times*, July 29, 1932.

11. Report of J. O. Patton, July 29, 1932, GP.

12. Walter W. Waters, *B.E.F.: The Whole Story of the Bonus Army* (New York: The John Day Company, Inc., 1933), pp. 225–26. Waters gave the time when he learned of the administration's plans as 5:30 P.M., July 27, 1932.

13. Waters, *B.E.F.*, p. 208.

14. Waters, *B.E.F.*, pp. 208–9. Douglas charged that Waters had de-

Some of the men began drifting away from the platform. (Waters later argued that they had left to collect their bed-rolls for the move to Camp Bartlett.) At this point, Glass-ford's secretary, Aldace Walker, interrupted Waters's speech to deliver the order for immediate evacuation of the one-block area. The order obviously involved more than the 200 men Waters had agreed upon, and it con-tained no mention of the four-day postponement. Waters was stunned. Glassford had promised to meet him that morning "sometime around 9 o'clock." Glassford had planned at that time to "tell him what was proposed to be done" and to suggest "that we get together and try to work out a solution [which] would obviate any con-troversy." Instead, Glassford had sent his secretary. At first Waters discussed the order with the Chief's secretary, but Walker could not enlighten him about its implica-tions. It now seemed to the BEF commander that the Commissioners and Glassford had deliberately misled him, and the realization struck him cruelly. He had al-ready absorbed considerable ridicule from the men and, in self-defense, had sworn to them that there would be no eviction that day. He had frequently been called a stooge of the police, and now, humiliated and angry, Waters loudly read the order to the men. "There you are!" he concluded. "You're double-crossed. I'm double-crossed." [15]

Waters's announcement sent the determined men swarming back into the buildings. Shortly afterward, Glassford and a force of 100 police converged on the old National Guard Armory. After blocking off traffic in the surrounding area and roping off the armory, the Police Chief, twelve officers, and six Treasury agents began leading the veterans out of the building one by one. The swelling crowd of excited veterans and spectators cheered each evicted protester. Many of the participants and spec-tators anticipated violence. Three of the evicted men wrestled with police, but after officers easily subdued

liberately "betrayed the men by not exposing the plan to use troops." Jack Douglas, *Veterans On The March* (New York: Workers Library Publishers, 1934), p. 233.
   15. Waters, *B.E.F.*, pp. 209–10; *Evening Star*, July 28, 1932; GP.

them, no further resistance developed. As the crowd had grown perceptibly around eleven o'clock, Glassford secretly ordered several hundred tear gas bombs rushed to the site, but shortly before noon the evictors had emptied the building completely without any significant trouble. All in all, the effort had gone remarkably well, and Glassford prepared to call a break for lunch.[16]

Meanwhile, Attorney General William D. Mitchell gathered his aides together for a meeting regarding the long-term evacuation plans. In the light of the White House conference of July 27 and subsequent press releases, no one could doubt that Hoover had decided to remove the protesters from government property. After repeated blunders the President had finally appointed his Attorney General to coordinate District and federal efforts. Reluctantly, Hoover agreed to use troops in the event of definite emergency, but he did not anticipate serious trouble or expect that troops would be necessary in the final resolution of the problem. This assumption is documented by the fact that he charged Attorney General Mitchell, not General MacArthur, with the responsibility for a coordinated, peaceable eviction. As Glassford and his assistants emptied the armory without incident, Mitchell began to map out his strategy for the days ahead.

First, the Attorney General requested permission from E. N. Chisolm, Jr., Acting Director of Public Buildings and Public Parks, to remove the veterans from all property under his jurisdiction. Then, he asked Chisolm and Heath to mark the principal encampments on a city map. The men discussed the various sites, and the Attorney General asked their advice on the order of the repossession. Perhaps the most important aspect of his preparations was the total absence of any undue haste or sense of emergency. Some time during the next few days, after he had decided the exact schedule for each eviction site, the

16. "Report of J. O. Patton," July 29, 1932; PDG, "Circumstances Leading Up to the Use of Federal Forces Against the Bonus Army, July 31, 1932," pp. 4–5, GP. Glassford, "Testimony Before the Grand Jury, August 1, 1932," PP 300, HHPL, pp. 2–3 (hereafter cited as GT). MTGJ, pp. 51, 67–68.

Attorney General planned to use United States marshals under his own command rather than Treasury agents and local police, as in the case of the initial repossession that morning. But many important arrangements remained to be made, and, not wanting to repeat previous errors, Mitchell approached them without a sense of hurry. In fact, he took great pains to impress his aides that the final plans must above all enable him "to force them *gradually* out of government property with the least amount of trouble." His careful, deliberate strategy showed no evidence of panic, no fear of imminent revolution, no expectation that troops would be needed.[17]

The President's tardy appointment of a cabinet officer with full responsibility for the undertaking came too late, however, and Mitchell's announcement of his new responsibility created the impression of great haste. Well before noon the Attorney General notified reporters of his new job and his initial plans. Unfortunately, he used the term *summary* for the evictions, which meant, in legal language, repossession that could be undertaken without a court order, but reporters and editors understandably interpreted it to mean *immediate*. Since the initial effort at the National Guard Armory was moving smoothly at the time he issued his statement, Mitchell's choice of words did not seem especially significant then. However, by the time his statement appeared in the evening papers— alongside reports of all the later violence—the word *summary* took on sinister implications.[18]

Just as Attorney General Mitchell felt no sense of urgency that morning, neither did Hoover. July 28 was, in fact, a very busy day for the President. According to James H. MacLafferty, a congressional liaison man, Hoover's chief concern was how he could make bankers cooperate

17. My italics. WDM [William D. Mitchell] "Memorandum for Mr. Caldwell," July 28, 1932; Heath, "Memorandum for the Attorney General," July 28, 1932; David D. Caldwell, "Memorandum for the Attorney General," July 28, 1932; E. N. Chisolm to Edgar C. Snyder, July 28, 1932, HHPL. A copy of the map indicating the eviction sites is in Department of Justice, File 95-16-26, RG 60, NA.

18. New York *Herald Tribune,* July 29, 1932; New York *Times,* July 29, 1932; *Evening Star,* July 28, 1932.

in his efforts to end the depression. MacLafferty was impressed by his determination: "It is rarely that I have seen Mr. Hoover as much in earnest as I saw him this morning." On July 28 Hoover also completed his selection of the directors for the Reconstruction Finance Corporation. Further, after a long conference with Secretary of the Treasury Mills, leading officials of the nation's major railroads met with Hoover and Secretary of Commerce Robert P. Lamont to discuss immediate federal loans. In addition, the President finished editing and finally approved Secretary of State Stimson's forthcoming major address on Japan.[19]

Shortly before noon, as Glassford's men stopped for lunch, several police officers rushed to the Chief with reports that Waters had made a speech at the Anacostia camp to encourage all veterans to converge on the eviction site.[20] Suddenly a number of trucks and several automobiles arrived. The drivers had eluded the traffic police, and they quickly dumped their angry cargo. Crowds of men on foot soon augmented their numbers. Glassford watched them closely as they massed in a park across the street. The police were most concerned by the hostile, belligerent mood of the crowd. Glassford immediately ordered reinforcements. Unknown to the Chief, Assistant Superintendent Lewis Edwards also telephoned police headquarters to send every available officer, on or off duty.[21] The police now tried to raise the Anacostia bridge to prevent cars and trucks from returning for more passengers, but the veterans had anticipated that move and oc-

19. James H. MacLafferty, "Diary," July 28, 1932, MacLafferty Papers, HHPL. New York *Journal of Commerce*, July 29, 1932. Treasury Secretary Mills clipped the news report. A copy is in the Ogden Mills Papers, Vol. 11, Container 196, Newspaper Clippings, p. 162. President's Appointments Calendar, July 28, 1932, HHPL.

20. GT, p. 3. Glassford's belief that Waters had called for reinforcements was supported by several police officers. "Report of J. O. Patton," July 29, 1932; Lloyd E. Kelley to PDG, September 11, 1932, GP. Waters later denied the charge; Waters, *B.E.F.*, p. 213. Waters's denial is supported by Charles F. Mugge to PDG, September 10, 1932, GP.

21. MTGJ, pp. 156–70, 191; GT, pp. 3, 16; "Statement of Lewis I. H. Edwards," August 3, 1932, PP 300, HHPL.

cupied the bridge. Only a large contingent could dislodge them, and all available police were speeding to the eviction site.[22]

Downtown, fears mounted among the police. Some historians later claimed that Communists started the Bonus Riot, but one of the two principal witnesses who could identify the Communists, J. O. Patton of the Crime Prevention Division, reported to other police officers that he recognized only thirty-five members of Pace's Communist outfit among the milling throng. More important, Patton cited no evidence of Communist organization or instigation before or during the riot. The other principal witness, Glassford, insisted that the reds were not responsible and that the rioting was "entirely due to an aggravated frame of mind on the part of the veterans." Far greater numbers of angry, non-Communist veterans from Anacostia and other camps continued to disembark from trucks. At about ten minutes after noon, three of these men, one carrying an American flag, began pushing their way through the crowd toward the evacuated building. They soon picked up a following and continued their advance. Glassford realized that they intended to reoccupy the armory, so he quickly gathered his own forces and ran to meet the veterans at a point where they would converge on police lines.[23]

As he shouted orders to halt, some of the men seemed surprised at his sudden tough attitude. Only yesterday he had refused to evict them, and they had cheered his support. Now someone shouted, "Give the cops hell!" as the charging veterans encountered fierce resistance. Clubbing the protesters with night sticks, the police at first held their own in hand-to-hand combat until a hail of bricks, rocks, scrap iron, and other remnants of the demolition forced Glassford's men to retreat behind several flimsy huts. The police were greatly outnumbered as more and

22. Indianapolis *Times*, July 28, 1932. United Press reported the effort to raise the bridge.
23. "Report of J. O. Patton," p. 3, GP. GT, pp. 3, 8. Glassford was convinced that the Communists were not involved.

more veterans crowded after the first wave of their buddies and continued the heavy pelting. One man, Bernard McCoy, ripped off Glassford's badge. Significantly, he was the only veteran among the rioters whom Patton cited as being a Communist. Other veterans, responding to Glassford's call for help, quickly wrestled the badge away from McCoy and returned it to a police officer—a marked gesture of respect for the Chief.[24]

The bombardment of bricks continued, and as Glassford at one point stood in the thick of the fray, pleading for an end to the fighting, a brick hit him in the side, and he collapsed. One of his men, Edward G. Scott, who had been awarded the Medal of Honor in the World War, instantly tried to protect his fallen commander. As he hovered over the Chief, however, a brick struck him in the head, and as he spun around at the blow, another brick to the temple knocked him unconscious. His skull fractured, the fallen police officer was attacked by the advancing wave of veterans. *Time* stated that he was trampled, and the New York *Times* reported that "a group of men

24. "Report of J. O. Patton," p. 3; GT, pp. 3–4; New York *Times*, April 29, 1932; "Battle of Washington," *Time* (August 8, 1932), p. 6. Patton's report is important because he was the only police officer who claimed that Communists were at the eviction site. Glassford, who was equally familiar with the Communists, was convinced that none of them were involved in the brick battle, a view that Patton's report does not contradict, with the one exception of the Communist who ripped off Glassford's badge. Significantly, Patton did not cite the other Communists in the crowd of onlookers as participants in the fighting. Glassford did not recognize any Communists before, during, or after the brick battle, and Patton limited his claim to the one involved in the battle. GT, pp. 3–4; PDG, "Circumstances Leading Up to the Use of Federal Forces," p. 7. Other observers, such as Will Castleman, who were far less qualified to identify the participants insisted, nevertheless, that the Communists had led the riot. Will Castleman to Hurley, December 1, 1932, HP. At least three historians have accepted this charge. John D. Weaver, "Bonus March," *American Heritage*, 14 (June 1963), p. 93. Weaver claims that "radicals" started the brick battle. Irving Bernstein accepted the Communists' explanation that they had been responsible for the riot in his one chapter about the bonus march; Irving Bernstein, *The Lean Years; A History of the American Worker, 1920–1933* (Boston: Houghton Mifflin Company, 1960), p. 451. Roger Daniels reprints the relevant part of the Patton Report. Roger Daniels, *The Bonus March: An Episode of the Great Depression* (Westport, Conn.: Greenwood Press, Inc., 1971), pp. 149–50.

jumped on his prostrate body and continued to hammer him with bricks." [25]

The fighting stopped as suddenly as it had begun. Glassford at first believed, and others widely reported, that the battle had ceased in response to his repeated pleas. Later he remembered that Eddie Atwell had rushed his BEF military police into a position between the police and the veterans and ended the hail of bricks. Atwell had restored peace, but the veterans remained sullen and angry. Although the battle had lasted only about five minutes, in the judgment of all the police and most reporters the encounter was a riot. By comparison to upheavals in the 1960s, it might not be considered a riot, but it qualified for one in 1932. Its duration was less important than the intensity of the fighting, the large number injured and bleeding, the fierce anger generated on both sides, and the occurrence of more violent action later on. Indeed, the incident was much more serious than the elapsed time of the fight suggested.[26]

Only Glassford refused to admit that he had momentarily lost control of events. In fact, the Chief later minimized the battle, as did most other critics of the administration.[27] For months, subsequently, another battle—one

25. "Battle of Washington," *Time* (August 8, 1932), p. 6; New York *Times*, July 29, 1932; New York *Herald Tribune*, July 30, 1932.

26. GT, pp. 3–4; "Statement of Ernest W. Brown," August 3, 1932, DCP; Atwell, *Washington, the Battle Ground*, p. ii. Accounts of the duration of the fight vary considerably. Paul Anderson, one of Hoover's harshest critics, claimed it lasted only "a few seconds"; Paul Y. Anderson, "Tear Gas, Bayonets, and Votes: The President Opens His Reelection Campaign," *Nation*, 135 (August 17, 1932), 139. Glassford recalled three to four minutes, J. O. Patton cited five minutes, Waters estimated six minutes, and the United Press reported ten minutes. PDG, "Circumstances Leading Up to the Use of Federal Forces," p. 5; "Report of J. O. Patton," p. 3; Waters, *B.E.F.*, p. 214; Indianapolis *Times*, July 28, 1932. Glassford later stated five minutes; PDG, Statement, Not Released, September 13, 1932, GP. Examples of observations that the battle was indeed a riot included the New York *Times*, July 29, 1932; *Evening Star*, July 29, 1932; Waters, *B.E.F.*, p. 215; *Herald*, July 30, 1932. For police insistence on the term *riot*, see MTGJ, pp. 50–52, 78–79, 96–97.

27. Glassford referred to the "brick battle" but also warned against "more rioting"; GT, p. 4. Glassford's secretary, who was also an eye-

of semantics—centered on the confrontation. Definition of the event depended usually upon either the individual's political bias or his use of the incident to further his political objectives. The leaders of the BEF, for example, blamed the Communists for initiating the fighting, while the Communist party at first denied responsibility. Eager to portray the battle as one between hungry men and reactionary authorities, the New York *Daily Worker* claimed that the "police deployed, advanced and fired point blank at the bonus marchers. The veterans fought back with their fists, bricks, and sticks." Other Communists, however, tried to take credit for the riot, but they were unsuccessful in convincing their irate superiors in Moscow. The confusion over responsibility allowed one to choose his definition and his villains. Whether the disturbance was a fight, brick battle, riotous condition, or riot, even Hoover's most severe critics agreed or at least suggested that it had been ugly and dangerous.[28] That the police did not draw

witness, later referred to the "first riot"; Aldace Walker to PDG, September 10, 1932, GP, and New York *Times*, September 13, 1932. Other critics of Hoover refused to use the term. Bartlett insisted that it was an "assault" rather than a riot, while Paul Anderson called it a "melee." The most partisan critics attempted to minimize the danger to the police during the fighting. Bartlett, *Bonus March*, pp. 32, 119; Anderson, "Tear Gas, Bayonets, and Votes," p. 139; Fleta Campbell Springer, "Glassford and the Siege of Washington," *Harper's Magazine*, 165 (November 1932), 641–55.

28. Excerpt from New York *Daily Worker*, July 29, 1932, in PP 299, HHPL. The principal leaders of the BEF blamed the Communists. Waters, *B.E.F.*, p. 214; Atwell, *Washington, the Battle Ground*, pp. 36–38; Indianapolis *Times*, September 12, 1932. Pace was in jail at the time of the riot, and his unconvincing accounts of Communist influence varied considerably; see Chapter 14 and U.S., Congress, House, Committee on Un-American Activities, *Hearings on Communist Tactics Among Veterans Groups*, 82d Cong., 1st sess., 1951, p. 1942 (hereafter cited as HUAC, CTVG); *Hearings on House Resolution 282, Investigation of Propaganda Activities in the United States*, 75th Cong., 3d sess., III, October-November 1938, pp. 2266–87. The New York *Times* reported that the Communists claimed credit for starting the battle; New York *Times*, July 31, 1932. The administration, of course, accepted reports of Communist participation, but other eyewitnesses refused to believe that the reds were responsible. See "Battle of Washington," *Time*, 20 (August 8, 1932), 5. Finally, although he did not have access to the Hoover Papers Maurice Sneller concludes that no one knows who started the brick battle. Maurice P. Sneller, Jr., "The Bonus March of

their revolvers testified to their self-discipline and training, for police of all ranks were genuinely frightened and freely admitted their fear to reporters. The crucial issue was not whether the battle constituted a "genuine" riot, or whether the Communists were responsible, but whether the police could maintain the uneasy truce in a potentially explosive crisis.

Knowing that six of their colleagues were hospitalized—two of them in serious condition—and many others were suffering from minor but painful wounds, the members of Glassford's force changed their attitude toward the veterans. For the past two months the police had shown tact, restraint, and helpfulness in dealing with the marchers. Because of the BEF encampment, they had been forced to postpone vacations, give up days off, and rush to their posts at odd hours for reserve duty. They had cooperated in the peaceable control without serious complaint, but now those months of friendly relations with the Bonus Army suddenly appeared wasted.[29] Further, the Chief alienated his men by repeatedly asserting that everything was under control, when obviously, they felt, it was not. Since they lacked the protective helmets, visors, and other equipment now routinely supplied during such disturbances, the police felt especially vulnerable. Verbal abuse helped to demoralize them, and threats by the BEF of what violence would happen after nightfall alarmed them.

Since individual police were now thoroughly convinced that they could not maintain control, they feared that another charge would force them to use their revolvers and cause heavy casualties. For months Glassford's men had respectfully supported him, but the disagreement over the need for troops marked the beginning of a serious split between the Chief and his force. Unknown to Glassford, Police Lt. Ira E. Keck, assigned by the Commissioners as their special agent at the site, raced

1932: A Study of Depression Leadership and Its Legacy" (Ph.D. diss. University of Virginia, 1960), p. 213.

29. *Post*, July 29, 1932; New York *Times*, July 29, 1932; *Evening Star*, July 28, 1932.

to the District Building, where he related the viewpoint of the force. While reporting the mounting concern of the majority of the men, he charged that the once friendly veterans had turned into a "mad, seething, howling mob [which] was going to wipe up the police." In his opinion and in the opinions of Assistant Superintendents Brown and Edwards, federal troops were needed immediately.[30]

Nevertheless, the Commissioners flatly refused to act on Keck's advice alone; first, they wanted to speak with Glassford. They ordered Keck to find the Chief and bring him back to their offices. When Keck returned to the eviction site, he found Glassford, Assistant Superintendent Brown, and Glassford's secretary Aldace Walker talking to Waters in Lee's Undertaking Garage. Glassford had taken Waters aside to discuss the veterans' "ugly mood," but Waters insisted that there was nothing he could do to modify it. He had completely lost control of them, he said—a statement he later denied. Waters's refusal to attempt to exert his authority was indeed a serious blow. At that point Keck informed Glassford that the Commissioners wanted his advice on the need for troops. According to Keck, Glassford replied, "Since Waters has lost control of his own men the police cannot control the situation any longer." [31]

A few minutes later, accompanied by Walker and Keck, Glassford met with the Commissioners and began to change his position. A show of force had been made, he argued, and one building evacuated. Therefore, enough had been accomplished to postpone clearing the entire block. Neither Glassford nor the Commissioners had the authority to postpone the Treasury Department's repossession order, but this did not dissuade him.

As for the use of troops, Glassford now began to hedge.

30. MTGJ, pp. 50–53; "Statement of Lewis I. H. Edwards," August 3, 1932, pp. 2–3; "Statement of Ira E. Keck," August 3, 1932, pp. 2–3; "Statement of Ernest W. Brown," August 3, 1932, pp. 3–4, DCP.

31. "Statement of Ira E. Keck," pp. 2–3; "Statement of Ernest Brown," p. 3, DCP. New York Times, July 29, 1932; Waters, B.E.F., p. 216. Testimony of Keck, Brown, and Edwards before the Grand Jury, MTGJ, pp. 53, 88–89, 96–97.

His attitude on this point later became a source of heated political debate. At the meeting in the District Building the Chief neatly sidestepped the issue with a set of confusing qualifications. On the one hand, if the Commissioners continued eviction from the one-block area, "federal troops *should* be called out to do so, because, the police being so greatly outnumbered, any attempt at repossession under police protection would *inevitably* lead to *more rioting* and possibly bloodshed." On the other hand, if further repossession were postponed, he assured them that his police could fully control the situation. Glassford, however, was not as calm or as confident as he later claimed to have been. When he left the District Building he told a group of waiting reporters that he had not requested assistance "at this time," but that he did "not want to go against the seething mob" again. Without another attempt at eviction, events soon belied Glassford's assurances. The question, then, hinged not on repossession but on control.[32]

Glassford left the Commissioners in a quandary. Considering earlier police reports and their own attitude toward the protesters, they were no doubt surprised by his assessment. His assurances contradicted Keck's story of the general police insistence on troops. They doubted the Chief's promises but did not know what action to take. They later claimed that while Glassford was in their office, Crosby called MacArthur and "requested that troops be held in readiness for a possible later call for assistance." The Commissioners now decided to conduct their own inspection of the area. Both questions—the need for troops and temporarily halting the eviction for that day—remained undecided.[33]

32. My italics. GT, pp. 4, 11, 12, 17; PDG to D.C. Commissioners, July 29, 1932, GP. Glassford did not send this letter to the Commissioners. Aldace Walker to PDG, September 10, 1932; PDG, "Circumstances Leading Up to the Use of Federal Forces," p. 5, GP. For the "seething mob" quotation, see both the *Evening Star*, July 28, 1932, and the *Times*, July 28, 1932.
33. Reichelderfer, Crosby, and Keck insisted that Glassford had requested troops; see their testimony, MTGJ, pp. 21–23, 31–32, 40–41, 53–54, and Douglas MacArthur to the Attorney General, August 2,

When Glassford returned to his officers and told them
that troops would not be needed, they were astonished.
Assistant Superintendent Brown was especially irritated,
as both he and Assistant Superintendent Edwards had
strongly urged him to convey their request to the Commissioners. Brown repeated his arguments and pointed
out that although every available police officer was on
duty, they were unable to reduce the size of the crowd or
to convince the men to disperse peaceably. Again and
again his officers expressed their fears, but Glassford ignored them.[34] Instead, after another fruitless conference
with Waters and a brief conversation with the Commissioners during their inspection tour, the Police Chief considered reducing the size of his force.

Glassford's extraordinary coolness under fire, whether
by bricks or artillery, may well have been a source of irritation and misunderstanding among his men. To his
credit, he scrupulously tried not to be a chief who cracked
heads first and asked questions later. His years in the
Army had strengthened his restraint, but the bombardment of bricks had badly shaken his men, who were less
battle-hardened and less willing to take what they consid-

1932, HP. MacArthur claimed that Crosby had informed him that
Glassford had requested troops to be held in readiness for immediate
action. Glassford later repeatedly insisted that the Commissioners did
nothing to indicate that they intended to call on troops. He never men-
tioned Crosby's call to MacArthur, yet if Glassford did witness the call,
it may have led him to jump to his explanation that the troop call resulted from a conspiracy, in which he charged that troops were summoned in response to the brick battle rather than to the shootings. The
Commissioners insisted that they alerted MacArthur while Glassford
was in their office, but that they did not formally request troops until
after the shootings. PDG, "Circumstances Leading Up to the Use of
Federal Forces," p. 5. In his testimony to the Grand Jury, Glassford
recalled that during the conference the Commissioners had asked him
questions about the need for troops (GT, p. 11). Crosby testified later
that "military authorities" had "evidently talked with the White
House" before he alerted MacArthur. The significance of this alleged
contact, however, is vague. If "military authorities" had contacted the
White House before he telephoned, it is evident that these "military
authorities" were not given permission to assemble troops (MTGJ, pp.
40–41). Crosby had cooperated closely with MacArthur and had conferred with MacArthur on the day before the riot. *Times*, July 27, 1932.
    34. Testimony of Edwards and Brown, MTGJ, pp. 88–89, 96–97.

ered unnecessary risks. They were brave enough, but they saw no point in being overwhelmed and beaten senseless or killed when such disasters could be avoided. Estimates placed the number of police at the site between 500 and 800, as compared to the 4,000 or 5,000 men in the restless crowd. Glassford's decision to reduce his force suggested that he may have been as concerned about the possible behavior of his nervous officers as he was about that of the sullen veterans. Perhaps he hoped not only to eliminate the less stable officers but also to reduce public concern by creating the impression that the crisis was over. Plenty of time remained before nightfall, and with some luck his strategy might work.[35]

Some time between 1:15 and 1:30 P.M., just after the Commissioners had completed their inspection and had left the area, a second incident, more serious and frightening than any previous happening, took place. In the old Ford Building, about fifty yards from the roped-off area, a fight broke out among several veterans. Their scuffling attracted a large crowd and four nearby policemen, who attempted to stop the fight and to prevent more men from entering the building. Suddenly, however, "a crowd of bonus marchers," shouting "Get Glassford! Get the Major!" pushed their way into the building and attacked the police with a barrage of bricks and stones. The Chief, who had not been inside the building, was attracted by the shouting and rushed in with a large contingent of police to find four of his officers "being attacked by an overwhelming number of veterans," whose vicious assault had put the police "in great danger of their lives." Police Officer George Shenault struggled with an assailant, who was beating him with his own club while another veteran tried to choke him. Shaking free long enough to draw his revolver, Shenault saw William Huska, another attacker, coming at him with a brick in his hand. Shenault fired, and Huska dropped with a bullet in his heart. Panic-

---

35. "Statement, Inspector Ogden T. Davis," August 3, 1932; "Statement, Inspector Thaddeus R. Bean," August 3, 1932; "Statement, Ira Keck," p. 4, DCP. GTGJ, p. 5; MTGJ, pp. 5, 62.

stricken, the police officer continued to fire wildly. Finally, after almost shooting Glassford, Shenault became calm and stopped shooting.[36]

The impact of this second confrontation was enormous. Although this assault was also of short duration, Huska was dead and one other veteran, Eric Carlson, fatally wounded. Three of the four besieged policemen were hospitalized, a fact Glassford's officers cited as additional evidence of his misjudgment. Without Glassford's timely arrival, their injuries might have been fatal. Their assailants had suddenly emerged from the seemingly unaggressive crowd and had attacked the police for no apparent reason. The crowd was far more dangerous, police officers unanimously agreed, than Glassford had judged it to be. None were Communists, but were, rather, the very men Glassford claimed he could control. The Chief now admitted that lives of police were in danger. Inspector Keck agreed and wasted no time in reporting the shootings to the Commissioners. They immediately telephoned the White House to request federal troops and quickly alerted MacArthur. Significantly, the President at first refused to comply. He told the Commissioners that until he received a written statement from them which included Glassford's views as well, he would not authorize the use of troops.[37]

At that point the Commissioners should have conferred again with Glassford, but evidently they did not. Rather, they relied on the unanimous opinion of ranking police officers. They assured Hoover that the Chief had requested the troops and rushed their written statement to the White House. They apparently interpreted the resurgence of violence, in absence of further efforts at eviction, as satisfying the prerequisite for Glassford's approval, for he had implied that federal troops should be

36. MTGJ, p. 5; PDG, "Circumstances Leading Up to the Use of Federal Forces," p. 6; "Report of J. O. Patton," p. 3. Waters greatly distorted the facts, claiming that Shenault was guilty of murder. Waters, *B.E.F.*, p. 217. While on duty two weeks later, Shenault was mysteriously killed. The murderer was never apprehended.

37. "Statement of Ira E. Keck," pp. 3–4; MTGJ, p. 54; Theodore J. Joslin, *Hoover Off The Record* (New York: Doubleday, Doran and Co., 1934), pp. 266–67.

called in the event of "more rioting." Glassford had then argued that only continued repossession would bring further trouble, yet that assurance had now been disproved. The Chief's equivocation no doubt confused his listeners, although it is possible, as Glassford later charged, that the Commissioners purposely misrepresented his views. That issue remains unresolved, and in light of conflicting testimony cannot be settled definitely. During later testimony before a grand jury Commissioners Crosby and Reichelderfer and Inspector Keck swore that Glassford had requested troops; Glassford and his secretary Aldace Walker claimed he had not. Given the unalterable convictions of the witnesses on both sides of the controversy, the most plausible explanation of events is a misunderstanding compounded by carelessness and mutual distrust. Reichelderfer insisted that even if Glassford had refused, he would have requested troops anyway.[38] Such statements do not excuse the Commissioners if, as Glassford charged, they failed to consult with him again after the shootings.

What has not been emphasized, despite its importance, is that the Commissioners evidently assured the President verbally of Glassford's alleged request, and promised to rush their written statement to him. The message that influenced Hoover read:

It is the opinion of the Major and Superintendent of Police, in which the Commissioners concur, that

38. See footnotes 29, 30, and 31. Without troops, Keck insisted, "there would have been bloodshed and to my mind the police would have gotten the worst of it." Edwards believed that if troops had not been called, the police would have had to use their revolvers for protection "and lots of people would have been killed . . . including police." Edwards further testified that the police were becoming exhausted and he doubted if they could have controlled the crowd throughout the night; MTGJ, pp. 61–62, 82, 88–89. Inspector Thaddeus Bean believed that "if troops had not arrived when they did there would have been more trouble and further bloodshed and loss of life"; "Statement of Thaddeus Bean." Assistant Superintendent Ogden T. Davis was elated at the sight of the approaching troops: "I was never more glad to see soldiers in my life," he stated. "There was absolute need of them"; see "Statement of Ogden T. Davis," DCP. There is no evidence that any of the other police officers on duty at the scene contradicted these sentiments. Another eyewitness, Congressman Donald

it will be *impossible* for the Police Department to maintain law and order except by the free use of firearms which will make the situation a dangerous one; it is believed, however, that the presence of Federal troops in some number will obviate the seriousness of the situation and result in far less violence and bloodshed.[39]

The Police Commissioners' formal communiqué did not specifically refer to the police officer's shooting of veterans, nor did it report the continued insistence of other ranking officers—Edwards, Brown, Davis, Bean, and Keck—that troops must be sent. Its omissions are suggestive but prove nothing, and the exact wording is relatively insignificant. Anticipating further trouble, the Commissioners may well have drafted at least part of the communiqué earlier, for immediately after their own inspection tour, which had followed the brick battle, Keck reported the shootings. When Hoover refused their first request for troops and demanded a written expression of Glassford's views, they may well have reassured him, then have added the statement of Glassford's approval and dashed it off to the White House. It is impossible to determine whether the Commissioners incorrectly assumed that the Chief would approve troops because of the new outbreak of violence or deliberately misrepresented his views. The letter closely paralleled the thinking of the police. At the same time, however, it misled the President regarding Glassford's opinion. Thus, believing that he was acting on both the Commissioners and Glassford's urging, Hoover agreed to communicate with MacArthur, who ordered the troops to assemble at the Ellipse behind the White House.

If Hoover had been seeking a pretext to use troops against the marchers, there had been opportunities before July 28 to claim disorder and send the Army into confrontation with the BEF. Indeed, if a plot had existed, the

F. Snow from Maine agreed with the police view; Donald F. Snow to Patrick J. Hurley, August 20, 1932, HP.

39. My italics, Reichelderfer to The President, July 28, 1932, PP 300, HHPL.

Commissioners need not have refused Keck's first request for troops after the brick battle, they need not have summoned Glassford to their offices for his firsthand account, and they need not have made their own inspection tour of the site just before the shootings began. Hoover, on his part, need not have refused the Commissioners' request subsequent to the shootings until they assured him of Glassford's approval and put it in writing.

Glassford's police gratefully received the news of the call for troops. From their viewpoint, as expressed both to reporters that afternoon and again in later testimony, it was essential to call in fresh, better-equipped, well-disciplined troops. Though he would not admit it at the time, Glassford did not feel sanguine about controlling the situation. His earlier order for several hundred tear gas bombs suggested that he had serious doubts about his ability to disperse the crowd and to maintain control by conventional methods. In fact, immediately before he heard about the call for troops, he devised a hasty and ill-conceived gas attack against the crowd. He counted on a stiff southerly breeze, which he hoped would blow the vapor toward the veterans and spectators, while his police followed at a safe distance. With only four masks available, a gas attack on an excited throng of 4,000 to 5,000 was obviously a risky undertaking. Without gas masks his men could not easily have subdued resisters or protected themselves from canisters thrown back at them. Later, he told MacArthur that "it was obvious that the evacuation of the incensed and determined veterans could not be accomplished by police action alone." [40] Unfortunately, once MacArthur's troops swung into action, the situation changed drastically.

40. GTGJ, pp. 6, 9–10; PDG to MacArthur, April 26, 1951, MacArthur Papers. The interview appeared in Glassford's home-town newspaper, the Laguna Beach (California) *Post*, April 12, 1951. Glassford had defended MacArthur's skillful use of the troops, gas, and tanks as early as September 29, 1932. *Post*, September 29, 1932; *Evening Star*, September 29, 1932. Still later, on July 13, 1967, Dwight D. Eisenhower, aide to MacArthur during the rout of the veterans, also revealed his belief that the police could not have moved the veterans without help. Interview, Dwight D. Eisenhower, July 13, 1967, Oral History Collection, HHPL.

10

The Rout of the Marchers

When Hoover finally summoned troops, he did so in response to the Commissioners' second request. Nevertheless, many observers considered his action both sudden and brutal. Forgotten was the conviction of the police that they could no longer hold the huge, threatening crowd at bay and their repeated pleas for federal troops. No one thought—few knew—of Hoover's quiet aid to the campers during the past two months or of his unprecedented patience and restraint. Instead, the events of July 28 seemed to prove that the President had finally revealed his true nature—that of a harsh, vindictive, or at least exceedingly fearful man, who had seized upon a pretext to use massive force against the hapless squatters. Again the belief prevailed that Hoover was in full control of the situation and, therefore, that the brutal rout of the marchers represented his insensitive and ruthless use of power. Unfortunately, in the months that followed, his actions served only to reinforce that impression, and for millions the Jekyll–Hyde image followed Hoover to his grave.

Throughout years of savage criticism after the rout of the BEF, Hoover did not blame anyone for the tragic dispersal. Many years later, however, he emphatically denied that he had ordered the rout. He declared that he had complied with the District Commissioners' urgent request—which had contained a statement of Glassford's approval—but, Hoover added, he had not directed the troops to drive the veterans out of the capital. He had ordered the Army only to move the rioting veterans out of the business district and to return them to their camps, where they would be placed under guard until a systematic investigation could identify the instigators of the riot.[1]

1. Donald J. Lisio, "A Blunder Becomes Catastrophe: Hoover, the

It is unfortunate that Hoover did not offer any proof in his memoir to substantiate his new explanation. His public statements at the time of the riot and afterward gave no hint that his orders were disobeyed. Indeed, his statement the day after the riot fully supported the rout and angrily scolded the retreating bonuseers. If Hoover's explanations were accurate, why had he not immediately disciplined those who had disobeyed his orders? Hoover's latter-day insistence that he had not ordered the rout appeared to be an old man's feeble attempt to find some justification for a serious mistake. Understandably, historians have discounted its validity.[2]

Legion, and the Bonus Army," *Wisconsin Magazine of History*, 51 (Autumn 1967), 37–50. The article established for the first time that MacArthur knowingly disobeyed the President's written orders, and also showed that he repeatedly disobeyed verbal orders to stop the rout. Roger Daniels, *The Bonus March: An Episode of the Great Depression* (Westport, Conn.: Greenwood Press, Inc., 1971) cites my article (p. 331, note 6) and agrees that MacArthur disobeyed orders. Herbert Hoover, *The Memoirs of Herbert Hoover: The Great Depression 1929–1941*, 3 vols. (New York: The Macmillan Company, 1952), III, 226–27.

2. Glassford raised the issue of discipline in a letter to Hoover that he apparently never sent. Hoover first made his claim in an article in *Collier's*, May 24, 1952, and Glassford was quite upset about it. He stated, "It would seem that if General MacArthur had exceeded his authority disciplinary action would have been in order." PDG to Hoover, draft letter, n.d., GP 679. This letter was enclosed in a copy of *The Nation*, dated August 17, 1932. Glassford had consistently argued that MacArthur was merely obeying Hoover's orders to rout the BEF. PDG to Joseph Choate, May 16, 1948, and PDG, "MacArthur and the Bonus Army," unpublished article, May 14, 1948, GP 679. Joslin had earlier insisted that Hoover's orders had been disobeyed. He noted that Hoover could have "crushed down on the commanding officers" but defended his inaction on the grounds that Hoover was not the "buck-passing" type of President. Theodore J. Joslin, *Hoover Off The Record* (New York: Doubleday, Doran and Co., 1934), p. 280. Bennett Milton Rich and John W. Killigrew rejected Joslin's defense. Both insisted that Hoover ordered MacArthur to clear all of the veterans out of the District. Bennett Milton Rich, *The Presidents and Civil Disorders* (Washington, D.C.: The Brookings Institution, 1941), pp. 175–76. John W. Killigrew, "The Impact of the Great Depression on the Army, 1929–1936," (Ph.D. diss., University of Indiana, 1960), p. 10. For brief accounts by two prominent historians who do not mention Hoover's later assertion that his orders had been disobeyed, see Arthur M. Schlesinger, Jr., *The Age of Roosevelt: The Crisis of the Old Order, 1919–1933*, 3 vols. (Boston: Houghton Mifflin, 1957), I, 256–65; Wil-

Despite the weakness of Hoover's defense, his explanation was correct. On the afternoon of the riot, he responded to the Commissioners' second request and directed his Secretary of War to assemble the troops. Hurley immediately telephoned the message to MacArthur, with the result that the President soon lost control over the swiftly moving events. Immediately after he had received the call from the Commissioners, MacArthur alerted his troops, ordered his reluctant staff aide Maj. Dwight D. Eisenhower into uniform, and personally began to coordinate the most impressive display of military might that Washington had seen in many years. Once in command, the General quickly showed his disdain for civilian interference in what he considered to be military affairs. In fact, MacArthur intentionally disobeyed the President's orders and, on his own volition, decided to drive the BEF out of the capital.

Basing his judgment partially upon an unconvincing Army Intelligence report and partially upon his own deep suspicion of "radicals," the young Chief of Staff argued that the rioters were actually Communist insurrectionists attempting a well-planned, intentionally bloody *coup d'état*. Supposedly, Waters was collecting machine guns and "gun-men from New York and Washington," and the BEF was plotting to establish a permanent encampment in order to compel the government to force the veterans out of the capital. "Word has been passed around in Syracuse," the report continued, "that the first bloodshed by the Bonus Army at Washington, is to be the signal for a communist uprising in all large cities, thus initiating a revolution." Therefore, when Hoover called for troops, MacArthur decided and later insisted that "the dispersion and expulsion from the District . . . became . . . the only logical answer." [3]

liam E. Leuchtenberg, *Franklin D. Roosevelt and the New Deal 1932–1940* (New York: Harper & Row, Publishers, 1963), pp. 14–17. Without the availability of supporting evidence at the time of their publications, there is no reason why either historian should have accepted Hoover's claim at face value.

3. Conrad H. Lanza, Assistant Chief of Staff, G-2, to Assistant Chief

Major Eisenhower was so shocked at MacArthur's decision to take personal command that he felt compelled to remind the Chief of Staff of his obligation to uphold the pride and dignity of the Army. "I told him," Eisenhower later recalled, "that the matter could easily become a riot and I thought it highly inappropriate for the Chief of Staff of the Army to be involved in anything like a local or street-corner embroilment. Of course," he added, "this was no 'street-corner' matter—but it still did not require the presence of the Chief of Staff in the streets." MacArthur quickly dismissed Eisenhower's objection. To the General, "it was a question of Federal authority in the District of Columbia, and because of his belief that there was 'incipient revolution in the air' as he called it[,] he paid no attention to my dissent." Instead, he ordered Eisenhower into uniform.

If Eisenhower had been given the opportunity to read the order when MacArthur explained his plans, he could easily have realized that his commander was redefining the question to suit his own prejudgments. As a good soldier, however, Eisenhower obeyed, swallowing his disagreement. In the Eisenhower Library is a copy of the order, with brackets added to set off the sentence that placed the troops under civilian control. There is no way of knowing whether Eisenhower saw the written order during the operation or received a copy later—whether he knew at the time, or later, that the rout did not represent the President's wishes. Yet even if the order was not available to him that afternoon, he had expressed his disapproval. In a more general context he later made the fol-

of Staff, G-2, 2d Corps Area, July 5, 1932, War Department, Records Division, RG 94, NA. Douglas MacArthur to The Secretary of War, August 15, 1932, "Report From the Chief of Staff to the Secretary of War on the Employment of Federal Troops in Civil Disturbance in the District of Columbia, July 28–30, 1932," p. 4, HP (hereafter cited as RCS). The Army Intelligence report was unconvincing in several respects. It contained no evidence that the rumor of gunmen had been carefully investigated or that precautions were being made to protect the nation's other large cities. Nor was any evidence ever produced to substantiate these rumors. Moreover, Waters was not a Communist; MacArthur in fact helped him to secure a job in the War Department three years later. *Evening Star*, January 22, 1935.

lowing assessment of MacArthur: "Most of the senior
officers I had known always drew a clean-cut line between the military and the political. Off duty, among
themselves and close civilian friends, they might explo-
sively denounce everything they thought was wrong in
Washington and the world, and propose their own cure
for its evils. On duty, nothing could induce them to cross
the line they, and old Army tradition, had established. But
if General MacArthur ever recognized the existence of
that line, he usually chose to ignore it." MacArthur's most
trusted subordinate, Deputy Chief of Staff Moseley, also
noted his dangerous "fault of believing that which fits in
with his personal ambitions and plans." Once he made up
his mind, there was nothing Eisenhower or anyone else
could do to dissuade MacArthur from his self-appointed
mission to save the Republic.[4]

Despite Glassford's own willingness in June to force
out the BEF, he suggested after the rout that the Army's
preparedness somehow proved the existence of a plot by
Hoover.[5] Troops and cavalry had undergone rigorous
training for riot duty in the event of any BEF emergency,
a precaution that may well have helped to save lives on
July 28 but for which the Army received little credit.
These precautions were understandable and do not prove
a conspiracy. There is no evidence that MacArthur consulted with Glassford about ways to coordinate the use of
troops with local police forces or that he contemplated the
possibility that the troops might be placed under civilian
control. The Army's plans went beyond aiding the local
police to maintain order, and an examination of these

4. Dwight D. Eisenhower, *At Ease: Stories I Tell to Friends* (New
York: Doubleday & Company, Inc., 1967), p. 216. For the marked copy
of the order, see Eisenhower Papers, 1916–1952, EL. While the working copies of *At Ease* are also at the Eisenhower Library, they are not
yet open to scholars. John Eisenhower checked the copies for the answers to several questions I asked concerning his father's account of
the rout and MacArthur's conduct as Chief of Staff. He found nothing
that adds to the published version. John S. D. Eisenhower to author,
July 25, 1972. George Van Horn Moseley, "One Soldier's Journey,"
unpublished diary, IV, 139, Moseley Papers, LC (hereafter cited as
GMP).
5. See Chapter 5, pp. 96, 102 and Chapter 12, pp. 266–67, 272–76.
New York *Journal American*, November 5, 1932.

preparations reveals the flaw which the advocates of a forced eviction, including MacArthur, Moseley, and Hurley, had failed to take into account. Although the various contingencies deployed the troops in different ways, the crucial factor in all of them was presidential approval of a proclamation declaring a state of insurrection. Thus, they greatly underestimated Hoover, the one man who had the power to scuttle these plans.

When MacArthur decided to drive out the BEF, he discarded previously arranged Army plans that, in the event of a serious disturbance, called for orderly transportation of the veterans to their home states in trucks upon the issuance of a presidential proclamation. He also rejected the advice of his Judge Advocate General on the legality of Army initiative and action. At some time on July 28 Judge Advocate General Blanton Winship sent MacArthur two long memos reviewing earlier discussions of the Army's proposal to truck the veterans back to their home states. Winship stated that on *"the discretion of the President, . . .* disturbances [might be termed] incipient insurrection or a threat thereof." In the earlier discussions to which Winship's memos referred, MacArthur probably had discussed dispersal, for Winship emphatically warned him that it was "obvious that a mere scattering of the members of this force at the places of their present encampments, or driving them beyond the borders of the District of Columbia, would not effect a permanent dispersion of the force, so as to bring the insurrection or threat of insurrection . . . to an end." [6] In the event of emergency the Army must transport all veterans to their homes under armed guard in Army trucks. For some time Hurley had favorably considered this plan and had urged Waters to let Army trucks take his men home. Waters, of course, refused.[7] It is impossible to say whether Mac-

6. My italics. Blanton Winship, "Memorandum for the Chief of Staff, Bonus Expeditionary Force," July 28, 1932; Blanton Winship, "Dispersion of the so-called Bonus Expeditionary Force by the Executive Power with the Employment of Military Force," July 28, 1932, HP. Also see PP 300, HHPL.

7. William D. Mitchell to HH, September 9, 1932, p. 10, PP 300, HHPL. The Attorney General's Report included this statement: "The

Arthur received Winship's memos before or after the riots of July 28, but the time is not important, for they establish the Army's prior examination and rejection of merely dispersing "insurrectionists."

Winship had emphasized to MacArthur that before the Army could act, Hoover must issue a proclamation declaring a state of insurrection. If this were done, it would remove legal restrictions against MacArthur's use of military force to restore law and order. Then not even writs of habeas corpus from federal courts could stop the Army from trucking the men back home. MacArthur and other Army leaders evidently tended to equate disorder with insurrection, for they had not prepared options for alternative uses of the troops. Instead, when the riot occurred, the Judge Advocate General drafted the insurrection proclamation, apparently confident that Hoover would sign it.[8]

Even with "a riotous condition" on his hands, however, the President was no more enthusiastic about the Army's plans on July 28 than he had been in early June during the red scare. At the White House conference of July 27, Hurley prevailed on Hoover to alert the troops, but Hoover set exact limitations on the possible use of troops, and these were then leaked to the press. Hoover stubbornly refused to give the Army carte blanche. On July 28 Hurley urged him to sign the proclamation and declare martial law, thus clearing the way for the Army to disperse the protesters, but Hoover would neither consider the disturbances as insurrection nor make the Army responsible for restoring peace.[9]

Secretary of War conferred with their leaders and urged them to disband, and made a definite offer to furnish them with Army trucks for part of the transportation and to arrange with National Guard units to transport them across the states and still they declined to leave." In 1949 Hurley claimed they had accepted the offer. Hurley to Otis Lee Wiese, August 5, 1949, MacArthur Papers (hereafter cited as MP).

8. Winship Memorandum, July 28, 1932, HP. The insurrection proclamation and Hurley's advice is in Hurley to HH, July 28, 1932, PP 300, HHPL.

9. Hurley to HH, July 28, 1932, PP 300, HHPL. Insisting that Hoover had ordered the rout, Bennett M. Rich was critical of Hoover for not issuing a proclamation warning of the coming of troops. See Rich, *Presidents and Civil Disorders*, pp. 174–75.

Critics have faulted Hoover for not signing a proclamation before unleashing the Army against the marchers.
They have failed to realize that Hoover would not sign
any document that would give the Army sweeping latitude. If Hoover had quickly grasped a flimsy pretext to
send troops against the marchers, one might suspect that
the President may not have received the insurrection
proclamation before he ordered the troops into action.
That speculation runs counter to the logic of the situation.
It was in the advantage of Hurley and the Army to press
Hoover to sign the document that would sanction the
Army's plans. Hoover was in fact so deeply skeptical of
Hurley's claims of insurrection that he refused to sign either the original or a revised form of the insurrection
proclamation, both of which can be found in the Hoover
Papers.[10] Three telephone exchanges with Hurley between 1:24 P.M. and 2:37 P.M. failed to change the President's mind. (During that period Hoover also conferred
with the Attorney General.) The troop alert and assembly
call had been issued immediately after the shootings, but
it was by no means inevitable that the troops would be
released. The fact has not been recognized that between
the time of the shootings and the time the troop deployment order was finally issued at 2:55 P.M., immense pressures were brought to bear upon the President. Indeed,
Hoover was so reluctant to sign an insurrection proclamation that Hurley decided to call upon MacArthur to help
persuade him.

When MacArthur arrived at the White House, Hurley
was waiting for him outside the Oval Office. George Drescher, a White House Secret Service agent who was on

10. Rich, *Presidents and Civil Disorders*, pp. 174–75; Daniels,
Bonus March, pp. 161–62 and note 6, p. 331. Daniels does not indicate
that the proclamation was one that was to be used in the event of insurrection; neither does he point out that it was revised, but again rejected, or that Hoover and Hurley also conversed by telephone at least
three different times between 1:24 P.M. and 2:37 P.M. To assume that
they did not discuss the two copies of the insurrection proclamation,
which Hurley had prepared and urged Hoover to approve, is hardly
plausible. President's Telephone Memorandum, July 28, 1932, HHPL,
also note 11.

duty at the time, witnessed Hurley's instructions to Mac-
Arthur. According to Drescher, these instructions were
firm: "You go in and tell the President," he instructed
MacArthur, that "you're just back from the demonstration" and that as the Metropolitan Police could not
cope with the disorders, the President must "send the
troops in." [11]

After Hurley and MacArthur entered Hoover's office,
Drescher tried to convince Lawrence Richey, himself a
former Secret Service agent, that the use of troops would
be a grave mistake. Drescher was convinced that Hurley
and MacArthur were giving the President bad advice.
More important, the fact that Hurley and MacArthur felt
compelled to exert combined personal pressure on the
President is a significant and previously unknown fact.
Quite possibly Hurley and MacArthur's plea, not the
Commissioners' earlier letter, was the decisive factor in
convincing Hoover that the summoned troops must be
used. Equally plausible is the possibility that Hoover ordered MacArthur to take personal command because
Hoover felt that he would best handle the troops in a deli-
cate situation.[12] Hoover had always trusted and highly
regarded his Chief of Staff and may have felt him best
qualified to exercise restraint. There is no record of what
happened in the Oval Office, but it is most significant that
even under intense pressure from Hurley and MacArthur,

11. George C. Drescher, Oral History Interview, June 1, 1967,
HHPL. Several months after this interview Dwight Miller, the senior
archivist at the Herbert Hoover Presidential Library, interviewed Drescher for two hours. Mr. Miller verified that Drescher's recall was "un-
hesitating and precise." Dwight W. Miller to author, March 17, 1972.
Drescher died on January 22, 1971, several months before his oral interview was transcribed and became available to scholars. Because of
the importance of his account I communicated also with Raymond
Henle, director of the Herbert Hoover Oral History Program, who reinforced Miller's statement of Drescher's reliability. Raymond Henle to
author, March 20, 1972.

12. Drescher interview. Hoover, *Memoirs*, III, 226; Douglas Mac-
Arthur, *Reminiscences* (New York: McGraw-Hill, 1964), p. 95; Perry
L. Miles, *Fallen Leaves: Memories of An Old Soldier* (Berkeley, Calif.:
Wuerth Publishing Company, 1961), p. 307.

Hoover remained adamant in his refusal to sign an insurrection proclamation or to accede to other Army measures. As a substitute, he gave Hurley and MacArthur clear and explicit instructions of his own.

The first plan Hoover communicated on July 28 severely limited the Army's responsibility. The President ordered the troops to clear the downtown area near the riot site at Third and Pennsylvania and then to herd the rioters back to their camps, where investigations would be conducted. To Washington's reporters the evening before, Hoover had leaked his exact plans for the limited evacuation the next day and the course of action in the event that an emergency required troops. The news stories stressed Hoover's firm hope that no incidents would occur and that troops would not be needed. If an emergency should occur, the Army's role was to be decidedly limited, involving only the movement of the protesters back to their camps for investigation. The plan described on July 27 in the newspapers matched Hoover's actual orders the next day and also his later account of them in his *Memoirs*.[13]

It is obvious that Hurley completely understood the President, for his first draft of the troop order directed MacArthur: "After having cleared the area where the riot had just occurred, you will maintain contact with the rioters until they have crossed the Anacostia Bridge, order them into the veterans' camps in Anacostia. Surround all veteran camps in Anacostia and hold all campers, rioters and marchers until the names of all of them can be tabulated and their fingerprints taken." Hurley concluded: "Those who have incited riot and *death* will then be arrested and delivered over to civil authorities for prosecution." Hurley's original draft varied from Hoover's stated plan in only one respect: The President ordered the men returned to their camps—granted, a difficult and confusing process; Hurley instructed MacArthur to force all the rioters back to the huge Anacostia camp and hold them

13. Hoover, *Memoirs*, III, 226–27. Also see Chapter 8, pp. 159–62, and Lisio, "A Blunder Becomes Catastrophe," pp. 39–42.

there. Indeed, except for this divergence, Hurley's draft exactly followed the President's instructions.[14]

The final order, which Hurley actually sent to MacArthur, expressed still further concern for a limited and humane use of troops. Stricken from the original draft was the first paragraph, which had echoed Hurley's belief that "the purpose of these non-veterans is to incite further riot, bloodshed and murder." The final order reflected Hoover's view that the rioting was a civil rather than a military matter, an issue of law and order to be settled by civil authorities and civil courts rather than by troops and martial law. This order clearly stated that the Army was merely to *"cooperate fully with the District of Columbia police force which is now in charge."* Therefore, Glassford—not MacArthur—was to determine the nature and extent of the Army's responsibility. Furthermore, the final order did not mention herding the veterans back to Anacostia but instructed the troops to "surround the *affected* area," clearing it without delay and turning over "all prisoners *to the civil authorities.*" "In your orders," the dispatch continued, "insist that any women and children who may be in the affected area be accorded every consideration and kindness. Use all humanity consistent with the due execution of this order." [15] Joslin, in his account, insisted that Hoover was so reluctant to commit troops that he suggested having the soldiers carry police sticks rather than firearms. According to another version, Hurley declined the use of "peace clubs" because "there were

14. My italics. The order is marked NOT SENT and initialed by Hurley. It is in a folder labeled "July 28, 1932," in HP. This first draft of the order further established that the administration was responding to the shootings rather than to the brick battle, where no deaths had occurred. Lisio, "A Blunder Becomes Catastrophe," p. 41.

15. Folder, July 28, 1932, HP. The final order is cited as Hurley to MacArthur, July 28, 1932, War Department, Office of The Adjutant General, RG 94, NA. My italics. The exact time at which the order was issued, 2:55 P.M., was added in ink. Lisio, "A Blunder Becomes Catastrophe," p. 41, discusses both drafts of the order; Daniels, *The Bonus March*, p. 167, discusses only the final draft. Despite the clear restraint of the final order, however, Daniels contends that Hoover feared revolution and that he used troops against the BEF at the slightest pretext (p. 172).

only 600 soldiers against thousands of bonuseers. I didn't want to see the United States Army defeated by a mob." [16]

The final troop deployment order was indeed more restrained than Hurley's original draft. Hoover was not to approve the revised directive until 2:55 P.M., one hour and fifteen minutes after MacArthur had summoned his troops to assemble at the Ellipse, and approximately an hour and a half after the shootings. Despite their best efforts neither Hurley nor MacArthur was able to persuade Hoover to sign the insurrection proclamation. Since Hoover had carefully placed the troops under civilian control, such a proclamation was not necessary. The contrast between the final order and the proposed insurrection proclamation was so great that it amounted to a clear rebuke.

Don Lohbeck, Hurley's authorized biographer, supports Hoover's explanation. Lohbeck admits that the President had stated "certain methods for suppressing the riot," with which Hurley did not agree. He further admits that Hoover's order limited Hurley and that "Hurley did not comply" with Hoover's methods for suppressing the riot. Then he rather feebly tries to defend Hurley by arguing that the President's instructions were not in writing and "not in the form of a directive or order." [17] Lohbeck's defense is very shaky, for an examination of both the drafted and final versions of the order establishes that Hurley fully understood Hoover's directions and that neither Hurley nor the Army was given a free hand. Nevertheless, soon after 2:55 P.M., when the order was issued to MacArthur, the Chief of Staff decided to force the veterans out.

The reasoning behind MacArthur's decision was pa-

16. Joslin, *Hoover*, p. 268. W. L. White, "Story of a Smear," *The Reader's Digest*, 59 (December 1951), 53. White claimed that both Hoover and Hurley remembered that Hoover had requested the use of sticks rather than guns. Both White and Joslin agree on this point and neither Hoover nor Hurley objected to its accuracy. Despite the later official insistence on insurrection, Hoover obviously was not frightened or concerned about taking special precautions against revolutionaries.

17. Don Lohbeck, *Patrick J. Hurley* (Chicago: Henry Regnery Company, 1956), pp. 110, 112, 487.

tently faulty. From the time of the shooting incident until
the troops arrived at the eviction site, well over three
hours later, there had been no additional violence. Mac-
Arthur had no good reason to sweep far beyond the eviction site and drive defenseless families out of their shelters. Many of them had not been at the scene of the
downtown riot, and there was no evidence of insurrection
or of Communist efforts to create violence. To be sure, the
huge crowd had ignored police requests to disperse. The
greatly outnumbered and frightened police force obviously needed some assistance to clear the affected area,
and that is what Hoover's order provided.

When MacArthur received the order, he realized that
Hoover had thwarted the Army's plans that had been
based on the insurrection proclamation. MacArthur thus
concluded that forced dispersion became "the only logical answer." Despite the order's specific instruction, he
did not consult with Glassford about possible alternative
methods of dealing with the crowds. Instead, within less
than an hour after receiving the order and well before all
of his troops had arrived at the Ellipse, MacArthur informed Glassford that he intended to drive out the Bonus
Army.[18]

From his office in the State War and Navy Building he
had earlier reached Brig. Gen. Perry L. Miles, the commanding officer of the Sixteenth Brigade, who was to
serve as field commander. MacArthur ordered Miles to assemble his men and equipment at the Ellipse behind the
White House. An hour later fully equipped troops began
pouring out of Fort Myer and Fort Washington, two
nearby Army posts. As Glassford talked with MacArthur
the soldiers continued to arrive at the Ellipse. An entire
battalion of infantry, one squadron of cavalry, one platoon
of tanks, and one machine-gun unit comprised the spe-
cially trained riot force—520 men, 35 officers, and numerous horses, trucks, and other paraphernalia. At the
same time reserve units from three other forts in Maryland and Virginia hurried to Fort Myer. The large, heavily

18. RCS, pp. 4, 6.

armed force presented a frightening display of military power with which MacArthur intended to convince even the most belligerent veteran that resistance was hopeless. By 4:30 that afternoon, almost three hours after Mac-Arthur's assembly order, the U.S. Army was ready to march against its former comrades-in-arms. Half an hour later the foot soldiers, cavalry, and tanks had moved from the Ellipse into the troubled area.[19]

MacArthur planned first to clear the eviction site near the Capitol Building at Third and Pennsylvania avenues, where the riot earlier that day had taken place. Next, he would push the veterans in a general southwesterly direction, blocking off access to the White House and Capitol Hill, and move against the Communist camp at Thirteenth and B streets. Then, after feeding and resting his troops, he would complete the operation by clearing everyone from the huge camp on the Anacostia flats.[20]

19. The most complete presentation of troop movements is the report of the field commander Gen. Perry L. Miles. P. L. Miles to Douglas MacArthur, "Report of Operations Against Bonus Marchers," August 4, 1932, PP 300, HHPL, pp. 1–3 (hereafter cited as Miles, "Report"). MacArthur's detailed account in RCS reveals more about the Chief of Staff's rationale. The training of the riot troops is discussed by Maj. A. D. Surles, "Memorandum Report on Bonus Riot to Commanding General 16th Brigade," Records of the U.S. Army Continental Commands, 1920–1942, Selected Documents, 1932, RG 394, NA (hereafter cited as Records of U.S. Army).

20. RCS, pp. 5–7. D. Clayton James, MacArthur's biographer, defends MacArthur against charges of brutality and argues that "MacArthur's only active participation in the operation was his order to continue the advance across the Anacostia Bridge." D. Clayton James, *The Years of MacArthur* (Boston: Houghton Mifflin Company, 1970), p. 410. James does not cite my 1967 article, which established that MacArthur knowingly disobeyed written orders. James F. Vivian and Jean H. Vivian deserve recognition for first publishing Gen. George Van Horn Moseley's role in the operation; James F. Vivian and Jean H. Vivian, "The Bonus March of 1932: The Role of General George Van Horn Moseley," *Wisconsin Magazine of History*, 51 (Autumn 1967), 26–36. More important, while the issue of the use of brutality must remain debatable, the evidence that MacArthur was in active command throughout the entire operation is overwhelming. His "only active participation" was not, as James argues, limited to disobeying orders not to cross the bridge; he repeatedly issued orders to Miles and personally supervised their implementation. MacArthur's Assistant Chief of Staff, Gen. George Van Horn Moseley, had no doubts about who was

Just before he moved his troops down Pennsylvania Avenue, MacArthur informed Glassford that he "had orders from the Chief Executive to drive the veterans out of the city. . . . We are going to break the back of the BEF," he informed the Chief. "Within a short time we will move down Pennsylvania Avenue, sweep through the billets there, and then clean out the other two big camps. The operation will be continuous. It will all be done tonight." He then sent Glassford on a special mission to notify the bonus leaders that all camps on federal property must be evacuated before nightfall.[21] Finally, with the impressively disciplined cavalry in the lead, followed by six tanks and the steady tread of massed infantry, the riot force began its advance. At the eviction site one reporter recalled that many of the veterans were "very militant. A few were drinking. . . . The crowds were milling, and the police were nervous and upset." The military spectacle, like a parade, drew crowds, who watched the approaching troops with grim fascination.[22] Ignoring the earlier fatalities, few of the onlookers believed that either the infantry or cavalry would attack them. In fact, when the troops first arrived, the sightseers greeted them with cheers and applause. Once again the huge crowd anticipated another fascinating semicomic melodrama between the BEF and the government.[23]

---

in command, for he later congratulated MacArthur: "Later when the test came, you executed a perfect solution to the problem." Moseley to MacArthur, November 3, 1942, RG 10, MP; Miles, *Fallen Leaves*, pp. 308–9. PDG to Hoover, n.d., draft letter, GP. Glassford did not send this letter but in it he stated that MacArthur "was at all times in direct control of the troop operation carrying out his masterful plan of eviction."

21. RCS, p. 6; PDG to MacArthur, April 26, 1951, MP. Interview in the Laguna Beach (California) *Post*, April 15, 1951, which Glassford sent to MacArthur. Glassford quoted MacArthur in a radio network speech to a veterans' meeting in Philadelphia at the height of the election campaign. *Evening Star*, November 4, 1932. For Washington, D.C., newspapers the city is omitted from the citation. The full quotation is from the Hearst exposé, which Glassford wrote after he resigned. New York *Journal-American*, November 5, 1932.

22. Memoir of Samuel B. Bledsoe, the Oral History Collection of Columbia University, I, 44. Jack Douglas, *Veterans On the March* (New York: Workers Library Publishers, 1934), p. 6.

23. *Evening Star*, July 29, 1932.

MacArthur's first priority should have been an attempt to control and gradually clear the crowds peaceably. After that, if he did not agree with the President's order to surround the affected area, he could have requested further instructions on how to deal with the more recalcitrant veterans who occupied the buildings. To be sure, some of the veterans outside might also have resisted efforts to separate and gradually remove the crowd, but as Mac-Arthur never attempted it, the degree of resistance he might have met remains problematical. Instead, he methodically deployed his men at the eviction site and, he later insisted, issued verbal warnings for the crowd to leave immediately. Many members of the crowd heard no orders, however, and they later insisted that they had never been issued. Unworried spectators watched General Miles march his troops back and forth for thirty minutes until they were in their exact positions for the attack. By this time the encounter appeared to be a standoff. Then, at about 5:30, 200 soldiers suddenly moved in to evacuate a building at Third and Pennsylvania, and a group of veterans, shouting defiance, let loose a hail of bricks. The troops immediately retreated, donned gas masks, and within minutes attacked veterans and spectators alike with tear gas, bayonets, and cavalry charges.[24] MacArthur did not deal separately with the entrenched veterans and the curious spectators, and he failed to surround and imprison the resisters, to be turned over to civilian authorities. Instead, he forced the resisters into the

---

24. New York *Times*, July 29, 1932; RCS, p. 7; "Memorandum of Testimony Presented to the Grand Jury," Department of Justice, File 95-16-26, RG 60, NA (hereafter cited as MTGJ). "Glassford, Testimony Before the Grand Jury," PP 300, HHPL, pp. 6–7 (hereafter cited as GT); Miles, "Report," p. 4; New York *Times*, July 29, 1932. *Time* incorrectly reported that, immediately upon their arrival, the troops attacked the veterans and spectators without any warning; the *New Republic* created the same impression; "The Battle of Washington," *Time*, 20 (August 8, 1932), 6; "In the Rear of the B.E.F. During the Washington Battle," *New Republic*, 71 (August 10, 1932), 326; John D. Weaver, "Bonus March," *American Heritage*, 14 (June 1963), 94. Later, Glassford could not recall his testimony before the grand jury and denied that the veterans had earlier hurled bricks or were obstinate. See Glassford's marginal annotations of Theodore J. Joslin, "Hoover Off The Record," *Redbook*, 60 (October 1934), 20, GP 679.

street, mixed them with the crowd, and indiscriminately attacked them all.

The attack at first surprised and then infuriated the spectators. Forced out into the streets, the veterans and some of the onlookers hurled tear gas bombs back at the soldiers. Then, terrified by the charging, saber-swinging cavalry and the slow but relentless advance of the infantry, many of them, panic-stricken, scurried off to the southwest, while soldiers quickly cut off access to the White House and the Capitol.[25] Almost immediately the troops felt the full measure of the shock and hatred directed against them by veterans and bystanders alike. Under the barrage of insults and profanity they became annoyed, then "thoroughly angry" at what they considered to be the universal expression of contempt. Maj. George Patton became furious, and his cavalry launched one or two punishing charges against resisters.[26] At several points, notably at Maine and Missouri avenues and Maryland Avenue and C Street, large concentrations of the civilians, pursued relentlessly by the military, retaliated with showers of bricks, striking at the soldiers whenever there was opportunity. These groups became so hostile that several officers expected them to organize a counterattack.[27]

"Yellow! Yellow!" taunted the crowd, both daring and rebuking the troops.[28] At first some of the soldiers took

25. RCS, p. 7; MTGJ, p. 52; GTGJ, pp. 6–7.

26. Martin Blumenson, ed., *The Patton Papers 1885–1940*, 2 vols. (Boston: Houghton Mifflin, 1972), I, 894–97. Patton was angered by the resistance and used the flat of his saber freely.

27. Surles, "Memorandum Report"; Lt. Col. L. A. Kunzig, "Summary Report," July 30, 1932, Records of U.S. Army; "Summary of Events, 2d Squadron, Third Cavalry," Records of U.S. Army. The detailed reports of battalion and company commanders fully reveal the extent of the resentment against the troops. The cavalry justified the use of drawn sabers, in part at least, as a means to prevent rioters from grabbing the horses' reins and unseating the troopers. H. W. Blakeley, "When the Army Was Smeared," *Combat Forces Journal*, 2 (February 1952), 29. Night sticks would have served the same purpose.

28. Quoted from the Baltimore *Sun*, July 29, 1932, in Louis L. Snyder and Richard B. Morris, eds., *A Treasury of Great Reporting* (New York: Simon and Schuster, 1949), p. 480.

the taunts in good humor, but soon, enraged, they stepped up the attack. The cavalry, jabbing, slashing, whacking with their sabers, were followed by a wall of determined infantrymen pushing and prodding with their bayonets as they advanced through the blue haze of tear gas. Mac-Arthur's assault proceeded with a precision and efficiency that was too much for even the most recalcitrant veterans. The retreating veterans and then the soldiers set fire to some of the huts, and the flimsy shacks burned quickly. One tattered man begged a soldier to let him return to his hut where all of his money was hidden, but the mounted trooper shouted him away and rode his horse into the man. A popcorn vender whose machine was stalled received the warning to start it quickly or it would be no good to him. A drunk, finding it difficult to steer any course, was told to get moving. He tried to argue, but a stiff beating with a saber changed his mind. At a gasoline station nearby a newspaper reporter was phoning in his story. "Out of there!" yelled a trooper, but the reporter continued to send his message; into the station sailed a gas bomb. The efforts of a few of the pursued to return the whizzing bombs had little effect on the well-equipped, stubbornly advancing troops. There was nothing to do but grab what possessions they could and run.[29]

General MacArthur, resplendent in his immaculate uniform, directed his riot force with evident pride. The disbelief, terror, anger, and brutality that surrounded him was no doubt mild in comparison with his earlier war experiences. Everything was proceeding smoothly. As he planned, he moved his men after the fleeing crowds until they reached the second objective, the Communist camp at Thirteenth and C streets. Along the way, several smaller camps were routed and the huts set on fire by

29. A thorough investigation reveals that both the marchers and the soldiers set fire to the huts. MacArthur to the Attorney General, August 2, 1932, HP; RCS, p. 9; MTGJ, pp. 57–59, 85, 121; GT, p. 19; Dwight D. Eisenhower, *At Ease*, p. 217; Kunzig, "Summary Report, July 30, 1932." Snyder and Morris, *Great Reporting*, pp. 479–83. While Bledsoe was telephoning his report to his newspapers a young cavalry trooper attacked him with the flat of his saber. Bledsoe, *Memoir*, I, 45, Oral History Collection of Columbia University.

both the retreating veterans and the soldiers. The Communists had already evacuated their camp, and as the crowds were dispersing without further difficulty, the Chief of Staff halted his men at 6:30 P.M. for over two and a half hours to feed and rest them. During the lull MacArthur reportedly refused a request from the District Commissioners to evict veterans from small camps located near the Library of Congress. He also recalled his refusal of Glassford's request to remove squatters near the Seventh Street wharves. His strategy remained direct and unchanged; the next and final objective was the huge camp on the Anacostia flats.[30]

While his troops relaxed, MacArthur directed Glassford to inform the inhabitants of the Anacostia camp to evacuate immediately. Army Intelligence reports, later confirmed by several police eyewitnesses, indicated that Eddie Atwell had delivered an emotional speech to the campers, urging them to gather firearms and vowing to kill the first soldier who entered the camp. However, those reports neither deterred nor hurried MacArthur. If MacArthur feared insurrection, he had ample opportunity during this break in the operation to go to the President and attempt to convince him to change the order and allow complete dispersal. But MacArthur did not do this. At 9:10 P.M., after the troops had been fed and rested, the advance toward the last big camp resumed.[31]

30. Paul Anderson incorrectly assumed that MacArthur delayed the troop movement to the eviction site for one hour while waiting for his full-dress uniform to be delivered to him. Paul Anderson, "Tear Gas, Bayonets, and Votes: The President Opens His Reelection Campaign," *Nation*, 135 (August 17, 1932), pp. 138–40. For a photograph of MacArthur supervising the rout, see my article, "A Blunder Becomes Catastrophe," p. 41. RCS, pp. 7–8; MacArthur to The Attorney General, August 6, 1932, HP.

31. MacArthur to The Attorney General, August 6, 1932, HP. Clement H. Wright, "Memorandum For Chief of Staff," July 28, 1932, Records of U.S. Army; MTGJ, pp. 62–63, 103, 136–37, 192–93; GT, p. 10. Wright informed MacArthur that Atwell had instructed his men to fire on the first troops to cross the Anacostia Bridge. Police Lt. Roy D. Kelly testified that Atwell not only refused to evacuate the camp, but predicted that "someone is going to die tonight." Reports of his repeated defiance were reiterated by newsmen. The *Post* claimed that Atwell shouted, "We will kill the first man that steps over the line,"

As the troops approached the Eleventh Street Bridge, the crowds lining nearby streets shouted insults, and individual attacks on soldiers became common. The New York *Times* reported that the real battle took place then, on the drive toward Anacostia: "Down toward Anacostia the troops went, in a bruising affair all the way, with persons in the streets swinging blows at the soldiers as they swept past, the cavalry wielding sabers and the infantry prodding with bayonets." General Miles quickly positioned his units according to plan, and Glassford assumed the responsibility for controlling the spectators. To clear the area near the bridge Glassford personally directed a gas assault against the crowd. MacArthur later recalled the Chief's attack with pride, but those spectators who had dutifully obeyed police orders, only to find themselves surrounded by gas bombs anyway, did not share the General's enthusiasm.[32]

Earlier, while the troops cleared the downtown area, Hoover fretted. According to Joslin, who maintained telephone communication with military officers, the Secret Service, police, and newspapers, Hoover's first question "invariably . . . was whether anyone had been hurt, and each time he received with a sigh of relief the information that the expedition was proceeding without untoward incident." [33] At some point during the evening, however, Hoover realized that MacArthur was disregarding his orders, and he acted to stop the rout. Waters believed that a newsman had called Senator William E. Borah, Senator James E. Watson, and Representative Kenneth D. McKellar, urging them to plead with the President. The New

and that the veterans were armed and ready to repel the troops. *Post*, July 29, 1932. The claim that the veterans were armed, however, has never been substantiated.

32. New York *Times*, July 30, 1932. Miles, "Report," pp. 6–7. MacArthur to The Attorney General, August 6, 1932, HP; RCS, p. 11. M. S. Breckenridge, "The Victory At Anacostia," *New Republic*, 72 (August 17, 1932), 20.

33. Joslin, *Hoover*, p. 275. Katurah Brooks and Phillips S. Brooks, Oral History Interview, September 1, 1970, HHPL. Mrs. Brooks was a maid in the White House, and her husband was one of the butlers. Both recall the regularity with which MacArthur's staff car arrived at the White House bearing reports during the rout.

York *Times* claimed that Senator Borah, at least, had called Hoover in the evening of July 28 to protest the troop movement and had been told that no eviction would take place that night.[34] Whatever his source of information, as soon as Hoover realized that MacArthur was ignoring his instructions, he determined that he must be stopped.

Hoover immediately told Hurley to forbid the troops to cross the Anacostia Bridge leading into the camp, and Hurley relayed the order. Rather than send a written directive, he dispatched Deputy Chief of Staff Moseley to inform MacArthur of the President's instructions. Moseley shared Hurley and MacArthur's view of the protesters, but, according to his own account, he clearly delivered the order: "Mr. Hurley . . . directed me to inform General MacArthur that the President did not wish the troops to cross the bridge that night, to force the evacuation of the Anacostia camp. I left my office, contacted General MacArthur, and as we walked away, alone, from the others, I delivered that message to him and discussed it with him. He was very much annoyed in having his plans interfered with in any way until they were executed completely." [35] Eisenhower, who was with MacArthur, confirmed that the orders arrived. At one point, he added, MacArthur snapped that he was "too busy" and did "not want either himself or his staff bothered by people coming down and *pretending* to bring orders." [36] It is clear that MacArthur

34. Walter W. Waters, *B.E.F.: The Whole Story of the Bonus Army* (New York: The John Day Company, Inc., 1933), pp. 231–32; New York *Times*, July 30, 1932. My examination of the Borah Papers at the Library of Congress did not uncover any references to the rout. Neither the Borah Papers at the Idaho State Historical Society nor the McKellar Papers contain any references to the BEF; Merle W. Wells, director, Idaho State Historical Society to author, December 9, 1969; Mrs. Sue Wise, librarian, Memphis Tennessee Public Library to author, December 9, 1969. The same is true for the Edward P. Costigan Papers at the University of Colorado; A.D. Mastroguiseppe, Jr., to author, October 29, 1971. James E. Watson's account is thoroughly confused. See Chapter 8, footnote 43.

35. George Van Horn Moseley, "One Soldier's Journey," II, 144–45, MP. Vivian and Vivian, "The Bonus March of 1932," pp. 26–36.

36. My italics. Eisenhower, *At Ease*, pp. 217–18.

had fully understood the President's orders repeated by his Deputy Chief of Staff and that he could have appealed to the President if he disagreed. As Moseley put it, "After assuring myself that he understood the message, I left him." Apologetically he added, "As I told him, I was only instructed to deliver the message to him, and having done that, I returned to my office." Almost equally revealing, Moseley claimed, "Later, I was asked from the White House if I had delivered the message, and stated that I had. Still later, I was instructed to repeat the message and assure myself that General MacArthur received it before he crossed the Anacostia Bridge." [37]

This time Moseley sent Col. Clement B. Wright, who delivered the same order. One must question Hurley's judgment in not sending a written directive the first time, but there can be no doubt that the Chief of Staff received the instructions. Years later even MacArthur admitted this.[38]

37. Moseley, "One Soldier's Journey," pp. 144–45. Dwight D. Eisenhower, July 13, 1967, Oral History Collection, HHPL. F. Trubee Davison reported that another Assistant Secretary of War, Frederick H. Payne, and Moseley may have been trying to cover up for MacArthur by suggesting that a messenger had been intercepted. Davison at first thought that only one messenger had been involved, but he shrewdly guessed that MacArthur received the order "verbally, not in writing, through this messenger, or Payne, or Moseley or somebody else." Davison interview, Oral History Project, HHPL. Moseley later corrected the interception story in his detailed private diary, "One Soldier's Journey." Considering the accounts of Eisenhower, Moseley, and Miles (see pp. 212–13), and MacArthur's admission that he received the order, the insubordination is irrefutable. Further, MacArthur had already exceeded Hoover's written order limiting his action to surrounding and clearing the affected area.

38. MacArthur, *Reminiscences*, p. 95. MacArthur recalled that at "the Anacostia Flats I received word from the Secretary of War, as we were in the midst of crossing the river, to suspend the operation at my discretion. I halted the command as soon as we had cleared the bridge, but at that moment the rioters set fire to their own camp. This concluded the proceedings for the night." This version does not coincide with either the Moseley or the Eisenhower account. In his oral interview Eisenhower recalled that Hoover had sent both Moseley and Wright with the order: "Don't allow any of the troops to go across the Anacostia Bridge"; Eisenhower Interview, July 13, 1967, Oral History Collection, HHPL. If MacArthur was not in "active participation," as James insists, one wonders why Hoover's repeated orders were sent to him rather than to General Miles; James, *MacArthur*, p. 410, and especially note 20, Chapter 13.

Moseley revealed that "Colonel Wright contacted General MacArthur immediately, and explained the situation to him fully. . . . Colonel Wright reported to me that the troops had not crossed the Anacostia Bridge, but were advancing on the bridge." [39] The written order of 2:55 had stated Hoover's instructions succinctly enough, and both officers Moseley and Wright repeated the President's intent that same evening, but MacArthur refused to be stopped. Earlier, feigning that he was acting on presidential orders, he expressed his determination to Glassford: "It will all be done tonight."

General Miles, the officer in immediate command of the troops, also verified that the President's instructions were received near the Anacostia Bridge. In an account which he later wrote at MacArthur's personal request, and which was personally corrected and approved by MacArthur, Miles stated that the Chief of Staff "in what the world has since learned is a characteristic way, sent word back that it was too late to abandon the operation, that the troops were committed, that we had encountered no machine guns, and that some of the troops [the leading elements] had crossed the bridge already." [40] Obviously the "leading elements" could have been recalled, especially as they met no armed resistance; equally clear was the lack of any danger to the troops or evidence of revolution.

After MacArthur crossed the bridge, he once again had ample opportunity to ponder Hoover's orders. According to Miles, "Before our troops had completed the approach to their respective positions, a man, claiming to have come from the camp commander arrived at my car seeking Gen. MacArthur." That man was Eddie Atwell, who had realized the futility of his earlier call to arms. Carrying a white flag, he approached the Chief of Staff to beg an hour's delay to allow an orderly evacuation of the entire camp. Miles "recommended a further delay on our part,"

39. Moseley, "One Soldier's Journey," p. 145.
40. See p. 204. Miles, *Fallen Leaves*, p. 309. Miles's account directly contradicts Lohbeck's claim in his biography, *Hurley*, p. 112. According to Miles there would have been no need to fear bivouacking the troops "under the guns of traitors."

believing that it "would make no foreseeable difference in the ultimate eviction." [41] MacArthur immediately agreed—a questionable decision if he feared that his troops risked attack from well-armed traitors. Moreover, considering the messages MacArthur had received from Moseley and Wright, he should have told Atwell that the BEF would not be required to evacuate the Anacostia camp that night and should have instructed him to inform the other occupants, but he did not. Thus, although MacArthur had claimed that it was "too late" to obey a presidential order, it was not too late to grant an hour's delay in the action. More important than Hoover's orders was MacArthur's determination to evict the BEF.

As MacArthur moved his forces across the bridge, Atwell approached him, received the hour's delay, and was to claim credit for personally supervising an orderly retreat well before the soldiers started their final mopping-up operations later that night. Although MacArthur granted the delay, his troops continued to surge across the bridge and to position themselves for attack. The protesters, terrified by the huge force, retreated into the night, leaving their burning huts behind them. According to Eisenhower, "While no troops went more than two or three hundred yards over the bridge, then that whole encampment started to blaze." Setting fire to their own huts was a last desperate gesture of defiance, "a pitiful scene," Eisenhower recalled, "these ragged, discouraged people burning their own little things." [42] MacArthur thereby ac-

41. Miles, *Fallen Leaves,* pp. 309–10.
42. Atwell's account is in *B.E.F. News,* August 6, 1932. This is also cited in Glassford's "Foreword" to Atwell, *Washington, the Battle Ground: The Truth About the Bonus Riots* (Patriotic Publishing Society, 1933). Eisenhower, *At Ease,* pp. 217–18, and Oral History, HHPL. MacArthur included the details in RCS, p. 8. D. Clayton James argues that MacArthur's decision to disobey orders may have been prompted by intelligence reports that the veterans were preparing to fire on the soldiers as they crossed the bridge. If MacArthur expected armed resistance, he could easily have sent scouts or patrols to ascertain the accuracy of the reports, but he did not. The facts suggest instead that MacArthur was not overly concerned about rumors of a bloodbath. James, *MacArthur,* pp. 401–2, 410; note 40 and Moseley to MacArthur, November 3, 1942, MacArthur Papers.

complished his final objective without another bruising assault. Seeing their makeshift homes at Anacostia ablaze, the veterans at Camp Marks fled while the Washington sky glowed with the orange haze of burning huts and tents.

Beyond the shadow of doubt, MacArthur was insubordinate—not for the last time in his famous but erratic career. He would not limit himself to clearing the riot site at Third and Pennsylvania or to surrounding and then surrendering resisters to civil authorities. He ignored repeated orders, attacked marchers and spectators, crossed the bridge leading to the large encampment, and harassed the beaten bonus marchers out of the city, along with their wives and children. Later, he would defend his actions with the statement that he could not permit his army to "bivouac under the guns of traitors." [43]

As the BEF retreated, MacArthur concluded that he had broken the back of the "revolt." He left General Miles at the outskirts of the emptying camp, under orders to make a sweep through it later that night and evict the few remaining stragglers. Soldiers eventually added their own torches to the shantytown and dispersed rock-throwing spectators at the edge of the camp, but for the present little else remained to be done. MacArthur told Eisenhower and reporters on the scene that "this concluded proceedings for the night." Then the Chief of Staff gave Eisenhower a ride back to town and dismissed him for the night. Eisenhower advised him against meeting the press. It "would be the better part of wisdom, if not valor," he urged, as this was a political matter best left to the politicians.[44] MacArthur would not be dissuaded, however, and he triumphantly hurried to the White House.

After years of experience with public relations, he had

43. Lohbeck, *Hurley*, p. 112. Evidence gathered from the records of Hoover, Hurley, Moseley, Lohbeck, Eisenhower, Davison, MacArthur, and Miles conclusively establishes that the President's repeated orders were understood but were not obeyed. Lisio, "A Blunder Becomes Catastrophe," pp. 39–42.

44. MacArthur, *Reminiscences*, p. 95; RCS, p. 8; Eisenhower, *At Ease*, pp. 217–18; Oral History Collection, HHPL.

anticipated from the beginning the importance of newsmen and motion pictures, and before his advance down
Pennsylvania Avenue he had personally invited reporters
"to go to any spot at any time they desired, and to see everything they possibly could." Supremely confident of his
well-trained and disciplined riot force, he arranged transportation for the press throughout the entire encounter
and preserved films of the troops evicting the veterans.
Basically, he was well pleased with the "very fair presentation of the facts as they were seen and interpreted by
the reporters." Because no one had been shot by the soldiers, many of the newsmen were indeed favorably impressed by what they considered to be the relatively restrained, although relentless action by the riot force.[45]

After leaving Eisenhower, MacArthur met Hurley, and
they went together to report to the President. The meeting lasted thirty minutes; unfortunately, no record of the
encounter remains. During a later conversation Hoover
told Assistant Secretary of War F. Trubee Davison that he
had been furious with MacArthur and had "upbraided"
him for disobeying orders.[46] On the night of the rout,
Hoover should have demanded that Hurley and Mac-
Arthur make a complete public explanation of the reasons for the disobedience or resign their posts. Confused,
Hoover did not make the demand, and the blunder
plagued him for the rest of his life.

45. RCS, pp. 13–14. In 1916 MacArthur was chief of military information for the Secretary of War. He performed so well that newspaper
reporters sent him a letter of commendation. James, *MacArthur*, pp.
130–32.
46. F. Trubee Davison, Interview, Oral History Collection, HHPL.
Davison emphasized Hoover's use of the term *upbraided* and its meaning. Davison recalled that Hoover had "bawled MacArthur out" for disobeying his orders and then "took the rap right down the line, when
MacArthur was the guy who should have taken the rap." Because of
the importance of Davison's information I corresponded with him several times, and at his invitation I interviewed him at his home on Long
Island on April 22, 1972. Davison's careful answers reinforced evidence I had gathered from a variety of other sources. His additional information was of such importance that I wrote a summary of the interview, which he and I both authenticated as accurate to the best of our
knowledge. Each of us has a signed copy of the summary.

Why Hoover allowed Hurley and MacArthur to go undisciplined, and why he finally accepted MacArthur's insistence on the presence of a dire revolutionary threat are matters best understood in terms of his preoccupation with what he considered to be more important problems connected with the depression, especially the implementation of the new legislation recently passed by Congress, and in terms of his remarkably close personal relations with his two chief military advisers. By July 28, 1932, Hoover was under considerable stress. Problems generated by an ever-worsening depression, bankers who refused to pass on the benefits of RFC's support, a badly split Republican party, attacks from political foes, the pressures of a difficult reelection campaign, and deteriorating foreign relations had taken a heavy toll of his energies. To his close aides the President openly worried about these and related problems. His sense of urgency was matched by his long, arduous work day and the seeming futility of his prodigious efforts. Under these circumstances, Hoover had not felt that he could give the questions surrounding the BEF his close, personal attention.[47]

Increasingly, the harried Chief Executive depended upon his trusted subordinates. One of those he most admired and relied on was MacArthur. At first glance, the President and Chief of Staff appeared quite unlike one another. Hoover was a pacifist, a poor speaker, a worse politician, a shy, almost introverted man who was most widely known as a selfless humanitarian. By contrast, MacArthur was a war hero, an accomplished orator, and a skillful persuader, who often referred to himself in the third person as "MacArthur," a man of destiny. Far from disdaining politics, the new Chief of Staff engaged in political battle with congressional leaders who insisted on reducing the size and expenditures of the Army. His opposition to the Geneva Disarmament Conference was no less intense. Thus, on the surface, it would appear as if Hoover would have reason to dislike the man.

47. For an example of Hoover's busy schedule, see "President's Day," July 28, 1932, *U.S. Daily News,* and Presidential Calendar, July 28, 1932, Box 3, HHPL.

Actually, Hoover and MacArthur were similar in several important respects. Both were strong-willed, determined men who were experienced administrators, held similar political views and sets of moral values, and had climbed to the peak of their respective professions. Hoover and MacArthur admired these qualities in each other, and the President had personally selected MacArthur over thirty senior officers to reorganize the Army. Moreover, by late 1931 Hoover's antimilitarism had softened, and he now defended the Army against critics and budget-slashers in Congress. MacArthur had reason to be grateful for the high honor and the President's continued support, and as he could be both charming and highly persuasive, he had apparently convinced Hoover of his complete loyalty and devotion. The Chief of Staff already possessed the style, forceful personality, intelligence, and professional competence that greatly impressed many world leaders before his career ended. Finally, he had done nothing prior to the Bonus Riot that would have led Hoover to doubt either his loyalty or his judgment.[48]

Many of the qualities Hoover admired in MacArthur could also be found in Hurley. He too could be exceedingly charming and persuasive, and his critics acknowledged him to be a "political spellbinder." An indication of his skills is that Hoover counted on him to campaign strenuously in the fall. Hurley had been an early supporter of Hoover in Oklahoma, which Hoover carried in 1928, and his loyalty to Hoover and his policies had always been beyond question. He was like MacArthur in that he put much stock in his "word," a characteristic that would cause an enormous amount of trouble for both men later in their careers and was causing more immediate trouble for Hoover.[49]

Thus, when MacArthur and Hurley reported to Hoover the night of July 28, the evidence available indicates that

48. Hoover, *Memoirs*, II, 220–39; for correspondence, see notes 2–4, Chapter 14. D. Clayton James made an earlier, similar comparison, but did not relate it to the rout. See James, *MacArthur*, pp. 344–45, 352–54.

49. Lohbeck, *Hurley*, pp. 23–60. Paul A. Anderson, "Republican Handsprings," *Nation*, 135 (August 31, 1932), 189. Hoover, *Memoirs*, II, 219; III, 233.

he was both irate and bewildered. Despite his irritation, his persuasive subordinates apparently managed to shake his earlier trust in the essentially peaceful nature of the protesters by claiming that the marchers' goal had been nothing less than bloody insurrection. Probably they also told him that the troops had already been committed when the verbal orders arrived and that stopping the troops at the Anacostia Bridge would have exposed them to attack from well-armed and dangerous subversives. At any rate, those themes dominated MacArthur's subsequent oration to the press as well as Hoover's remarks the next day.

For two months Hoover had remained calm while those around him and newspaper editors throughout the country had overreacted to each new wave of rumors of Communist activities. At one time or another many officials, including Vice President Curtis and Glassford, had favored calling out the troops. The Communists were happy, of course, to have the publicity, and they did their best to add to the growing fears. Finally, after repeated assurances from Hurley and MacArthur, Hoover began to believe that the law-abiding veterans had returned home and that those who remained had fallen under Communist control. Apparently having lost faith in his earlier restraint, he accepted the explanation of his trusted advisers that the veterans were acting in accordance with a red plot. He could not bring himself to believe that his respected and loyal supporters would willfully deceive him. Hoover had no way of knowing exactly what had happened, and no other advisers came forward to convince him to the contrary. In his uncertain state of mind he finally became convinced of the revolutionary intent of the BEF, and then directed his anger at the marchers rather than at his subordinates.

At the time, moreover, the President may also have felt that any action against Hurley and MacArthur would be futile, inasmuch as they had presented him with a *fait accompli*. Soon after crossing the bridge, MacArthur had told Eisenhower and reporters around him that the operation was over—information he apparently also gave to Hoover, for immediately after the meeting Hoover retired

for the night.[50] If Hoover had been plotting the rout as an
effective part of his campaign, he probably would have
wanted to stay in touch with any further developments,
but, reassured by MacArthur and Hurley, he anticipated
no more unusual events that night.

A careful examination of the extraordinarily complicated evidence establishes the nonexistence of a conspiracy planned by Hoover. He had certainly tried to stop
MacArthur, but, circumvented by the General's repeated
disobediences, events had passed beyond his control.
Camp Marks and other smaller camps burned, and the
BEF's sojourn in Washington was quickly brought to an
end. Hoover had tried in vain to stop the rout, but, however he may have felt about his advisers' insubordination,
he accepted their insistence on defining the marchers' resistance as insurrection. On the following day he expressed relief that the government had checked the alleged Communist threat in time. Hoover's acquiescence
to the "red plot" argued by Hurley and MacArthur mired
him deeper and deeper in a position that offered few avenues for retreat.

Having accepted their version, Hoover further weakened his position when he allowed Hurley and Mac-
Arthur to explain the incident to the press. While he now
evidently supported their basic premise, the extremity of
their claims may have come as a surprise to him the following morning. Hurley and MacArthur greeted the
newsmen in the role of victors instead of as humbled
men, and MacArthur made the most of the opportunity.
He told reporters at the 11:00 P.M. news conference that
the Army had saved the nation from incipient revolution.
Cooperating closely with Hurley, he emphasized that the
mob "was animated by the essence of revolution." Because the Bonus Army had misconstrued as a sign of
weakness the gentleness and consideration shown them
in the past, they were "about to take over in some arbitrary way either direct control of the Government or else
to control it by indirect methods." In fact they were insur-

50. President's Calendar, July 28, 1932, HHPL. Hoover retired at
11:15 P.M.

rectionists, he argued, with not more than one veteran in ten among them. These subversives were plotting to overthrow the government by force and to institute a reign of terror. The Secretary of War enthusiastically supported the Chief of Staff's explanation.

He had made his case as to the revolutionary nature and intent of the mob; MacArthur next sought to defend the President. Hoover had shown extraordinary patience—so much that "he didn't have much margin" left and "would have been very derelict indeed in the judgement in which he was handling the safety of the country." The whole world was watching, continued MacArthur, and with subtle implication added, "Had *he* [Hoover] not acted with the force and vigor that he did, it would have been a very sad day for the country tomorrow."

MacArthur was careful to place the responsibility for the decision upon the District Commissioners. "All of these moves of course had been at the solicitation of the District Commissioners, the District Government." Hurley also emphasized that point. "The movement," he stressed, ". . . since the clearing of the first area had been on the request and at the direction of the Civil Government." MacArthur added, "The Civil Government has functioned throughout. We have not taken over the city at all. We haven't taken over any functions of the Government and the Commissioners are in complete control of their city now as they were this morning, except that when they call on us we are going to help them." [51]

When asked by a reporter if the Army had plans to truck the men out of the city, MacArthur replied with a lie. "The Army," he insisted, "has had nothing to do with this problem until today, until called upon by the Commissioners who needed sufficient force to protect the institutions of this community." [52] Hurley was ebullient. "It was a great victory. Mac did a great job. He is the man of the hour," the Secretary reputedly exclaimed. "But," he

51. My italics. "Interview with Secretary of War by the Press at 11:00 P.M., July 28, 1932," pp. 1–4, PP 298, HHPL. MacArthur actually did most of the talking.
52. Ibid. Compare his denial, given in this note, about Army plans

paused, then cryptically added, "I must not make any heroes just now." [53]

MacArthur and Hurley talked with the press shortly before General Miles began to move his troops into Anacostia to prod the onlookers and stragglers out of the area. Since the veterans had much earlier set fire to their huts, Miles's men added their own torches to finish the burning. They had given Eddie Atwell more than one hour's extension, and he had led the BEF out of the camp in an orderly retreat. When MacArthur crossed the bridge, the sight of the massive force advancing toward them overwhelmed the veterans, and they began abandoning camp. With their huts in flames and no other course but retreat, they had soon faded into the night.[54] Thus, long before the news conference ended, the BEF had evacuated its camps.

After meeting the press, MacArthur returned to observe the mopping-up operation at Anacostia without summoning his aide, Major Eisenhower. For this inspection, the General was accompanied by the Secretary of War, nattily dressed in spats. The appearance of these two at the principal eviction site, as Miles directed the final dispersal of spectators at the east edge of the camp, confused some reporters and created an unfortunate impression, which later redounded against the President. The gas attack against the spectators, the sight of the soldiers burning huts, and now the appearance of MacArthur and Hurley suggested that the real Battle of Anacostia had just begun. Many persons therefore assumed that the drive against

for the use of trucks to the exchange between Judge Advocate General Blanton Winship and MacArthur. See note 6.

"*Question:* The Staff had no plans for trucking these people one day's ride for instance?

"*MacArthur:* None whatsoever. The Army had nothing to do with this problem until today, until called upon by the commissioners who needed sufficient force to protect the institutions of this community." The Army, in fact, had been involved in planning for the possible use of troops since early June and did indeed have elaborate plans for trucking the veterans back to their states.

53. "The Battle of Washington," *Time*, 20 (August 8, 1932), 7; J. Fred Essary to John S. Martin, August 9, 1932, HP.

54. Miles, "Report," pp. 7–8; RCS, p. 10.

the camp had started *after* the two had gone to the White House to report to the President and meet the press, and they jumped to the conclusion that the Anacostia rout must, therefore, have had the President's full approval.[55] They did not know that the majority of marchers had fled the burning camp before MacArthur and Hurley went to the White House and that MacArthur had much earlier informed Eisenhower, some reporters, and undoubtedly the President that the operation had been completed. Once again, appearances were misleading.

The charred remains of shacks, stinking open latrines, and withered poplar trees were all that remained of the teeming camp at Anacostia. Sad souvenirs of a futile occupation were strewn everywhere—scorched pots and pans, broken bits of furniture, little piles of cabbage, onions, and potatoes, a rocking horse, and a baby's crib. That same night thousands of veterans and hundreds of their women and children wandered in ragged, confused groups through the streets of the District, looking for a place to rest. Some searched for their wives or children, who had become separated from them during the commotion, while others attempted to escape a sudden rain by huddling together under whatever shelter was close at hand. Blocked by state police from entering either

55. Anderson was a national correspondent for the St. Louis *Post-Dispatch* and a frequent contributor to *The Nation*. He assumed that MacArthur returned to the Anacostia camp after receiving Hoover's approval; Anderson, "Tear Gas, Bayonets, and Votes," p. 40. Lee McCardell's story won honorable mention in the competition for the 1933 Pulitzer Prize, but it too created erroneous impressions, especially that of one battle which lasted until past midnight, long after MacArthur had reported to Hoover. Snyder and Morris, *Great Reporting*, p. 477, 479, 482. In 1941 Bennett Rich insisted that Hurley and MacArthur had gone to the White House to get Hoover's approval. They "persuaded" Hoover, he claimed, "to allow the War Department's plans to be carried out without interruption." Rich concluded that it was "inconceivable that any troop movements were carried out contrary to his [Hoover's] express command." Rich, *The Presidents and Civil Disorders*, pp. 174–75. Rich should have acknowledged that the basis of his conclusion was a New York *Times* article which was admittedly based on "belief" rather than fact. See New York *Times*, July 30, 1932. Daniels, *The Bonus March*, p. 172, also speaks of "the midnight rout from Anacostia," but he does not use it in an effort to suggest Hoover's approval.

Virginia or Maryland, they had no place to go—and no place to stay. They were frightened, exhausted, humiliated, angry, utterly depressed, and very hungry.[56]

MacArthur still acted as though these wretched people were dangerous. As dawn broke, the city swarmed with military riot patrols. The mopping-up troops used tear gas and "the flat sides of sabers freely" as they drove out those who had crept back into several smaller camps where the huts had not yet been burned. The soldiers also were tired, and they vented their resentment at the contemptuous booing and name-calling from fleeing veterans and the spectators. None too gently they herded the last of the BEF out of the District to the Maryland border. There, after considerable pressure from the Secretary of War, state-owned trucks finally arrived to haul the refugees to Johnstown, Pennsylvania, where Mayor Eddie McCloskey, a blustering ex-prize fighter, had offered the hospitality of his town.[57]

Those who were fortunate enough to escape further harassment by the troops organized impromptu military formations for the march out of the District. Preceded by an assortment of salvaged flags, the first parade contingent momentarily panicked the police as their retreat neared the White House. Later groups were assigned police escorts as they moved along Massachusetts Avenue to Wisconsin Avenue and on out to the Maryland state line. Impressed by the orderly, dignified exodus, residents and tourists lined the streets to cheer the men as they marched past. Their applause helped bolster sagging spirits somewhat, but the protesters were overwhelmingly bitter, especially toward the President, whom they blamed for the brutal rout. When reporters called out to the passing Oregon contingent, asking if they were

56. *Post*, July 29, 1932; *Evening Star*, July 29, 1932; Slater Brown, "Anacostia Flats," *New Republic*, 72 (August 17, 1932), 15. Malcolm Cowley, "Flight of the Bonus Army," *New Republic*, 72 (August 17, 1932), 13.

57. Miles, "Report," pp. 9–11. Miles outlined in detail the Army's operations against the veterans on July 29 and July 30. New York *Times*, July 30, 1932, and *Evening Star*, July 30, 1932, for reports of continued troop brutality on July 29.

headed toward Johnstown, one of the leaders shouted that they were "heading for the United States, wherever that is." [58]

The retreating Bonus Army was as unwelcome in the states and communities through which it fled as it had been during its original march to Washington. Some veterans were trucked through Pennsylvania directly to the Ohio state line, others were hurriedly dumped near Johnstown, and thousands of others had to make it on foot as best they could. In Johnstown the exhausted and penniless refugees were met by the panic-stricken townspeople and city council, who demanded that Governor Gifford Pinchot and Mayor Eddie McCloskey rid the city of the Communists, criminals, and deadbeats descending on them.[59] The mayor responded by repeating his invitation and declaring, "To hell with everybody! Let them come!" [60] Unfortunately, for all his good intentions, McCloskey's hospitality was severely limited. He had nothing to offer the veterans except a park on the outskirts of town, where they could sleep in the open. Heavy rains, hot, steamy days, a lack of food, shelter, and sanitary facilities soon turned the campers at Ideal Park into a chaotic, sick, despondent, and extremely bitter group.[61] The hasty reorganization of a band of Khaki Shirts and repeated talk of fascism now alarmed even some of their most sympathetic supporters, but the veterans were in no condition to do anything but talk.[62]

58. *Evening Star*, July 30, 1932; New York *Times*, July 29, 30, 1932; *Post*, July 31, 1932.

59. *Evening Star*, July 30, 1932; Cowley, "Flight of the Bonus Army," p. 13; New York *Times*, July 31, 1932.

60. New York *Herald Tribune*, July 31, 1932.

61. Douglas, *Veterans*, p. 264; Cowley, "Flight of the Bonus Marchers," pp. 14–15. For a thorough analysis of the Johnstown camp, see J. Prentice Murphy, "Report on Bonus Expeditionary Force Emergency Camp," August 10, 1932, GP.

62. "Bullets for the B.E.F.: Hoover Relief, New Style," *New Republic*, 71 (August 10, 1932), 329. The *New Republic* expressed concern over the "sinister and concealed motives" of some of the BEF's "respectable" leaders who advocated the Khaki Shirt effort. "There are enough wealthy Americans who favor Fascism," the editor noted, "and are willing to spend money to aid its cause here, to make such a movement extremely dangerous." After a visit to Johnstown, Cowley, one of the editors of the *New Republic*, concluded that fascism was more

Responding to the protesters' desperate plight and to the outrage of his townspeople, Mayor McCloskey asked Hoover for help from the Red Cross. On July 29, the day following the riot, while the rout was still under way, the President had privately arranged for the Red Cross to aid and transport home the women and children of the BEF. Instead of responding at once, the Red Cross would not commit itself or its resources until the President had telephoned twice personally, and by late afternoon when the news was announced, most of the women and children had already left the capital.[63] Now, in response to McCloskey's plea, Hoover quietly arranged free food and transportation to Chicago and Saint Louis through Daniel Willard, president of the Baltimore and Ohio Railroad. At Waters and McCloskey's urging the veterans agreed to board special trains for the westward journey. Unfortunately, arrangements to carry them beyond the Chicago or Saint Louis terminals were left to the cooperation of other railroads. Since none accepted the responsibility, the men and their wives and children had to get home by whatever means they could find.[64] It was a pitiable and tragic ending for those who two months earlier had eagerly hopped freights to Washington, buoyantly singing "Hinkey Dinkey Parley Vous." Driven out by the young Chief of Staff who had become a general while leading them in the World War, the veterans of the Bonus Army had become, in a very real sense, refugees from their own government.

likely to emanate from the federal government than it was from the tattered remnants of the BEF. Cowley, "Flight of the Bonus Army," p. 15.

63. James L. Fieser to HH, July 29, 1932, PP 300, HHPL. Fieser, Vice-Chairman of the Red Cross, wrote two letters to Hoover on July 29, 1932.

64. Newton, Memo, August 3, 1932, PP 297, HHPL. Newton related that Daniel Willard of the B. & O. had agreed to transport the veterans to Chicago and Saint Louis free of charge. Arrangements beyond these points would depend upon the willingness of other railroads to cooperate. For excellent details, see "BEF's End," *Time*, 20 (August 15, 1932), 9; New York *Times*, August 3, 5, 1932. Murphy, "Report of Bonus Expeditionary Force Emergency Camp," pp. 16, 20; Gertrude Springer, "What Became of the BEF," *The Survey*, 68 (December 1, 1932), 640–42.

11

Governance and Candor

From the arrival of the BEF in the capital until long after its dissolution, Hoover committed one embarrassing blunder after another. Following the events of July 28, the President's mistakes became far more serious and their effects more lasting. Subsequent to the brutal eviction of the Bonus Army, Hoover unwisely reinforced the impression that the whole operation had been his idea. One of his gravest mistakes was to accept uncritically MacArthur and Hurley's explanation. His later public defense of the rout led to a series of errors that were to embarrass him acutely at the height of the presidential campaign. In less than three months the administration thoroughly discredited itself, turned Glassford into one of the President's most effective political foes, and silenced many of his strongest supporters, whose help would have been invaluable during the last weeks before the election.

At first, press reactions to the forced eviction were highly favorable. Rumors of a Communist conspiracy had been rampant during June and July in Washington and in other parts of the country, and alarmed editors lavished praise upon the President for his decisiveness in the face of radicalism and anarchy. Newspapers lauded him as a President who had placed the national welfare above partisan politics or temporary political advantage. At first, Hoover emerged from the wreckage of the Bonus Riot as the hero of the day, and to some the savior of the Republic.[1]

1. Herbert Hoover, *The State Papers and Other Public Writings of Herbert Hoover*, William Starr Myers, ed., 2 vols. (New York: Double-day, Doran and Co., 1934), II, 244–45 (hereafter cited as HHPW). New York *Times*, July 30, 31, 1932; New York *Herald Tribune*, July 29, 30, 31, 1932. Both the *Times* and the *Herald Tribune* published editorial

Nevertheless, the President awoke the morning after the rout with renewed anger over the entire event. Anger—not fear—was his chief reaction. That anger was to contribute significantly to his personal disaster. Paradoxically, Hoover was irritated with both MacArthur and the marchers. According to two contemporaries, Arthur J. Curtice and F. Trubee Davison, on the morning of July 29 Hoover again confronted a "very nervous" MacArthur and "upbraided" him.[2] Presented with a *fait accompli* the evening before, Hoover had retired before Hurley and MacArthur had met the press. The morning's irritation may have been a reaction against MacArthur's grandiloquent claims to reporters or to the misleading impression created by General Miles's midnight encounter with spectators on the eastern outskirts of the Anacostia camp—especially since newsmen recorded Hurley and MacArthur's presence at the scene. Or Hoover may have experienced a renewed sense of doubt about the entire operation. The period July 28 through July 30 was a time of acute private vacillation and uncertainty for Hoover. Publicly he would not repudiate his advisers, but privately he was torn between aggravation and trust.

According to Curtice, a business partner of Herbert Hoover, Jr., and a member of the Hoover inner circle,

comments, supporting the President, from a variety of newspapers. Hurley established a highly detailed newspaper survey that tabulated the reactions of 102 newspapers during the period July 30 to August 5, 1932, HP. Additional newspaper comments are in Bonus Files, PP 298, HHPL; E. Francis Brown, "The Bonus Army Marchers to Defeat," *Current History*, 36 (August 1932), 688; "The Progress of the World," *Review of Reviews*, 76 (September 1932), 18. David Brion Davis, ed., *The Fear of Conspiracy: Images of Un-American Subversion From the Revolution to the Present* (Ithaca, N. Y.: Cornell University Press, 1971), p. xvii. Davis identified another category of conspiracy seekers as "defenders of threatened establishments." From "the New England Federalists of the 1790's to the businessmen leaders of The Liberty League in the 1930's," the charge of "conspiratorial subversion may have been a strategic device to convince potential supporters that any threat to their own power imperiled the social order." For another good example, see "Recent Revolutionary Activities," *National Republic*, 20 (September 1932), 26–28.

2. See footnote 46, Chapter 10. F. Trubee Davison, Oral History; Arthur A. Curtice, Oral History Interview, October 8, 1967, HHPL.

after the scolding that morning MacArthur offered his resignation. The story, circulated among Hoover's closest
friends, continued that the President refused to accept it
and decided to shoulder the responsibility himself.[3] Thus,
despite Hoover's renewed irritation, MacArthur managed
to retain the President's loyalty. By that morning he could
have armed himself with editorials which lauded Hoover
for having saved the nation from a Communist revolution.
Certainly, after MacArthur and Hurley's press conference
the preceding night, Hoover's options were more severely
limited. His actions toward his Secretary of War and Chief
of Staff must now produce either an embarrassing showdown or an appearance of support. To work his way out of
the maze that was entrapping him he would have to repudiate the press conference and thus at least indirectly censure his two friends. This he could not bring himself to
do, especially as he was not convinced of their outright
disloyalty. Others would protect MacArthur, suggesting
misunderstandings or breakdowns in communications.
Moreover, thanks to Hurley and MacArthur's per-
suasiveness and his own self-doubts, his attitude toward
the marchers had now changed.

Hoover's anger at MacArthur was justified. But to understand his anger toward the BEF one must bear in mind
his legislative efforts in behalf of the veterans and his
long patience and substantial aid for the unwelcome
marchers, once they arrived in Washington. Hoover had
not been a frightened man, waiting for a pretext to turn
force against the BEF, nor had he been intolerant toward
Communists or protesters generally, as many have
argued. He had trusted the marchers to terminate their
peaceful protest voluntarily, and he had trusted Mac-
Arthur to restore order in a restrained and careful manner. Presented with a *fait accompli,* his chief reaction was
not fear, but anger—anger at both MacArthur and the
marchers. At first he kept both irritations private. Eventually, however, the facile Hurley and MacArthur won their
way back into his good graces, and the demonstrators

3. Curtice, Oral History, HHPL.

would henceforth bear the brunt of Hoover's exaspera-
tion. At that point, the confused, worn, unwise President
abandoned his earlier tolerance and, unfortunately, in
the months and years ahead was increasingly to become
a seeker of conspiracy. In so doing, he committed himself
to a position that involved his administration in reprehensible tactics which, in turn, became a key factor in his personal tragedy.

It was during this process of readjusting his position
that Hoover materially altered his first explanation of the
need for troops. The President's statement on July 28, in
contrast with later pronouncements, was calmer and more
measured. It stressed the need "to carry forward the Government's construction program" as the reason for evacuating buildings on the riot site. Although he believed
that "many [were] communists . . . and the veterans . . .
[were] no doubt unaware of the character of their com-
panions and [were] being led into violence" during the
disturbances, it is significant that on the day of the riot
Hoover did not claim that the riot had resulted from a
Communist conspiracy or argue that it had been an attempt at insurrection. Instead, he stated on July 28 that he
had "asked the Army to *assist* the District authorities *to
restore order*" and "asked the Attorney General to investigate the whole incident." [4]

However, on July 29 after the conference with Mac-
Arthur, it was clear that he had finally accepted the Chief
of Staff's assurances. Now the President lashed out at
"subversives," "mob rule," and "organized lawlessness."
He should have remained uncommitted until the Attorney
General could have investigated the matter; instead, the
exasperated President launched an immediate attack. As
military and police patrols were still driving the tired, for-
lorn, but orderly bands out of the District, he released two
documents, one directed to the press and one to Commissioner Reichelderfer, which was also made public. Both
of Hoover's statements attacked the fleeing veterans in his

4. My italics. HH, Press Statement, July 28, 1932, PP 300, HHPL.
The statement did not refer to the shootings; neither did his statement
on the following day, July 29.

most scolding manner. Almost as if they had betrayed his trust in the nonviolent character of their protest, he now singled them out as targets for the entire nation's blame.

Now he was precisely parroting the MacArthur–Hurley line, insisting that the rioters had blatantly challenged "the cherished process of self-government" and the Constitution. It was "obvious that, after the departure of the majority of the veterans, *subversive* influences obtained control of the men remaining in the District . . . secured repudiation of their elected leaders and *inaugurated and organized* this attack." He reminded the Commissioners that "there is no group, no matter what its origins, that can be allowed either to violate the laws of this city or to intimidate the Government." To the press he thundered, "Government cannot be coerced by mob rule. . . . There can be no safe harbor in the United States of America for violence." [5]

Hoover's outrage on July 29 overcame his usual caution and restraint. Totally absent from his remarks was any expression of regret at being forced to use troops against his fellow citizens or any indication of sympathy for the fleeing thousands. His statements were so self-righteous and so harsh, in fact, that many Republicans preferred to believe that they had been written by one of Hoover's secretaries and released without his knowledge. His critics later charged that his press releases owed more to politics than to the lessons of history or to the facts of the previous day. At the same time, however, most editors unquestioningly accepted the explanations of Hoover, Hurley, and MacArthur and acclaimed the President a national hero. Hoover's position appeared almost unassailable, for the routed veterans themselves blamed the radicals, and the Communist party was quick to accept full credit for the violence.[6]

5. My italics. HH to Reichelderfer, July 29, 1932, DCP. A copy of the letter is in PP 300, HHPL. Press Conference Statement, July 29, 1932, HHPW, II, 245.

6. *B.E.F. News*, August 6, 1932; New York *Times*, July 31, 1932; *Times*, July 30, 1932; *Post*, July 31, 1932. For Washington, D.C., newspapers the city is omitted from the citation. Hundreds of letters and

Some editors placed the greatest share of the blame on congressmen who had encouraged the veterans to remain in the capital so long; others recalled Walter W. Waters's formation of the Khaki Shirts and his pledge to "clean out the high places in government." Waters's statement convinced the New York *Times* that Hoover had faced serious challenges from the Communists on the left and from the new "American Hitler" on the right. With the exception of the influential Hearst and Scripps-Howard chains and some independent dailies, such as the Baltimore *Sun*, most of the press offered extravagant praise. The administration's case seemed further strengthened by the arrest on the afternoon of July 29 of forty alleged Communists and radicals. During a secret meeting in an abandoned church they had reputedly plotted to "overthrow law and order in the Capitol." The group included James Ford, the Communist party's nominee for Vice President of the United States.[7]

During the first days after the riot, Hoover enjoyed a good press. Most editors seemed satisfied by assurances from officials high in the administration that proof of a revolutionary Communist plot would soon be forthcoming, but a small group of critics was not so easily swayed. The members of the BEF were not Communists or radicals, they argued, but loyal, patriotic Americans who had served their country well. As proof, they pointed to the fact that when the Senate rejected the bonus, the thousands of petitioners gathered at the steps of the Capitol had not rioted but had reacted by singing "America." Defenders of the BEF interpreted the veterans' continued

telegrams of support are in PP 298, 299. Deets Pickett to Newton, September 9, 1932; Pickett to Bruce Bliven, September 9, 1932; Newton to Pickett, September 10, 1932, PP 297, HHPL. Bliven, president of *The New Republic*, had written Pickett about the rumors inspired by Hoover's harsh press releases. Pickett had denied the rumors, as had Newton.

7. New York *Times*, July 30, 1932; *Post*, July 29, 1932; New York *Times*, July 30, 1932; "Swords or Charity," *Commonweal*, 16 (August 10, 1932), 358; New York *Times*, July 30, 1932; *Post*, August 2, 1932; *Evening Star*, August 1, 1932; *Herald*, August 1, 1932. The New York *Times* reported 36 arrested, the New York *Herald Tribune*, 40. New York *Times*, July 30, 1932; New York *Herald Tribune*, July 30, 1932.

discipline after repeated defeats as proof of patriotism, not communism.

Despite the growing reaction, no one could reasonably deny that the administration had been patient. The marchers were clearly unjustified in resisting the repeated attempts to remove them from illegally occupied government buildings. No responsible person defended the veterans' actions during the riot—the stoning and mauling of the police and the subsequent attack which precipitated the fatal shooting. Hoover's critics tried to play down the two incidents. They ignored the fact that the police had worked for hours to disperse the crowd of spectators and threatening veterans, only to fail. Clearly, the situation at that point threatened more violence. What angered the President's critics most was the Army's use of troops, tanks, and tear gas not merely to clear the downtown area in an orderly manner but to drive the unarmed marchers and their families out of the capital.[8]

One of their best arguments gained strength when Hoover's bitter comments of July 29 brought a damaging rebuttal. In Hoover's published letter to Commissioner Reichelderfer, he directed a thinly veiled attack at Police Superintendent Glassford, in which he implied that the need for troops stemmed from Glassford's repeated refusal to enforce the law. MacArthur's press statement of July 28 had claimed that the Bonus Army had misconstrued the gentleness and consideration shown them in the past as a sign of weakness. Hoover argued that the veterans "were undoubtedly led to believe that the civil authorities could be intimidated with impunity because of attempts to conciliate by lax enforcement of city ordinances and laws in many directions." Glassford quickly

8. Adolph J. Sabath to HH, July 30, 1932, PP 300, HHPL; "Heroes," *Time*, 20 (August 8, 1932), 5, 7; "Cowardice and Folly in Washington," *Nation*, 135 (August 10, 1932), 116; "Bullets for the BEF: Hoover Relief, New Style," *New Republic*, 71 (August 10, 1932), 328–29; "Foreign Sympathy For the B. E. F.," *The Literary Digest*, 114 (August 13, 1932), 11. Numerous letters and resolutions denouncing Hoover are in PP 299 and PP 300, HHPL. Bennett Milton Rich, *The Presidents and Civil Disorders* (Washington, D.C.: The Brookings Institution, 1941), p. 175.

replied. That same afternoon he astonished reporters and
the President with the assertion that he had never been
consulted after the shooting incident and indeed had
argued against the need for troops.[9]

Glassford's vigorous defense was an unexpected blow
to the administration. After all, he knew more about the
events leading up to the rioting than any other public official, and his honesty was above question. Hoover had
recognized this when he had instructed the District Commissioners to obtain Glassford's opinion before he would
consider ordering out the troops. Now the Police Chief
claimed that although a "riotous condition" had existed,
he had maintained complete control and at no time
requested troops. He was severely critical of MacArthur
for driving the men out of the buildings into the street,
where they were far more difficult to control, and for his
insistence that he had faced "incipient revolution."

Until Glassford publicly contradicted the Commissioners' assurance that he had requested the troops, Hoover's press releases had expressed the indignation of a
man certain that his stand was undeniably correct. The
Commissioners had declared that Glassford approved the
troops, and Hurley and MacArthur had argued that the
imminent Communist insurrection had made the dispersal of all veterans that night absolutely essential. Now,
however, the Chief's denial startled and shook the President. Once again he began to entertain serious doubts
about his course. Eager to set the record straight, Hoover
on July 30 requested that Hurley and MacArthur either
publicly acknowledge their responsibility for the rout or
at least inform a member of Congress who could then defend him against the critics. Both MacArthur and Hurley
refused.

After carefully discussing the suggestions, Hurley informed the President that they had decided against his
request. MacArthur claimed that "it would be bragging"

9. HH to Reichelderfer, July 29, 1932. *Evening Star*, July 29, 1932;
Herald, July 30, 1932. PDG to D.C. Commissioners, July 29, 1932, GP.
This letter was not sent to the Commissioners, but it is a good example
of Glassford's views on July 29, 1932.

and that it would put him "in the role of a hero in a situation of that kind." Hurley declined for the same reason. He stated that he would not have the President "think for a moment that I don't want to do it, because I could do it and be a kind of hero." Both contended that they should not be the ones to "hit the foot lights."

More important, they argued that, since the Communist threat had indeed been serious, their action was both necessary and correct and therefore needed no public justification. Besides, Hurley contended, as support for the President was already "99 percent," it would be unwise "to defend a just action." "That," he warned, "would be trying ourselves, and you know how fickle the public is." Rather than defending himself, the President ought to enjoy the glory, "standing at the head where he should be, [with] nobody against him except Scripps Howard and a bag of scatterbrains." [10]

Hoover should then have insisted that MacArthur and Hurley announce their responsibility, either personally or through a congressman. If they continued to refuse, he should have demanded their immediate resignations. MacArthur had clearly disobeyed orders, and while Hurley's role is more ambiguous, he had certainly supported the Chief of Staff. Unfortunately, Hoover again vacillated. Perhaps he was encouraged by the strong support he was receiving from the newspapers and by the arrest of the forty alleged radicals. Favorable press reaction had not, however, stopped him from requesting the public disclosure in the first place. Probably more significant, Hoover had come to believe that the Communists had indeed precipitated the disorder, and Hurley had managed to convince him, despite Glassford's rebuttal, that if given time, he could prove the riot had been a serious threat to the government.

Perhaps, too, the exigencies of the election campaign

10. Richey Telephone Memorandum, July 30, 1932, PP 300, HHPL. Richey recorded Hurley's exact telephone message to Hoover. William D. Mitchell to D.C. Commissioners, August 1, 1932, PP 300, HHPL; Luther H. Reichelderfer to The Attorney General, August 2, 1932, DCP.

added weight to Hurley's warning that a sudden public explanation would serve only to raise unnecessary doubts and also affected Hoover's decision not to raise these doubts. At that point he was still hopeful that he could defeat Roosevelt. In the long run, however, the consequences would have been far less damaging to him both politically and personally if he had demanded the announcement. But Hurley and MacArthur had spun a cunning argument, and the overburdened, worried President was soon caught in its web. A more seasoned politician might have insisted upon protecting himself, but Hoover acquiesced to their arguments and accepted full responsibility for their actions. It was a fateful blunder, for it required that he prove the existence of a revolutionary plot.

The adverse reaction was not long in coming. Glassford's dramatic denial, set alongside Hoover's insensitive charges on July 29, prompted most critics to blame the President personally. His too-hasty condemnation of the veterans suggested that he had been in complete charge of the rout and fully approved the treatment of the marchers. In the critics' view, his statements now revealed the true nature of the man, a mean-hearted coward who had cynically ousted the veterans and then manipulated the press to his own political advantage. *The New Republic* conceded that Hoover might have been justified in calling troops to clear the riot area, but like most other critics, it could find no justification whatever for routing the veterans from their camps and driving them from the capital.[11] Obviously these ragged, bewildered men and women, tramping out of the city under armed escort, were not Communist revolutionaries. They were loyal Americans, poor but peaceful, and they deserved far better treatment than they had received. Only a weak, timid, panic-stricken man or a stupid, sadistic brute could have authorized such an action, they charged. The veterans

11. "Bullets for B. E. F.," *New Republic*, p. 328; James R. Cox to HH, July 28, 1932, PP 299, HHPL; "Cowardice and Folly," *Nation*, p. 116.

judged Hoover a murderer, who had ordered soldiers to
fire on defenseless citizens. Senator Kenneth McKellar
called Hoover's use of troops "the highest species of tyr-
anny." [12]

In view of Hoover's scolding press statements on July
29, one might conclude, as most historians have at least
suggested, that Hoover acted out of fear. One scholar has
argued that Hoover called out the troops at the "slightest
pretext" because of a "fundamental misunderstanding of
the nature of American society. [Hoover] felt, I think, that
the situation in Washington in 1932 was somewhat analo-
gous to that in Petrograd in 1917, and he did not want to
be the Kerensky of the American revolution, which he
regarded as a distinct possibility." Considering Hoover's
numerous attempts at restraint before and during the rout,
such a claim is unsupported and inconsistent. Yet the
writer agrees with the previously established facts that
MacArthur's rout of the so-called revolutionaries was an
act of disobedience and that Hoover had tried to stop
it—an uncharacteristic action for a man who supposedly
feared revolution. Most other historians have argued similar fear, but primarily because they assumed that Hoover
ordered the rout.[13]

At the time, harsher critics also speculated about Hoover's motives. Beneath a façade of respectability, they
said, Hoover was actually a brutal cynic who deliberately
provoked the riot and planned the sudden rout of the
helpless veterans in order to create a sensational beginning for his reelection campaign.[14] By thus diverting the
campaign to a defense of law and order and an offense

12. Statements of Norman Thomas and Senator McKellar in New
York *Times*, July 30, August 2, 1932; Fiorello LaGuardia to HH, July
30, 1932, PP 298, HHPL. The Grand Rapids (Michigan) *Chronicle* incorrectly reported that the veterans had been "shot down by soldiers
acting under the orders of the Chief Executive." Grand Rapids
Chronicle, August 5, 1932.

13. Roger Daniels, *The Bonus March: An Episode of the Great Depression* (Westport, Conn.: Greenwood Press, Inc., 1971), p. 172. See
note 13, Chapter 3, for other examples. Other critics, who were not
aware of the disobedience, are cited in note 2, Chapter 10.

14. Paul Y. Anderson, "Tear Gas, Bayonets, and Votes: The President Opens His Reelection Campaign," *Nation*, 135 (August 17, 1932),

against the threat of communism, Hoover hoped to camouflage the real issues—financial crisis and hard times.
Clearly, these proponents of the conspiracy theory did not
know that it was only after the rout that Hurley and Mac
Arthur finally persuaded Hoover that a threat had existed
and that MacArthur's action had been necessary. Hoover
had not been afraid; quite the contrary. Further, by the
time he accepted MacArthur and Hurley's explanation,
the alleged threat had been checked. Yet, as he and his
supporters then campaigned against a Communist-led
BEF, some critics quite naturally assumed that a fearful
and calculating Hoover had been in charge throughout
the crisis. William R. Rice, commander of a local American Legion post, congratulated the President for finally
revealing to the nation his "sadistic principles of government." One irate citizen noted that Hoover had helped
the starving people of the world, but, he accused, "as
soon as your own get near enough to ask for food you
order them shot down." "Fear produces cruelty, always,
and fear blunders stupidly. What was there to fear?"
asked the New York *Evening Journal*.[15]

The rout violated a deep-seated sense of fair play and
trust in the basic goodness and loyalty of the American
people, many of whom felt betrayed and insulted. The
rattle of sabers, they thought, belonged to the tragedy of
the Old World, where autocractic and totalitarian governments gave little thought to human dignity. To drive
American citizens out of the national capital with American troops was a slander against the nation and against the
great democratic spirit Hoover had so often exalted in his
speeches. Floyd Gibbons, the popular radio broadcaster
and war correspondent, summed up much of the reaction

138; "Political Gesture," *New Republic*, 72 (September 21, 1932), 139.
Jack Douglas, *Veterans on the March* (New York: Workers Library
Publishers, 1934), pp. 233, 228; John H. Bartlett, *The Bonus March and
the New Deal* (New York: M. A. Donohue and Company, 1937), p. 113;
B. E. F. News, November 5, 1932; J. W. Wilford Statement, August 9,
1932, GP; *News*, August 10, 1932.

15. William R. Rice to HH, July 29, 1932, PP 299; R. V. Kohl to HH,
August 1, 1932, PP 298, HHPL. New York *Evening Journal*, August 1,
1932.

when he compared the bedraggled band of fleeing veterans to World War I refugees. The only difference was that the members of the BEF were "American refugees fleeing from the fire and sword of the Great Humanitarian." [16]

On August 2 William Huska, the Distinguished Service Cross winner whom a beleaguered police officer had shot in the riot, was buried in Arlington National Cemetery. A delegation of his comrades returned to the capital to provide him with full military honors. The next day Eric Carlson, the other veteran who had been shot, also died.[17] That same day Hurley led off the administration's rebuttal, motivated partly by demands for a congressional investigation and partly by pleas from worried Republican leaders for a better defense.[18] He attempted to correct many of the erroneous charges that had been given widespread publicity, especially the belief that Hoover had ordered the troops to fire and that federal troops, rather than a policeman, had killed Huska and Carlson. Characteristically, Hurley went beyond mere defense. Claiming that the sinister purpose of the bonus march had been "to intimidate, coerce, and compel the Congress to make appropriations for them," he asserted that fully a third of the protesters were not veterans.[19]

After "the genuine veterans" had accepted transportation loans, said Hurley, those who remained had fallen under the control of "Red agitators." He stated that on July 28 the police had encountered a "definite organized

16. George Kleinholz, *The Battle of Washington: A National Disgrace* (New York: BEF Press, 1932), pp. 1–4. Kleinholz reproduced an editorial that appeared in the New York *American*, July 30, 1932. New York *Evening Journal*, August 1, 1932.

17. New York *Times*, August 3, 1932.

18. Senator McKellar, Congressman Adolph J. Sabath, and others demanded a congressional investigation; "Causes of Disturbance," *Nation*, 135 (August 24, 1932), 154; New York *Times*, August 2, 1932; Sabath to HH, July 30, 1932; Republican Congressman Robert L. Hogg to Newton, July 30, 1932, PP 60; William T. Davis to Lawrence Richey, August 2, 1932, PP 298, HHPL.

19. Grand Rapids (Michigan) *Chronicle*, August 5, 1932; Hurley Press Statement, August 3, 1932, PP 300, HHPL.

attack of several thousand men [who] were entirely controlled by Red agitators whose sole purpose was to bring about disorder, riots, bloodshed and death." Following "a second riot," troops dispersed the mob, but "no one was injured after the coming of the troops." He further asserted that no property was destroyed by the troops, who had performed the "duty of restoring law and order . . . with directness, with effectiveness, and with unparalleled humanity and kindness." As if those claims were not enough, the Secretary added that the troops had evicted no women and children and that the Red Cross had "immediately" announced that it would care for and transport home all of the families in the BEF.[20]

Hurley's "candid" rebuttal was ethically outrageous and politically disastrous, for it revealed his willingness to distort the facts and, even more clearly, the enormity of Hoover's blunder in accepting Hurley's explanation for the rout. The Republican National Committee also trusted Hurley's explanation and widely circulated it as the official account. Critics, for their part, lost little time in tearing it to shreds. They easily refuted the assertion that "no one was injured." The Washington *Post* had reported that sixty persons were treated for injuries; *Time* cited fifty-five; and the New York *Herald Tribune* listed fifty-three. Many with lesser injuries did not seek hospital treatment. In fact, eyewitness accounts by reporters and journalists contradicted most of Hurley's account.[21]

Within a few days after the rout the rapid deterioration of the administration's position had become apparent. Hurley now quietly modified his earlier public support of MacArthur's claims of insurrection and revolution. By August 3 he contented himself with emphasizing the radi-

20. Hurley Press Statement. The Red Cross did not agree to help until late in the day on July 29. James L. Fieser to HH, July 29, 1932, PP 300, HHPL.

21. Pamphlet published by the Republican National Committee, *Bonus Marchers and the Federal Troops* (Chicago, 1932), in PP 299, HHPL. *Post*, July 29, 1932; "Heroes," *Time*, p. 6; New York *Herald Tribune*, July 30, 1932. Anderson, "Tear Gas, Bayonets, and Votes," pp. 138–39.

cal nature of the riot and its Communist leaders, and he made no further mention of a revolutionary coup.[22]

Hurley's shift did not stop other Republican leaders from repeating and even embellishing upon rumors of guns and dynamite available to the rioters and the charge of a plot to overthrow the government. Significantly, no one in the administration informed the press that no arms had been found. Along with other Republican leaders, Royal C. Johnson was convinced that the public reaction against the administration resulted from a carefully concealed conspiracy by bonus agitators and unprincipled Democrats to make the rout of the BEF into a campaign issue through systematic lies. Those closest to the President, especially his secretaries, believed that the chief danger lay in a conspiracy of radical newsmen and editors, who were carefully and deliberately distorting the facts. To the Republicans this conspiracy explained why many Americans, despite clear evidence to the contrary, had come to believe the widespread rumor that the troops had brutally shot and killed defenseless petitioners. Thus, the forced eviction quickly became an important and highly emotional campaign issue, with members of both parties charging conspiracy.[23]

Two days before Hurley's disastrous "explanation" to the press, Attorney General Mitchell had been unable to uncover any proof that anarchists, radicals, or Communists had organized or led the attack. On August 1 Assistant Attorney General Nugent Dodds called a high-level

22. Hurley issued two press releases which were very similar. The shorter release is labeled "Statement By the Honorable Patrick J. Hurley, Secretary of War, on 'Bonus Marchers in Washington.'" The longer release, which includes much more detail, was issued on August 3, 1932. The shorter release is in PP 297, and the August 3 release is in PP 300, HHPL.

23. Royal Johnson to Richey, September 8, 1932, PP 300; Louis McGrew to Richey, August 5, 1932, PP 102–B. McGrew believed that the Democratic National Committee was "giving aid to the Bonus men who are going from town to town in Pennsylvania." He charged that some of these men had attached a sign to their car, reading "Hoover Murdered Our Buddy." Edgar Rickard, Diary, July 29, 1931, Rickard Papers, HHPL. The belief in a conspiracy of hostile reporters preceded the rout by at least one year.

conference that included James Sloan of the Secret Ser-
vice, J. Edgar Hoover of the FBI, Leo A. Rover, the
United States District Attorney, Inspector Davis of the
Metropolitan Police, and other officials of the Veterans
Administration, the Immigration Service, and the Military
Intelligence Division of the War Department. None could
contribute any information that could have supported
Hurley's charge.[24] Their task was to gather every scrap of
evidence that could be used in the grand jury inquiry or-
dered by the President and already under way.

In this inquiry the presiding judge, Oscar K. Luhring,
tried to assist the administration by informing the jurors
that a mob "made up mainly of communists, and other
disorderly elements" had engaged in a "violent attack
upon law and order." [25] Soon, however, it began to appear
that the evidence for these charges would not be as easily
obtained as Hurley and others had indicated. Justice Department agents made a careful investigation, as did Immigration officials, who had often gathered information
for deportation proceedings against suspected "radicals."
Despite their efforts, the Metropolitan Police had to release twenty-eight of the forty alleged subversives who
had been rounded up on July 29. Among those released
was James Ford, the candidate for Vice President on the
Communist party ticket. Emmanuel Levin and the others
were held for several more days, but they too were finally
discharged at the District line.[26] The utter lack of evidence to sustain indictments was a severe blow to the administration. Far from uncovering proof of a revolutionary
plot to overthrow the government, authorities had to con-

24. "Bonus March Conditions," Report, PP 300, HHPL. Dodds to
Hurley, September 2, 1932, HP.
25. For Judge Luhring's charges to the jury, see "Memorandum of
Testimony Presented to the Grand Jury," Department of Justice, Division of Records, File No. 95-16-26, RG 60, NA, pp. 2–3 (hereafter cited
as MTGJ); *Evening Star*, July 29, 1932. The American Civil Liberties
Union severely criticized Luhring. New York *Times*, July 31, 1932.
26. New York *Times*, July 31, 1932. For further information on federal action against radicals, see William Preston, Jr., *Aliens and Dis-
senters: Federal Suppression of Radicals, 1903–1933* (Cambridge,
Mass.: Harvard University Press, 1963), pp. 238–39, 242–46, 267, 275.

tent themselves with indictments against only three veterans, who were charged with assaulting the police. None of the three were Communists. All were "genuine" veterans, including a holder of the Distinguished Service Cross.[27]

Although the grand jury had produced no evidence to support a red plot, Hurley and other spokesmen acted as though it had. As did other administration staffers, he attributed much of the carping to political partisans or the lunatic fringe. Hoover's White House staff was furious over inaccurate and politically damaging newspaper accounts and editorials, especially those which accused Hoover of ordering the troops to shoot down the marchers. To them, the radical reporters and commentators had long been the chief enemy,[28] and they bent every effort to influence news coverage and editorials. To be sure, Hoover's supporters had reason to be angry at inaccurate charges, but such errors did not justify the tactics used to correct the critics' mistakes.

According to Raymond Clapper, chief of the United Press Washington Bureau, the first sign of an irate reaction came when Walter Newton canceled the White House subscription to the Washington *Daily News* because of its "revolutionary tendencies" in commenting on the rout. Out of respect for Hoover, the *Daily News* decided not to reveal Newton's blunder, and the United Press also decided that it would be in poor taste to publicize the incident. Although most of the press had initially supported the President, Hoover staffers continued to imagine a conspiracy by the press, and on July 29, the day following the rout, his aides discussed a nationwide effort to counter critics such as the Hearst and Scripps-Howard chains. The methods to be employed against critics would

27. New York *Times*, August 17, 1932; *Times*, August 15, 1932; *Herald*, August 18, 1932. Glassford urged U. S. Attorney Leo A. Rover to release the three veterans who had been indicted for throwing bricks. He argued that a trial would make them martyrs. PDG to Leo A. Rover, August 20, 1932, GP.

28. Rickard, Diary, July 29, 1931.

include threats by influential Republicans to withdraw advertising and cancel subscriptions. By August 15 Clapper "saw evidence" that the Republican leadership was launching a determined and "carefully organized 'letter-writing' and protest campaign among party leaders to force newspapers into line." [29]

These efforts to silence the press and other critics were doomed to failure. The morning after the rout, for example, Theodore Joslin, Hoover's press secretary, erroneously informed reporters that the telegrams of protest flooding the White House came from either Communists or Communist organizations. Later, when a group of writers including Sherwood Anderson and Waldo Frank, then a contributing editor of *The New Republic*, insisted on presenting their protest to the President, Joslin seized the opportunity to propagate the thesis of the radical press. Ushered into the White House, the newsmen were not allowed to see Hoover but were taken to Joslin's office, where he lectured them on the duty of all writers "to spread the truth" and then thoroughly publicized the visit.[30] On leaving the White House, the writers said they adjourned to a nearby speak-easy, but federal agents who followed them claimed that they had actually gone to the local headquarters of the Communist party. Sherwood Anderson was shocked and angered by this crude, information-warping maneuver. In a remarkably gentle comment he warned Hoover and the nation that the President "was surrounded by yes-sayers" who were determined to shelter him from the hard realities of life in America.[31] In

29. Raymond Clapper, Diary, August 1, 1932, Clapper Papers, LC. Rickard, Diary, July 29, 1931. Rickard related that these methods were discussed by top officials at least a year prior to the rout. Clapper, Diary, August 15, 1932.

30. Theodore Joslin, *Hoover Off the Record* (New York: Doubleday, Doran and Co., 1934), pp. 262, 275–76; *Evening Star*, July 29, 1932. "Statement of Theodore G. Joslin to committee of writers," August 10, 1932, PP 297, HHPL; New York *Times*, August 11, 1932; Clapper to Joe, August 16, 1932. Clapper was convinced that the "blundering attempts" to explain away the rout tended "to destroy confidence" in Hoover.

31. "This Week," *New Republic*, 72 (August 24, 1932), 29–30; "Of-

Hoover's dealings with the bonus marchers, this was undeniably true.

MacArthur exhibited a similar defensiveness. When Richey forwarded an ACLU protest to him, the Chief of Staff was understandably angered by its contents, which commented on rumors of orders to shoot to kill, but his retort went far beyond merely challenging the error. "The Civil Liberties Union have [sic]," he charged, "made frequent attacks upon the Army in every possible way. Their basic purpose, of course, is the destruction of all constituted authority." [32] In their several ways, Joslin, Richey, Hurley, and MacArthur all strove to shield the President and propagate the belief that Hoover's detractors were radicals, Communists, or fellow-travelers whose criticism was beneath consideration. When hecklers interrupted Charles Curtis's speech at Las Vegas, demanding to know why he had not helped feed the veterans in Washington, the Vice President shot back, "I've fed more than you have, you dirty cowards! I'm not afraid of any of you." In spite of their belligerence, the efforts to discredit critics actually masked growing apprehension.

Administration officials were well aware that the American Legion, heretofore one of the great bulwarks of the Republican party's strength, was close to open revolt against Hoover. The Legion's national officers had already tactfully refused an appeal by Assistant Attorney

---

ficial Misrepresentation of Eviction of Bonus Marchers," *New Republic*, 72 (August 24, 1932), 29. Sherwood Anderson, "Listen, Mr. President ——," *Nation*, 135 (August 31, 1932), 191–92.

32. John Haynes Holmes, et al. to Hoover, August 12, 1932; Richey to John Haynes Holmes, August 13, 1932; PP 300, HHPL. MacArthur to Richey, August 12, 1932, War Department, Office of The Adjutant General, RG 94, NA. Donald J. Lisio, "A Blunder Becomes Catastrophe: Hoover, the Legion, and the Bonus Army," *Wisconsin Magazine of History*, 51 (Autumn 1967), 42, note 20. Holmes replied that the ACLU protest did not contain lies but was based on information from reliable correspondents and other sources. Holmes to Richey, August 15, 1932, PP 300; the protest was filed in "Criminal Records, Exhibit A," PP 300, HHPL. On August 13, a committee of 41 prominent Americans, including John Dewey, Roy W. Howard of the Scripps-Howard newspaper chain, and representatives of the ACLU, sent a strongly worded protest to Hoover. New York *Times*, August 14, 1932.

General G. Aaron Youngquist to publish the administration's official explanation of the riot and rout in the Legion's monthly journal.[33] In addition, judging from reports by state officials, James Barton, the Legion's national adjutant, felt certain that a large majority of the state conventions would approve bonus resolutions for presentation at the Legion's national convention in September. Other administration supporters feared that the angry legionnaires might force through a resolution of censure, which in the last weeks of the campaign might give Hoover the *coup de grâce*.[34]

To counter critics in the Legion, Richey admonished leading Republicans to tell legionnaires that forthcoming evidence would soon prove that 800 of the rioters were "ex-criminals and refugees from justice" and that 400 more were Communists.[35] This statement was unsupported but it aptly illustrated the increasing frustration and recklessness at the White House. Actually, opposition

33. "Heroes," *Time*, p. 5. G. Aaron Youngquist to National Commander, American Legion, August 5, 1932, BEF Folder, ALP. Theodore Roosevelt, Jr., argued that the administration had put down Communists who had "tried to incite riot and revolution." Copy of speech in French Strother Papers, HHPL.

34. James Barton to Mose G. Hubbard, August 9, 1932, ALP. For numerous resolutions from local posts demanding immediate payment and denouncing Hoover, see BEF Folder, 1932, ALP. "Heroes," *Time* (August 8, 1932), p. 10. Some state conventions heralded the controversy that was to follow at the national convention in Portland. At the New York state Legion convention, for example, Assistant Secretary of War F. Trubee Davison, a candidate for the gubernatorial nomination, tried to defend the administration by charging that the rioting had been instigated by a bunch of Communist-led tramps and hoodlums. The New York delegation booed, hissed, and passed resolutions demanding the bonus and censuring Hoover. Lisio, "A Blunder Becomes Catastrophe," pp. 43–44. Later, Davison regretted the speech. Interview with F. Trubee Davison, April 22, 1972.

35. Mark Requa to Newton, August 24, 1932, PP 60; Requa to Richey, August 12, 1932, PP 297; Richey to Requa, August 13, 1932, PP 300, HHPL. Requa urged Hoover to organize a friendly committee that represented one of the Legion posts in Washington, D.C., which would send out a pamphlet "as an authoritative statement of the Washington Post of the Legion" to every local post in the United States. Richey replied that it was practically "impossible to get any Legion post in the District to do as you want [because] these posts are in the hands of radicals."

from the Legion was not the threat Hoover's advisers feared. While the smaller VFW condemned the President for his "unnecessary, criminally brutal, [and] morally indefensible" use of troops,[36] most state Legion conventions merely passed resolutions favoring the immediate payment of the bonus. Republican leaders had controlled the state resolutions committees, which in all but eight states refused to pass censure motions.[37] Passage of the bonus resolution was a foregone conclusion, but as Roosevelt also opposed immediate payment, it should not have excited Republicans to frenzied activity. Yet it did. *Time* reported that all was already lost, and that the prospect for defeat in Portland "sent cold chills up and down the spine of the Republican high command." Its editors predicted that Hoover was "lying low, having abandoned all efforts to try to stop the Legion's stampede for the Bonus." The President had "no relish for a fight in which he was doomed to defeat." [38]

Regardless of warnings in the press, Hoover's advisers were determined to vindicate the President before the Legion's national convention. Suddenly, on September 1, Assistant Attorney General Nugent Dodds informed J. Edgar Hoover that Hurley had asked him "personally to compile at once a summary of all information . . . now in

36. "Military Rout of the B.E.F.," *Foreign Service* (October 1932), 9.

37. J. Edgar Hoover to Richey, August 26, 1932, FBI Miscellaneous Cases File, HHPL. FTH to "Managers of All Regional Offices and Combined Facilities, Personal and Confidential," August 8, 1932, PP 300, HHPL. Hines supplied his numerous officials with documents detailing the official explanation of the rout and instructed them to present the documents to the appropriate convention committees. His purpose was to stop both censure and resolutions supporting immediate payment of the bonus. The New York *Evening Post*, August 16, 1932, contains an excellent article by Harold Brayman, "Legion to Press for Cash Bonus." Hines stopped drives for censure in Illinois, Kansas, California, Maryland, and South Dakota. FTH to Newton, August 15, 1932, PP 300; Newton to FTH, August 19, 1932; S. H. Conner to Newton, August 20, 1932, PP 286; FTH to Newton, September 1, 1932, PP 299; Newton to FTH, August 31, 1932, PP 297, HHPL. *Time* later reported, however, that Illinois and Maryland had passed censure resolutions. "Heroes," *Time*, 20 (September 12, 1932), 10.

38. New York *Times*, August 30, 1932; "Heroes," *Time* (September 12, 1932), pp. 9–10.

the hands of the Department of Justice." Dodds ordered the FBI chief to submit an immediate report and refused requests for more time. No matter what shape the information might be in, Dodds exclaimed, "I must have access to it as it is now." [39]

The decision to confront his critics and overwhelm them presupposed that the President had evidence to support the charges of a radical plot to overthrow the government, or at least of a riot organized and led by Communist agitators. In fact, he had no such evidence. Since July 28, the day of the riot, the administration had involved several government agencies in a search for proof of its thesis. Government attorneys had been taking depositions from principal witnesses while the FBI diligently investigated rumors of Communist plots. Much of the inquiry was disheartening, for little new evidence emerged. The charge of the Communists supplying guns and ammunition and other sensational claims could not be verified.[40]

The investigation did prove that the troops had not started the burning of BEF camps but merely completed the process after some veterans had first set fire to the huts.[41] Photographs of the riot were produced as evi-

39. Dodds to J. Edgar Hoover, September 1, 1932, PP 300, HHPL.

40. Dodds to Herbert B. Crosby, September 8, 1932; J. Edgar Hoover to Richey, September 9, 1932, PP 300, HHPL. Royal Johnson had repeatedly insisted on the validity of the red plot. See *Post*, August 16, 1932. Mitchell to Hoover, September 9, 1932, PP 300, HHPL. Mitchell included the charge in the first draft of his report to Hoover.

41. The troops' burning of the camp became a sharply controversial issue; GT, p. 19; RCS, p. 10; Dwight D. Eisenhower, *At Ease: Stories I Tell To Friends* (New York: Doubleday & Company, Inc., 1967), pp. 217–18. George Van Horn Moseley to Hurley, December 7, 1932; P. V. Kieffer to Moseley, December 14, 1932, War Department, Office of The Adjutant General, RG 94, NA. Hoover demanded a complete investigation, which finally established that the troops were ordered to finish burning the huts, but the huts were set ablaze initially by the retreating veterans. Moseley, "One Soldier's Journey," unpublished diary, IV, 146, Moseley Papers, LC; P. V. Kieffer to Deputy Chief of Staff, December 14, 1932; Moseley, Memo for Secretary of War, December 17, 1932, War Department, Office of The Adjutant General, RG 94, NA. Moseley rejected Richey's suggestion that photographs of troops burning huts were "posed." General Miles's investigation revealed that a lieutenant of infantry had given the order when police

dence. On September 6, Walter Newton supplied the Republican national committeeman in charge of publicity, Henry J. Allen, with photos of the veterans hurling stones at policemen. He instructed Allen to show the pictures to doubters as evidence that "this was a real onslaught on the forces of law and order" and that "no one could foretell what possible consequences might follow." Since few denied that a riot had occurred, the photographs proved little, but Allen thought they could be put to good use. Furthermore, the chief criticism centered, not on the need for troops to help maintain order, but on the use of troops to drive the bonuseers out of the capital.[42]

More important, despite their vigilant efforts, none of the investigating agencies—neither the Secret Service, the Metropolitan Police, the FBI, the Immigration Bureau, the Veterans Administration, the Military Intelligence Division of the War Department, nor the Attorney General's office—could uncover any evidence to support the charge of Communist insurrection or Communist leadership in the rioting.[43]

Ironically, the reason for this complete lack of evidence did not lie in any skillful evasiveness on the part of the Communists but rather in their repeated ineptness, their failure to anticipate and take advantage of the confrontation, their lack of real revolutionary fervor. Between presence and intent, and actual accomplishment lay a huge gulf. Pace and his chief lieutenant, Walter Eicker, were in jail during the riot for picketing the White House, so Em-

requested him to complete the burning and that other soldiers had apparently followed this example. Miles was willing to accept the responsibility, but he insisted that no orders to burn the huts had been authorized. P. L. Miles, Memo to Moseley, September 23, 1932, War Department, Records of the U.S. Army Continental Commands, RG 394, NA.

42. Newton to Henry J. Allen, September 6, 1932, PP 297; Henry J. Allen to Newton, September 8, 1932, Republican National Committee, Allen File, HHPL. The censure resolutions are cited in notes 36 and 37.

43. Dodds to Hurley, September 2, 1932, HP; "Bonus March Conditions," Report, PP 300, HHPL. Lisio, "A Blunder Becomes Catastrophe," p. 45.

manuel Levin took command. In effect, this meant that
the reds were practically leaderless, for Levin much preferred making speeches or conducting press conferences
to leading revolution in the streets. Instead of precipitating the attack on the police or leading his men against
the troops when they arrived, Levin called another meeting at the Pythian Temple. From nine o'clock until eleven
o'clock that evening, while MacArthur advanced on Anacostia, routed the BEF, and triumphantly returned to
town to meet the press, Communist orators harangued 200
of the faithful. One speaker flatly denied that he or his
comrades had been the cause of trouble. Revolutionary
rhetoric flowed, but a police spy who covered the meeting
was unable to report that Levin, Ford, or any other Communist claimed a part in the violence or admitted being in
its vicinity.[44] Later, however, they would happily accept
the credit to mute the fury of their superiors. Glowing
headlines in *Pravda* and immediate efforts by the Communist party to inaugurate a second bonus march were
nothing more than a façade to placate Moscow's fury over
the complete lack of revolutionary leadership on July
28.[45]

44. Report of S. M. Scott, "Communist Meeting in Pythian Temple,
July 28, 1932," July 29, 1932, DCP; Douglas, *Veterans*, pp. 246–47;
Douglas was a Communist propagandist whose eyewitness account is
obviously biased, yet it is surprisingly detailed and presents an interesting point of view. He described the meeting in vivid detail: "While
the meeting was going on runners from the Anacostia Bridge brought
moment-to-moment news of the attack, which were read to the crowd.
There was booing and jeering as Levin pointed to the sky-line of
Washington turning bright red. The torch had been set to Anacostia." In
this dramatic setting Levin "spoke like a man inspired." Significantly,
he did not lead the "two thousand" in revolutionary activities; Scott reported only 200 at the meeting. Joseph Z. Kornfeder, a high-ranking
Communist in 1932, identified Douglas as a Communist who had been
trained at the Lenin School in Moscow. See U.S., Congress, House,
Committee on Un-American Activities, *Hearings on Communist Tactics Among Veterans' Groups*, 82d Cong., 1st sess., 1951, pp. 1945–46
(hereafter cited as HUAC, CTVG).
45. *Times*, July 30, 1932; New York *Times*, July 31, 1932. William Z.
Foster later admitted that WESL "was not able to maintain the leadership of the swiftly developing struggle. Another factor in this inade-

Although the forty alleged radicals were released and repeated investigations failed to produce evidence supporting their claims, the President and his advisers remained blindly convinced that the riot was the fruit of a Communist plot. They decided to play down that charge for the moment, however, in favor of another approach. For some time Attorney General William Mitchell had been investigating the personal character of the men who comprised the BEF. With the help of the Veterans Administration and the FBI he had checked the military and civilian records of the 5,091 veterans who had applied for transportation loans and who had left Washington before the riot occurred. To prove that they were bona fide veterans entitled to the transportation loans, the applicants had agreed to allow the Veterans Administration to check their fingerprints against those in their service files. The fingerprints were turned over to the FBI, which could identify only 4,723 of 5,091 as genuine veterans; 1,069 of those had police records before they came to Washington.[46]

Assistant Attorney General Dodds, who had ordered J. Edgar Hoover to rush all data to him at once, at first discounted this information as irrelevant. Dodds told Hurley that "this tabulation cannot be considered particularly valuable as it has nothing to do . . . with any persons who were here during the riot." Dodds was correct, and he might have added that the data had nothing to do with communism or radicalism either.[47] Furthermore, only 829 or 17.4 per cent of those fingerprinted had actually been convicted of a crime, and their police records were mostly for minor offenses. Above all, it was certainly dishonest to impugn those who had remained in Washington by mak-

quacy was some initial hesitation in the Party leadership as to the potentialities of the movement." William Z. Foster, *History of the Communist Party of the United States* (New York: International Publishers Co., Inc., 1952), pp. 290, 282–84. For further evidence of the Communists' ineffectiveness, see Chapter 14.

46. J. Edgar Hoover to Richey, September 1, 1932; Dodds to J. Edgar Hoover, September 1, 1932, PP 300, HHPL. Dodds to Hurley, September 2, 1932, HP.

47. Dodds to Hurley, September 2, 1932, HP.

ing a haphazard sampling of the BEF, using pre-Washington arrests of those who had accepted transportation loans and who had left town before the riot. A study of the 362 bonuseers who were arrested during June and July, while in the capital, proved equally fruitless, for it did not indicate convictions; most of the arrests were for such non-criminal offenses as intoxication, begging, mental observation, and routine investigation. Oddly enough, Dodds suddenly changed his mind and concluded that the records could, nevertheless, be used to reveal "the rather questionable make-up of the BEF as a whole." [48]

There is ample reason to be sympathetic to Hoover before his vacillation and eventual acceptance of MacArthur and Hurley's explanation. As investigation after investigation proved his two advisers to be wrong, however, it is not possible to defend Hoover's willingness to allow the distortions to continue. The misleading of the people is the basis for sound criticism of Hoover—not his alleged search for a "pretext" to call out troops or the reputed fears of a Communist revolution that were attributed to him in retrospect. The critics had deeply seared Hoover,[49] and by September he had come to accept increasingly rediculous and unfounded charges against his foes. Moreover, he now believed the MacArthurs, the Joslins, the

48. Lewis I. H. Edwards to Crosby, September 8, 1932, PP 300, HHPL. Dodds to Hurley, September 2, 1932, HP. The compilation of the police records of the veterans who applied for transportation loans does not include their fingerprint records. While it appears that the FBI made a conscientious effort, the evidence is confusing and, in any case, irrelevant. See the 248-page Report of September 6, 1932, Department of Justice, File No. 95-16-26, RG 60, NA. Well before Attorney General Mitchell released his report, Hines objected to the use of fingerprint data to determine the number of marchers who were not veterans, for the evidence of the government was incomplete. See Hines's statement, "Information From Veterans Administration Relative to Bonus Marchers," September 8, 1932, Department of Justice, File No. 95-16-26, RG 60, NA, and "Report of the Administrator of Veteran Affairs Relative to Transportation of Veterans," Historical Studies, Soldier's Bonus, Adjusted Compensation, p. 7. This report is in the Office of the Administrator of Veteran Affairs. It establishes that some fingerprints were being taken between July 7 and July 15.

49. *Time*, 20 (September 19, 1932), 9–10; HH to Hurley, September 6, 1932, HP.

Richeys, and the Hurleys, and would eventually conclude that the entire affair had been a leftist plot against him. As a result, the miseducation of the public continued. Yet each uncandid effort to explain away the rout further solidified the impression that the President had been responsible for the entire affair.

On September 12, 1932, the night before their convention, as 18,000 legionnaires gathered in Portland, the President surprised them by releasing the Attorney General's official report on the Bonus Army. The document was so obviously inaccurate, so poorly reasoned, so tactless and politically inept that few Republican leaders could either believe or defend it. The shift in strategy immediately became obvious. The administration no longer emphasized the charge that BEF rioters were Communist insurrectionists. Instead, Attorney General Mitchell's report tried to demonstrate that an impressive percentage of the veterans were criminals. It was impossible, the report stated, to understand the conditions that caused the riot unless one knew "something of the character of the Bonus Army." Using a decidedly unrepresentative sampling and the number of arrests rather than the number of convictions, the Attorney General declared that 22.6 per cent of those veterans who had returned home on government loans before the riot were men with criminal records. Since these men were "the most sensible and least disorderly," Mitchell reasoned, it followed that "a considerable portion" of those who had remained were Communists, radicals, or disorderly elements. It was therefore possible, Mitchell concluded, that "the Bonus Army brought into the City of Washington the largest aggregation of criminals that had ever been assembled in the city at any one time." Criminals in the BEF, cooperating with the Communists who precipitated the riot, had attacked the police, caused the death of two veterans, and overwhelmingly threatened the safety of the city and the federal government. With this circuitous, tortured logic the Hoover administration wandered deeper and deeper into a maze of its own devising.

Attorney General Mitchell included some words of

praise for the honorable veterans in the Bonus Army. He tried to correct the erroneous impression he himself had created on the day of the riot with his reference to "summary" evictions. The administration had not planned an immediate evacuation of the other sites, he insisted. Rather, "it was hoped that their evacuation could be gradually accomplished." In a statement accompanying Mitchell's report, Hoover too tried to soften the indictment by adding that "the extraordinary proportion of criminal, communist, and nonveteran elements should not be taken to reflect upon the many thousands of honest, law abiding men" who had petitioned the government.[50] Hoover's clumsy effort to mollify the veterans was lost, however, in the wave of outrage that greeted the new charges. Although much of the information included in the long report was based on thorough documentation, the Attorney General's allegations concerning Communists, the criminal character of the BEF, and the justification for the rout did not fit the facts he presented. While much of the data was accurate, much of Mitchell's interpretation was not. The reprehensible attempt to discredit the entire BEF by associating it with criminals and Communists added insult to injury and fooled no one.

Among the numerous distortions and half-truths in the Attorney General's report was the charge that Glassford had failed to assign detectives to circulate among the crowd at the eviction site and that thus it was impossible to identify the Communists who had instigated the riot. This criticism of the popular Police Chief was further in-

50. William D. Mitchell to HH, September 9, 1932, PP 300, HHPL. The full text of the public report and Hoover's accompanying statement are in the New York *Times*, September 12, 1932. Also see HHPW, II, 274–77. For further examples of Mitchell's documentation, see William D. Mitchell to the Commissioners, August 1, 1932; Reichelderfer to the Attorney General, August 2, 1932; Dodds to Crosby, September 8, 1932; Secretary, Board of Commissioners to Glassford, August 5, 1932, DCP; Mitchell to MacArthur, August 2, 1932; MacArthur to Mitchell, August 2, 1932, War Department, Office of The Adjutant General, RG 94, NA. In the Hoover Papers, PP 300 contains much additional evidence. The testimony of the grand jury was also important in compiling the report. The affidavits of the police officers are in DCP.

dication of the reckless nature of the Attorney General's counterattack. Except for his press statement that he had not requested troops, Glassford had refrained from public criticisms. Now, however, he had little choice but to reveal his earlier secret testimony before the grand jury and thus refute the misrepresentations put forth by the Attorney General and sanctioned by the President.[51]

The Chief stated that he had ordered his plain-clothes detectives to move among the protesters, but they were instructed to withdraw to safe positions if any violence erupted. In answer to Mitchell's charges about detectives at the Anacostia camp, he specifically named those who had been on duty. He accused the administration of misleading the American people on the character of the bonus marchers. The veterans were not criminals who had cooperated with the Communists. Since only 12 of the 362 arrests during June and July had been of a criminal nature, the BEF was a far cry from being the biggest accumulation of criminals in the city's history. Police records and statistics further established that "there was less crime in the District of Columbia during either June or July than during the month of August after the veterans had been evicted." More significant, neither Communists nor criminals had been responsible for the riot. Pace had never been able to collect more than 210 followers, and they were easily controlled by the District police and the

51. MTGJ, pp. 106–8, GT, p. 18. J. O. Patton was on duty. He reported both the brick battle and the shootings. Mitchell to HH, September 9, 1932. Mitchell charged that on the day of the riot Glassford had ordered detectives out of the Anacostia camp. Four days before he released the report to the American Legion, Mitchell asked the Commissioners to determine why Glassford had issued the alleged order. Nugent Dodds to D.C. Commissioners, September 8, 1932, DCP. Ogden Davis's testimony is in MTGJ, pp. 106–8. Glassford immediately replied to Mitchell's inquiry. He repeated essentially what he had told the grand jury—that detectives were on duty at the camps that day. Thus, Mitchell's criticism of Glassford in the final report clearly establishes that the Attorney General believed that the Chief was lying. Glassford to Crosby, September 8, 1932, DCP. Crosby forwarded Glassford's letter to the White House; PP 300, HHPL. For charges that Waters incited the men at Anacostia and his denial, see Chapter 9, note 20.

active BEF military police. Detectives had not been able to identify any conspirators because there was no conspiracy. The riot and later shootings had been both sudden and unorganized. Glassford was personally well acquainted with the leaders and the small sprinkling of radicals, and, having been on duty at the eviction site himself, he stated that the riot was caused only by the men's "aggravated frame of mind." [52]

Glassford's exact, point-by-point rebuttal was all the more effective for its calm presentation. It captured national headlines and whipped the already angry legionnaires into more furious denunciation of the President. Newspapers of every political view attacked or regretted the administration's ineptness. The Chicago *Tribune* tried to defend the administration, but it did not contradict Glassford's assertions. Few believed the President or his Attorney General. Most people read the Mitchell report with disbelief, then outrage. Even Republican leaders were silenced, and later attempts by the Justice Department to undermine Glassford's testimony were ignored. The Legion passed a bonus resolution, but effective maneuvering by administration loyalists prevented the passage of a motion to censure Hoover. The controversy, inflamed by Attorney General Mitchell's report and further intensified by Glassford's rebuttal, shattered Hoover's remaining credibility in the last months of the campaign.[53]

After the release of the Mitchell report, no criticism of the President seemed too harsh. Critics charged that Hoover had dishonored himself and the Presidency. He

52. New York *Times*, September 13, 1932. The *Times* reprinted Glassford's complete statement in reply to Mitchell. Copy of press release dated September 12, 1932 in GP. Glassford again repeated his opposition to troops. New York *Times*, September 14, 1932. For a copy of Glassford's press release, see New York *Times*, September 13, 1932.

53. "The Bonus Bomb," *Literary Digest*, p. 12; "Political Gesture," *New Republic*, 72 (September 21, 1932), 139–40; Paul Y. Anderson, "Mourning Becomes Herbert," *Nation*, 135 (September 28, 1932), 280–81; "Storm-Signals in the New Bonus Drive," *The Literary Digest*, 114 (September 10, 1932); New York *Times*, September 13, 1932; Chicago *Tribune*, September 14, 1932. Additional details concerning the Legion fight and the bonus and censure resolutions are in Lisio, "A Blunder Becomes Catastrophe," pp. 43–50.

deserved no better treatment than he had shown the heroes of the Great War. *America,* a Roman Catholic weekly, caught the sense of indignation in a pithy superlative: "For its cynical disregard of truth this statement is probably unsurpassed in Federal annals." [54] *The New Republic* noted that the quarrel between the Hoover forces and their critics rather resembled an intense marital squabble—each side hurt and shocked by the other's distortion, angry, and vindictive. According to the editors, the greater fault lay with the administration. By using Mitchell's slurs against the veterans, Hoover had acted "in the spirit of a man who would quarrel with his wife about the household bills and plunging out of doors in anger, would shout to the neighbors false accusations against her personal honor." [55] Floyd Gibbons summed up the bitter reaction in his remark that there was a lower percentage of criminals in the Bonus Army than there had been in "at least one of the presidential cabinets in which Herbert Hoover has served." [56] The Democrats broadcast suspicions that Hoover had deliberately provoked the riot to manufacture a campaign issue; the Republicans countered with the equally ridiculous accusation that the Democrats had formed an alliance with the radicals to smear Hoover and undermine the Republic.[57] Conspiracy theories abounded, and charges and countercharges—most without foundation—stirred the controversy into an emotional frenzy that continued for many years after the Legion convention was forgotten. Mayor James Curley of Boston contributed what came to be, for several generations, the most vivid symbol of the whole sad event when

54. *America: A Catholic Review of the Week,* September 24, 1932, p. 583; *Herald,* September 12, 13, 1932.

55. "Bullets for the BEF: Hoover Relief, New Style," *New Republic,* 71 (August 10, 1932), 329.

56. Gibbons's article, PP 298, HHPL; cited also in Lisio, "A Blunder Becomes Catastrophe," p. 47. New York *Times,* September 14, 1932. The same sentiments were also expressed by Paul Y. Anderson, "Mourning Becomes Herbert," *Nation,* pp. 280–81.

57. "Tear Gas, Bayonets, and Votes," *Nation,* p. 138; New York *American,* October 30, 1932. Glassford charged that Hoover deliberately provoked the riot for his own political gain.

he declared that Hoover had ordered the troops to shoot down the defenseless veterans "like dogs." [58]

58. New York *Times*, September 13, 1932; Chicago *Tribune*, September 14, 1932. The *Tribune's* editors blistered Curley as an "accomplished demagogue." They charged that Glassford's rebuttal was "being taken up by the Democrats as ammunition for them" but refused to print one word of criticism against the respected Police Chief. Clarence J. McLeod of Michigan informed Hoover that "most service men in Detroit believe that the man killed was killed by Federal troops not by local Police Dept." McLeod to Hoover, n.d., PP 298, HHPL. An article in *Reveille*, 8 (November 1932), 9, stated that Hoover treated veterans "like dogs" while treating the wealthy to billions.

12

The Conspiracies Compounded

After his dramatic rebuttal of the Mitchell report, Glassford's reputation as a national hero became greater than before the Legion convention. At the same time, the President and his assistants were denounced as ruthless villains. As late as July 16, only twelve days before the rout, the *BEF News* had expressed the generally held view that Hoover was a man of integrity, whose personal honesty was not in question, but that view had been shattered. Now, it seemed that, armed with nothing but truth and courage, the local cop had exposed the unscrupulous lies of a once-respected President. He had stood alone against the vast power of the United States Government and almost alone had humbled his gigantic adversary. To many, Glassford represented "sterling stalwart honesty in the muck and filth of Washington's federal hypocrisy and official falsehood." [1]

It was an appealing scenario, which conformed perfectly to familiar stereotypes. Newsmen and politicians alike stressed the triumph of good over evil and contrasted Hoover's diabolical conspiracy with Glassford's heroic public service.[2] This oversimplified view—which seemed so true at the time and in the years that followed—unknowingly obscured, however, a far more complicated chain of events, both on the day of the riot and in its aftermath. Believing in a Hoover conspiracy against the BEF as well as against himself, Glassford charged the

1. Floyd Gibbons to PDG, September 12, 1932, GP.
2. "Glassford Sees It Through," *Nation*, 135 (September 28, 1932), 269; Eddie Atwell to PDG, September 12, 1932; Arthur Capper to PDG, July 26, 1932; Gifford Pinchot to PDG, September 13, 1932; Joseph P. Tumulty to PDG, September 22, 1932; Eddie McCloskey to PDG, September 13, 1932, GP.

President with a plot to further his campaign. Appearances seemed to support his allegations, and when the administration's defense collapsed, few questioned the respected Police Chief. In the weeks ahead Glassford was to become increasingly suspicious and bitter toward the President, an antagonism he brought to a climax with a devastating election-eve attack on Hoover.

Granted, Glassford deserved his immense popularity. For ten weeks he had treated the bonus marchers with tolerance and restraint. He had handled dozens of difficult problems with good sense and grace, and on various occasions he had generously dipped into his own pocket to help the shabby, hungry men. A revealing display of affection for the Chief occurred less than a week after his famous rebuttal at Portland. On September 17, fifty-five of the capital's reporters and columnists held a dinner at the National Press Club in his honor.[3] Some newsmen may have felt fraternal ties with the former reporter, but Glassford had won their greatest acclaim for his honesty, his kind management of the BEF, and his devastating exposure of the administration. The dinner was both a tribute to Glassford and another warning to the administration that, supported by such politically powerful friends as the Washington press corps, the Chief had become a dangerous adversary during the final weeks of the campaign. Hoover fully realized the significance of the newsmen's dinner. Because there had been rumors that he would demand Glassford's dismissal after the Portland convention, the President made a point to deny any such plans. In fact, he promised reporters that he would not interfere in the controversies between the Commissioners and the Chief.[4]

Considering Hoover's new reputation as a liar and a conspirator, some reporters were skeptical. They in-

3. *Post*, September 17, 1932. *Editor and Publisher: The Fourth Estate*, September 24, 1932, p. 4. On December 29, 1932, the *Nation* announced its selection of Glassford for its 1932 Honor Roll. For Washington, D.C., newspapers the city is omitted from the citation.

4. *Times*, September 14, 1932; *Daily News*, September 13, 1932; Baltimore *Sun*, July 26, 1932.

terpreted his statement as a sign to the Commissioners that they could remove Glassford at their discretion, as long as they did not implicate the White House.[5] That interpretation is strained and unconvincing, for obviously Hoover had little to gain by firing Glassford. In fact, there were definite advantages to keeping Glassford in office, at least until after the election. Hoover's credibility had been so badly damaged at the Portland debacle that he could not afford any more crises, especially any that would involve the popular Police Chief. Glassford could hurt him immensely if he were fired or if he resigned. The President's promise not to interfere, therefore, was an indication to the Commissioners that they should remain calm and help disarm his critics. Hoping to reduce the criticism, he agreed to a well-publicized meeting with an official delegation from the first (and last) national convention of the quickly disintegrating BEF.[6]

Just as Glassford's national fame reached its peak, his prestige within his own police department began to tumble. At first the members of the Metropolitan Police had cooperated willingly with their new superintendent. They liked and respected him, and during the long BEF encampment had willingly endured sudden alerts, extra hours, and delayed vacations, while exercising great patience with the bonuseers. Glassford, in turn, was truly proud of their performance. But when Glassford insisted on stern discipline against two high-ranking officers for inefficiency during the riot, he touched off a revolt within the department. Despite many months of association with his men, he obviously did not understand them.

The problem was one of identity—the police thought of themselves as civilians doing a thankless, dangerous job,

5. *Times*, September 14, 1932.
6. Hoke Smith to HH, October 7, 1932; FTH to Joslin, October 12, 1932. The FBI investigated "conditions" at the new BEF camp near Uniontown, Pennsylvania, but nothing came of the action. Everett Sanders to Richey, October 8, 1932; Richey to J. Edgar Hoover, October 12, 1932; J. E. Hoover to Richey, October 14, 1932, PP 300, HHPL. For an excellent article on the disintegration of the BEF, see Gertrude Springer, "What Became of the BEF," *Survey*, 68 (December 1, 1932), 640–42. *Evening Star*, October 7, 1932; *Times*, October 18, 1932.

while Glassford, the retired general, expected them to act as battle-toughened soldiers. He overlooked the fact that they were neither equipped, trained, nor psychologically prepared to face the brick battle, the shootings, the hostility, the threats of massive retaliation, and the stubborn refusal of veterans and spectators to heed repeated requests to disperse. Harassed by angry men whom they had befriended for two months, the police were convinced that they could not control the crowd, and they feared the outbreak of widespread violence. Several officers had been seriously battered, and they had repeatedly implored Glassford to ask the Army for assistance. Thus, when he later denied the need for troops, the Chief stood essentially alone.

With this dispute, relations between Glassford and his force began to disintegrate, but a more devastating split came in October. Soon after the Legion convention, when Glassford attempted to discipline two assistant superintendents, he met extensive and unexpected opposition from his men. First, the Chief made an example of Ogden T. Davis, the head of the Crime Prevention Bureau and long a rival in the department. Davis had ordered his detectives to cooperate in the raid on July 29 by the Secret Service, which had resulted in the arrest of the forty alleged radicals, but he had not asked permission from Glassford to participate in the raid. More important, during the grand jury investigation he had criticized Glassford for withdrawing detectives from the eviction site on the day of the riot, and Attorney General Mitchell had used that testimony in his report to the Legion. Yet Detective J. O. Patton, who had been there, had submitted a report on the riot. When the Mitchell document appeared, Glassford revealed what he had earlier told the grand jury—that in addition to himself, plain-clothes detectives who could identify the bonuseers had been on duty at the eviction site, and he named the detectives who had been stationed at Anacostia.

Glassford transferred Assistant Superintendent Davis to another, less prestigious assignment and thereby served notice to his force that he would not tolerate actions that he considered disloyal. At the same time, he demanded the demotion or the resignation of Assistant Superintendent Frank Burke on charges of "inefficiency," although he refused to explain the charges. Since Burke was Chief of Detectives, it appeared that he was to be punished for the same reason as Davis. This time, however, Glassford had gone too far. Davis was obviously guilty of disloyalty, but the even sterner action against Burke threw virtually the entire force into revolt. Furthermore, as only the District Commissioners had the authority to administer such drastic discipline to an assistant superintendent, Glassford seemed to be forcing a showdown with them. The Chief had made it clear that the Commissioners must choose between Burke and himself, and he undoubtedly expected that the public vote of confidence would bring pressure on them to support him. Once again the professional soldier failed to appreciate the viewpoint of the professional cop, particularly on the sensitive issue of job security. The force considered Burke's penalty unduly harsh, and the men reacted quickly with loud, public protests.[7]

The local police association led off the attack against the Chief. Entire police precincts threatened wholesale resignations, and all levels of the department joined the campaign. The widespread outrage within the force enabled the Commissioners to dodge the Chief's ultimatum and instead to work out a compromise that theoretically would satisfy Glassford while keeping Burke on the force.

7. For the details of Mitchell's confusion of Glassford's testimony, see Mitchell report, Mitchell to HH, September 9, 1932, HHPL; Nugent Dodds to D.C. Commissioners, September 8, 1932, DCP. Ogden Davis's testimony is found in MTGJ, pp. 106–8. Also see Glassford to Crosby, September 8, 1932, DCP. Crosby fowarded Glassford's letter to the White House, PP 300, HHPL. Glassford's complete public reply to Mitchell is found in the New York *Times*, September 13, 14, 1932. Also see copy of press release dated September 12 in GP. For details of the problems in the police department see *Evening Star*, September 12, October 1, 1932; *Daily News*, September 29, 1932; *Post*, October 2, 3, 7, 1932; *Times*, October 6, 1932. There is no evidence that Davis saw the Patton report, yet as Chief of the Crime Prevention Bureau, he should have been able to learn that at least one of his detectives was on duty at the eviction site and that he had filed a report.

Surprised and chagrined by the department's vehement reaction, Glassford at first accepted the compromise, but on the following morning, October 20, after brooding over his humiliating defeat, he submitted his resignation.[8] He carefully recorded his version of almost all important incidents during and after the bonus march, but, oddly enough, he did not include either his evidence against Burke or the circumstances of his own sudden resignation.

Theories of conspiracy revived. Few reporters doubted that the worthy Superintendent had been the victim of a vicious plot, but they could not decide whether to blame the Commissioners or the "police machine." None suggested that Glassford might be partially responsible for the dissension; most believed that Hoover had played a larger role in Glassford's resignation than the Chief's own actions.[9] The Commissioners had tried to conciliate Glassford before his resignation, but it was easy for his many admirers to believe that they had not offered enough and that they, the police officers, and perhaps also the President had forced him out.

Thus, Glassford left his department a national hero,[10] to all appearances scandalously misused by the Hoover administration. There is no evidence to suggest that the President wanted Glassford's resignation. As both Hoover and Glassford realized, the ouster of a popular officer could only lose votes.[11] In view of an earlier warning to

8. *Daily News*, October 21, 1932; *Herald*, October 20, 21, 1932; *Times*, October 21, 1932; *Post*, October 20, 1932.

9. *Daily News*, October 21, 1932; *Herald*, October 20, 21, 1932; *Times*, October 21, 1932; *Post*, October 20, 1932. The *Herald* charged that a plot existed to force Glassford to resign as early as October 3, 1932. On October 2, 1932, the *Post* had suggested that Glassford was angling for an appointment as one of the District of Columbia Commissioners. Glassford denied the rumor.

10. The San Francisco *News* stated: "No soldier in peace time has come closer to making himself a national hero"; San Francisco *News*, October 21, 1932. The same idea was expressed by the Philadelphia *Record*, October 22, 1932. For numerous examples of nationwide newspaper praise, see Newspaper Clippings, GP.

11. On October 13, 1932, Walter Newton sent the Commissioners a letter from Congressman John C. Schafer, denouncing Glassford as a

the President that Glassford planned to "spill his guts" just before the election, there is every reason to assume that Hoover was dismayed by the timing of Glassford's resignation.[12]

Glassford left his job embittered by the events of the last several months. He never understood his men's unexpected reaction to his discipline, and, prompted by his supporters' speculations, he thought more and more in terms of conspiracy. Rumors that Hoover was displeased with him had persisted almost since the veterans had arrived in the capital, and the President's criticism on July 29 of his lax enforcement of regulations to control the marchers publicly opened the breach between them. Even without supporting evidence, Glassford's suspicions are understandable. As he put it, the administration was plotting "to make me the goat." [13]

Against the first criticisms of his actions Glassford limited his defense to the specific charges leveled at him by the administration.[14] That restraint had proven highly effective, and he had won the public's respect for his careful rebuttals. Immediately after his resignation, however, he decided to enter the presidential campaign. No longer a member of the police force, he was completely free to attack Hoover.

In contrast with his skillful rebuttal of the Attorney General's charges, Glassford now became less careful with the facts. He publicly insisted that the BEF had been "discriminated against," in comparison with the hunger marchers of Coxey's Army. Especially striking

---

"publicity hound" who had given the Democrats a "large size club" with which to beat Republicans during the campaign. Schafer's letter is in DCP.

12. On October 15, Hoover received a report that Glassford would release a statement "that will knock your hat off just about ten days to two weeks before the election. He is going to spill his guts about the whole situation in Washington as it pertains to the Bonus Army and other things." "Report," October 5, 1932, PP 298, HHPL. Owen P. White hinted at much the same belief at the conclusion of his interview in *Collier's*. Owen P. White, "General Glassford's Story: An Interview," *Collier's*, 90 (October 29, 1932), 32.

13. PDG to Christopher C. Coles, August 10, 1932, GP.

14. Ibid.

were his bold suppositions that the proposed permanent encampment was never intended to be permanent but actually a means of moving the men off federal property and that eventually, it was hoped, the marchers would have become dissatisfied and returned home voluntarily.[15] To be sure, Coxey's Army had disintegrated in that manner after the men had put the matter to a vote. Waters, by contrast, had at first used BEF military police to intimidate those who sought transportation loans, and he repeatedly vowed to stay in Washington another thirteen years if necessary. Glassford continued to fault the administration for not accepting his plan to evacuate the men to Camp Bartlett, but he failed to mention that the plan aborted when Bartlett suddenly withdrew his offer of the use of his land.

However, the ex-Chief's cruelest blow was his insistence that "of course we got nothing from the federal government but the people of the District of Columbia were magnificent in helping us out." Glassford may have been unaware that Hoover had channeled the Army rations, bedsacks, tents, rolling kitchens, aid station, field hospital, and medical supplies through inconspicuous outlets such as the National Guard and Veterans Administration. There is evidence, however, that he knew the source of at least some of these supplies. On June 16, the day the field hospital was erected, he told a friend that he was "getting more and more support from the powers that be." A more likely explanation for his comment is that Glassford was too angry at the time of his resignation to credit Hoover and his administration with their due.[16]

Immediately after his resignation Glassford accepted an attractive offer to write for the Hearst newspapers a series on the events surrounding the Bonus Riot, and on October 30—only ten days after his resignation and nine days before the election—the first installment of his eight-part exposé appeared.[17] The series introduced Americans to

15. White, "Glassford's Story," pp. 10, 11, 32.
16. Ibid. PDG to Rush Sturges, June 16, 1932, GP.
17. PDG to William Randolph Hearst, June 21, 1933, GP. Glassford complained to Hearst that he had not received at least $600, which

yet another thesis based on conspiracy, one that Glassford had for some time believed but had not yet made public. The American people might well have become tired, by this time, of all the charges of conspiracy. There was no newspaper conspiracy against the administration, Hoover's "red revolution" had not materialized, and the *B.E.F. News* had never produced any evidence of its charge that officials high in the administration were plotting to establish a dictatorship.[18] Still, Glassford's articles, released in the last days of the campaign, provided sensational reading. With the help of the Hearst staff he created the impression that his chronicle exposed the real inside story, the hidden, sordid truth about Herbert Hoover's calculated plot to promote violence and thus create a winning law-and-order issue.

Glassford based his theory of Hoover's conspiracy on two major assumptions. The first was his oft-repeated belief that troops were not needed and that Hoover had seized upon a manufactured need to bring in the Army and drive out the BEF. Glassford's second assumption was that the troops had arrived quickly and therefore, he speculated, they must have been called out "one half hour before" the shootings took place. He implied that Hoover might have had good reason to call out the troops if he had waited until after the shootings. The hasty troop call was clearly unjustified, however, and proved, according to Glassford, that Hoover had planned the attack several weeks earlier, hoping thereby for law and order to become an important factor in the campaign.[19] As he saw

Hearst owed him for writing the articles. He insisted that in addition to the eight articles at $100 each, Hearst representatives had promised him $250 each for four articles on police work, but had accepted only two of them. Glassford further complained that he had not yet received all of his profits on syndicate sales of the eight articles to other newspapers. First article is in New York *American*, October 30, 1932.

18. *B.E.F. News*, November 5, 1932.

19. Copies of the series are in Newspaper Clippings, GP, and in PP 298, HHPL. New York *American*, October 30, November 4, 5, 1932; *Herald*, October 31, November 2, 3, 4, 5, 6, 1932. Following his views closely, Fleta Springer suggested the Glassford conspiracy thesis; Springer, "Glassford and the Siege of Washington," *Harper's Magazine*, 165 (November 1932), 654. Irving Bernstein relied heavily on the com-

it, Hoover had callously provoked the violence as a pretext for sending in troops, which were not needed. *Time* reported this charge as early as August 8, but neither *Time* nor Glassford gave any proof of the assertion.[20]

Historians have not examined carefully Glassford's incorrect charge that the troops had been called out before the shootings.[21] Glassford remembered that the shooting started at about 1:45 P.M. On another occasion he placed the incident some time "before 2 P.M." His failure to be precise is understandable; he had been thoroughly occupied trying to stop the fight and the wild shooting by Officer Shenault, so he could only approximate the time.[22] Records from the Army message center accurately establish that MacArthur alerted the troops at 1:35, and that five minutes later, at 1:40, he ordered them to assemble at the Ellipse behind the White House.[23] Using either of

pelling Glassford Papers and accepted the Police Chief's charge that the troops were called out before the shootings took place. Although he reflected Glassford's shock at a "drastic change" in administration policy, Bernstein did not repeat the Chief's charge of political conspiracy. Irving Bernstein, *The Lean Years: A History of the American Worker, 1920–1933* (Boston: Houghton Mifflin, 1960), p. 452. John D. Weaver, "Bonus March," *American Heritage*, 14 (June 1963), 94.

20. Hurley had publicly stated that it was only after the "second riot" that the Commissioners requested the troops; "Statement by the Honorable Patrick J. Hurley, Secretary of War, on 'Bonus Marchers in Washington,' " PP 297, HHPL. A shorter version of this press release, which makes the same distinction between the two riots, is dated August 3, 1932, PP 300, HHPL. Hurley was in error, however, on a number of specifics, including the exact wording of the Commissioners' written request to Hoover. New York *American*, November 5, 1932; "Riots," *Time*, 20 (August 8, 1932), 6.

21. Waters, *B.E.F.*, pp. 217, 222, 227; Arthur Hennessy, "Bonus Army of 1932" (Ph.D. diss., Georgetown University, 1957), p. 332.

22. PDG, "Circumstances Leading Up to the Use of Federal Forces," p. 6; GT, p. 9; his reply to Attorney General Mitchell, New York *Times*, September 13, 1932, in which he cited "about 1:45 P.M." Roger Daniels, *The Bonus March: An Episode of the Great Depression* (Westport, Conn.: Greenwood Press, Inc., 1971), pp. 153, 163, 165, 172, 175. Materials in note 19. A year later, in 1933, Waters placed the time of the shootings around 2:00, but his greater concern on the day of the riot was his belief in an alleged plot to assassinate him, and with the outbreak of shootings his bodyguard whisked him off to a hotel where he hid for two hours; Waters, *B.E.F.*, p. 222.

23. "Report of Operations Against Bonus Marchers, 1932," War De-

Glassford's estimates of the shooting time, 1:45 or 2:00, one might erroneously conclude that Hoover had indeed precipitately responded to the brick battle.

One commentator states that, after Hoover summoned troops, fate supplied him with "two convenient corpses." [24] In other words, Hoover quickly seized upon an inadequate pretext, but the shootings then took place and thus seemingly provided justification for the precipitate troop call. Despite some kind references to the President, this view essentially reinforces the impression of the fearful Hoover that has passed down through the years. This interpretation also contends that the time marked in ink on the troop deployment order—2:55 P.M.—was a deliberate falsification of the record by Hurley.[25]

Neither Glassford nor those who have accepted much of his version have recognized that between the 1:40 troop assembly call and 2:55, when the troop deployment order was finally issued, a significant and intense debate took place. Hurley had urged Hoover to sign an insurrection proclamation, but the President refused both the original and revised versions. Nor did several telephone conversations change his mind. In spite of Hurley and MacArthur's pressure on him in the Oval Office, Hoover refused to consider the disorders a military operation, and Hurley's first draft of the troop deployment order had to

partment, III Corps Area, RG 98, NA; "Mr. Alf's Record at Message Center," July 28, 1932, Records of U.S. Army Continental Commands, 1920–1942, Selected Documents 1932, RG 394, NA; Perry L. Miles to Douglas MacArthur, August 4, 1932, "Report of Operations Against Bonus Marchers," PP 300, HHPL (hereafter cited as Miles, "Report").

24. Daniels, *Bonus March*, p. 153.

25. Daniels, *Bonus March*, p. 175. Daniels correctly rejects the charge that Hoover was plotting a reelection campaign issue (p. 172). However, his nuances are disturbing. He suggests that Hoover may have been in league with the Commissioners (p. 145) who, he claims, saw the plan to repossess buildings as a "military operation" (p. 146). Daniels portrays it as a "chess game" (p. 142) and "showdown" (p. 143) in which the most "combative" men were to be evicted first. (See my comments concerning the first repossession site, pp. 156–57). He also accepts and elaborates on the charge that Hoover seized upon a flimsy pretext to call out the troops before the shootings (pp. 153, 163, 165, 172) and accuses Hurley of falsifying the time marked on the final order (p. 175). He offers little evidence to corroborate Glassford's incorrect estimate of the time of the shootings (pp. 154–55).

be revised significantly before Hoover would approve it. Considering Hoover's stubborn refusal to give the Army carte blanche, the final version also undoubtedly underwent careful scrutiny before the time of approval could be marked on it. Indeed, the final version issued at 2:55 clearly placed the operation under the control of civilian authorities, but MacArthur overrode the President's instructions.

No one has refuted Glassford's estimate of when the shootings took place. This timing is important, for he used this detail to propagate a view of Hoover as a fearful and callous schemer who deliberately provoked the riot in order to gain reelection. A careful examination easily disproves these claims. By the time Glassford's articles for Hearst appeared in late October and early November, the chronology of the afternoon's events had become a matter of some political concern. In the last days before the election Hoover's integrity was in question, and Glassford was determined to prove him a ruthless conspirator. Immediately following the riot, however, almost no one suspected that the exact time of the shootings might ever be used to influence the election or to impugn the President's reputation. The earlier testimony is less biased, in fact, and eminently more reliable than Glassford's later emotional recollections.

Indeed, it is quite clear that the shootings took place before 1:45, Glassford's earliest estimate—and in fact before the troops were summoned at 1:40 to assemble. On July 29, the day following the riot, the Associated Press outlined the chronology of the previous day's events. It designated the time of the shootings at 1:25, fifteen minutes before MacArthur telephoned the message center to summon troops to the Ellipse.[26] *Time* magazine set the

26. New York *Times*, July 29, 1932. Byron Price, chief of the Washington Bureau of the Associated Press, was an eyewitness to the shooting of Huska; Byron Price, Oral History Interview, March 21, 1969. In response to my written inquiry concerning the time sequence compiled by the Associated Press, Price informed me that, according to standard procedure, such time sequences were "put together on the news desk from information from a dozen reporters"; Byron Price to author April 13, 1972.

shootings at 1:25, as did the New York *Herald Tribune*. Still another objective witness was Doak Carter, chief of staff of the BEF. Carter could not foresee any political significance in his assessment, and he would never have knowingly exonerated Hoover of blame. He reported the shootings at 1:30.[27]

In addition to the reports of various representatives of the press and of Doak Carter of the BEF, three police officers also stated that the shootings had occurred considerably earlier than the 1:40 assembly call. Assistant Superintendent Ogden T. Davis recorded that he had arrived at the site at about 1:30 because he had heard that "a great deal of shooting was going on down there." Lewis I. H. Edwards, another assistant superintendent, reported 1:15, and Thaddeus R. Bean, an inspector, swore that the shootings took place at 1:10.[28] Thus, at least seven witnesses placed the shootings between 1:10 and 1:30, well before MacArthur's 1:40 call to assemble, long before the troops actually arrived at the Ellipse, and still longer before they began dispersing the BEF. It is not reasonable to believe that the three policemen, the Associated Press, *Time*, the *Herald Tribune*, or Doak Carter had reason to falsify the record.

Using any of these reports by reliable witnesses, it is evident that Lt. Ira Keck, the Commissioners' agent at the scene, had time to telephone his superiors. According to the Commissioners' testimony, they quickly reached both the President and MacArthur, then rushed their formal request. The rapid telephone calls from Keck to the Commissioners to MacArthur gave the Chief of Staff time to reach the message center. First, at 1:35, he called in the alert, then five minutes later he phoned in the order to assemble.

Ordering troops to assemble and holding them in readiness were understandable precautions, yet they did not commit the Army to action. Glassford misjudged the time

27. "Battle of Washington," *Time*, p. 6; New York *Herald Tribune*, July 29, 1932; Indianapolis *Times*, September 12, 1932.
28. "Statement of Ogden T. Davis," August 3, 1932; "Statement of Lewis I. H. Edwards," "Statement of Thaddeus Bean," DCP.

of the shootings and also was clearly in error in his sense of hasty troop deployment. MacArthur called in the assembly order at 1:40, and after important changes in the wording Hurley issued the final written order at 2:55. According to General Miles, although his "previous orders had assigned the Ellipse as the assembly position," he did not receive the call from MacArthur until "about 3 P.M." informing him that he "would soon receive definite orders. . . . A few minutes later the definite order arrived by telephone." But even with the 1:40 assembly call, the first troops did not arrive at the Ellipse until 3:13. Other units from the various nearby posts straggled in during the next hour, while the 3d Battalion, 12th Infantry, did not arrive until 4:16. At 4:30 troops marched from the Ellipse, and at 5:00 they moved into the troubled area. By contrast, on July 16, when Congress had adjourned, newsmen reported that armed tank troops had waited two hours, anticipating trouble, while only a few blocks from the Capitol a force of Marines also stood ready. On July 28, however, the 254 men of the 3d Battalion, 12th Infantry, were out on the rifle range, and the entire morning at Fort Myer had been routine.[29] They arrived at the Ellipse 1½ to 2½ hours after the assembly order. At approximately 5:30—four hours or more after the shootings—the Army began routing the veterans and spectators from the area. Glassford and other critics failed to make these dis-

---

29. "Mr. Alf's Record at Message Center"; Perry L. Miles, *Fallen Leaves: Memories of An Old Soldier* (Berkeley, Calif.: Wuerth Publishing Company, 1961), p. 306. According to Miles's Report, he did not join MacArthur and have an opportunity to see the written order until 3:59 P.M.; Miles, "Report," pp. 1–4. For activities at Fort Myer on the morning of July 28, see H. W. Blakeley, "When the Army was Smeared," *Combat Forces Journal*, 2 (February 1952), 29; D. Clayton James, *The Years of MacArthur, 1880–1941* (Boston: Houghton Mifflin Company, 1970), pp. 396–98, 409. James puts the shootings at 2:15 P.M. and argues that the administration was involved in a "conspiracy to maneuver the B.E.F. into precipitate action that would justify the use of the Army to get a quick eviction." For events of July 16, see Chapter 7, pp. 132–38. Although the troops moved into the riot area at 5:00, they maneuvered for another half hour and did not begin the rout until approximately 5:30; RCS, p. 7, and New York *Times*, July 29, 1932. The *Times* indicated that the gas attack occurred some time between 5:20 and 5:40.

tinctions. The administration did not falsify the time line on the final order, and by no stretch of logic were the troops used prematurely, as the popular and persistent myth suggests.

Attempts to ascribe exact times to such incidents often produce more errors than conspiracies. Glassford's conspiracy theory rested on a very shaky premise. The evidence clearly refutes the attempt to prove that a sly or frightened Hoover prematurely called out the troops before the shootings. Too many unbiased sources challenge Glassford's basic claims. He was mistaken both in his estimate of the time of the shootings and in his charge of rapid troop deployment. Furthermore, it must be recalled that the President believed that the Chief had requested the troops. Whether the Commissioners incorrectly assumed Glassford's approval after the resurgence of violence or deliberately misrepresented his views, Hoover became a victim of the misunderstanding.

One of the saddest ironies in the story of the Bonus Army is that the person who was most able to stop Mac-Arthur—Police Chief Glassford—did not. When Mac-Arthur arrived at the Ellipse, where the troops had begun to assemble, Glassford immediately sought out his old schoolmate to ascertain the Army's instructions. He told MacArthur that his men were exhausted, a statement MacArthur later used as a justification for the rout.[30] After MacArthur explained his plan, Glassford had almost two hours to do something about it—from about 3:45 until 5:30, when the rout began.

Instead of challenging the need for such a drastic action, the Chief, according to his own testimony, volunteered to place "the Metropolitan police force at his disposal." Glassford recalled, "By agreement between MacArthur and myself, the Metropolitan Police under my command took no part in the actual eviction, but assumed the functions of keeping traffic lanes necessary to the eviction clear, and keeping the thousands of curious spectators at a distance from the fracas." As MacArthur put it,

30. RCS, p. 6.

this was an "important" part of his plan, and he was pleased to have Glassford's full cooperation. Thus, although the Police Chief later denounced Hoover for sending troops, at the time he willingly helped MacArthur to use them as he pleased.[31]

During the Death March Glassford had stopped the Marines by getting in contact with a friendly senator, who quickly spoke to the President. Considering his political contacts, and in light of his strong public statements denouncing the troop call, Glassford's uncomplaining but "important" cooperation with MacArthur raises disturbing questions about his judgment. If Glassford were so upset and angry about Hoover's decision to send troops, why did he not at the time demand that MacArthur show him the orders, or reach a sympathetic senator, check with the White House himself, or in some other way refuse to cooperate with the General? Hoover's instructions had placed Glassford—not MacArthur—in charge, and a reading of the order would have made that fact clear to the Chief.

After having challenged the President, the Vice President, the Speaker of the House, the Capitol Police Board, the District Commissioners, and a variety of congressmen on a number of important issues concerning the BEF, it is curious that Glassford offered no opposition to MacArthur's decision, but, in fact, willingly cooperated.

In April 1951, after President Truman relieved MacArthur of command in Korea for refusing to obey orders, Glassford sent his old friend a copy of an interview in

31. PDG to John T. Rogers, January 19, 1946, GP; RCS, pp. 6–7. MacArthur conferred with Glassford about "the projected troop movement" at "about 3:45 P.M." The troops did not begin their march until 4:30 P.M. and did not arrive at the eviction site until 5:00 P.M. Another half hour passed before the troops acted against the veterans. MacArthur believed that Glassford fulfilled an "important" function. MacArthur to the Attorney General, August 6, 1932, PP 300, HHPL. MacArthur informed the Attorney General that the "police authorities and police generally coordinated and cooperated in the most hearty fashion from the time the troops were summoned. Their cooperation was such as to cause General Miles, the immediate commander of the Army detachment, to write a letter of appreciation to General Glassford." MacArthur claimed the cooperation "was, of course, voluntary, as they were not under my orders or command."

which he had praised the General's use of troops during the ouster of the BEF. Glassford now stated that the troops had assembled at the rear of the White House "*a few hours after the riot*," and not once in all the years after the rout did he offer anything but the highest praise of MacArthur's "brilliant and magnificently" executed plan. MacArthur proudly recalled that the last time he saw Glassford that evening, the Chief was personally commanding a police detachment "clearing the mob by use of tear gas bombs" near the Anacostia camp.[32] Indeed, Moseley documented that Glassford had expressed to him his pleasure that MacArthur had evacuated the huge camp that night because the veterans would have been uncontrollable the next morning.[33]

The key element in Glassford's belief that Herbert Hoover had plotted the rout was the Chief's devotion to Douglas MacArthur. Both of their fathers had been professional soldiers, and MacArthur had known and highly valued Glassford's father. "Happy" Glassford, the West Point plebe, had followed the career of upperclassman MacArthur with open admiration. While at West Point, Glassford had predicted that MacArthur would some day be President. Among West Point career men and general officers of the United States Army, and especially for Glassford, the notion that the President's orders might be violated by the Chief of Staff was unthinkable. When Mac-

32. My italics. MacArthur to the Attorney General, August 6, 1932, PP 300, HHPL; PDG to MacArthur, April 26, 1951, MacArthur Papers (hereafter cited as MP). Glassford enclosed a newspaper clipping of an interview which he had granted to his home town newspaper, the Laguna Beach (California) *Post*, April 26, 1951.

33. Maurice Paterson Sneller, "The Bonus March of 1932: A Study of Depression Leadership and Its Legacy," (Ph.D. diss., University of Virginia, 1960), pp. 284–85. Sneller doubted whether Moseley had heard Glassford correctly. Glassford's constant praise of MacArthur's action and his own energetic cooperation suggest, however, that Moseley's recollection was accurate; see note 34. Furthermore, Moseley took the precaution to have his driver, Sgt. John W. Powder, verify Glassford's praise in a signed statement, which Moseley preserved; statement by John W. Powder, November 11, 1932, Moseley Papers, LC. Glassford did not criticize the rout of the veterans from the Anacostia camp. His criticism was limited to the initial decision to begin any evictions, to send troops, and to making him "the goat." PDG to HH, draft letter, n.d., GP 679.

Arthur informed him that "he had orders from the Chief Executive to drive the veterans out of the city," Glassford did not question him, even when MacArthur characterized his plan as one that would "break the back of the BEF." [34]

Although Hoover, as President, was commander-in-chief of the armed services, he was also a politician. Glassford viewed politicians with disdain, if not contempt, as men who would knowingly use deception to stay in power, and his articles for Hearst reiterated that theme.[35] By contrast, he tended to view military officers as selfless servants of the nation. Glassford adamantly refused to consider the possibility that the decision to drive out the BEF was MacArthur's rather than Hoover's. In

34. PDG to MacArthur, April 26, 1951, MP. *Evening Star*, November 4, 1932. Glassford criticized MacArthur for his statement to the press, insisting that the veterans had been "animated by the essence of revolution." PDG to Aldace Walker, May, 1952, GP 679. MacArthur's statement, Glassford recalled, was "the only rotten thing I have ever known him to do." In the same letter Glassford claimed to be surprised to learn that Attorney General Mitchell had taken the sworn statement of the Commissioners concerning Glassford's request for troops. The Commissioners' letter to Hoover, which claimed Glassford's request, had been published in Washington newspapers on July 29. Not until twenty years later, in 1952, in the letter to his former secretary, Aldace Walker, did the former Chief conclude that Hoover was not to blame. "Mr. Hoover cannot be accused of prevarication," Glassford informed Walker. "He knew nothing about the Bonus Army personally and in the article is setting forth what was reported to him by some of his gutless subordinates." The Hoover article to which Glassford referred appeared in *Collier's*, May 24, 1952. It reiterated Hoover's belief in a Communist plot and revealed for the first time that his orders had been exceeded. Although Glassford now blamed Hoover's "gutless subordinates," he did not agree with all portions of the article. As head of a "Draft MacArthur" committee, he felt that if he and Walker were to refute any of Hoover's account, it might hurt MacArthur's chances for winning the Republican presidential nomination. Possibly for that reason Glassford never sent Hoover a drafted letter in which he wondered why Hoover had not disciplined MacArthur if the General had exceeded his authority. PDG to Hoover, draft letter, n.d., GP 679. Glassford had no way of knowing about Hoover's efforts to stop the rout, or of MacArthur and Hurley's influence on Hoover after the rout.

35. PDG, "Veteran Participation in Politics," July 16, 1933, Box 15, GP 679. David Brion Davis, ed., *The Fear of Conspiracy: Images of Un-American Subversion from the Revolution to the Present* (Ithaca, N.Y.: Cornell University Press, 1971), p. xxiv. Davis cites reaction against "the expediency and compromise of conventional politics" as a source of frustration, which nurtures conspiratorial explanations.

fact, while later addressing veteran rallies under the aus-
pices of the Democratic National Committee, Glassford
repeatedly cited MacArthur's statements as his principal
evidence of a conspiracy by Hoover. Significantly, Mac-
Arthur never suggested that Glassford might have misun-
derstood or misquoted him. Not even in 1951, when Mac-
Arthur virtually forced Truman to relieve him of
command in Korea, would Glassford believe that his
trusted friend was capable of deliberately disobeying orders.[36]

Glassford's damaging charges greatly distressed Hoover
during the final days of the campaign. Administration officials sought unsuccessfully to destroy Glassford's credibility by releasing his warning to the Commissioners,
given early in June, which had indicated the possible
need for federal troops. By making that letter public, the
administration hoped to convince voters that he had approved troops for a lesser emergency. The last-minute
counterattack was a case of too little too late, and Hoover
obscured it with a clumsy, tactless remark in St. Paul on
November 6. As Joslin put it, Hoover was "out on his feet.
. . . I knew something was wrong the minute the radio
began bringing his address over the air. He spoke halt-
ingly and without emphasis. His voice was tired. He lost
his place in the manuscript again and again. I learned
later that a man sat directly behind him gripping an
empty chair throughout the time he was speaking, so that,
if he should collapse, the chair could be pushed under
him and he would not fall to the platform." Overcome by
weariness and deeply wounded by the many charges leveled against him, Hoover struck back at his critics and in
so doing climaxed his last campaign speech with another
stunning blunder. "Thank God," he cried, "you still have
a government in Washington that knows how to deal with
a mob." [37] The outburst was sad testimony to Hoover's

36. PDG to MacArthur, December 17, 1946; PDG to MacArthur,
April 26, 1951, MP; PDG to Aldace Walker, May, 1952, GP 679.

37. Theodore J. Joslin, *Hoover Off The Record* (New York: Doubleday, Doran and Co., 1934), p. 324. *Herald,* November 4, 7, 8, 1932;
New York *Times,* November 6, 1932.

deep hurt at being labeled a murderer, to his bitter frustration over the rout, and to Glassford's effectiveness.

Speculation concerning conspiracy dominated the thinking of almost everyone involved in the rout. Stories of imagined conspiracies proliferated and compounded to distort the event completely. Participants and political commentators alike sought simple, emotionally appealing explanations for the complex chain of events and for the abundance of contradictory testimony. Hoover clung tenaciously to his belief that the bonus march was part of a Communist plot. At the same time, Glassford became unalterably convinced of a conspiracy by Hoover against himself and against the BEF as well. Both Hoover and Glassford's fancied conspiracies were related, in part, to the trust they placed in MacArthur.

Throughout the long years of criticism the effect of the bonus rout during the campaign and on Hoover's reputation became for him a deep and bitter source of hurt. Stung by the public's reaction, the President brooded over references to himself as "the murderer of American veterans" and to his Chief of Staff as "the tool of the Fascists." Those who repeated such views he would come increasingly to label "commisar[s]." Although troubled by recurring doubts about MacArthur's disobedience, Hoover nonetheless held stubbornly to his belief that a Communist plot was responsible for the disturbances. Clearly, the administration's defense was politically disastrous and ethically reprehensible. Hoover had unwisely trusted the men who disobeyed him, and he believed instead that the mounting criticism was the work of Communists, radicals, and Democrats, who conspired to ruin his good name. Almost "every Democratic speaker," he said, "in the 1932 campaign implied that I had murdered veterans in the streets of Washington." [38]

The rout haunted him throughout the rest of his life. For years, whenever the time for a presidential campaign

38. Herbert Hoover, *Memoirs* (New York: The Macmillan Co., 1941), III, 225–32. Herbert Hoover, "The 1932 Campaign," *Collier's*, 129 (May 24, 1952), 32.

approached, Hoover's political opponents revived their charges against their favorite villain. For example, as late as 1943 the CIO Political Action Committee circulated a leaflet in anticipation of the return of World War II servicemen. A picture of troops in a welcome-home parade contrasted sharply with a photo from the Bonus Riot, showing the brick battle between veterans and police. The caption beneath the photo asked, "Will they come home to this?" The leaflet incorrectly declared that Hoover's answer to the hungry veterans had been troops, tanks, and cavalry.[39] In the outpouring of intense hatred against him, the President was wrongly portrayed as a mean, vindictive, frightened, brutal man. Glassford's conspiracy theory was effective in damaging Hoover's reputation and contributed significantly to his personal tragedy. Yet the President—and especially his advisers—had structured the administration's defense, and for their miseducation of the public they must bear much of the responsibility for that tragedy.

39. Hoover, *Memoirs*, III, 225–32; CIO Political Action Committee, Campaign Leaflet, November 23, 1943; copy in PP 298, HHPL.

13

Roosevelt and the Bonus Marches

Hoover and his advisers had once hoped that, during the summer months after Congress adjourned, a period of relative quiet would prevail. For a time the President clung to his belief that he could win the election over Roosevelt. After the riot, however, especially when the defense of the rout failed, administration officials gave in to despair. According to Joslin, as of September 15, three days after Glassford's highly publicized rebuttal of the Attorney General's report, there "was no question that the President was hopelessly defeated." Although the economy showed signs of improvement, "every disgruntled individual was against him." [1]

The depression was obviously the decisive factor in destroying Hoover's political career, but the BEF controversy dealt the most serious blow to his reputation as a forthright leader and man of personal integrity. The use of force now seemed to be his chief response to hungry people. Mark Sullivan, the well-known correspondent and a friend of Hoover, predicted that the rout might very well become the determining factor in November.[2] As for the bonus as a national cause, it was not much more popular than previously,[3] and immediate payment never became the major campaign issue that many had predicted.

1. Theodore Joslin, *Hoover Off the Record* (New York: Doubleday, Doran and Company, 1934), pp. 218, 315, 322. "I'll tell you what the trouble is," Hoover stated. "We are opposed by 6,000,000 unemployed, 10,000 bonus marchers, and ten cent corn. Is it any wonder that the prospects look dark?"

2. "The Bonus Bomb Bursts Into the Campaign," *The Literary Digest*, 114 (September 24, 1932), 12.

3. The evidence is overwhelming. Ibid.; "Behind the Bonus Battlefront," *Literary Digest*, 114 (October 1, 1932), 11; Alfred E. Smith, "A Halt to Veteran Legislation," *Review of Reviews*, 86 (July 1932), 43;

One reason for the weakness of the bonus as an issue was Roosevelt's long opposition to it. He had cooperated with the administration's pleas to urge the veterans back to their respective states. As governor of New York, Roosevelt had offered both transportation and jobs to the contingent from his state, but they felt that fighting for the bonus was more vital to their future, so they chose to remain in Washington. During the campaign Roosevelt avoided, as far as he was able, any discussion of the bonus. Only after Calvin Coolidge asserted that Roosevelt's silence on the issue was retarding economic recovery and after intense pressure from Hurley and other Republicans did he bring the issue into his campaign, on October 19 in Pittsburgh.[4]

Roosevelt had received considerable advice on how to handle the bonus issue. Felix Frankfurter, the Harvard law professor whom Roosevelt was later to appoint to the United States Supreme Court, urged that "the rejection of the cash bonus" was imperative—and for the same reasons Hoover had so often cited. Frankfurter also insisted that it "must be linked up with the cruel and unstates-

"The Legion Raid," *Christian Century*, 49 (September 28, 1932), 1159–61; New York *Times*, September 11, 16, 1932; Chicago *Tribune*, September 24, 1932; "Portland Thorn," *Time*, 20 (September 26, 1932), 8–9; "Exacting Tribute From a Nation," *Woman's Home Companion*, 59 (August 1932), 4; Walter Lippmann, "The Demands of the Veterans," *Woman's Home Companion*, 59 (August 1932), 13; Walter Davenport, "Taking Allowances," *Collier's*, 90 (August 20, 1932), 12–13, 46–47; *Post*, July 26, 1932; New York *World Telegram*, September 17, 1932. Edward L. Bernays to Henry M. Robinson, September 20, 1932, PP 297, HHPL. For Washington, D.C., newspapers the city is omitted from the citation.

4. Robert G. Simmons to Newton, July 2, 1932; Memo, September 6, 1932, PP 297, HHPL; New York *Times*, September 21, 29, October 7, 12, 20, 21, 1932. Felix Frankfurter was privately disappointed in FDR's silence and consistently urged him to speak out against the bonus. Nevertheless, he defended Roosevelt to critic Walter Lippmann. Felix Frankfurter to Walter Lippmann, October 13 and 26, 1932, in *Roosevelt and Frankfurter: Their Correspondence, 1928–1945*, Max Freedman, ed. (Boston: Little, Brown and Company, 1967), pp. 89–91. Elmer Thomas had urged FDR to remain silent. Elmer Thomas to Franklin D. Roosevelt, October 17, 1932, Thomas Papers, University of Oklahoma. Campaign pamphlet, Democratic National Committee, *Pledges, Promises, and Proposals of the Democratic Party* (n.p., 1932), p. 14.

manlike treatment of the BEF—the President's failure to take the sober and responsible leaders of the men into common counsel and the slanderous miseducation of the country regarding the BEF by Attorney General Mitchell's report disseminated by the President." [5] By contrast, Congressman Rankin, chairman of the Committee on World War Veterans Legislation, implored Roosevelt not to throw away four million votes by opposing the bonus. It would be better to say nothing, he advised, especially as four million votes would "control this election." [6]

Roosevelt rejected both viewpoints. He stated his opposition to the bonus, but to his credit, he refused to mention the rout. One might argue that numbers of other Democratic politicians were already keeping that matter before the public. Roosevelt indeed held deep feelings about the rout, but he shared them only with his most intimate advisers. In his speech at Pittsburgh he repeated his opposition to immediate payment, which he had voiced as early as April, and brushed aside Coolidge's charge as "baseless and absurd." "I do not see how," he repeated, "as a matter of practical sense, a Government running behind two billion dollars annually can consider the anticipation of bonus payment until it has a balanced budget, not only on paper but with a surplus of cash in the treasury." [7]

The Republicans remained unsatisfied. William Allen White insisted that Roosevelt had evaded the issue, since he had not categorically condemned the veterans' demand as unjust or economically catastrophic; this latest example of artful dodging was nothing other than "a dirty

5. Felix Frankfurter to Samuel Rosenman, September 29, 1932, Election of 1932 file, Frankfurter Papers, LC.

6. J. E. Rankin to FDR, October 19, 1932, Democratic National Committee, Mississippi, FDRL. The letter obviously arrived too late, but it does represent the conflicting advice.

7. New York *Times*, October 20, 1932; Franklin D. Roosevelt, *The Public Papers and Addresses of Franklin D. Roosevelt*, Samuel I. Rosenman, ed. (New York: Random House, Inc., 1938), VI, 809. FDR remained consistent. FDR to R. D. Baker, October 29, 1932, Democratic National Committee, Georgia, FDRL.

trick." By championing the repeal of prohibition and holding out a vague promise of the bonus, Roosevelt had "dunked his bonus in beer." "Bitter bread it will be for him on the day of reckoning," White angrily predicted.[8]

By now the bonus issue had become heavily clouded. It included both the question of immediate payment and the explosive rout,[9] but it was the rout of the marchers that dominated opinion on the matter. Democrats were delighted with Roosevelt's skill and Hoover's blundering, and they made the most of their opportunity. Some politicians like Louisiana's fiery Huey Long declared that the bonus affair was the hottest issue of the election, and after considerable hesitation Jim Farley, chairman of the Democratic National Committee, allowed him to stump for the national ticket. James Van Zandt, national commander of the VFW, and ex-Marine General Smedley Butler joined him in castigating the President. To everyone's surprise, Long did so well on the campaign circuit that in Farley's opinion he might have carried Pennsylvania also for Roosevelt if he had been allowed to campaign there.[10]

Rexford Tugwell, a member of the "Brains Trust," observed that Hoover's outrageous handling of this incident "had a tremendous impact, all of which was favorable to the Roosevelt cause. . . . No Democrat was even remotely involved, and there was nothing whatever to do except to watch with incredulous gratification. If it had been planned by a political strategist, the affair could not have been more perfectly arranged." [11]

Frankfurter also recognized the political advantages of

8. "Where Roosevelt Stands On the Bonus," *Literary Digest*, 114 (October 29, 1932), 5–6; New York *Times*, October 21, 1932.

9. Roy V. Peel and Thomas C. Donnelly, *The 1932 Election: An Analysis* (New York: Farrar & Rinehart, Inc., 1935), p. 141. These two scholars referred to the bonus issue as "the most potent under-cover question in the campaign."

10. New York *Times*, September 13, 1932; interview with James Van Zandt, April 14, 1972; James A. Farley, *Jim Farley's Story: The Roosevelt Years* (New York: McGraw-Hill, Inc., 1948), pp. 170–71. The best account of the campaign is in Frank Freidel, *Franklin D. Roosevelt*, III: *The Triumph* (Boston: Little, Brown and Company, 1956).

11. Rexford Guy Tugwell, *The Brains Trust* (New York: The Viking Press, Inc., 1968), pp. 359, 316, 295–96.

the controversy and the effect it had on Roosevelt's candidacy. He recalled a conversation at the Governor's Mansion in Albany in which Roosevelt had explained how he would have handled the protesters. If he were President, Roosevelt had said, he would have called the veterans' leaders together at the White House and told them that they could not have the bonus because there was not enough money in the Treasury and the nation "can't borrow it to pay off your certificates." But he would have given them jobs developing the Shenandoah National Park and would thereby, he hoped, stimulate states and municipalities to offer similar types of job-producing public works. His proposal had the advantages of attacking unemployment while simultaneously defusing the protest. If the bonus marchers had rejected such an idea, they would have had only themselves to blame, and the nation would have viewed their activities in a less sympathetic light.

Probably no one knew better than Roosevelt how much the rout had helped the Democratic cause. He watched his exhausted opponent with wonder and perhaps some sympathy, for both had served in the Wilson administration, and Roosevelt had then regarded Hoover as a fine candidate for the Presidency. Now he wondered to Tugwell what it was "that made so great a man so inept a national leader," for Hoover had once been so effective. "But when he had become President, he had hardly seemed the same man who had saved the Belgians and then the rest of Europe and Russia from starvation, had been so effective a food administrator during the war, and had then gone on to be the strong man in the Harding and Coolidge cabinets." Now, in the wake of the Bonus Riot and as a result of "country-wide publicity, the belief that Hoover was completely devoid of human sympathy was more than ever fixed in people's minds." [12]

Roosevelt fully recognized the narrowness of the protest. As he considered the rout, he pondered certain themes which had been a part of the tragedy of the

12. Tugwell, *Brains Trust*, pp. 316, 350–59, 425–28.

past three depression years: the heightened class-con-
sciousness of the disadvantaged and the appalling indifference or antagonism toward the poor on the part of some of
the more fortunate. He told Tugwell that these attitudes
had become familiar to him, for "he had heard [these
views] repeated over and over by the most surprising people, many of whom were otherwise humanitarian and
some of whom were well-known philanthropists." He had
been amazed by the kind of people who had characterized the poor as "shiftless irresponsibles," gathered "in
dirty camps where there was no rent to pay." These people, many of them business and financial leaders, considered begging and sleeping on park benches a "menace"
and riding across the country on freight cars a dangerous
"defiance of authority." FDR recognized the implications
of class conflict and no doubt realized that these were the
same people who felt that MacArthur had known exactly
how to cope with the situation.

Roosevelt had also heard the argument that "concentration camps far from the cities would have to be substituted for Hoovervilles." By way of contrast, he reminded
Tugwell that during his depression-plagued years as governor of New York he had never called out the National
Guard even though the "fat cats" had wanted him to several times. His "answer had always been that suppression
was not good enough"; indeed, "if revolution was feared,
this was not the way to avoid it." The poor on the Anacostia flats or on the banks of the Hudson "were too beaten to
be dangerous except to health." Relieving business would
not "relieve the massive alienation" or guarantee recovery.[13]

If Roosevelt had needed any reassurance of victory, the
rout of the marchers supposedly bolstered his confidence.

13. Tugwell, *Brains Trust*. For an example of the type of thinking
Roosevelt feared, see "Mob Rule and Presidential Candidates," *Review of Reviews*, 86 (October 1932), 14–15. In defending Hoover the
editors claimed that "thousands of ignorant men, led by fanatics and
demagogues, were engaged in attacking the authorities of the District
of Columbia." Tugwell related FDR's conviction that "the revolution
he spoke of could hardly be avoided if another President should fail as
Hoover had failed."

According to Tugwell, "If Roosevelt had had any doubt about the outcome of the election, I am certain he had none after reading *The Times* that day." His "political problem was smaller than he would have believed before the incident happened." Roosevelt believed, Tugwell claimed, that "MacArthur and the army had done a good job of preventing Hoover's re-election." Later, Frankfurter told of sitting with FDR on the porch of his Hyde Park home, listening to radio reports on the rout. Roosevelt allegedly turned to him and said, "Well, Felix, this will elect me." [14] Clearly, Roosevelt's supporters were overly impressed with the impact of the event on the coming election.

Most significant for his actions as President was the force with which the bonus rout helped drive home to FDR the deep social cleavage in the nation and the possible difficulties posed by alarmists, such as the Army Chief of Staff, who was to continue in that role for two years before he would relinquish his post. Roosevelt was sharply suspicious of MacArthur, whom he considered "a potential Mussolini" and indeed "the most dangerous person" in the United States. He feared him as a "brilliant soldier" who talked "in a voice that might come from an oracle's cave" and who thought his own pronouncements "infallible." Roosevelt's intense feelings resulted, in part, from his observation of MacArthur's handling of the rout and quite probably from his reading of the General's virtuoso performance at the press conference following the rout. MacArthur's obvious satisfaction with his troops' actions while driving out the veterans profoundly disturbed him. "Did you ever see anyone more self-satisfied?" he asked Tugwell.[15]

14. Tugwell, *Brains Trust*. Memoir of Gardner Jackson, The Oral History Collection of Columbia University, p. 369; Frankfurter to Jackson, March 30, 1960, Gardner Jackson file, Frankfurter Papers, LC. Frankfurter was at Hyde Park with Roosevelt the weekend of July 30, as the last of the protesters were being evicted from the District and the rout was making front-page headlines in the New York *Times*. New York *Times*, July 30, 1932; Freedman, *Roosevelt and Frankfurter*, p. 78.

15. Tugwell, *Brains Trust*, p. 434. Tugwell first reported Roose-

Roosevelt saw MacArthur as the American counterpart to the European strongman. His suspicions about Mac-Arthur's political ambitions have been challenged, at least indirectly, however, by a biographer of the General. The writer insists that "nothing in MacArthur's corre-spondence, addresses, or actions during the remaining years of the Great Depression suggests that he had presi-dential or dictatorial ambitions. . . . The general's behav-ior during the bonus affair," he concludes, "more nearly resembled that of a nineteenth-century English noble than a twentieth-century totalitarian mass leader." [16]

There is evidence that suggests that Roosevelt had rea-son to be suspicious, that MacArthur saw in his post as Chief of Staff political as well as military opportunities. Eisenhower was appalled at his superior's behavior on July 28. MacArthur's insistence on personally overseeing the eviction, his curt refusal to listen to high-ranking officers "pretending to bring orders," and his eagerness to meet reporters after the rout impressed Eisenhower as rash and ill-advised actions, unsuitable to the Chief of Staff and harmful to the good name of the United States Army. These were obviously the acts of an ambitious man. Although Eisenhower did not specifically link these decisions to politics, he criticized other activities in which MacArthur consistently refused to draw the line between military and political matters. As Ike put it, his own duties for MacArthur often verged "on the political, even to the edge of partisan politics." [17]

Assistant Secretary of War F. Trubee Davison gave fur-ther evidence of MacArthur's ambition. He was especially

velt's reactions in abbreviated form in *The Democratic Roosevelt: A Biography of Franklin D. Roosevelt* (New York: Doubleday, Doran and Co., 1957), p. 349. I did not find any references to the bonus rout in the Tugwell Papers at FDRL.

16. D. Clayton James, *The Years of MacArthur, 1880–1941* (Bos-ton: Houghton Mifflin, 1970), pp. 412–13. James added: "MacArthur's intense dedication to duty, honor and country were commendable, and he doubtless felt that he was following those principles as he donned his uniform on that July 28th."

17. Dwight David Eisenhower, *At Ease: Stories I Tell to Friends* (New York: Doubleday & Company, Inc., 1967), pp. 213, 217–18.

impressed by MacArthur's comparison of his own political future to that of Franz von Papen, the new Chancellor of Germany. (Von Papen entered office in May 1932, but held it only until December, giving way to Gen. Kurt von Schleicher and one month later aiding Adolf Hitler to become Chancellor.) MacArthur had met von Papen as a young military attaché in 1914 during the U.S. occupation of Veracruz.[18] Von Papen later wrote of his admiration of the "virile and handsome" Captain MacArthur, "always in immaculate uniform." [19] The German officer similarly impressed MacArthur, both then and when he became Chancellor.

In May 1932, on the day that von Papen assumed the chancellorship, MacArthur made a dramatic announcement to the War Council, composed of the Secretary of War, the two Assistant Secretaries, and the Chief of Staff. On that day, MacArthur noted, the ambitions of the two men had been fulfilled—but *"in reverse."* As MacArthur put it, "one wanted to be head of a great army, the other head of a great state. I speak . . . of von Papen and MacArthur." According to Davison, "Von Papen had wanted to be Chief of Staff of the German Army, but instead became Chancellor of Germany, while MacArthur—who had become Chief of Staff of the Army, wanted, most of all, to become President of the United States." Davison was struck by MacArthur's having "hooked himself up with von Papen" but concluded that the only significance of the General's pronouncement was the revelation from "MacArthur's own lips that he wanted to be President." [20]

18. "Interview with F. Trubee Davison," pp. 4–6, Oral History Collection, HHPL.

19. Franz von Papen, *Memoirs* (New York: E. P. Dutton, 1953), pp. 18–19, 29–60, 151, 157–58, 225–49. Koppel S. Pinson, *Modern Germany: Its History and Civilization* (New York: The Macmillan Company, 1966), pp. 474–78. Von Papen was a prominent figure in American news during the late spring and summer of 1932. See *Daily News*, July 27, 1932.

20. My italics. "Interview with F. Trubee Davison," p. 6. "Anyway," Davison concluded, "there was the ambition that eventually ruined his life and eventually led to his being fired by President Truman, because he was doing exactly the same thing to Truman that he was doing to Mr. Hoover." For information on MacArthur's later politi-

Davison was also "impressed with MacArthur's natural, theatrical ability," and he considered him "one of the most attractive men I have ever met [and] probably the most brilliant field general we ever had." Despite his admiration for the man, the Assistant Secretary became increasingly "distressed by General MacArthur's political ambitions, by his political maneuverings as chief of staff, and by his repeated tendency to lie when it suited his purposes to do so." Moreover, the General "would not tolerate opposition and often interpreted disagreement as a sign of personal disloyalty," a somewhat awkward situation for an assistant secretary who favored expanding the Air Force, a policy MacArthur opposed.[21] At first glance it might appear that Davison was overly critical of MacArthur, but Moseley also noted some of these same traits, and the closeness of Moseley's relationship with the General was unquestionable. Indeed, MacArthur considered Moseley one of his closest advisers and a most loyal friend.[22] Nevertheless, Moseley observed that his commander was unable to discern the truth when his personal ambitions were involved and thus tended to believe whatever suited his purposes.[23] He agreed that MacArthur was "a prima donna [who] must occupy the center of the stage, but that is where he belongs, for he is the best actor." Moseley felt a leader like MacArthur was exactly what the Army needed.[24]

cal ambitions, see O'Laughlin to MacArthur, December 23, 1943; MacArthur to O'Laughlin, February 19, 1944; O'Laughlin to MacArthur, February 4, 1948, Box 54, O'Laughlin Papers, LC. O'Laughlin died in March 1949.

21. Interview with F. Trubee Davison, April 22, 1972. F. Trubee Davison to author April 17, 1972. Both Davison and I have typed, signed copies of the interview.

22. MacArthur to Moseley, September 30, 1935, Scrapbook of Selected Papers 1899–1942, Moseley Papers, LC (hereafter cited as GMP). MacArthur told him: "You were always my strongest supporter, my wisest adviser, and my most loyal friend." MacArthur had appointed Moseley as his Deputy Chief of Staff.

23. Moseley, "One Soldier's Journey," p. 139. Moseley also explained that "only one thing" took precedence over his devotion to MacArthur "and that is my duty to our Republic as a whole" (pp. 137–38).

24. Moseley, "One Soldier's Journey," unpublished diary, IV, 137, GMP. Interview with F. Trubee Davison, April 22, 1972.

As MacArthur's press conference indicated, he hoped that he would gain national recognition and a good deal of support in some quarters for routing the veterans. At the same time he also may have had the more current interests of the Army in mind. The immediate praise the press heaped upon the Army for not having fired a shot and for its highly disciplined restraint was precisely the favorable publicity Army spokesmen needed to disarm the critics and budget cutters in Congress. During the rout MacArthur's actions did not indicate that he equated the disturbance with "insurrection." Reporters were treated with every consideration and provided with Army transportation. His troops were fed and rested before proceeding to Anacostia, a lull during which he could have appealed to the President personally for a change of orders.[25] Afterward, however, when he met the press, the General may well have emphasized his thesis that the disturbance resulted from a revolutionary plot, in order to convince Congress and the nation that a strong Army was crucial to national security, especially during a danger-breeding depression. It is equally plausible that he was primarily concerned with justifying his repeated refusal to obey Hoover's orders, in the event that his insubordination should become known. A blend of these factors—justification for disobeying Hoover's orders, personal ambition, and the promotion of the Army, seems to be the most likely explanation. Moseley aptly summarized MacArthur's success. Rather than serving as a routine chief of staff, MacArthur "brought the Army to the front page." [26]

Roosevelt, of course, was not privy to the reflections of Army officials, and his distrust of MacArthur resulted primarily from the rout and from his assessment of the man. Nevertheless, in 1934 he agreed to the unusual procedure of extending the Chief of Staff's tenure beyond the normal four years. This he did only after his Secretary of War, George H. Dern, and Democratic House Majority Leader Joseph W. Burns insisted that MacArthur's knowledge of

25. RCS, p. 14.
26. Moseley, "The Bonus March, 1932." Moseley believed that MacArthur was so powerful that President Roosevelt and his advisers decided it was best not to fire him as Chief of Staff.

complex legislation before the Congress was essential to the success of the Army's reorganization and the defenses of the United States.[27] With strong political support of MacArthur from Burns and support in the cabinet from Dern, FDR acquiesced despite intense opposition from Senator Kenneth McKellar and Josephus Daniels. MacArthur stayed on as Chief of Staff, but Roosevelt gave him a warning which he never forgot. "Douglas, I think you are our best general," MacArthur recalled him saying, "but I believe you would be our worst politician." MacArthur later commented, "With his rare sense of humor, I wonder which side of that remark he thought was the compliment." [28]

By May 1935 Roosevelt concluded that MacArthur was maneuvering for reappointment as Chief of Staff. This the President blocked. He did allow him to remain on active duty while he organized the defense force in the Philippines. When that final task was completed Roosevelt cabled congratulations on MacArthur's accomplishments and at the same time accepted his resignation.[29]

Roosevelt continued to have trouble intermittently with the politically oriented general, but not half as much aggravation as he had with the veterans' groups.[30] FDR

27. Stephen Early to George B. St. George, April 23, 1935; James W. Burns to Louis Howe, July 6, 1934, OF 25-T, FDRL. Howe sent Burns's note to FDR on July 13, 1934. Burns had already insisted to FDR that MacArthur be retained as Chief of Staff. Early told St. George that "Secretary Dern was adamant in continuing MacArthur as Chief of Staff after the expiration of his appointment."

28. Kenneth McKellar to FDR, October 2, 1934, OF 25-T; Josephus Daniels to FDR, March 14 and October 8, 1934, PPF 86, FDRL; Douglas MacArthur, *Reminiscences* (New York: McGraw-Hill, Inc., 1964), pp. 96–97.

29. Unknown to MacArthur, Roosevelt skillfully prevented the General from influencing the appointment of his successor as Chief of Staff. Farley, *Jim Farley's Story*, p. 55; a copy of MacArthur's resignation and Roosevelt's reply is in Harry H. Woodring to FDR, October 11, 1937, PPF 4914, FDRL. Roosevelt agreed with Hugh S. Johnson that MacArthur had a plan to gain reappointment as Chief of Staff. Hugh S. Johnson to FDR, April 30, 1935; FDR to Johnson, May 2, 1935; Johnson to Margaret LeHand, September 4, 1935; FDR to Johnson, September 9, 1935, OF 25-T, FDRL.

30. Gardner Jackson to Marvin H. McIntyre, March 11, 1932; McIntyre Memo For the President, March 12, 1942, PPF 3453; Irving

knew more about handling political opponents than he did about the complexities and inequities of veteran law, and that inexperience quickly became obvious. Soon after taking office, he forced through the hastily conceived Economy Act, which among other cuts stopped benefits for thousands of veterans with service-connected disabilities. If he had limited his cuts to nonservice-connected benefits, he would have fared better. But the severity and injustice of his actions created a deep anger among almost all ex-servicemen.[31] A second bonus march quickly developed, and in this march the Communists were able to gain far more influence than they had wielded during the two-month protest in 1932.

As soon as Roosevelt realized the seriousness of his error, he acted quickly to prevent the need for force in controlling the marchers. First, he mobilized support by the leaders of the veterans' organizations in a blistering attack on the march.[32] Then, benefiting from his observations of Hoover's successes and mistakes, he issued a new regulation that prohibited loitering in public parks or

Brant to FDR, August 26, 1942, PPF 7859, FDRL. For a flurry of letters concerning MacArthur's claim that FDR attempted to cut the Army officer corps by a third, see Stephen Early to S. T. Williamson, June 25, 1942. MacArthur was undoubtedly bitter toward FDR. As early as 1938 he told Moseley that he was "alarmed at the marked swing toward the left" and believed that the best way to prevent the "shaking of the very foundations of our country [was] by defeating the present administration. . . . I hope," he added, "that America will awaken to the true situation before it is too late." MacArthur to Moseley, March 9, 1938, Selected Papers, GMP.

31. Stephen Early, Memorandum to General Hines and enclosures, May 13, 1933; Early to Roy Roberts, May 12, 1933; L. S. Ray to Early, March 13, 1933, OF 95; James E. Van Zandt to FDR, September 22, 1933, PPF 87, FDRL. Early informed Roberts that FDR was now aware of the injustices of the Economy Act. A copy of the portion of the Economy Act relating to veterans and FDR's numerous Executive Orders modifying it is in Veterans Administration, *Public Law No. 2, 73d Congress, and Executive Orders* (Washington, D.C.: Government Printing Office, 1933), in Republican National Committee Files, Correspondence, HHPL.

32. Hines to Robert E. Coontz, March 23, 1933; Louis Howe was deeply angered over the second march. Howe to Mr. Kelly, April 25, 1933; Howe to FDR, April 22, 1933; March 30, 1933; OF 391, FDRL. The Secret Service was especially active. W. H. Moran to Howe, May 18, 1933, OF 391, FDRL.

grounds and ordered Veterans Administrator Hines to establish a camp for the marchers at Fort Hunt.[33] Hines had
supervised the field hospital Hoover had ordered established at the abandoned post in 1932, and he had had
considerable experience as Hoover's chief assistant during the first march. Located about fifteen miles from the
Capitol via the newly opened Mount Vernon Highway,
the camp and its occupants were effectively isolated from
Washington. Unlike Hoover, Roosevelt refused to establish
a conveniently located camp at Anacostia or in the closer
government buildings.

Previous accounts of the Second Bonus March have dramatized Eleanor Roosevelt's unexpected appearance at
the bonus camp. While her visit was both kind and politically astute, it was merely a symbolic gesture, which, of
course, did not furnish the food, equipment, and other essentials that helped to ensure that the demonstration remained peaceable. Far more effective was this President's
good use of the able Veterans Administrator. Previously
uncited records recently found in the Veterans Administration establish that Hines fulfilled FDR's orders with
such skill, speed, and meticulous attention to detail that
much of the bonus marchers' discontent was quickly reduced.[34]

In fact, the anticlimactic Second Bonus March soon became a complete fiasco. Although the men could lobby in
the capital and were permitted to parade, their isolation
encouraged them to spend most of their time in
prolonged, bitter arguments between the left-wing Communists led by Levin and the right wing headed by Mike
Thomas, at one time the commander of the Anacostia
camp.[35]

33. Frank T. Hines to Howe, May 9, 1933, Box 60, Howe Papers,
FDRL; U. S. Grant, III, to FDR, May 11, 1933, 25-H, FDRL.

34. The evidence is too voluminous to cite in detail. The correspondence and numerous reports are in Historical Studies, Adjusted
Compensation, housed in the Veterans Administration Building, Washington, D.C.; correspondence in Howe Papers, Box 59, and in FDR,
OF 391, FDRL. Hines to FDR, May 25, 1933, OF 95, FDRL. George
H. Dern to Hines, June 6, 1933, RG 94, 240 Bonus, NA. There are
many important letters in this file.

35. An interesting, if biased, account is Henry O. Meisel, *Second*

While the factions squabbled and shouted at one another, Roosevelt implemented the plan he had discussed with Frankfurter while still governor of New York. He provided jobs for the protesters by creating the Federal Emergency Relief Administration, which in turn established a division of Emergency Conservation Work, the forerunner of the Civilian Conservation Corps. In an ironic twist, Roosevelt now ordered reluctant Army officers to care for the veterans. Rather than driving them out, MacArthur's officers now established and supervised the new conservation camps. Under Roosevelt's prodding, most of the marchers enrolled in the conservation work, the others were transported back to their homes, and the bonus camp was closed. The marchers had been well treated and skillfully controlled, but they did not win their bonus.[36]

In December 1932, as he served his final months in office, Hoover had remained calm during a Communist-led march.[37] The Second Bonus March had passed similarly, without serious incident, and bonus demonstrations in

Bonus Army, 1933 (Shawano, Wis.: Economy Printing Service, 1934). The Emmanuel Levin Papers are disappointing as sources, since they consist mainly of newspaper clippings and leaflets about the Second Bonus March; Emmanuel Levin Papers, Department of Special Collections, The University of California, Los Angeles. The Bonus Army newspaper clippings file, Washingtoniana Collection, in the Washington, D.C., Public Library is useful. Documents in OF 391, FDRL, are especially revealing. New York *Herald Tribune*, May 11, 1933; *Evening Star*, May 11, 13, 14, 18, 20, 30, 1933; *Daily News*, May 11, 13, 1933; *Herald*, May 13, 20, 1933; *Post*, May 15, 17, 1933. The best and fullest account of the Second Bonus March is in Roger Daniels, *The Bonus March: An Episode of the Great Depression* (Westport, Conn.: Greenwood Press, Inc., 1971), pp. 220–26.

36. Alfred B. Rollins, Jr., *Roosevelt and Howe* (New York: Alfred A. Knopf, Inc., 1962), pp. 386–88. Rollins overemphasizes Howe's importance in the second march. Daniels, *Bonus March*, p. 339, note 24; Eleanor Roosevelt, *This I Remember* (New York: Harper and Brothers, 1949), pp. 111–13; New York *Times*, May 17, 1933.

37. Nugent Dodds to Attorney General, Memo, October 5, 1932; PDG to D.C. Commissioners, October 11, 1932; George J. Matowitz to PDG, October 8, 1932, Records of the Department of Justice, RG 60, NA. Joslin, *Hoover*, pp. 329–30; New York *Times*, December 1, 6, 8, 1932. Elliot E. Cohn to HH, December 1, 1932; Howard K. Beale to HH, December 2, 1932; Hurley to Mitchell, December 7, 1932, Records of the Justice Department, RG 60, NA.

1933 and 1934 attracted little attention.[38] The major bonus invasions had ended. Veterans no longer supported demonstrations. Among the more effective reasons for their drop in interest were the new jobs and Roosevelt's swiftness in restoring most of the benefits the Economy Act had removed from veterans with service-connected disabilities. These measures he skillfully managed through a series of executive orders.

Finally, after defusing the Second Bonus March, providing jobs in federal conservation projects for all interested veterans, and restoring the most obviously needed benefits, FDR launched a thinly veiled attack upon the American Legion. He was well aware of the politics the Legion had played so well during the Republican years since the war. The new national commander, Louis A. Johnson, was an avowed Democrat whom Roosevelt could rely upon, but the Republican forces within the well-organized and politically powerful Legion were strong and would attempt to embarrass and harass the new President for the insensitive Economy Act.[39] To meet this challenge FDR decided to confront the Legion in person.

On October 2, 1933, he lectured the national convention on the duty of soldiers and citizens to promote national unity and to defeat the enemies of that unity—sectionalism and class distinction. "You and I," he told them, in a statement that sounded like it came from Herbert

38. New York *Times*, May 23, 1933; *Evening Star*, May 22, 1933; *Daily News*, May 27, 1933; Meisel, *Second Bonus Army*, pp. 12–17. The FBI kept watch over the veterans. Frank M. Parrish to Ernest W. Brown, March 14, 1933; Frank M. Parrish to Attorney General, May 10, 1933, Records of the Department of Justice, RG 60, NA. Parrish was acting head of the Criminal Division of the Justice Department. Robert Fechner to Louis M. Howe, March 20, 1934; H. A. Drum to The Adjutant General, United States Army, March 21, 1934; Secretary of War to The Adjutant General, March 21, 1934, War Department, Records of The Adjutant General, RG 94, NA. Copies of the camp newspaper, *VET: Rank and File*, May, 1934, in Levin Papers. For a report of the 1934 BEF parade down Pennsylvania Avenue, see *Evening Star*, May 18, 1934; Daniels, *Bonus March*, p. 230.
39. Louis Johnson to FDR, March 28, 1933; Johnson to Early, March 3, 1934, OF 64, FDRL.

Hoover, "are well aware of the simple fact that as every day passes, the people of this Country are less and less willing to tolerate benefits for any one group of citizens which must be paid for by others. . . . No one [merely] because he wore a uniform must therefore be placed in a special class of beneficiaries over and above all other citizens." Roosevelt further warned them that "the fact of wearing a uniform does not mean that he can demand and receive from his Government a benefit which no other citizen receives."

His criticism of veterans' demands was even stronger, though less moralistic, than that of his predecessor. Further, in an obvious criticism of Hoover's 1930 Disability Act, he denounced pensions for nonservice-connected disabilities. He assured the men that his executive orders would restore service-connected benefits, but he stood firm against nonservice-connected appropriations. Eventually he would reverse that position as he became educated to the numerous inequities in the legislation for veterans. For the time being, however, those who did not have service-connected status but were in need received his promise of help but no special benefits, no bonus.

Roosevelt warned the Legion's officials that he no longer intended to allow them a free hand in using the Legion for partisan politics. Political differences he would tolerate, but the charter and character of the Legion "keeps it out of partisan politics, [and] the strength and very existence of the Legion depend upon the maintenance of that principle." The legionnaires might continue to present their case to Congress and to lobby for the balance of the bonus, but Roosevelt was determined to prevent the veterans from continuing to think and act like a special, privileged class and from developing into a militant, partisan opposition.[40] In implementing this program

40. A copy of the speech is in OF 350, American Legion, FDRL. Johnson believed FDR's speech was crucial in revising the thinking of the legionnaires. Johnson to FDR, October 9, 1933, ibid. On August 13, 1935, FDR admitted that granting pensions for all veterans who served prior to the World War was the only equitable solution. Press Release, OF 95, FDRL. Daniels, *Bonus March*, pp. 227–28.

he was successful, partly because he kept a watchful eye on Republican leaders in the Legion, who were known for their desire to embarrass him. FDR also skillfully used his allies, and on at least one occasion William Gibbs McAdoo helped ensure that a national commander favorable to the President was elected.[41]

Roosevelt, like Hoover before him, played at veteran politics because he had little choice. He liked VFW's Van Zandt and tolerated the Legion, but the veterans' leaders knew that the President was deeply serious in his dogged efforts to eliminate the privileged-class concept that had dominated the veterans' policies. They continued to press for the bonus, and he continued to oppose it. In 1935 Congress passed the bill, and FDR delivered a personal veto lecture to the assembled Congress. Once again he stressed his opposition to the special privilege which he insisted the bonus represented.[42]

With Roosevelt attacking their familiar special-status reasoning, the veterans now deemphasized that argument. By 1936 inflation and deficit spending had finally become more acceptable than in 1932, and the veterans' spokesmen emphasized that the bonus would promote a beneficial inflation that would help combat the depression.[43] FDR was not impressed, but the Congress respected the veterans' power and could accept their argument. The next year, 1936, before Roosevelt issued his second veto, it was a foregone conclusion that Congress would quickly override it.[44] Thus, seven years after Patman began his

41. William Gibbs McAdoo to M. H. McIntyre, October 7, 1935, OF 64, FDRL. McAdoo enclosed a detailed report from R. Dean Warner.

42. McAdoo to McIntyre, October 7, 1935, OF 64, FDRL; report from Warner. Early to McIntyre, November 21, 1934; Early to Johnson, November 22, 1934, and other correspondence in OF 64, American Legion and Veterans of Foreign Wars, OF 84, FDRL. Both organizations continued lobbying on issues of national consequence. FDR, *Public Papers*, IV, 182–93, especially p. 193.

43. The VFW began to emphasize the inflationary advantages as early as September 1933, but FDR was unconvinced that their concern for economic recovery was uppermost. James E. Van Zandt to FDR, September 22, 1933, PPF 87, FDRL. Interview with Van Zandt, April 14, 1972.

44. FDR, *Public Papers*, V, 67–69. A long, fascinating political

fight, the tireless leader of the bonus forces witnessed the final victory for the $2,491,000,000 bill.[45]

Ironically, Roosevelt twice vetoed the bonus for the same reasons that caused Hoover to oppose it. At the time both were fiscally conservative, both strongly opposed the special class orientation of veteran reasoning, yet both were willing to allow peaceful protest and lobbying by their opponents. FDR did not originate significant new policies toward the veterans. Hoover had long insisted on need as one of the chief criteria for federal aid, but the veterans themselves had rejected that point and Congress repudiated the "pauper's oath." Hoover finally discarded the need principle in favor of equity and pensions to all veterans, regardless of service-connected disabilities, but Roosevelt later rescinded benefits for nonservice-connected disabilities and reintroduced the need provision.[46]

It was Roosevelt rather than Hoover who best educated the nation about veteran politics. Hoover had been exceptionally generous and patient with the veterans and their protest, allowing broader permissiveness in the choice of their camps, for example, than FDR would tolerate. Unfortunately, Hoover's defense of the rout marked an important turning point in his thinking and the end of his careful restraint. It ruined his chances to be a respected leader and teacher, a role he could otherwise have main-

struggle took place between 1933 and 1936, but it is not appropriate to this volume. ASCF 1933–1936, Patman Papers; files of correspondence at the national headquarters of the American Legion. Details of FDR's maneuverings concerning the veto of the two bills are in Freedman, *Roosevelt and Frankfurter*, pp. 312–13; Farley, *Jim Farley's Story*, pp. 53–54, 58–59, and especially Harold L. Ickes, *The Secret Diary of Harold L. Ickes: The First Thousand Days, 1933–1936*, 3 vols. (New York: Simon and Schuster, 1953), I, 158, 356, 525. Ickes was especially irritated with FDR's secrecy on whether he would veto the bonus bill. Daniels, *Bonus March*, pp. 233–41.

45. Interview with Wright Patman, June 21, 1968. Patman explained his long fight and the final ceremonies in a mimeographed letter; Patman to "Dear Friend and Comrade," June 6, 1938, Patman Papers.

46. Daniels, *Bonus March*, pp. 227–28. Daniels credits Roosevelt with first suggesting the origins of the welfare state when FDR reintroduced the need provision. He does not evaluate or discuss Hoover's support of legislation for the veterans or his formulation of many of the policies upon which FDR later insisted.

tained despite political defeat. Roosevelt has often been criticized for his unwillingness to take political risks in educating the people on controversial issues. In this case, however, he had learned much from Hoover's efforts and mistakes, and he emerged a strong and determined educator. He directly and repeatedly challenged some of the least admirable values held by the powerful veterans' organizations. In personal appearances before both the Legion and the entire Congress he lectured the people on the need to reject the veterans' special status as a concept alien to a democratic society.

Obviously, the many urgent needs of veterans, such as disability allowances, hospitalization, and rehabilitation programs, could not be dismissed, for they are clearly a part of the cost of war. But there was a marked difference between the service-connected disability benefits rescinded by FDR's Economy Act and the opposition of these two Presidents to immediate payment of the bonus. The compromise reached under Coolidge would have compounded interest to increase the bonus payment by 1945, but it postponed a just payment at a time when the nation could most easily have afforded to pay it. Under Wilson, Harding, and Coolidge a prosperous nation had been unwilling to pay the aftercost of war. Notwithstanding the onset of hard times, Hoover had increased the more pressing hospitalization and disability benefits, service-connected or not. Both Hoover and Roosevelt were correct to reject the special pleading for the bonus as a means of relief—especially when provision of jobs and relief for all of the unemployed were higher priorities and a more equitable means of promoting recovery.

Hoover had been more generous than Roosevelt and had criticized veteran lobbies for similar reasons. He had done more for the veterans and protesters than contemporaries or historians realized. His failure was not recognizing or responding skillfully to the symbolic significance of the march. After the rout, critics naturally used the misleading symbolism against him, and many Americans continue to think of him primarily as a man who turned tanks against the poor, one of the country's less admirable Presidents. Obviously, the times called for sensitivity and for the practice of artful politics. Roosevelt also rejected the idea of special status for hungry veterans. But at the same time he recognized the class-conscious alienation of millions of others equally in need, as well as the attitudes of "fat cats" who preferred to ignore them and to deal harshly with dissent. Roosevelt did not carry the stigma of business favoritism, and in his efforts to educate the public against the veterans' special class orientation, he maintained far greater credibility and popular support. Moreover, he had learned much from Hoover's successes in dealing with the veterans but even more from his mistakes.

14

Presence, Intent, and Conspiracy

No one could deny that some Communists were present at the scene of the brick battle or that their leaders had often threatened to provoke violence. For many citizens their mere presence and intent were sufficient evidence to prove that the Bonus Riot was part of a red revolutionary conspiracy. Although Hoover came to believe in a plot by Communists and Democrats to smear him, he continued to harbor a few nagging doubts about the event, at least until several years afterward. The doubts involved MacArthur.

In October 1934, for example, over two years after the rout, the former President became exasperated by repeated assertions from MacArthur devotees that the Chief of Staff had merely been obeying orders, an assertion MacArthur neither denied nor corrected. "If McArthur [*sic*] is putting out this kind of stuff," Hoover threatened, "I shall tell what really did happen, and it will do McArthur [*sic*] no good." [1] Ten years later, in 1944, Hoover again became irritated by the pro-MacArthur propaganda. This time reporters emphasized that the General had been made the scapegoat for the rout. In response Hoover authorized John Callan O'Laughlin, a close friend of both Hoover and MacArthur and owner and editor of the *Army-Navy Journal,* to write a book on the Bonus Riot

1. Hurley to HH, December 27, 1933; HH to Hurley, January 4, 1934, Post-Presidential Papers, Box 53, HHPL. The attacks continued despite his efforts to stop them. HH to Richey, December 4, 1934; Edgar Rickard to Editor, Parkersburg (West Virginia) *Sentinel,* October 26, 1948, Post-Presidential Papers, Box 39, HHPL. Other letters by Rickard attest to the continuing effort to combat the slander that Hoover had ordered MacArthur to fire on the veterans. HH to Richey, October 23, 1934, Bonus March Temporary File, HHPL.

and, more important, to ask MacArthur to indicate the exact instructions Hoover had given him on July 28.[2]

Instead of replying to O'Laughlin, the General wrote directly to Hoover, assuring him that nothing anyone "might say would shake my absolute faith in your demonstrated loyalty to the subordinates who served you during your term of office." He denied having criticized Hoover at any time, expressed his "complete devotion," and praised Hoover's "great moral courage" in handling the BEF.[3]

MacArthur's repeated assurances removed the potential for a serious breach between the two men, and by 1946 Hoover was pressing the victorious general to return and fight the vital political battle against the socialists at home. Two years later Hoover supported MacArthur's abortive candidacy for the Presidency, and again in 1949 he personally urged him to return, for, as he put it, "reinforcements" were needed "if our way of life is not to be lost in the wilderness of a 'Welfare State'." [4] By now Hoover's aversion to leftists and his faith in MacArthur were complete.

Eleanor Roosevelt became a participant in the battle— indeed, a symbol of what Hoover now opposed and feared in the nation's life. In July 1949, she reinforced Hoover's belief that there had been a conspiracy against him when

2. John Callan O'Laughlin to MacArthur, May 5, 1944, O'Laughlin Papers, LC. Pearson's interpretation is in Drew Pearson and Robert S. Allen, "The Real General MacArthur," *Liberty Magazine* (March 7, 1942), pp. 20–22. This account argues that MacArthur was a scapegoat. Hoover later wrote MacArthur denouncing Pearson as a scoundrel. "There is one point on which President Roosevelt, Secretary Hull, and I agree," he stated, "—that is that Pearson is the most complete skunk in American journalism." HH to MacArthur, April 26, 1944, Post-Presidential Papers, Box 78, HHPL. One month earlier, in March 1944, either Hoover or his secretary Edgar Rickard had drafted a letter to the editor of the Portland *Oregon Journal* denying that Hoover had ordered MacArthur to drive the BEF out of Washington. Draft letter, March 25, 1944, PP 298, HHPL.

3. MacArthur to HH, May 19, 1944, MacArthur Papers (hereafter cited as MP).

4. HH to MacArthur, October 17, 1946; MacArthur to HH, October 31, 1946, MacArthur Papers. O'Laughlin to MacArthur, April 2, 1948, O'Laughlin Papers; HH to MacArthur, October 19, 1949, MacArthur Papers.

she stated in her autobiography, serialized in *McCall's*, that Hoover had ordered the troops to "fire on the veterans." [5] It was an attack the former President would not allow to go unanswered. By 1949 Hoover had become unalterably convinced that MacArthur had put down a Communist coup. A series of events that year seemed to confirm the growing apprehension over the Red Menace: revelations that a leading British scientist had passed the United States' atomic secrets to the Soviet Union, Russia's explosion of the A-bomb, the conviction of eleven Communist leaders for advocating violent means to overthrow the government, the sensational trial of Alger Hiss, and the successes of Mao's forces in China. Moreover, in addition to assurances from Hurley and MacArthur, a new spate of "confessions" appeared from unreliable, overly repentant ex-Communist leaders, who insisted that a serious internal red threat had existed and had been crucial in the Bonus Riot. [6] Hurley had twice campaigned unsuccessfully for the Senate in New Mexico on the theme of international and internal red menace, and Hoover turned to the crusading anti-Communist to answer Eleanor Roosevelt. [7]

5. Eleanor Roosevelt, "This I Remember," *McCall's*, 77 (July, 1949), 109.

6. Benjamin Gitlow, *The Whole of Their Lives* (New York: Charles Scribner's Sons, 1948), pp. 221–30. Jacob Spolansky, *The Communist Trail in America* (New York: The Macmillan Company, 1951), pp. 49–51. Both authors are so patently in error on the facts that they are entirely unreliable. Each however is clear on the charge that Moscow singled out Hoover for character assassination. Max Eastman's introduction to Gitlow's book, on Gitlow's expulsion in 1929; J. Edgar Hoover, *Masters of Deceit: The Story of Communism in America and How to Fight It* (New York: Henry Holt and Company, 1958), pp. 69–70.

7. Don Lohbeck, *Patrick J. Hurley* (Chicago: Henry Regnery Company, 1956), pp. 155–436; 440–43, 453–55, 467. Barbara Tuchman emphasizes Hurley's conviction of a conspiracy and concludes: "Hurley opened the journey toward the tawdry reign of terror soon to be imposed with such astonishing ease by Senator Joe McCarthy." Barbara W. Tuchman, *Stillwell and the American Experience in China, 1911–1945* (New York: The Macmillan Company, 1971), pp. 525–26, 513, 514. Also see Roger Daniels, *The Bonus March: An Episode of the Great Depression* (Westport, Conn.: Greenwood Press, Inc., 1971), pp. 257–61.

Thoroughly aroused by this latest misrepresentation of the Bonus Riot and by his now well-established fears, Hoover informed Hurley of the need "to scotch this perpetual myth the New Dealers are trying to build up about the Bonus March" and emphasized that Mrs. Roosevelt's statement in *McCall's* presented an excellent "opportunity to blow the whole thing right out of the water." Hoover suggested to Hurley that they could threaten a libel suit if the editors should refuse to print Hurley's rebuttal.[8] As expected, *McCall's* cooperated, and in November Hoover and MacArthur applauded Hurley's lengthy repetition of the theory of the 1932 "red plot." Hoover had reason to be upset by the erroneous and persistent charges against his reputation, based on the false reports of his treatment of the marchers, but once again he relied upon the wrong defense and the wrong man. While some of Hurley's article was factual, much of it consisted of the same kinds of distortions and charges of Communist conspiracy that had characterized the administration's defense in 1932.[9] Eleanor Roosevelt apologized,[10] but

8. HH to Hurley, July 8, 1949, Hurley Papers (hereafter cited as HP). Hoover included a draft of a rebuttal from which Hurley drew freely; HH to Editor, *McCall's Magazine*, July 11, 1949; Hurley to HH, July 14, 1949; HH to Hurley, July 20, 1949, HP. Hoover informed *McCall's* that "in view of the facts her statement goes further than smear and into libel."

9. A copy of the article Hurley submitted is in Hurley to Otis Lee Wiese, August 5, 1949, MP. Hurley to Wiese, September 9, 1949, HP. Hurley referred to his article as "the outline of the authentic history of the Bonus March." MacArthur agreed; MacArthur to Hurley, August 27, 1949, HP. MacArthur was convinced that Hurley's article would "prove a real contribution to historical accuracy and tend to unmask the deceit with which the communists have since sought to misrepresent that incident." Patrick J. Hurley, "The Facts About the Bonus March," *McCall's*, 77 (November 1949), 2, 142–43.

10. Chicago *Tribune*, October 30, 1949; *Times Herald*, November 1, 1949. For Washington, D.C., newspapers the city is omitted from the citation. Also see Post-Presidential Papers, Box 39, HHPL. Eleanor Roosevelt, *This I Remember* (New York: Harper and Brothers, 1949), p. 112. The files of the Republican National Committee at the Eisenhower Presidential Library contain the best collection of newspaper clippings on bonus rout politics in the 1950s: Westbrook Pegler, New York *Journal-American*, June 5, 6, 1951, and George E. Sokolsky, Washington *Times Herald*, July 18, 1949. There are numerous others in this file.

once again a sensational conspiratorial explanation of history had been widely popularized, one that Senator Joseph McCarthy and a host of like-minded journalists and radio commentators were soon to propagate.[11]

The ex-Communist most prized by Hoover, Hurley, MacArthur, and by the New York *Journal-American* was John T. Pace. The former field commander of the red element in the 1932 march had become a frequent witness before the House Un-American Activities Committee and in 1919 was the star of a new exposé by the Hearst chain. Under screaming headlines ("Moscow Ordered Riots in 1932 Bonus March"), Howard Rushmore, a reporter for the chain, claimed that Pace revealed that Stalin had ordered a revolution. Since the Communists "controlled every action" of the Bonus Army, they were able to use every "Red-Fascist trick to get President Hoover to call out the Army." However, "MacArthur put down a Moscow-directed revolution without bloodshed; and that's why the Communists hate him even today." According to Rushmore, Moscow had ordered Pace and the entire American Communist party to smear Hoover and MacArthur as murderers, a campaign that succeeded after the "parlor pinks" took up the cry. Coming from the acknowledged Communist leader of the BEF, this confession seemed the long-awaited, triumphant vindication of Hoover, Hurley, and MacArthur.[12]

11. MacArthur congratulated Hurley; MacArthur to Hurley, August 27, 1949, HP. Allen J. Matusow, ed., *Joseph R. McCarthy* (Englewood Cliffs, N.J.: Prentice-Hall, Inc., 1970), pp. 5–8. Lohbeck, *Hurley*, p. 457. Senator McCarthy was primarily interested in Hurley's charges concerning the success of the Communist revolution in China. Joseph R. McCarthy, *Major Speeches and Debates of Senator Joe McCarthy* (Washington, D.C.: Government Printing Office, n.d.), pp. 191, 196; also pp. 68–69, 242, 244, 250, 256, 265, 272.

12. New York *Journal-American*, August 28, 29, 30, 1949. For Pace and another ex-Communist leader's testimony, see footnotes 17 and 18; either Pace or Rushmore and other reporters distorted or enlarged upon his sworn testimony. At least one newspaper had claimed that Communists were responsible for the riot; New York *Sun*, November 16, 1938. The three articles from the New York *Journal-American* and one from the Washington *Star* were read into the *Congressional Record* on August 31, 1949; U.S., Congress, Senate, *Congressional Record*, 81st Cong., 1st sess., 95, pt. 9, 1949, pp. 12529–32.

As HUAC supporters repeated the Hearst charges, it was easy to assume that Pace's interview paralleled his testimony, but this was not the case.[13] In fact, a careful comparison of the doom-filled Hearst stories and the actual HUAC testimony on the bonus march establishes an opposite conclusion. Either Pace or the Hearst reporter had left out many important facts in the articles, or Rushmore misrepresented Pace's statements. The Hearst interview stated, for example, "My Communist bosses were jumping for joy on July 28 when the Washington police killed one veteran." But Pace and Joseph Z. Kornfeder, another ex-Communist, had already told HUAC that the Communist bosses had certainly not jumped for joy—indeed, they considered the Communists' participation in the bonus march a glaring failure. Nevertheless, the Hearst stories created the impression that the Communists had masterminded the bonus march, that a revolution had been at hand, and that the march had been an important link in the continuing Communist threat. These were the tactics of communism, the newspaper stories implied, and the nation should beware.

Actually, Pace had been in jail on the day of the riot. He admitted to HUAC that he was not released and briefed by party officials until "2 or 3 weeks after that." Despite these facts, his well-publicized Hearst interview suggested that he was finally confessing the hidden truth about his role in a Moscow-directed insurrection attempt on July 28, 1932, thereby finally putting an end to "the big lie."[14] Pace had testified before the House Un-American Activities Committee intermittently for thirteen years, in 1938, 1949, and 1951, and an examination of those appearances in fact establishes the reds' dismal failure.

Pace's 1938 testimony went almost unnoticed—perhaps because it did little to support the charge of a revolutionary threat. He admitted that he was "put on the pan in

13. Daniels, *The Bonus March*, pp. 265–66, examines Pace's appearances before the Committee but asserts that "Pace's [HUAC] testimony was in substance quite similar to the Pace-Rushmore articles."
14. New York *Journal-American*, August 28, 29, 30, 1949.

New York City" after the rout for not carrying out Moscow's intent. On two different occasions, he emphasized,
he had called off Communist parades. "I knew that it
would end in a riot, [and] I averted a couple or three riots
in Washington. I had instructions not to, but I did, anyway, because I knew it was not right." [15]

Some newsmen and Republican leaders accepted the
widely publicized interview by Rushmore in 1949 as an
accurate representation of his testimony. Walter Trohan,
the Chicago *Tribune*'s Washington correspondent and
radio broadcaster, insisted that this new "evidence" established "the long hand of Soviet planning in Washington." [16] Actually, that second testimony, like the one in
1938, further demolished the charges of a Communist-
planned and -directed riot or revolutionary threat. The testimony in 1949 was in some respects confused and contradictory. On the one hand, Pace avoided specifics, backing
away from claiming credit for the Communists either for
starting the brick battle or for the shooting incident. On
the other hand, he suggested that the Army's action had
been justified. The nearest he came to claiming credit for
the Communists for instigating the riot, however, was his
statement that "the Communist Party . . . was gaining influence [resulting] in more militant and direct action,
which we *hoped* would bring us into sharper clashes with
the Government and law-enforcement agencies and
which, in my opinion, resulted in the Government being
placed in a position of having to call out the Army." He
parroted the MacArthur line by offering the speculation
that "had this thing gone another week, the Communists

15. U.S., Congress, House, Committee on Un-American Activities,
*Hearings on House Resolution 282, Investigation of Un-American Pro-
paganda Activities in the United States*, 75th Cong., 3d sess., October-
November, 1938, pp. 2284–87. See New York *Sun*, November 16, 1938.

16. Newspaper Clipping File, Republican National Committee, Ei-
senhower Library. Chicago *Tribune*, June 1, 1951. The Reprint of
Statement by Representative H. Alexander Smith in the *Congressional
Record*, August 31, 1949, "Hoover and the Bonus: Communist Plot
Told," was widely distributed. Copies are in EL, Hoover Institution,
and HHPL. Walter Trohan, Radio Broadcast, June 30, 1951, Trohan
Papers, HHPL.

would have gained the leadership of the bonus expeditionary forces, thereby resulting in forcing the Government to take the action that they did take, at a time when the results would have been more disastrous." [17] Pace thereby admitted that the Communists had not, when the riot occurred, gained the leadership they wanted, and he could only speculate on what he had hoped they would have achieved in another week.

Moreover, Pace admitted in his testimony in 1949 that the "Communist Party of the United States was severely criticized by the representative of the Comintern," Mario Alpi, whom Pace had met when he was called to New York for his rebuke. He further stated that Alpi had sarcastically called the American party "a swivel-chair organization" and compared the march to "an alarm clock" waking the American Communists "out of a deep sleep." At least two higher-ranking Communist leaders agreed with that view. Joseph Z. Kornfeder, another ex-Communist and a member of the party's central committee at the time of the riot, told HUAC that the Communists had never constituted a threat to the federal or the District government, that the march was a spontaneous movement, and that the reds had "missed the boat" by not starting and organizing it. According to Kornfeder, Waters's "group may have been affected by communist agitation, [but] it was certainly not led by Communists." William Z. Foster, chief of the American Communist party, agreed; he later noted that the bonus movement "took on such a swift mass character that it largely escaped WESL [Workers' Ex-Service Men's League] control." More significant, Kornfeder corroborated Pace's story of the Communists' failure and told HUAC that the fiasco set off a power struggle within the party. William Weinstone, an experienced organizer, eventually received much of the blame for the Communists' failure in the bonus march. Both Weinstone and Earl Browder were called to Moscow for a hearing, and

17. My italics. House, Committee on Un-American Activities, *Communist Tactics Among Veteran Groups*, 82d Cong., 1st sess., 1951, p. 1942 (hereafter cited as HUAC, CTVG). Pace's testimony of August 23, 1949, was read into the record: pp. 1925–46, 1942.

Weinstone was reprimanded and demoted.[18] The gulf between the Communists' intentions and their accomplishments was impressive.

The Hearst series and the barrage of other anti-Communist stories of the era had, nevertheless, firmly ce-
mented in the people's minds the impression that the
Bonus Riot had constituted an actual threat to the government. The nature of the questions asked by HUAC probably accounts largely for these incorrect impressions. The
Committee avoided embarrassing questions concerning
the Communists' failures and concentrated instead on the
philosophy of the party, the aims of the Communists, and
the techniques they tried to use. These threatening details received the publicity. By revealing the names of actual Communists, by recording inflammatory slogans and
the expressions of revolutionary intent, the reports undoubtedly convinced many citizens that HUAC had uncovered a dangerous conspiracy. At the same time, HUAC
members passed over the central question—had the Communists really posed a serious danger? [19]

On April 11, 1951, Truman relieved MacArthur of his
Korean command, and the controversy again captured national headlines. Within less than a week a writer for the
New York *World-Telegram and Sun* noted that the "No. 1
anti-MacArthur story being used by his critics concerns
the General's leading troops on the bonus marchers in
1932." Senator Robert S. Kerr of Oklahoma charged on
the Senate floor that MacArthur was as wrong now as he
had been in 1932, but Walter Winchell and other Mac-
Arthur supporters dismissed such "smears." Later, in

18. HUAC, CTVG, pp. 1942, 1928, 1945; William Z. Foster, *From
Bryan to Stalin* (n.p.: International Publishers, 1937), p. 228.

19. Chicago *Tribune*, June 1, 1951; Sandusky (Ohio) *Register-Star-
News*, June 21, 1951. The New York *Mirror* added to the clamor by
calling the bonus marchers "besotted skid row derelicts who didn't
know the barrel of a rifle from the butt"; New York *Mirror*, July 13, 14,
1951. William L. White, "Story of a Smear," *Reader's Digest*, 59 (December 1951), 49–53. For more examples of press reaction, see PP 298,
HHPL. The Committee's unwillingness to ask embarrassing questions
of friendly witnesses is discussed in a thorough analysis by Robert K.
Carr, *The House Committee on Un-American Activities 1945–1960*
(Ithaca, N.Y.: Cornell University Press, 1952), pp. 290–94.

1958, MacArthur categorically denied Truman's charge that he had disobeyed direct orders. In a letter to Edward R. Murrow, who had recently interviewed Truman, MacArthur sought to discredit Truman by assuring newsmen that "I have never knowingly disobeyed, either in letter or spirit any order given me in my fifty-nine years of military service." As if that statement were not enough, MacArthur considered such criticism by Truman and others as evidence of a left-wing conspiracy against him.[20]

Indignant supporters of the General demanded in 1951 that HUAC recall Pace to testify again, and he was duly summoned. Pace's final testimony added little information about the bonus march. He did say that temporary economic conditions had been responsible for the protest. Aside from that, he spoke of his subsequent experience as chairman of the Un-American Activities Committee in the Detroit District Association of the American Legion. He warned HUAC of Communist sabotage, espionage, and acts of mutiny in the armed forces, communism in the colleges and universities of Michigan, and the dangers of immigration by reds. He concluded by congratulating the Committee, and the Committee in turn congratulated him.[21]

HUAC and its publicizers continually played up the Communists' hopes and rhetoric rather than the clear evidence that established their ineffectiveness and utter failure. The Committee searched for evidences of conspiracy

20. New York *World-Telegram and Sun*, April 16, 1951. For a detailed examination of the Truman–MacArthur controversy, see Richard H. Rovere and Arthur M. Schlesinger, Jr., *The General and the President and the Future of American Foreign Policy* (New York: Farrar, Straus, and Young, 1951). Winchell claimed that Glassford "was the one man who could tell the facts." PDG to MacArthur, April 26, 1951; Glassford enclosed an interview citing Winchell's remarks; the Laguna Beach *Post*, April 26, 1951. Gen. Courtney Whitney sent Walter Trohan a photostatic copy of MacArthur's letter to Edward R. Murrow. MacArthur to Murrow, February 4, 1958, MacArthur file, Trohan Papers, HHPL. Douglas MacArthur, *Reminiscences* (New York: McGraw-Hill, Inc., 1964), pp. 96–97.

21. Chicago *Tribune*, June 1, 1951; Sandusky (Ohio) *Register-Star-News*, June 21, 1951; New York *Mirror*, July 13, 1951. Other newspapers' reactions are in PP 298, HHPL. HUAC, CTVG, pp. 1954–64.

and explained complex historical events in simplistic conspiratorial terms. To be sure, Levin, Pace, and others claimed that they had come to Washington with orders to provoke violence, but they did not carry them out. They delivered inflammatory speeches, distributed leaflets, compiled scrapbooks, picketed the White House, stole a policeman's revolver, and went to jail. HUAC and those who advocated the broad legal definition of conspiracy could thereby avoid the question of responsibility. For many, the marchers' presence, intentions, and sometimes illegal picketing were "proof" enough that, when a riot and then shootings occurred, the disturbances had been the work of a red revolutionary conspiracy.[22]

Despite the Communists' philosophy, intentions, rhetoric, and presence, there is no substantial evidence that they organized or initiated the riot. Neither did they effectively exploit the disorder it created. During the rout, when revolutionary insurrectionists might have been expected to engage their capitalist adversaries in bloody combat, the Communists abandoned their camp before the Army arrived and gathered at the Pythian Temple for another round of speeches. During this time Pace sat in a jail cell for having paraded without a permit. Inspector Patton's report identified only 35 Communists at the riot site, and only one, Bernard McCoy, took part in the brick battle; no Communist was identified at the later shootings. Also previously unrecognized was the fact that none of the Hoover administration's investigating agencies— the Secret Service, the Metropolitan Police, the FBI, the Immigration Bureau, the Veterans Administration, the Military Intelligence Division of the War Department, or the Justice Department—could uncover any evidence to

---

22. Edwin R. A. Seligman, ed., *Encyclopedia of the Social Sciences,* 8 vols. (New York: The Macmillan Company, 1937), II, 237; George S. Gulick and Robert T. Kimbrough, eds., *American Jurisprudence,* 2d ed. (Rochester, N.Y.: The Lawyers Co-operative Publishing Company, 1964), XVI, 127–59; Francis J. Ludes and Harold J. Gilbert, eds., *Corpus Juris Secundum* (Brooklyn, N.Y.: The American Law Book Company, 1967), 15A, 593–984.

support the charge of either Communist insurrection or Communist leadership in the rioting.[23]

Nonetheless, in the rising tide of anticommunism in the early 1950s, HUAC valued Pace's credentials as a former Communist. His testimony was only one piece of the Committee's elaborate antisubversive rationalization, but for many Americans it seemed to vindicate the rout and at the same time to help promote the witch-hunting of the McCarthy era.[24]

23. Daniels, *Bonus March*, pp. 149–50, suggests that the Communists started the riot and speculated that Glassford suppressed the Patton report because it blamed the Communists. However, while Patton claimed that some Communists were present at the eviction site, he limited Communist responsibility to one participant in the brick battle.

24. New York *Mirror*, July 13, 14, 1951; White, "Story of a Smear," pp. 49–53. Glassford challenged the red plot thesis that White repeated in his article. PDG to John Chamberlain, January 25, 1952, GP.

15

Conspiracy As History

After the rout of the bonus marchers, the protest became a confusing political symbol. On one extreme, it was remembered as the revolt of an angry Communist-led mob and on the other, a valiant struggle by noble representatives of the nation's forgotten poor. The evidence reveals both characterizations to be inaccurate. Communism held no monopoly on anger or violence among the people during the depression, and the bonus marchers, though penniless and hungry, were actually a minority of the nation's poor, a special-interest group seeking government aid denied to the equally needy majority. Unfortunately, after the eviction of the marchers at gunpoint, Hoover accepted the advice of men who could not distinguish between legitimate protest and the real danger of insurrection. Because Hoover unwisely acquiesced to his advisers' theory of conspiracy and because his opponents' criticisms deeply wounded him, he first attempted to cover up his administration's blunders, then ignored important evidence that discredited the red plot theory, and finally participated in the effort to mislead the public.

Hoover's over-all record in dealing with the veterans was better than most suspected, either then or since. The bonus became a political issue during the twenties, but a prosperous nation refused to pay the aftercosts of war. Following the bonus compromise reached under Coolidge, Hoover attempted to correct many of the injustices visited upon veterans by increasing benefits and providing greater equity to soldiers of all wars, especially in the most pressing areas of disability pensions, hospitalization, construction of hospitals and soldiers' homes, and the creation of the Veterans Administration.[1] After those large expenditures and with the onset of the depression, which affected a far greater number of nonveterans, he refused to view the renewed enthusiasm for the bonus as an equitable means of relief for victims of the depression.

Neither his critics, the marchers, nor historians acknowledged his numerous legislative efforts to benefit ex-servicemen or knew of his secret but substantial aid to the protesters and their families. Before the rout he had demonstrated a capacity for flexibility, a calmness under intense domestic and international pressures. To be sure, he was not always flexible and had long exhibited a closed mind toward direct federal relief; regarding protest, however, he had been tolerant and controlled. He had repeatedly rejected the counsel of force, restrained self-proclaimed national guardians, and defended the civil liberties of protesters, Communist and non-Communist alike. For two months an unspoken, uncoordinated bargain had been sustained: In return for their maintaining a peaceable demonstration Police Chief Glassford and Hoover had supplied the men and had effectively checked those who demanded force. Unquestionably, the unorthodox Glassford merited the immense praise he received for his humane treatment of the tattered men, but much of the praise came at the President's expense.

Reflecting a popular assumption, one critic suggested that the violence was inevitable.[2] Such fatalism ignored the many mistakes and misjudgments made during the days and hours beforehand—by Hoover, his subordinates, the Commissioners, the protesters, and Glassford. On several occasions Glassford and Hoover had wisely drawn back from the brink of open conflict. The brick battle was not decisive. Even after the shootings Hoover refused to

1. Hines had also attempted to find jobs for the veterans in their home towns but ran into intense opposition from local leaders who did not believe the veterans were entitled to preferential treatment over the thousands of other unemployed equally in need. See FTH to HH, July 1, 1932, PP 300, HHPL.
2. See Chapter 9, note 2.

comply with the Commissioners' request for troops until they assured him of Glassford's approval. The troop assembly call to the Ellipse did not commit the troops to any specific action; indeed, Hoover rejected issuing the insurrection proclamation. His final order placed civilian authorities in charge. After the Commissioners incorrectly assured Hoover that Glassford wanted troops, however, and when MacArthur disobeyed his orders, Hoover's hopes for an orderly end to the protest gave way to the despair of the rout. Ironically, Glassford's trust in MacArthur removed a potent obstacle to the brutal eviction.

Like other alarmists, MacArthur argued for a broad, sweeping definition of what constituted serious disorder. He met the so-called massive threat with a corresponding response and thereby turned his back on other less drastic alternatives. The evidence establishes, however, that he did not feel threatened at the time. For example, despite his later statements to the press, he admittedly found no arms among the vehemently anti-Communist marchers at the Anacostia camp. Earlier, he had not sent special detachments to surround the Communists or to determine if they were at their camp, which was already deserted when the troops arrived. Neither did he surround the so-called revolutionaries at the Pythian Temple, and while the Army routed the men and their families from the huge Anacostia camp, the Communists, undisturbed, listened to the usual party harangues. He justified the use of force against the entire Bonus Army and thousands of onlookers because he allegedly suspected the intentions of an ineffectual few. Actually, he failed to take special precautions against these Communists, whom he would later blame for the disorders; instead, he used the Army for attack rather than for control.

The Chief of Staff's action pointedly illustrates the sometimes fragile balance between civilian and military power in a democracy. As other Presidents both before and since have discovered, their generals do not always shun politics or execute orders faithfully. On the fateful night of July 28, 1932, as the inhabitants of Anacostia fled their burning camp, MacArthur and Hurley journeyed to the White House and presented Hoover with a *fait ac-compli*, then triumphantly met the press. General Miles recognized the strategic value of such tactics. In August 1952, when he sent MacArthur his written account of the BEF eviction for MacArthur's approval, Miles added: "I have many times thought how unfortunate the country is that you were so restricted in advance by orders not to go beyond the Yalu in Korea. A *fait accompli* there at that time would probably have led to the conclusion of that war long before it caused our present long casualty lists." [3] Whatever the rationale—shortening casualty lists, quelling so-called insurrectionists, or defeating Communists—such an attitude of insubordination points up the dangers of trusting with responsibility those military men who disdain civilian control.

Also disturbing was the silence of general officers who refused to criticize MacArthur or to reveal the truth about his actions to the proper authorities. MacArthur insisted that his orders allowed him considerable latitude and that they permitted him to use his discretion. His misuse of presumed latitude was neither new in military history nor the last example of it. Obviously, the nation cannot afford to excuse or overlook insubordination by generals who disobey orders or those whose misguided sense of loyalty requires them to cover up for their fellow officers. Neither should Presidents grant immunity for such behavior or expect to be forgiven for so doing.

Once courted by both political parties, Hoover had been the voice of forbearance and restraint during Father Cox's protest, during the Communist demonstration in 1931, and during the red scare in early June, which followed the bonus marchers' arrival. He had insisted that an illegal, overt act against the government was necessary before civil liberties could be infringed. By his repeated efforts to avoid confrontations, he also demonstrated that such an overt act had to be very serious. Even after the brick battle and shootings, he limited the use of troops.

---

3. Perry L. Miles to MacArthur, August 28, 1952, RG 10, VIP File, MacArthur Papers.

Unfortunately, after the rout his attitude underwent a significant change. He lost his faith in the protesters' peaceful intent, abandoned his practice of restraint, and became markedly defensive and bitter. More important, he turned increasingly toward explanations for the riot that depended on charges of conspiracy. When he accepted MacArthur and Hurley's version and on the following day publicly approved the rout, he tacitly sanctioned the use of military force against protesters, on the grounds of suspected conspiracy.

Because of the brutal rout, Hoover's opponents were convinced that they now had proof of what they had for some time suspected about his character, that he was a mean-spirited, easily panicked bigot, more worried about Communist rhetoric than about starving people. This composite view pictures a Hoover so fearful of revolution that he either approved a plan to use troops to drive out the protesters or, at the very least, precipitately seized upon an inadequate pretext for use of the Army as soon as he had the opportunity. He was a President who failed completely to understand the nature of American society. These erroneous interpretations continue to be repeated and have sustained a lasting impression of Hoover as villain, one that he and his advisers helped to create. As a result, his was an ironic and tragic fate, for which he bore more than his own full measure of blame.

In many respects the story of the bonus march has misled both contemporaries and historians. Hoover had not plotted violence against the marchers nor seized upon an inadequate "pretext" to call out troops against them. He did not authorize the rout, but tried to stop it. The veterans were by no stretch of the imagination forgotten heroes. Their demonstration was not a hunger march that represented the interests of all the poor. For their stature in history, one might wish that the Bonus Expeditionary Force had led the fight to bring relief for all of the unemployed, but it did not. In fact, congressmen feared that passage of the bonus would sabotage their long efforts to secure relief legislation. Some thought of the protest as "another Coxey's Army"; one admirer has viewed it as the genesis of the CCC or perhaps of the New Deal, but it was not that either.[4]

What the bonus march did reveal was the relative lack of sustained, dramatic protest among the disadvantaged. Timid and leaderless, some nonveteran paupers joined the BEF demonstration, but they were an indistinguishable and negligible minority. The Bonus Army rejected efforts to broaden its purpose, and the BEF's commander, Waters, achieved election as "dictator" on that stand. Lacking leadership and organization, the poor of the nation crowded into the homes of more fortunate relatives, tramped the country looking for work, or drifted into Hoovervilles. The really forgotten men were too inarticulate, too disorganized, and too dispirited to form their own march on the capital. No lobby represented them. Because the BEF was the largest protest to go to Washington and its members were poor and unemployed, sympathizers tended to overlook its narrow special interest. The protest, therefore, became a misleading symbol— especially after the Army's eviction of the defenseless marchers.

The worsening depression endowed the veterans' protest with special appeal, reflecting a heightened sense of class consciousness. To thoughtful observers the wretched encampment raised questions about the depression and national attitudes toward poverty. Although the men were portrayed as "the poor," an effective element in their appeal may well have arisen from the fact that many, if not most, were either displaced middle-class Americans or had experienced a degree of upward social mobility. The men were shaven, as clean as their circumstances permitted, orderly, and respectful of the authorities. They openly displayed their patriotism and on

4. John Henry Bartlett, *The Bonus March and the New Deal* (New York: M. A. Donohue and Company, 1937); "Bullets for the B.E.F.: Hoover Relief, New Style," *New Republic*, 71 (August 10, 1932), 328; "This Week," *New Republic*, 72 (September 28, 1932), 162–63; "The Bonus Expeditionary Force," *Christian Century*, 49 (August 10, 1932), 774–75. Roger Daniels, *The Bonus March: An Episode of the Great Depression* (Westport, Conn.: Greenwood Press, Inc., 1971), p. 172.

various occasions zealously persecuted those who did not share their view of Americanism. Except for alarmists, described by Roosevelt as people who feared all protest and dismissed all the poor as "shiftless irresponsibles," many citizens who sympathized with the BEF viewed the orderly marchers as rather ideal protesters. After all, they were not "lazy parasites" on society. They were a special kind of poor. They were like many other Americans whom the depression had dealt a cruel blow, robbing them of their possessions and of their self-respect.

In more prosperous times middle-class Americans could easily abstract chronic poverty and keep it at a safe psychic distance; in better days they could ignore the persistent problems of malnutrition, poor health care, inadequate housing, and job training. These and scores of other worries hounded the disadvantaged both before the stock market crash and long after the middle class recovered and turned to other matters. The depression brought many Americans face to face with prolonged deprivation for the first time in their lives, and during the depression years, at least, poverty struck a responsive chord. The bonus marchers inspired nationwide sympathy, but they refused to demand reforms to combat unemployment and poverty, their appeal for the poor was incidental, and the poor remained underrepresented. Before the onset of the depression, most of the veterans, like many other citizens, had earned respectability, savings, and homes. To be sure, they were a poignant group, but their plight best portrayed the crisis of the middle class.[5]

After the rout, the protest reached its highest level of respectability as a democratic safety valve, an act of petition and persuasion, which had been forceably suppressed. The brutal eviction further endowed the lot of the unemployed veterans with a special appeal, for it seemed to epitomize Hoover's insensitivity and callous reaction to the disadvantaged, raising further doubts about the ability and willingness of the government to

5. See Chapter 4, especially pp. 82–86; Chapter 6, pp. 109–12, 114, 118–21.

meet the economic crisis. The Great Depression ended
Hoover's administration, but the rout and the administration's ethically reprehensible defense shattered his remaining credibility and moral authority. Rather than educating the nation by informing the public of the actual
nature and sequence of events, Hoover chose to protect
MacArthur, who had disobeyed his orders. While some
may believe that the President's willingness to shoulder
the responsibility was commendable, his acceptance of
MacArthur's explanation contributed to a more profound
tragedy than his own. The miseducation of the public not
only shattered trust in the President but also shook people's faith in the institutions that were established to ensure justice as well as order.

According to one historian, "More than the battling unemployed in Detroit or the submerged characters in the
Scottsboro case, the angry war veterans seemed to sym-
bolize the American tragedy in 1932." [6] Race hatred and
labor conflict were intrinsically far more significant problems than the bonus protest, but only the BEF "hunger
marchers" had directly confronted the government and
received their humiliation at gunpoint from the United
States Army. While the misinterpretations of Hoover's
role in the dispersal unjustly dishonored him, the sad fate
of the marchers shocked and dismayed the American public. Understandably, his quick defense of the action
prompted many to believe that this was political violence
against unarmed, downtrodden political opponents—an
insult to the principles of American democracy. These
tactics were associated with foreign dictatorships, not
with the republican institutions of a free people.

In the long view, one of the most significant calamities
that resulted from the bonus protest was the eventual
abandonment of reason and restraint by partisans on both
sides. The protest vividly illustrated the conspiracy men-
tality, which has too frequently distorted vision, fostered
hatreds, and divided Americans. Neither party had a mo-

---

6. Jonathan Daniels, *The Time Between the Wars: Armistice to
Pearl Harbor* (New York: Doubleday & Company, Inc., 1966), p. 191.

nopoly on devil theories, for Democrats assumed a pre-
mediated, sinister plot by Hoover as readily as Republicans charged an attempted Communist-inspired revolution. Both sides used such variously shaded terms as
plot, conspiracy, and *cabal* interchangeably and indiscriminately. Sinister intent was often assumed, and the
degree of danger often grossly exaggerated. Proponents of
conspiracy interpretations usually ignored the distinction
between one's reputed attitudes and his ability or willingness to translate them into action. Partisans often saw
what they wanted to see, ignored facts that would damage
their case, and eagerly selected the "evidence" that might
prove them correct. With some facts and an exceedingly
fragmented view of reality, the quest for conspiracy represented the extreme extension of partisanship.

Prejudiced, insufficient, or erroneous information led in
many instances to an inaccurate perception of events both
during and after the bonus march of 1932. Given the
troubled times, the crises, the Communists' rhetoric, and
skewed or partial information supplied by trusted subordinates, Hoover eventually abandoned his faith in the
protesters, acquiesced to the theory that the BEF had constituted an actual threat to the nation, and came to believe
that the rout had, therefore, been justified. In a similar
fashion Glassford's fragmentary information convinced
him that the President, probably in league with the Commissioners, wanted to make him the scapegoat for the disturbances. He had considerable justification for his error
in judgment: his belief that MacArthur was obeying presidential orders, Hoover's intemperate statements on the
day following the rout, Hurley's later fabrications, and
the distortions in the Attorney General's report. Then,
disgusted by what he had witnessed over the past several
months, by Hoover's criticism of his lax enforcement, and
by his own troubles in the police department, Glassford
went on to conclude that Hoover was a devious man who
had deliberately provoked the riot and had approved the
rout in order to pose as savior of the Republic and to ensure his reelection.

Administration officials, Glassford, Patman, Waters, the

Communists, segments of the press, and a few historians explained particular conditions in terms of conspiracy.[7] The inclination toward belief in conspiracies by important national leaders helped to promote mistrust, division, misunderstanding, and the belief in several different conspiracies operating at the same time. David Brion Davis has correctly pointed out that real conspiracies have existed in America from Benedict Arnold to the present time. However, most striking in the story of the bonus march was the indiscriminate use of the term and the frequency with which participants labeled as conspiracy events that were in fact nonconspiratorial. Clearly, Richard Hofstadter's definition of "paranoid style" might be broadened to include a larger spectrum of people, who are not necessarily paranoid but who, for various personal or politically partisan reasons, become seekers of more limited, specific conspiracies.[8] Both HUAC's publicizers

7. The record of the press presents a certain amount of paradox. Editors were guilty of chronic sensationalism and of promoting conspiratorial theories. But the divergence of opinion provided a corrective force, and the reports of day-to-day events were more accurate than not. This accuracy becomes especially evident when one compares the press accounts with information in private manuscripts and official documents. Shortly before the riot, for example, MacArthur considered an Army report which claimed that Waters was assembling guns and gunmen in New York and Washington and that the rumor had circulated in Syracuse that the first BEF bloodshed in Washington would be the signal for a Communist revolution in the nation's major cities. By contrast, reporters who circulated among the men came to know their hopes, grievances, factionalism, proud loyalty, and basic conservatism. Naturally, this understanding was piecemeal, but evaluated as a whole, coverage in the local papers shows reporters to have been well informed—far better informed than Army Intelligence. After the rout the press initially supported the President, but when criticism of the administration began to mount, Joslin and Hurley counterattacked, imagining a conspiracy by the press against the administration. In their view, newspapers could promote charges of conspiracy as long as they were the "right" conspiracies.

8. Among the most prominent analyses of conspiratorial thought in America is Richard Hofstadter's *The Paranoid Style in American Politics* (New York: Alfred A. Knopf, Inc., 1968). Hofstadter described the paranoid spokesman as one who "traffics in the birth and death of whole worlds, whole political orders, whole systems of human values. He is always manning the barricades of civilization. He constantly lives at a turning point: it is now or never in organizing resistance to conspiracy. Time is forever just running out." He concluded that the

and Hoover's critics demonstrated that the mode of defining controversial events as conspiracy can promote division and distrust and perpetuate distortion indefinitely, especially when the so-called conspiracies masquerade as history. Hoover had not plotted the riot; nor was the Bonus Riot proof of the continuing Red Menace, as argued by HUAC's publicizers in the late 1940s and early 1950s. Nevertheless, both erroneous explanations have persisted. The twisted view of the past strengthened HUAC's broader charges of continuing subversion and thus helped contribute to the McCarthy-bred hysteria. The symbolic misuse of the Bonus Riot was only one part of the anti-Communist rationale. HUAC's far-reaching quest for subversion represented a culmination of conspiratorial thinking, which seriously divided the nation and poisoned consideration of more crucial national and international issues.

The application of the legal definition of *conspiracy* as "an agreement, manifesting itself in words or deeds, by which two or more persons confederate to do an unlawful act" also requires careful judgment.[9] While ideas may

paranoid spokesman regards "a 'vast' or 'gigantic' conspiracy as *the motive force* in historical events. History *is* conspiracy, set in motion by demonic forces."

David Brion Davis suggests a variation that allows for "muted versions" of the paranoid theme and that does not limit its proponents to regarding conspiracy as the motive force behind all historical events. Thus, men may be plot-prone and seek conspiracy in particular events, but not regard all events as part of a conspiracy. Davis contends that while there have been genuine conspiracies from Benedict Arnold to the present and while "we all have our paranoid moments," there has been a tendency to search for "enemies and to construct terrifying dangers from fragmentary and highly circumstantial evidence." David Brion Davis, ed., *The Fear of Conspiracy: Images of Un-American Subversion From the Revolution to the Present* (Ithaca, N.Y.: Cornell University Press, 1971), pp. xiv–xix. Hofstadter's essay is reprinted in Davis, pp. 2–9.

9. Edwin R. A. Seligman, ed., *Encyclopedia of the Social Sciences*, 8 vols. (New York: The Macmillan Company, 1937), II, 237; George S. Gulick and Robert T. Kimbrough, eds., *American Jurisprudence*, 2d ed. (Rochester, N.Y.: The Lawyers Co-operative Publishing Company, 1964), XVI, 127–59; Francis J. Ludes and Harold J. Gilbert, eds., *Corpus Juris Secundum* (Brooklyn, N.Y.: The American Law Book Company, 1967), 15A, 593–984.

well serve as blueprints for behavior, the legal definition of *conspiracy* fails to account for publicity-seeking rhetoric or for the fact that those ideas or plans are not inevitably translated into action. Indeed, the belief that men's words are enough to indict them for criminal conspiracy poses numerous tangled problems, including dangers to freedom of speech. By legal definition some of the bonus marchers could be considered *conspirators*. Some Communists had spoken openly of violence against the established order. Then a riot occurred. For many critics of protest the riot was proof enough of the veterans' subversive character. Such critics took no cognizance of the facts that only a few of the veterans had participated in the riot and that the participants were overwhelmingly non-Communists. The proponents of conspiracy failed to make another distinction: Those responsible for the riot did not conspire against or intend to overthrow the government. They were angry men who resisted efforts to remove them from federal buildings. Their continued resistance justified the use of limited force, but it was not a threat to the government. The problem was crowd control, not conspiracy.

The reliance on such simplistic explanations for complex historical events has not diminished since the McCarthy era. Protest has continued to generate allegations of conspiracy.[10] The demonstrations of the 1960s and early 1970s sprang from the grievances of a wide range of minority groups with different philosophies, different goals, and different strategies. These protests again raised crucial questions about the right to dissent and the reasonable limits of such dissent. These confrontations again underscored the need for careful assessment of the degree of real danger posed by disorder, the appropriate response to it, and the nature of justice in the United States. Certainly rhetoric cannot be dismissed entirely, and those who speak of insurrection or other unlawful actions invite scrutiny by those entrusted to maintain order. Yet, the charge of a dangerous conspiracy based only on professed

10. Davis, *Fear of Conspiracy*, pp. 319–24.

intent also poses a threat to democratic freedoms. A relatively accurate reconstruction of historic reality has become increasingly difficult as wide-ranging charges of conspiracy have proliferated. In many ways, the Bonus Riot of 1932 gave a shocked and uncomprehending America a glimpse of the troubled future.

Bibliographical Essay

The sources available for this study are so numerous and varied that only the principal ones are discussed in this essay. Many others that are useful on particular incidents are cited in the notes. Most helpful are the major manuscript collections. Their limitation is that, almost invariably, each contains an abundance of evidence that either directly or indirectly promotes suppositions of conspiracy. Thus, more than one collection tempts the researcher with its seemingly plausible and documentable evidence of conspiracy. When checked against evidence from other sources, however, none of these have proved valid.

The best and most varied collections are in the Herbert Hoover Presidential Library in West Branch, Iowa. Hoover and his chief advisers advanced one of the two more important explanations of the riot as conspiracy. Nonetheless, the papers preserved by the administration were more effective in refuting all of the alleged conspiracies than any other single source. The Office of the Attorney General collected a great amount of evidence on both the riot and the rout. These affidavits, official investigations, FBI reports, letters of inquiry, the transcript of Police Superintendent Glassford's testimony before the grand jury, photographs, denunciations of the principals by critics, and revealing letters and memoranda from government officials, politicians, and participants are essential to an understanding of the event.

Along with these materials—which best document the administration's miseducation of the public—are other sources at the Hoover Library that establish a view of the President that historians were unable to substantiate until 1966, when the Hoover Library was opened to scholars. In these papers, for example, is the evidence of his lack of fear either before or during the riot and his disagreements with Hurley and MacArthur both before and after the eviction of the veterans from the capital. The huge collection, which is by no means predominantly favorable to Hoover, offers ample opportunity for revising both the traditional credits and criticisms. Understandably, since scholars who wrote about the President before 1966 did not have access to important materials, they have presented Hoover as a frightened or devious man who failed to value civil liberties adequately and too quickly seized an opportunity to drive out the protesters.

Other important manuscript collections at the Hoover Library include those of the President's secretaries Lawrence Richey, French Strother, and Edgar Richard Rickard. The Hanford Mac-Nider, Ray Lyman Wilbur, James McLafferty, and Walter Trohan papers are also valuable sources. The Edgar Rickard diary and Henry J. Allen file in the Republican National Committee Papers at the Hoover Library, as well as the Raymond Clapper Papers at the Library of Congress, are especially valuable on Hoover's relations with the press both preceding and following the rout.

Equally important are the papers of the Republican National Committee and the Oral History Collection, which has now been indexed. The recollections of Dwight D. Eisenhower; Arthur A. Curtice, a family friend and business associate of Herbert Hoover, Jr.; Assistant Secretary of War F. Trubee Davison; and Secret Service Agent George Drescher are most informative, especially as they corroborate other evidence containing more immediate observations. Recordings in the Columbia University Oral History Collection are also useful. Correspondence with eyewitnesses to the riot and rout included Associated Press Bureau Chief Byron Price who, in a letter to me, confirmed that the Associated Press usually relied on the observations of many reporters to establish accurate chronologies of events, such as the time of the shooting incident.

F. Trubee Davison's recollection at the Hoover Library has been supplemented by my own interview with the Assistant Secretary at his home on Long Island, New York. Davison added a number of important details on MacArthur, how he learned about Hoover's "upbraiding" of MacArthur, the attempts of military officials to cover up for the Chief of Staff, and further recollections on his relations with Hoover. His memory was excellent, his information accurate, and he unhesitatingly refused to answer questions beyond his experience. Both Davison and I hold signed summaries of the long interview.

The Hoover Library is noteworthy also as an important center for the study of veteran politics, especially Hoover's relations with the veterans before the bonus march. This source has been neglected in other accounts of the bonus march, which have failed to place the President's relations with the veterans in proper context. Veterans Administration Chief Frank T. Hines's highly detailed letters to Hoover are indispensable to an understanding of the complex veterans' legislation introduced in Congress. Charts, graphs, and elaborate studies of prior veteran benefits provide the researcher with dependable and useful information. There are also many letters from various ex-servicemen's organizations, outlining their demands, and memoranda showing Hoover's reactions to them. Hoover's controversial reorganization of the three veterans' agencies into the Veterans Administration, his one major bureaucratic reform, can be traced in his correspondence and in the minutes kept by his special Committee on Veteran Affairs. Unfortunately, the Hoover Library does not also offer the related congressional reports, hearings, and special studies, which must necessarily supplement the President's materials.

Veteran politics and legislative power cannot be fully appreciated without access to both the Wright Patman Papers, now deposited at the Lyndon Baines Johnson Presidential Library in Austin, Texas, and the even more extensive files at the national headquarters of the American Legion at Indianapolis, Indiana. The Patman Papers I consulted were those principally concerned with his various bonus bills. At the time, the materials were still in Washington and in considerable disarray, but Congressman Patman allowed me access to them and granted an interview. His papers are undoubtedly one of the better collections for recent American political history. The file on his effort to impeach Secretary of the Treasury Andrew Mellon provides one indication of the collection's extensiveness. Patman's bonus drives were intricately related to the persistent lobbying efforts of the American Legion, which has records that are even more voluminous and are open to scholars. The VFW does not have records for this period, but its magazine *Foreign Service* is a good source. The papers of Senator Robert Wagner of New York, housed at Georgetown University, provide information on liberal opposition to the bonus. Patman's battle with the Legion after 1932 about the method of financing the payment is too long and involved to be included in this study. In my interview with Patman and in a much longer one with James Van Zandt, lobbyist and past national commander of the VFW, each man stressed his belief that Hoover had specifically ordered Mac-Arthur to drive the veterans out of the city. Both provided me with many insights into the thinking of the bonus advocates and the zeal with which they pursued their goal, and Hoover.

The Pelham D. Glassford Papers at the University of California, Los Angeles, is the second principal collection of sources for this study. Fascinated by his new job and its accompanying publicity, Glassford preserved immense quantities of newspaper clippings, letters, reports, and memoranda. He even attempted a diary of daily events. The result is an unusually detailed source on his handling of the bonus march and his reactions after the rout. While the Hoover Papers remain the best source on veteran politics, Hoover's thoughts, the government's actions before and after the rout, and its catastrophic defense, Glassford's collection is indispensable to an understanding of the day-to-day story of the protest and his management of it. Seven large volumes of newspaper clippings are especially useful, and my citations to the Washington, D.C., newspapers are taken from this source. Without reporters' extensive daily observations, the significance of some of the documentary material and correspondence and the sequence of events would have been elusive.

Unlike the Hoover Papers, which only occasionally provide glimpses of Hoover's personality, the Glassford collection is dominated by the obviously appealing, charming character of the Police Superintendent. Indeed, because the Chief was an exceedingly likable, admirable man, his papers pose a special challenge. The immense evidence pays repeated tribute to his engaging personality, his humane treatment of the marchers, his enlightened use of police power, and his courage in exposing the administration's blunders and reputed "plotting." This laudatory collection has encouraged several historians to rely heavily on Glassford's interpretation of events. Yet, it cannot be relied upon to provide the bulk of the evidence necessary to unravel many of the complicated and controversial issues. While of great value, the Glassford Papers must be used carefully, especially for events after July 26, when the Chief became increasingly bitter toward the administration and finally

ended his Washington career with the Hearst articles charging a
Hoover campaign conspiracy. Many years later, in 1948, he
wrote an unpublished, highly biased, self-serving article, "Mac-
Arthur and the Bonus Army," in which he defended the Army
and his good friend MacArthur, while again charging Hoover
with creating "situations obviously intended to incite the veterans to riot." This view has been repeated or gone unchal-
lenged by several historians cited in the notes.

The evidence in the Hoover and Glassford papers offers interesting contrasts. In the Hoover collection are many letters,
editorials, and other expressions of criticism as well as favorable
responses. Included are reports of investigations by many government agencies, which actually disprove Hoover's belief in a
Communist revolutionary threat. Without these a strikingly different view of the event would emerge. Also included are important documents from the files of the District of Columbia
Commissioners and the Department of Justice, which establish
that the police insisted on the use of troops and record Glassford's testimony before the grand jury. Glassford did not have
access to much of this information, and his papers argue mistak-
enly that the police had everything under control. The Glassford Papers furthermore do not include any evidence of Hoover's aid to the marchers, the President's repeated refusal to
heed the advocates of a forced eviction, or his unwillingness to
issue an insurrection proclamation, as it would give the Army
too much latitude. The Hoover collection, despite its own particular biases and preoccupation with the Communist conspiracy, is more balanced and informative than the voluminous and
compelling papers of the popular Police Chief.

The materials in several less extensive but valuable collections were essential to this study. The Patrick J. Hurley Papers
at the University of Oklahoma document the full extent to
which Hurley understood Hoover's orders and the elaborate defense he constructed both publicly and behind the scenes. Don
Lohbeck, who wrote Hurley's authorized biography, had access
to the Hurley Papers yet could not provide a convincing refuta-
tion of Hoover's charge that the Secretary of War had not carried out his orders. The evidence in the collection clearly de-
nies Lohbeck's findings. The first draft of the troop order is
especially significant, and Judge Advocate General Blanton

Winship's memoranda outlining the Army's prior plans in the event of "insurrection" are included in this collection. Most of the documents, however, are concerned with Hurley's defense against critics of the rout. The latest scholarly study on Hurley is Russell D. Buhite, *Patrick J. Hurley and American Foreign Policy* (1973).

The George Van Horn Moseley Papers at the Library of Congress are essential to an understanding of the thinking and actions of leading military figures. Especially revealing is his diary and a red leather-bound volume entitled "The Bonus March, 1932," in which Moseley included personal commentary, military reports, affidavits, and notes. James F. Vivian and Jean H. Vivian first published the incident involving Moseley's relaying of Hoover's orders to MacArthur not to cross the Anacostia Bridge. Their article, "The Bonus March of 1932: The Role of General George Van Horn Moseley," *Wisconsin Magazine of History*, 51 (Autumn 1967), records Moseley's earlier plans, made in June, as well as his detailed account of his version of the rout. The Vivians deserve recognition for their contribution, but as they did not consult any other collections, they could not establish a conclusive case. The actions at the Anacostia Bridge, taken out of their proper context, could be viewed as a last-minute change of heart by the President, a quick decision not to let the eviction and all his "plotting" continue. The Vivians do not create that impression, but MacArthur's supporters have tried to suggest that MacArthur was only following orders and that the messages did not reach the General at the bridge in time, thus exonerating him of responsibility.

My article, "A Blunder Becomes Catastrophe: Hoover, the Legion, and the Bonus Army," *Wisconsin Magazine of History*, 51 (Autumn 1967), appeared in the same issue as the Vivians' article and used documentation from Hoover, Hurley, Lohbeck, and Eisenhower to prove for the first time that MacArthur knowingly disobeyed his written orders as well as repeatedly ignored the high-ranking officers who conveyed the President's instructions not to cross the Anacostia Bridge. The article examines Hoover's heretofore unrecognized request that Hurley and MacArthur publicly reveal their disobedience either personally or through a congressman, and Hoover's crucial blunder in acquiescing to MacArthur and Hurley's insistence on a "red plot."

Paul W. Glad reprinted the article in *The Dissonance of Change, Nineteen Twenty-Nine to the Present* (New York: Random House, Inc., 1970). While other historians have agreed with this analysis of MacArthur's disobedience, they have not added significantly to a fuller understanding of MacArthur's role—either his pressures on Hoover both before and after the rout, his crucial relationship with both Glassford and Hoover, or his political ambitions. Evidence from several other research centers further supports and enlarges upon my earlier analysis and fills in other significant areas, such as Hoover's prior relations with the veterans, his aid to the marchers, and his attitude toward protest generally.

The Douglas MacArthur Papers at the MacArthur Memorial, Norfolk, Virginia, which I visited on two occasions, also yielded some valuable pieces of evidence. MacArthur left very little information concerning his relationship to the bonus march and rout. More revealing is Glassford's laudatory 1951 interview in the Laguna Beach (California) *Post,* a copy of which he sent to the General. It corroborates MacArthur's determination to drive out the veterans and establishes Glassford's later admission that troops had indeed been needed, an impression not conveyed by the Glassford Papers. MacArthur's own account of the events of July 28 through 30, 1932, is his long report to Hurley, which can be found in the Hurley, Eisenhower, and Hoover papers. This official report is supplemented by MacArthur's *Reminiscences* (1964), in which he laments the distortions of facts, reiterates his belief in a Communist conspiracy, and states that he did receive Hoover's order.

In a quest for additional, possibly extenuating material concerning MacArthur's actions, I appealed, unsuccessfully, to Mrs. Courtney Whitney, widow of a trusted aide, and to Col. Lawrence Bunker, president of the MacArthur Memorial Foundation. Since the MacArthur archival materials fall under the jurisdiction of the City of Norfolk, I also wrote to Mayor Roy B. Martin, who told me that most of MacArthur's records pertaining to matters prior to 1942 were destroyed in the Philippines and that all material under the city's jurisdiction relating to the bonus march has been made available to me. Nevertheless, it is quite unlikely that papers destroyed in the Philippines or those possibly remaining in the Whitney estate would substantially alter the abundance of evidence that establishes MacArthur's disobedience of Hoover's orders. The scarcity of material explaining MacArthur's actions is illustrated by his eagerness to have General Miles's account.

The correspondence between MacArthur and the immediate commander of the troops, Gen. Perry L. Miles, is among the best evidence at the Memorial. Miles's memoir, *Fallen Leaves: Memories of an Old Soldier,* is even more revealing. MacArthur solicited and personally edited this account. Despite Miles's praise of the Chief of Staff, the memoir establishes that the operation could have been halted. Miles also corroborates other evidence that there was no armed resistance at Anacostia and no reason for MacArthur to profess later that he had not wanted his troops to "bivouac under the guns of traitors." Despite the scarcity of materials at the MacArthur Memorial, it is clearly one of the important research centers for study of the rout.

Motion pictures of the dispersal are favorable to MacArthur. Of the two at the MacArthur Memorial, one is an official Army Signal Corps silent film showing the well-disciplined troops in action; the other is a biographical film which insists that MacArthur was merely obeying orders, an insistence to which MacArthur clung tenaciously. Still another film, often shown at the Hoover Library, is a production by David Wolper on the life of the former President, dramatically narrated by Mike Wallace. This interpretation and coverage of the rout is similar. Ironically, it too contends that the President ordered the rout of the veterans.

An abundance of evidence can be found in the National Archives. The Secretary of the Treasury's Correspondence, Soldiers' Bonus, RG 56, includes several boxes of letters concerning the controversy over immediate payment of the bonus, both in the 1920s and 1930s. More useful are the Records of The Adjutant General's Office, which contain the Army's investigation of Communists in the BEF, Hurley's final order to MacArthur, MacArthur's denunciation of the American Civil Liberties Union, and other material related to the protest. Evidence on the riot and rout collected by the Attorney General includes valuable correspondence, the alleged criminal records of veterans who had applied for transportation loans, the transcript of the District of Columbia grand jury proceedings, reports, and highly informative correspondence. (Glassford's testimony was removed and placed in the Hoover Papers.) The records of the Attorney General must be used in conjunction with the voluminous, additional materials gathered by the Justice Department, but reposited at the Hoover Library. However, the evidence collected by the Justice Department requires careful evaluation. Not all of it was used by the Attorney General. Some of the information is simply not reliable, while other affidavits are of questionable validity. Merely because the documents are included in the collection does not attest either to their verity or to their use by the administration.

The Records of the U.S. Army Continental Commands, Selected Documents, 1932, in the National Archives provide a highly detailed description of troop actions on July 28–30, 1932. Reports of the company commanders are usually factual and are primarily useful in revealing the frustration and the extent of opposition experienced by the troops during the rout. Messages sent by MacArthur to alert the troops and later messages and orders issued during the rout are included in this source. Also included in this collection is evidence of Hoover's extensive aid to the marchers, which he channeled through the Army, the National Guard, and Veterans Administrator Hines.

The massive collection of the papers of Franklin D. Roosevelt at Hyde Park, New York, is especially valuable on the lessons he learned from observing Hoover's successes and mistakes and on his relationship with MacArthur. Among the more interesting materials is evidence that Hoover's choice of the first repossession site was not motivated by a desire to engineer a violent confrontation. Instead, the FDR Papers contain the lengthy correspondence and report, which indicate that the salvage contractor had pressed for repossession of that area because his losses were mounting daily. The Louis Howe Papers contain some information on the camp at Fort Hunt, but the best source on the Second Bonus March is a group of papers uncovered at my behest by the Special Assistant to the Director of Veteran Affairs, Warren MacDonald, at the Veterans Administration in Washington, D.C. The rich collection, entitled Historical Studies, Soldier's Bonus, Adjusted Compensation, establishes Hines's hitherto underestimated skill in ensuring successful management of the second encampment. The Felix

Frankfurter Papers at the Library of Congress contain some useful information, including an excellent letter in which Frankfurter reports a conversation Roosevelt had with him on how he would have handled the BEF protest. The Rexford Tugwell Papers, also at the Roosevelt Library, do not contain reference to the rout, although his book, *The Brains Trust*, gives a good account of Roosevelt's reaction to the event.

The Dwight David Eisenhower Papers at his presidential library in Abilene, Kansas, contain several interesting sources, the most valuable of them being one of the best files of newspaper clippings on the efforts of several reporters and journalists to utilize ex-Communist Pace's claims to prove the menace of communism and the political fate of those who opposed the reds in 1932. Many of these articles appeared in the pre-McCarthy and early McCarthy era of the late 1940s and early 1950s. The clippings revealed an error by Eisenhower's opponents during the 1952 campaign, who incorrectly assigned him a higher rank during the rout and thus placed a larger share of responsibility on him. Also at the Eisenhower Library are numerous copies of the Chief of Staff's report to the Secretary of War and related documents, which suggest that Eisenhower may have worked with MacArthur in drafting the report. Mrs. Mamie Eisenhower was not available for an interview or correspondence, but her son John Eisenhower considered my request to open the working copies of *At Ease* to all scholars. Unfortunately, this action was delayed indefinitely, but he has informed me that the only marginal comment related to the rout is not significant. The library also contains a copy of the troop deployment order, with brackets added to set off the section that specified civilian control of the operation.

The records of the District of Columbia Commissioners are disappointing as sources of information concerning this event. Considering the degree to which the Commissioners were involved in the action, little of documentary value is in their records. Telegrams to state governors, secret reports by detectives covering the Communists' meetings, and the sworn affidavits of ranking police officers on the details of the brick battle and the need for troops are among the few useful items. Much of the Commissioners' correspondence and their orders are scattered throughout the Hoover and Glassford papers. The

Emmanuel Levin Papers at U.C.L.A. are even more disappointing, since they consist almost entirely of newspaper clippings. A search for the papers of BEF commander Walter W. Waters proved futile. His highly biased and often inaccurate account is in Walter W. Waters and William C. White, *B.E.F.: The Whole Story of the Bonus March*. Copies of the *BEF News* are in the Library of Congress.

Books and oral recollections by participants have been valuable sources of information. Herbert Hoover, *Memoirs: III, The Great Depression, 1929–1941* (1952), is excessively defensive and often inaccurate, yet it does contain some essential verifiable information. Dwight David Eisenhower, *At Ease: Stories I Tell to Friends* (1967), is a good corrective to MacArthur's *Reminiscences* (1964) and is in accordance with facts established from other sources. Theodore J. Joslin, *Hoover Off the Record* (1934), is exceedingly protective of the President. It was edited by Hoover before publication and is inaccurate about the details of the rout and the alleged red plot. Efforts to gain access to the working copies of the book were fruitless. Joslin's work is perhaps the most successful in "humanizing" Hoover, but his statements must be corroborated by evidence from other accounts. The volume is a supplementary source that offers many nuggets to the discriminating reader. George Kleinholz, *The Battle of Washington: A National Disgrace* (1932), and Edward T. Atwell, *Washington, The Battle Ground: The Truth About the Bonus Riots* (1933), are brief and biased, but they provide some interesting details on noncontroversial matters.

Three dissertations relating to the bonus march are available. John W. Killigrew, "The Impact of the Great Depression on the Army, 1929–1936" (University of Indiana, 1960), contains one chapter on the bonus riot which provides information on the Army's preparations. His article, "The Army and the Bonus Incident," *Military Affairs*, 26 (Summer 1962), explains the "White Plan," but defends MacArthur and the Army against criticisms and depends primarily on military reports on the rout. Arthur L. Hennessy's dissertation, "The Bonus March: Its Roots, Growth, and Demise" (Georgetown University, 1957), makes good use of the evidence and is especially valuable on the bonus issue during the early 1920s. Lacking access to the Hoover or Glassford papers and other sources, Hennessy's information and conclusions are necessarily limited by the amount of printed material and information at the National Archives and District of Columbia Building. Similar limitations affect Maurice Paterson Sneller, Jr., "The Bonus March of 1932: A Study of Depression Leadership and Its Legacy" (Ph.D. diss., University of Virginia, 1960). Sneller wrote a good, critical study based on a larger number of sources, including the Moseley Papers, but was also hampered by the inaccessibility of important manuscript collections. Both the Hennessy and Sneller studies are straightforward, essentially factual accounts. I disagree with them on too many points to cite their work in my notes. The Sneller dissertation, for example, relates Moseley's version of the bridge crossing, but Sneller wrote his account before the opening of the Hoover Library and had not examined the first draft of the order in the Hurley Papers. Therefore, he could not establish a conclusive case to reveal MacArthur's deliberate disobedience of written orders. These and many other differences are not criticisms of the scholarship in these dissertations, but they are faults that arise mainly from lack of access to additional information which was later available to me.

Other secondary works range from general impressions created by prominent historians to anecdotal accounts and outright distortions argued by partisans. Arthur Schlesinger, Jr., *The Age of Roosevelt: The Crisis of the Old Order, 1919–1933* (Boston, 1957); John D. Hicks, *Republican Ascendancy, 1921–1933* (New York, 1960); and William E. Leuchtenberg, *Franklin D. Roosevelt and the New Deal, 1933–1940* (New York, 1963), acknowledge the importance of the bonus march and are naturally critical of Hoover, for they attribute the rout to his unwarranted fears. Schlesinger has the most complete account of the event, but neither he nor the others had access to the Hoover Papers. Irving Bernstein, *The Lean Years: A History of the American Worker, 1920–1933* (Boston, 1960), relied heavily on the Glassford Papers. As a result, his otherwise excellent, concise chapter on the BEF suffers from his acceptance of Glassford's interpretation of events. It must be noted, however, that Bernstein did not have access to the Hoover Papers. He does not repeat Glassford's explanation of the rout as the result of a conspiracy by Hoover. Three valuable recent publications by scholars are Jordan A. Schwarz, *The Interregnum of Despair:*

Hoover, Congress, and the Depression (1970); Craig Lloyd, *Aggressive Introvert: A Study of Herbert Hoover and Public Relations Management 1912–1932* (1972); and David Brion Davis, ed., *The Fear of Conspiracy: Images of Un-American Subversion From the Revolution to the Present* (1971).

Anecdotal reminiscences by minor participants or observers, based on recollections long after the event, have often proven unreliable and must, therefore, be carefully corroborated. Several later remembrances of specific incidents were verifiable, but others, such as James E. Watson, *As I Knew Them* (1936), were not. An interesting anecdotal account is in Gene Smith, *The Shattered Dream: Herbert Hoover and the Great Depression* (1970). Other historians and chroniclers have also been less careful of their evidence. One of the most persistent claims is that Communists were responsible for the riot, but that Hoover was remiss in calling out the troops. This is argued by John Henry Bartlett in *The Bonus March and the New Deal* (Chicago, 1937), a pro-BEF, anti-Hoover polemic by the man who suddenly withdrew permission for the veterans to use his land for a permanent camp. Bartlett's confused account blames the Communists for the disorders but criticizes Hoover for evicting the marchers and thus playing into the hands of the Communists. Bernstein and a later account by Roger Daniels also credit the Communists, as do two others who are highly critical of Hoover: James D. Weaver, "Bonus March," *American Heritage*, 14 (June 1963), and Jonathan Daniels, *The Time Between the Wars: Armistice to Pearl Harbor* (New York, 1966). Weaver blames "radicals," but his use of the term is not clear. His study is also dependent upon Glassford's interpretation and is much too brief to deal thoughtfully with a number of important questions. A children's book by Robert Webb, *Bonus March on Washington* (New York, 1970), also repeats this emphasis. All of these works are in error regarding the Communists' role in the rioting. A reading of Pace's three testimonies before HUAC, Police Inspector Patton's report, and the many fruitless investigations by the Hoover administration will establish the astonishing ineptness of the reds.

More disturbing are those works which emphasize one conspiracy explanation or another. In his useful volume written before the Hoover Papers were available, Harris Gaylord Warren,

Herbert Hoover and the Great Depression (New York, 1959), acknowledges the difficulty of assigning responsibility but suggests that the District Commissioners plotted "to goad the BEF into causing disorder." Hoover himself was among the most persistent advocates of another view that the riots were rooted in conspiracy. In 1940 his article "Russian Misadventure," *Collier's*, 105 (April 27, 1940), was reprinted in his book, *Further Addresses Upon the American Road, 1938–1940* (New York, 1940). In "The 1932 Campaign," *Collier's*, 129 (May 24, 1952), he again argued the red-plot thesis and again in Volume III of his *Memoirs*. Numerous errors appear in Hoover's accounts, and they must be used with considerable caution.

Many of Hoover's supporters also argued the existence of a Communist conspiracy. They include Don Lohbeck, *Patrick J. Hurley* (Chicago, 1956), and Frazier Hunt, *The Untold Story of Douglas MacArthur* (New York, 1954). Another partisan, Eugene Lyons, *Our Un-Known Ex-President* (New York, 1948), placed the blame on "extremists" and argued that Hoover had no choice but to use the Army to force the veterans from Washington. W. L. White, "Story of a Smear," *The Reader's Digest*, 59 (December 1951), undoubtedly reached a wide audience and was one of the most effective of the Communist-conspiracy explanations of the rout used during the McCarthy era. White relied on repentant Communists Gitlow and Pace and on Hurley, whose "authentic history," "The Facts About the Bonus March," *McCall's*, 77 (November 1949), had earlier reached a sizable readership. MacArthur's *Reminiscences* repeated the same kinds of charges. H. W. Blakeley, "When the Army Was Smeared," *Combat Forces Journal*, 2 (February 1952), is based in part on White's article and argues that "the Army has been the chief victim" of the red smear tactics. Two volumes repeat Attorney General Mitchell's argument that the BEF represented a conspiracy of "hoodlums and Communist agitators." They are William Starr Myers and Walter H. Newton, *The Hoover Administration: A Documented Narrative* (New York, 1936), and Ray Lyman Wilbur and Arthur M. Hyde, *The Hoover Policies* (New York, 1937).

One of the most recent examples of a book which argues a conspiracy thesis is by MacArthur's biographer, D. Clayton James, in *The Years of MacArthur, 1880–1941* (1970). Rather than a Communist conspiracy as the cause of the riot, James, like Glassford, argues an administration conspiracy. According to James, MacArthur "was an active leader in the administration's conspiracy to maneuver the BEF into precipitate action that would justify the use of the Army to get a quick eviction." Later, he argues that MacArthur's "only active participation" in the rout was limited to his refusal to obey Hoover's orders not to cross the Anacostia Bridge. He offers no proof whatever of conspiracy fueled by the administration or Hoover. Ample evidence was available to document MacArthur's disobedience, but James does not use it. The rout of the bonus marchers was certainly a crucial chapter in MacArthur's long career, yet James does not make full use of the evidence in the Hoover Papers or in the other sources he cites.

The first monograph by a professional historian is Roger Daniels's *The Bonus March: An Episode of the Great Depression* (1971). Except for his agreement with my 1967 article, that MacArthur knowingly disobeyed Hoover's orders, our interpretations are quite different. Those who are interested in these differences should compare my 1967 article with his book and consult the notes in this volume. Basically, Daniels's interpretation relies heavily on the Glassford Papers. While he obtained materials from the Herbert Hoover Presidential Library, he did not examine many significant and extensive collections there. A careful analysis of the major explanations based on conspiracy theories and an examination of the papers at the American Legion National Headquarters and the MacArthur Memorial would also have been appropriate.

Daniels has made a number of contributions from which I have benefited. The publication of his book enabled me to delete long sections from my manuscript. His study should be consulted for details on the bonus legislation of the 1920s, the atrocity myths that lingered long after the rout, the Second Bonus March, and the legislative battles during the Roosevelt administration. I have cited these contributions in the notes.

Index